CRITICAL
INSIGHTS

Herman Melville

CRITICAL
INSIGHTS
Herman Melville

Editor
Eric Carl Link
University of Memphis

SALEM PRESS
A Division of EBSCO Publishing
Ipswich, Massachusetts

Cover Photo: © Bettmann/CORBIS

Editor's text © 2013 by Eric Carl Link

∞ The paper used in these volumes conforms to the American National Standard
for Permanence of Paper for Printed Library Materials, Z39.48-1992 (R1997).

Library of Congress Cataloging-in-Publication Data
Herman Melville / editor, Eric Carl Link.
    p. cm. -- (Critical insights)
Includes bibliographical references and index.
ISBN 978-1-4298-3726-2 (hardcover)
1. Melville, Herman, 1819-1891--Criticism and interpretation. I. Link, Eric Carl.
PS2387.H416 2012
813'.3--dc23
                    2012007779

PRINTED IN THE UNITED STATES OF AMERICA

Contents_____

Resources

About This Volume

Eric Carl Link

One might naturally assume that an author as celebrated as Herman Melville would have a vast body of scholarship written about him and his works. This is true. For the past hundred years, and certainly since the Melville revival of the mid-1920s, readers have pored over his works, critics have put them under the metaphorical microscope, and teachers have brought his body of work into the classroom and made it an ongoing object of analysis. There is little serious debate about Melville's centrality in the canon of American literature, and Melville's masterpiece, *Moby-Dick* (1851), has taken its rightful place among the small handful of works that might legitimately claim ownership of the title of world's greatest literary achievement. With all that has been written and said about Herman Melville, what room is there for yet another collection of essays such as the one you are holding now? The answer is simple and immediate: plenty.

One of the hallmarks of truly great works of literature—and the majority of Melville's writing certainly falls into that category—is that they continue to reward new generations of readers. Much has been said and written about Herman Melville simply because there is much to say and write. His works are beautiful, elegant, disturbing, experimental, and challenging. They reward the effort the reader puts into them. One hesitates to assert that works like *Moby-Dick* and *Pierre* (1852) are like Old Testament urns that mysteriously never run out of oil; but after a hundred years of dedicated scholarship, Melville's work continues to fuel serious intellectual endeavor.

The essays contained in this volume are ones that students can learn from, teachers can take into the classroom, and scholars can appreciate. No collection of this size could ever claim to be exhaustive or even comprehensive, and that claim will not be made here. What these essays, taken together, *do* provide is a point of entry into Melville studies. There are essays here that will provide new readers of Melville with overviews of his life and work, and well as essays that will introduce students and scholars to the broad range of scholarly opinions on Melville's canon. Other essays will offer detailed and original readings of some of Melville's major works, illustrating for the student how detailed literary analysis is done and making new ideas and concepts available to the teacher, as well as providing new avenues for ongoing scholarly pursuit for the advanced student and scholar.

The essays in this volume are grouped into three categories. In part one, "Career, Life, and Influence," I offer an overview of Melville and his work, and Greg Conley provides a brief biographical sketch, noting that Melville's physical travels took him around the world, but his intellectual travels took him even further. In the next section, "Critical Contexts," John David Miles offers "Melville's America," in which he notes that a vision of Melville as the brooding artist cloistered in an endless philosophical fugue is but a partial portrait of the man. Rather, Melville was a writer of his times, and his works reflect the preoccupations of the age, from westward expansion to Wall Street economics to slavery and race relations in America. John Samson, in "The Critical Response to Herman Melville," then takes readers on a tour of historical trends in Melville scholarship and commentary from the mid-nineteenth century to the present. Clark Davis, in "Melville and the Transcendentalists," looks at the complex relationship between Melville and the ideas of the major representatives of transcendentalism, particularly Ralph Waldo Emerson and Henry David Thoreau. Through an examination of themes and passages in texts spanning Melville's career—from *Moby-Dick* through *The Confidence-Man* to *Billy Budd*—Davis illustrates how Melville engaged transcendentalist thought with both a seriousness and skepticism that, on the whole, offered a provocative critique of the idealistic perspectives of Emerson and like-minded philosophers of the time. The section concludes with Nicole de Fee's "Transgressing the Border: The Complexities of Colonial Critique in *Typee*." This essay features a reading of Melville's first novel, *Typee* (1846), through the lens of postcolonial theory, which not only serves to introduce the reader to some of the critical language and concepts related to postcolonialism, but also to expose the complex web of political and social relations in the novel that allow Melville to comment in complicated and nuanced ways on Western imperialism and national identity.

The third and longest part of this collection, "Critical Readings," gathers together treatments of different themes, conventions, and motifs in Melville's canon, demonstrating how a number of philosophical and aesthetic issues influenced and guided Melville's writing, and are reflected in his works. David Dowling's "At the Axis of Reality: Melville's Aesthetic" ranges throughout Melville's oeuvre, examining elements of Melville's artistic philosophy through both the visual arts and the uniquely powerful pursuits and interests of Melville's roving intellect. What is evident in this analysis is that throughout his body of work, Melville creates an overall aesthetic vision suitable for nineteenth-century American sociopolitical realities, yet charged with the allegorical, symbolic, and mythic significance and beauty of classic art. Meanwhile, it has been a staple of Melville criticism for the past century to discuss his works as participating (either fully or in part) in the tradition of the gothic romance, although how this is so is a matter of some speculation, particularly when one notes that some of the conventions of the British gothic are not often present in the American gothic. Gale Temple, in "Melville and the Gothic Romance," using Freud's notion of the uncanny as a defining feature of the gothic romance, examines—in *Typee*, *Redburn*, and *Pierre*—the tension between the repressed, symbolic urges and desires of the uncanny other and the social and sexual mores of nineteenth-century American culture.

Moving from the aesthetic to the philosophical, John Wenke in "The Many Masks of Melville's God" takes up one of the topics that truly defined the intellectual life and literary career of Herman Melville. The "problem of the universe," as Melville sees it, rests in the human inability to truly know the nature and character of God—if, indeed, there is any God out there whose character can be known. In a chapter ranging widely through Melville's life, correspondence, and novels, Wenke engages the diverse ways in which Melville approaches the subject of God—from orthodox Christianity through paganism to universalism and beyond. Melville cannot, in the end, be said to have a single position on the subject. Instead, he continually questions and examines the human relationship with the divine throughout his career. Then, shifting from the philosophical to the sociopolitical, Shelby Crosby presents "Melville's Democratic America." Known in the popular imagination as a writer of sea tales with mythical sperm whales, mad captains, and loads of metaphysical symbolism, Melville's status as an author of the mid-nineteenth century, consumed by mid-nineteenth-century sociopolitical concerns, is easily overlooked. Yet a careful reading of his work reveals a Melville who was engaged in both metaphysical speculations and social commentary. Crosby demonstrates that in works like *Redburn*, "Benito Cereno," "Bartleby the Scrivener," and "The Paradise of Bachelors and the Tartarus of Maids," Melville examines some of the prevailing social issues of his time, including poverty, slavery, economic disparities, class warfare, and gender politics.

Part three of this volume gathers together essays devoted to extended analysis of particular works by Herman Melville, ranging from his first novel to his last. In "*Typee* and the Myth of Paradise," Jonathan A. Cook provides an in-depth examination of how Melville's first novel engages—in complex and at times ironic ways—the Eden myth. *Typee* rewards careful analysis: Even in this early work, as Cook demonstrates, Melville engaged ideas central to the Western sense of self and nationhood. As the title of her chapter suggests, Anna Krauthammer's "*Mardi*: Melville's Search for Narrative" focuses on Melville's third novel, *Mardi*. A remarkable departure from *Typee* and *Omoo*, which preceded it, *Mardi* was a commercial failure. Melville's audience, and the reading public at large, simply didn't know how to respond to this wide-ranging novel that mixed fantasy, allegory, satire, travelogue, philosophy, and social commentary. What one finds in *Mardi* is Melville working out narrative methodologies that would give shape and

significance to his later works, and in working out these methodologies, Melville uses *Mardi* to comment on a host of key themes, including race and racism, the nature of primitive innocence, and the sometimes savage nature of humankind. Then, Steven Frye, in "*Moby-Dick*
and Metaphysics," looks at Melville's masterpiece as a metaphysical
romance that not only reflects an interest in classical metaphysics and
German idealistic philosophy of the eighteenth and nineteenth centuries, but also focuses on religious and metaphysical conceptions drawn
from the Judeo-Christian tradition. Frye's essay reads *Moby-Dick* in
light of these religious and philosophical concerns, with a particular
focus on the symbolism of the great white whale itself.

In "*Pierre* and the Ambiguities of Antebellum America," Peter West
examines Melville's dark and complicated follow-up to *Moby-Dick*,
in which Melville offered to the world not a "bowl of salt water" but
a "rural bowl of milk." West looks at how *Pierre* reflects the ambiguities of its age. It is a novel that not only grows out of Melville's own
experience and biography, but one that reflects the tensions in the literary marketplace in the mid-nineteenth century and the age's struggles
with national identity, gender, sexuality, and art. Peter J. Balaam, in
"Melville's Anatomy of American Belief: *The Confidence-Man: His
Masquerade*," takes the reader on a tour through Melville's challenging and enigmatic final novel—that is, the final novel he would publish in his lifetime. Balaam reads the work as an anatomy—a work
that deviates from common narrative progression in order to explore
an intellectual pattern that can be seen twisting and twining through
the characters and episodes of a work. In this case, Melville presents
an *anatomy of belief*, in which conventional objects of faith, and even
conventional satiric responses to these objects of faith, are recast as
philosophically ambiguous. There is a central joke being worked out
in *The Confidence-Man*, and it seems at first like the joke may be at
the expense of God, or of the knaves and fools aboard the *Fidèle*, but
perhaps in the end the joke is really on us.

After *The Confidence-Man*, Melville's literary energies went primarily into the production of poetry instead of fiction. Brian Yothers, in "Metrical Melville: The Career of an Obscure Poet," examines Melville's career as a poet, arguing deftly for the sophistication, complexity, and importance of Melville's poetic works, and providing an overview of some of the key critical statements that have been made about Melville's poetic production. What one finds is that Melville was not a poet by afterthought, but that his poetry represents a major—if overshadowed—portion of his canon, and that the reader of Melville will find in his poetry material that testifies to Melville's ongoing intellectual pursuits in his post-*Confidence-Man* years. Finally, part three, and the volume itself, concludes with a chapter that interprets Melville's final book as a meditation on *how to read books*. In "*Billy Budd, Sailor*: Or, How to Read a Book," Wyn Kelley demonstrates the ways in which Melville's complex, unpolished, posthumously published *Billy Budd* focuses on questions of literacy. Kelley argues that Captain Vere, Claggart, and Billy Budd himself exemplify different kinds of reading, making *Billy Budd* itself a very modern exercise in exploring the dimensions of literacy and the way in which books make meaning for the reader.

CAREER, LIFE, AND INFLUENCE

On Herman Melville_____

Eric Carl Link

In 1888, Herman Melville was an old man in poor health. Born in 1819, he was fast approaching seventy years of age in 1888 and, although he could not have known it at the time, he would pass away just a few years later, in 1891. Melville had lived a life of both bold adventure and frustrating monotony, of great expectation followed by vilification and alienation. He had found instant success as a writer with the publication of his first novel, *Typee,* in 1846, yet by the time he published the difficult and philosophically dark novel *The Confidence-Man* in 1857—the last novel Melville would publish during his lifetime, and the last he would write save for *Billy Budd*, which was left unpublished at the time of his death—Melville had lost his audience and his fame. To all but a small band of friends, colleagues, and like-minded artists, Melville spent the last thirty years of his life largely disconnected from the reading public and forgotten by reviewers, artists, and fellow writers.

When in these later years of his life Melville did put pen to paper, it was generally to write poetry. After watching the United States soak itself with its own blood during the Civil War, Melville published a collection of poetry inspired by the conflict, *Battle-Pieces and Aspects of the War*, in 1866. Despite its merits—only Walt Whitman's *Drum Taps* surpasses it as a collection of Civil War poetry—it was a commercial failure and did not restore Melville to the front, or even middle, ranks of noted American artists of the day. He returned to print a decade later with the publication of his long epic poem *Clarel* in 1876. It was another commercial failure. Another decade and more of silence followed, interrupted, finally, in 1888 with the publication of another volume of poems, *John Marr and Other Sailors*. It was published by Melville himself in a small edition of just twenty-five copies—hardly enough even to call it *published*, let alone call it a literary event—and although few read it during what little was left of his life, it contains several of Melville's more intriguing and provocative verses. Consider the following four-line lyric, "The Tuft of Kelp":

> All dripping in tangles green,
> Cast up by a lonely sea,
> If purer for that, O Weed,
> Bitterer, too, are ye?

This simple four-line poem, in which the speaker apostrophizes a piece of seaweed that has washed up on a beach, contains within it one of the central paradoxes that Melville believed defined the relationship between the individual and God. The tension emerges in the seemingly strange juxtaposition of *purity* and *bitterness*. Most associate purity—and processes of purification—with something positive. One associates purity with innocence, with the joy of one's salvation, with cleanliness. In this poem, the tuft of kelp has been made more pure by having been cast up out of the sea onto the shore, where it may enjoy direct sunlight, sunlight unfiltered by murky fathoms of salty, unpalatable ocean water. Paradoxically, the process of purification has left the kelp more, not less, bitter—a conundrum emblematic of the fang lodged in Melville's brain throughout his career as a writer.

Why would the kelp grow bitter? The unexpected attitude of the kelp can be explained by noting that the natural environment for kelp is not on the shore. Its natural environment is in the sea. It is in the sea that the kelp can live and move and interact with its environment according to the natural inclinations of its being. In short, where does kelp wish to be?—in the ocean. Where has it had to go in order to find purification?—the shore. Thus, the kelp is caught: to enjoy what seems to be its birthright, the ocean, it must forego purification. But to seek purification it must leave its natural environment and present itself to the direct sunlight, alone, passive, without the company of other kelp or the self-determining freedom of the open sea. Cast up out of that sea, the kelp has found a measure of purity, but what it has lost in the bargain has lead to bitterness rather than joy. Contained within this four-line poem is an allegory: In order to serve God, humans must leave their natural environment, separate themselves from others, forego the natural drives and pleasures that define human experience itself, and in doing so they may be made pure in the eyes of God. But what kind of a God tells its creatures that they must deny their *God-given* natures in order to be clean in his eyes? Surely, such a God is inscrutable at best, mad at worst.

The Lonely Sea

Thus, the sea that casts the kelp upon the shore is a lonely sea, lonely because of the loss of the kelp, but also because of its separation from God. It may be difficult to say which pang cuts deepest. What is clear, however, is that the universe is a place of dark mysteries. To solve the riddles posed by this dark universe requires the wielding of an equally dark power. In the months just prior to the publication of *Moby-Dick*, Melville, in his essay "Hawthorne and His Mosses" (1850), attributed to the greatest of authors—such as William Shakespeare and Nathaniel Hawthorne—the "power of blackness." This power is the willingness to stare into the dark side of nature, the courage to confront the ambiguous within nature and within humankind, and the drive to explore those forces in nature and within the human psyche that reveal a dark side to human experience. Even the mighty pens of Shakespeare and Hawthorne, however, are not sharp enough to cut clean through to the truth. The best the artist can hope for is a *glimpse* of the truth—or, of such truth as might be out there. "In this world of lies," writes Melville, "Truth is forced to fly like a scared white doe in the woodlands; and only by cunning glimpses will she reveal herself, as in Shakespeare and other masters of the great Art of Telling the Truth,—even though it be covertly, and by snatches."

Achieving an apotheosis—such as Ralph Waldo Emerson and the other New England transcendentalists describe in their writings—may be an impossibility in Melville's world of dark mysteries, but that should not deter us from the quest for Truth. In fact, as Ishmael notes in *Moby-Dick*, to choose the comforts of the hearth over the tumult of the open sea may lead to a long, comfortable life, but it will be a life of intellectual stagnation and death. To seek truth, one must leave the safety and security of land and push out to sea. This is the lesson offered in the life and death of the minor character Bulkington. In the "Lee Shore" chapter of *Moby-Dick*, Ishmael notes with wonder that Bulkington—only recently landed on shore from a "four years' dangerous voyage"—has turned around and shipped back out to sea on the *Pequod*, as though the "land seemed scorching to his feet." Ishmael sees that Bulkington will die at sea, but in pursuit of something greater than himself; in such a death, Ishmael speculates, one finds the physical embodiment of a philosophical truth. Ishmael asks the reader:

> Know ye, now, Bulkington? Glimpses do ye seem to see of that mortally intolerable truth; that all deep, earnest thinking is but the intrepid effort of the soul to keep the open independence of her sea; while the wildest winds of heaven and earth conspire to cast her on the treacherous, slavish shore?
>
> But as in landlessness alone resides the highest truth, shoreless, indefinite as God—so, better is it to perish in that howling infinite, than be ingloriously dashed upon the lee, even if that were safety! . . . O Bulkington! Bear thee grimly, demigod! Up from the spray of thy ocean-perishing—straight up, leaps thy apotheosis!

Only in his death did Bulkington find his apotheosis, and the message for readers is clear: to pursue the Truth, one must leave, metaphorically, the comforts of home—the comforts of inherited and culturally accepted intellectual norms—and one must push out into the midst of an inhospitable sea. One may perish in the pursuit of Truth, but better to die in the pursuit of Truth than to live a long life of intellectual stagnation.

In *Moby-Dick*, the quest for that elusive Truth with a capital *T* is symbolically embodied in the chase for the white whale. For those of us who perhaps do not cut quite the same silhouette as the beloved and celebrated Bulkington, there still remains the possibility of heavenly reward. Even the low-ranking librarians who pursue the whale, rummaging, as Melville writes in the "Extracts" section prefacing *Moby-Dick*, through all the books in all the libraries of the earth in a quest after references to whales, though not appreciated in this world, will take the seats of long-pampered archangels in the next world. All humans, Ishmael notes in the first chapter of *Moby-Dick*, feel at some point the gravitational pull of the sea. We look into the sea and find "the image of the ungraspable phantom of life; and this is the key to it all." It is the key to understanding both why Bulkington would strive to keep the open independence of his sea, and also why the pursuit of the truth is a quest that is at once necessary, endless, and tragically futile. For Melville, this quest defines the metaphysical state of those willing to engage in deep, earnest, thinking. We leave the comforts of our intellectual home, push out into the sea, chase the ungraspable phantom of life, and die in our ocean-perishing, with only Ishmael escaping the wreckage of the *Pequod* to tell the tale.

In Search of a Well-Built Universe

Melville is a metaphysical novelist, meaning the major themes that consumed Melville throughout his career as a writer tended to focus on metaphysical questions, questions about the absolute nature of the universe: Is there a god? Is there a transcendent realm, a realm beyond the empirical world of the senses? What is the relationship between the individual and the transcendent? What is the meaning or purpose of life itself? What is evil and where does it come from? From his grappling with the complicated blending of good and evil in his first novel, *Typee,* through the inscrutable allegories built into his last novel, *Billy Budd*, Melville explored these questions and others in all of his major works.

One should not conclude from this fact, however, that Melville was so given to philosophical speculations that he turned a blind eye to the social realities of his age. As he demonstrates in some of his best-known works—"Benito Cereno," "Bartleby the Scrivener," *The*

Confidence-Man—Melville confronts directly, and with determination, some of the most troubling and complex issues in antebellum American culture. He takes on issues of race, racism, and slavery in "Benito Cereno." He looks at gender disparities and sexism in the marketplace in "The Paradise of Bachelors and the Tartarus of Maids." He explores the nuances of social justice, equality, crime and punishment, and class structure in works such as *Redburn*, "Bartleby the Scrivener," and *Billy Budd*. The intersections of warfare, politics, and history come to the fore in works as wide ranging as Melville's *Israel Potter* and *Battle-Pieces and Aspects of War*. Melville may have set the vast majority of his major works on the ocean, but he did not glamorize sea travel, and in a work such as *White Jacket* he subjects naval life and structure to pointed and poignant criticism—highlighted by his critique of the practice of flogging as a mainstay in naval justice. As Ishmael points out in "The Grand Armada" chapter of *Moby-Dick*, there "is no folly of the beasts of the earth which is not infinitely outdone by the madness of men." From *Typee* through *Billy Budd*, Melville illustrated Ishmael's observation, parading before the reader an encyclopedia of folly, not with the comedic burlesque of a Mark Twain, but with the wry sobriety of a sage who sees ambiguity where he has been told he will find clarity, who finds the universe, and the creator of the universe, complicit in the sustaining of a ruined Eden characterized more by darkness than light.

Thus, Melville's social vision complemented his metaphysical speculations, and both intellectual paths seemed to lead him to the same conclusion: the world is simply not well built. Humans are flawed, violent, maniacal, dangerous, obsessed, and those who manage to temper their madness and restrain their obsessions are often too meek and mild to be the shapers of civilizations and the directors of history. These human flaws are mirrored in the universe that surrounds us. It is a world in which human striving for love, for greatness, for meaning, for comfort, is met with silence and a cold wind. In chapter two of *Moby-Dick*, Melville notes that the universe is a drafty place, providing for neither physical nor intellectual comfort: "Yes, these eyes are windows, and this body of mine is the house. What a pity they didn't stop up the chinks and the crannies though, and thrust in a little lint here and there. But it's too late to make any improvements now. The universe is finished; the copestone is on, and the chips were carted off a million years ago." Such is the melancholy denouement of the human drama: The architect of this drafty universe built for his creatures a house lacking proper insulation from the elements, and the warranty has long since expired. Could we bring suit against the creator for his poor workmanship, we would. As Ahab notes in "The Symphony," toward the end of *Moby-Dick*, "Who's to doom, when the judge himself is dragged before the bar?"—if only there were a court that would hear the case.

Is there any place where one might find solace in the midst of the spiritual, intellectual, and physical struggles that result from a universe poorly built? Just as the ever-moving ocean surrounds the stable land, so in the individual one can find a small island of peace at the center of the storm, as Ishmael notes in the "Britt" chapter in *Moby-Dick*: "Consider them both, the sea and the land; and do you not find a strange analogy to something in yourself? For as this appalling ocean surrounds the verdant land, so in the soul of man there lies one insular Tahiti, full of peace and joy, but encompassed by all the horrors of the half known life. God keep thee! Push not off from that isle, thou canst never return!" But in order to pursue the truth about the nature of the universe, we must follow in Bulkington's footsteps and launch the little crafts of our being into the watery fields of the half-known life. A cruel joke by a bad architect—it is no wonder the kelp grew bitter.

Instincts and Acquired Wisdom

One takes the measure of a great writer through the power of the author's ideas, the fearlessness with which the author pursues the subject, and the craftsmanship and aesthetic beauty of the works themselves. Herman Melville is, by these standards, one of the greatest writers the world has ever known, and the intellectual energy that has been devoted to interpreting his works bears witness to this judgment. In retrospect, the public response to Melville during his lifetime was likely as inevitable as it was tragic: the early and enthusiastic embrace of *Typee* and, to a slightly lesser extent, *Omoo*; the confused reception of *Mardi*; a slight recovery in terms of sales with *Redburn* and *White Jacket*; the slow decline into obscurity starting with *Moby-Dick*; continuing through *Pierre*, Melville's dark inversion of the domestic novel; and ending for all practical purposes in 1857 with *The Confidence-Man*, arguably one of the most intellectually challenging and philosophically dark novels of the nineteenth century. It is a cliché to call something (or someone) "ahead of its time" as intellectual shorthand for explaining the newness and importance of an idea that is not immediately embraced. With Melville, however, there may be a small degree of substance behind the cliché. Perhaps it is no surprise that Melville experienced a revival in the 1920s and has enjoyed considerable regard ever since—perhaps it took a world war and the radical aesthetic experimentation that followed to create the right environment for Melville's greater works. In the increasingly industrialized and secularized version of America— and the Western world generally—that evolved in the early twentieth century, did the dark philosophical musings of *Moby-Dick*, *Pierre*, and *The Confidence-Man* simply seem more palatable? Or perhaps the institutionalization of American literary studies that took place in colleges and universities in the first half of the twentieth century provided an opportunity for literary scholars to fix literary masters such as Melville in the canon without regard for—or even despite—popular opinion.

Yet, for all of this speculation, the fact remains that Melville's career started strong, with both *Typee* and *Omoo* finding a welcoming audience among the reading public of the 1840s. That would change dramatically with the publication of his third novel. With *Mardi*, the shift in Melville's writing away from the faux-realistic South Seas adventure narrative of *Typee* and *Omoo* into the realm of imaginative and experimental allegory was such a radical undercutting of his core readership's expectations that Melville's popularity—and sales—dropped.

Melville knew he was doing something radically different in *Mardi*, as he made clear in a March 25, 1848, letter to his publisher, John Murray: "As for the policy," Melville writes, "of putting forth an acknowledged *romance* upon the heel of two books of travel which in some quarters have been [received] with no small incredulity—That, Sir, is a question for which I care little, really.—My *instinct* is to out with the Romance, & let me say that instincts are prophetic, & better than acquired wisdom." As an aesthetic choice, Melville's instincts may have been right, for he started on a path that would lead ultimately to *Moby-Dick*, *Pierre*, and *The Confidence-Man*. But in terms of his popularity in the nineteenth century, Melville couldn't have set himself on a more disastrous path.

As a self-described writer of romances, Melville was identifying his work—specifically *Mardi* in the letter from 1848, but other, later works as well—with an aesthetic tradition that spanned centuries and helped define American fiction in the nineteenth century. The term *novel* in the nineteenth century had two meanings. Broadly conceived, the term referred to any work of long, narrative, prose fiction; thus, works as radically different in plot, characterization, setting, and theme as Henry James's *Portrait of a Lady* and Melville's *Mardi* are both novels—they are both works of long, narrative, prose fiction. The term *novel* had a more specific, narrow meaning as well, however. A novel in the nineteenth century—narrowly defined—was a work of long, narrative, prose fiction that focused on realistic characters engaged in conflicts and activities representative of actual nineteenth-century society. In the words of Nathaniel Hawthorne in his preface to the *House of the Seven Gables* (1851), a novel presumes "to aim at a very minute fidelity, not merely to the possible, but to the probable and ordinary course of man's experience." In the novel, that is to say, the author attempts to accurately render social realities and create characters and plots that reflect a reader's own experiences in, or expectations about, the world in which we live and act.

The romance, on the other hand, was not restricted to the accurate depiction of the "probable and ordinary" course of experience. Hawthorne notes that the romance allows for a "certain latitude, both as to its fashion and material." When writing a romance, in other words, the author has more artistic freedom to develop characters, manipulate settings, and construct plots that veer, sometimes widely, from the real world. In his declaration that with *Mardi* he would "out with the romance," Melville is announcing his intention to exploit the freedom of composition and invention that is available to the romance but not the novel of social realism. Insofar as the novel of social realism reflected the cultural interests and social forces of the Western industrialized world, so the romance brought some of the conventions of the ancient epic and the medieval romance into this same world and reconfigured them for a nineteenth-century audience. The *modern romance*, as it was often called in the nineteenth century, blended together keen observation of the real world with elements that pushed—and crossed at times—the boundaries of the ordinary, the status quo, the expected. What was lost in abandoning the fidelity of social documentation in the novel was gained in the ability of the romance writer to use the freedom allotted him or her to use symbols, allegory, and myth as a means to bring the abstract into the world of the novel. There are no giant white sperm whales in a novel of social realism. There is nothing ordinary or probable about Moby Dick, the novel *or* the whale.

The Artist as Enceladus

Neither is there anything ordinary or probable about *Pierre*. Late in that dark, complex novel, the title character, in a reverie, sees a rocky outcropping, and it assumes in his mind the shape of an armless Enceladus—a giant from Greek mythology, one of the sons of Gaia—lower half trapped in the earth, striving with all his might to release himself from his rocky prison so that he might strike back in vengeance against the gods of Olympus. Enceladus seems to Pierre a mirror image of himself. Pierre, the artist, the writer, longs to ascend Mount Olympus and take his place in the heavenly realm, but he is caught, legs imprisoned in the rocky earth, condemned to a life of striving with no resolution for his frustration, anger, and despair. There is an analog here between Enceladus, Pierre, and Melville: Melville, too, strives.

Pierre was not well received by contemporary reviewers, who seemed, at times, to take almost too much delight in panning the book. One reviewer even went so far as to suggest that Melville should be locked up in a ward for the disturbed so that he wouldn't pose a danger to himself or society. The reviewer may or may not have been facetious. Sadly, as noted above, this kind of extreme and negative reaction to Melville's works, particularly those now considered among his finest—*Moby-Dick, Pierre, The Confidence-Man*—was too common. Melville was increasingly unwilling to compromise his artist vision, however. After unleashing his imagination in *Mardi*, taming it again for the sake of *Redburn* and *White Jacket*—efforts which, Melville acknowledged, were written for money, rather than to push forward his artistic and philosophical vision—was frustrating for Melville. The struggles of the literary artist, for Melville, should not spring from the attempt to contain one's vision and accommodate one's narrative to the expectations of a genteel audience. The struggles of the literary artist should be the struggle of Enceladus to free himself from his prison beneath Mount Etna in order to strike another blow against the gods. It should be Bulkington's tireless struggle to keep the open independence of his sea and not be dashed against the lee shore.

Art is born out of striving. Melville sensed this early in his career, formulated it as a theory, and acted on it in his greatest novels. In his poem "Art"—included in *Timoleon* (1891), the final book published by Melville in his lifetime—Melville compares the process of artistic creation to Jacob's struggle with the angel of God in the Old Testament:

> In placid hours, well-pleased we dream
> Of many a brave unbodied scheme.
> But form to lend, pulsed life create,

What unlike things must meet and mate:
A flame to melt—a wind to freeze;
Sad patience—joyous energies;
Humility—yet pride and scorn;
Instinct and study; love and hate;
Audacity—reverence. These must mate,
And fuse with Jacob's mystic heart,
To wrestle with the angel—Art.

It is all very well to placidly dream up fantastic works of art in idle hours, but to breathe life into those works, to give them form through words on a page, or paint on a canvas, or through chisel and stone, is a titanic struggle such as Enceladus himself might undertake. Jacob wrestled with the angel of God through the night and was blessed upon the break of day, but was also struck lame by the angel as a not-so-gentle reminder of the sovereignty of God. Art emerges out of the alembic in which contrary impulses are distilled: melting flames and freezing winds; humility and pride; the earthly and the transcendent; the chronometrical and the horological, as Plotinus Plinlimmon might argue in *Pierre*. Melville, therefore, might be understood as a novelist who engaged in his own struggle with the angel in order to produce the finest of art—and such struggles require a mixture of brashness and respect. There is an audacity juxtaposed with reverence in his fiction and poetry. He has the audacity to wield the power of blackness and fling open the doors to the darkest chambers of the universe, and he has a deep and profound reverence for human aspiration, for a squeeze of the hand, for the human drive to know and explore.

"Who ain't a slave?" asks Ishmael in the opening chapter of *Moby-Dick*. "Well, then, however the old sea-captains may order me about—however they may thump and punch me about, I have the satisfaction of knowing that it is all right; that everybody else is one way or other served in much the same way—either in a physical or metaphysical point of view, that is; and so the universal thump is passed around, and all hands should rub each other's shoulder-blades, and be content." Melville can hardly be said to be *content*, perhaps, and he took up his themes with the passion of an evangelist—joining with Father Mapple, another character in *Moby-Dick*, to preach truth in the face of falsehood—but he served up ambiguities and ironies rather than clarities. For Melville, the universe is an ambiguous place, and human nature is steeped in metaphysical ironies that slowly pull us under the water, where we either see visions of God's foot on the treadle of the loom of time—like Pip in *Moby-Dick*—and forever after speak the "sane madness of vital truth"; or we sink fathoms down and join Billy Budd in a watery grave, the oozy weeds twined about our wrists, fitting emblems of the physical and metaphysical shackles that define the human condition.

Biography of Herman Melville

Greg Conley

Herman Melville was born on August 1, 1819, in New York City to a well-to-do family that steadily lost money throughout his childhood. His father, Allan Melvill (the *e* was added to the family name after his death) was a merchant, and the son of Boston merchant Thomas Melvill, who loved to show visitors a jar of tea from his rebellious night dumping crates of it into Boston Harbor in 1773. Stress and illness wore Allan Melvill down until, in 1832, he died; Herman was twelve and had to leave school in order to bring in extra income for the family. He clerked in a bank, kept shop in his brother's hat store, worked on an uncle's farm, and taught school.

Melville didn't like most of these jobs, and eventually went to sea on a merchant vessel, the *St. Lawrence*. When he got home he tried to teach again, but gave that up to go back to sea. He signed aboard the *Acushnet*, a whaling vessel bound for the South Pacific, in December 1840. Eventually life on the whaler wearied him—he complained later about the lack of food, and the stories of the fertile and decadent islands nearby may have lured him from duty. In July 1842 he jumped ship at the Polynesian island of Nukuheva—one of the Marquesas Islands, the modern rendering of which is *Nuku Hiva*—along with a friend, Richard Tobias Greene. They wandered into the settlement of the Typee (Taipi) natives, known to be cannibals. The Typees welcomed them but wouldn't let them leave. Melville had hurt his leg in the jungle and Greene left to get medicine, but couldn't get back and eventually went home. Melville made his way out of the settlement after a few weeks' residence—helped by the crew of the *Lucy Ann*, a ship berthing at Nukuheva looking for more hands. Melville took advantage of a trading party to escape the natives and ship aboard the *Lucy Ann*.

In September 1842, Melville and ten other crew members refused to do their work; they hated the first mate, who was a vicious drunkard. By this time the ship had made it to Tahiti, and officials there imprisoned the mutinous crew members, Melville included, in a prison with no walls, just a roof to keep out the rain. Security was so lax (the prisoners were only hobbled at night) that Melville strolled away one day. He worked his way across the island, performing manual labor such as ditch-digging. To make it off the island he signed aboard the *Charles and Henry*—his third whaling vessel in two years.

He left the *Charles and Henry* in May 1843, though this time he didn't desert or go to jail. He had only signed on for one cruise, and that ended in the Hawaiian Islands at Lahaina, Maui. Melville left for Honolulu, where he spent three months, at one point working to reset bowling pins. Homesickness summoned him back to the East Coast in August, and he signed aboard the USS *United States*, a naval vessel. While on board, Melville might have seen around 150 floggings, a common punishment for offences in the Navy at the time. Other than the discipline, the voyage was uneventful, and he arrived in Boston a little over a year later, in October 1844.

Still needing work, Melville began to write a thinly fictionalized account of his time on Nukuheva, which he titled *Typee: A Peep at Polynesian Life*. Once finished, he took the manuscript to Harper Brothers and they rejected it; Melville gave up after this single rejection, but circumstances aided him. While he was voyaging, his older brother, Gansevoort, had curried political favor through speaking publically for the Democratic Party's cause; Gansevoort's reward was a political appointment in England. Gansevoort took the manuscript of *Typee* with him to London, and there showed it to Washington Irving, just back from visiting the Continent. Irving loved it, and told his British publisher to accept it. On that strength Melville found an American publisher soon after, and *Typee* was published in 1846.

Typee was popular in both countries, save with conservative religious groups, as it described how missionaries interfered with simple native lives. Many critics didn't believe the book was true—the very reason Harper rejected it. Some felt the events unlikely, but more thought it impossible for a sailor to have written so well. However,

Richard Greene, Melville's comrade on Nukuheva, reappeared soon after publication and assured readers the book was true. He sent one letter to Melville asking for some of the *Typee* profits, but soon apologized, and told Melville what had happened to him after they parted ways. This account was added to *Typee* in subsequent editions.

In August of 1846 Melville proposed to Elizabeth Shaw, though her well-established Massachusetts family wouldn't let the marriage happen until he was more financially secure, so he set to work on a second book, *Omoo: A Narrative of the South Sea*. This was a direct sequel to *Typee* and described everything from Melville's leaving Nukuheva to the end of his time in Tahiti. It was popular, though not as successful as *Typee*. This time, Harper published it in America; the head of the company took it without seeing it first, frustrated at having rejected a book as popular as *Typee*. *Omoo* was published in May 1847, and the advance gave Melville enough money to convince the Shaws he could make a living at writing; he married Elizabeth in August of that year.

His third book, *Mardi: And a Voyage Thither* (1849), started as another adventure yarn in the South Seas, but transformed into a metaphysical romance. Melville saw it as his first serious book, but very few liked it—though Nathaniel Hawthorne, who would be prominent later in Melville's life, enjoyed it. Generally it was badly received; people were disappointed Melville left his peculiar specialty of charmingly narrated real-life sea stories.

Melville wrote two more books in four months to save his literary reputation and make enough money to keep his household afloat (he supported many of his close female relatives as well as his wife). *Redburn: His First Voyage* (1849) drew from his experience on the merchant ship *St. Lawrence*; *White-Jacket: Or, the World in a Man-of-War* (1850) came from his time on the frigate *United States*. The latter novel execrated flogging and influenced government policy with its portrait of life under such cruelty: later in 1850, the U.S. Congress banned flogging as a punishment in the U.S. Navy. Melville said these two books were merely "jobs" done for money. Reviewers enjoyed them for the most part, though some felt *White Jacket* oversimplified the problems of flogging.

Five months after *White Jacket*'s American release, Melville invited several literary friends to spend a few weeks in Pittsfield, Massachusetts with his family. Nathanial Hawthorne, who lived nearby, accompanied them. Melville and Hawthorne enjoyed each other's company, and Hawthorne shocked his wife, Sophia, by inviting Melville over in turn—Hawthorne was already a notorious shut-in. The summer trip went so well that Melville bought a farm of his own near Pittsfield; he may have wanted to be near Hawthorne, who encouraged Melville's desires to try another serious literary work.

In early October 1850, Melville and his family moved to the farm he named Arrowhead, for the Indian artifacts he found there. It occupied 160 acres of land he thought he could till while writing and managing his career. Melville visited Hawthorne and his family frequently. The Hawthorne family loved him: Julian, their first son, said Melville was the person outside his own family whom he loved most in the world.

Melville began writing *The Whale*, later renamed *Moby-Dick*, at this time. He wrote furiously, and finished the novel while the first chapters were being printed by Harper in New York. It was published in 1851. The British edition failed to include the epilogue, leading most of the early British reviewers to hate the book; without the epilogue, the book seemed to break the rules of fiction: Ishmael can't narrate the book, as he appears not to survive—only in the epilogue does Ishmael explain how he survives the disaster of the *Pequod*. Most American reviewers took their lead from the British magazines, despite having a complete version of the book.

But before the reviews had even come in, Melville was at work on another novel; in writing to Hawthorne, he called it a "kraken"—a sea monster—in comparison to the whale he had just finished. Melville finished this book, *Pierre: Or, the Ambiguities*, by January 1852. *Moby-Dick* had sold so poorly that Harper offered Melville only twenty cents on the dollar, rather than the 50-percent profit he had enjoyed previously, for this new book. He accepted the deal, terrible though it was, but not without his own peculiar revenge: He wrote new passages for *Pierre*, making the titular character a writer so he could lament the evils of the publishing industry and reviewers. *Pierre* was the most domestic of Melville's novels: It centers on the vagaries of a rich family in New England. However, Melville weaves in gothic tropes, such as Pierre's false marriage to his half-sister, which hinted too much at incest for contemporary reviewers, who hated it; they were scandalized, and many went so far as to say Melville had lost his mind.

The next year, 1853, he finished a novel titled *The Isle of the Cross*; Harper refused it altogether, and Melville never showed it to anyone else, despite several chances he could have taken over the years. At some point in his life, he destroyed the manuscript. Several magazines, however, asked Melville for contributions, and his short stories date from this period. He started another novel, *The Tortoise-Hunters*, and might have cannibalized passages from it in what became "The Encantadas," first published in *Putnam's Monthly Magazine* in 1854 and later included in his short-story collection of 1856, *The Piazza Tales*. He serialized *Israel Potter*, the story of an American Revolutionary soldier hiding in England and France, in *Putnam's* between June 1854 and March 1855. Soon afterward, Putnam published it in book form. Melville's short fiction and serialized historical drama fared well in the reviews, but didn't sell well.

Melville left for a European trip in October 1856 to try to salvage his failing health. He went to Britain and spent some time with Hawthorne there, then visited Greece, Constantinople, Egypt, Jerusalem, Naples, Rome, and Venice, before coming home in May of 1857. While he was gone, his last novel, *The Confidence-Man*, was published, coincidentally on April 1, the day on which its events occur. In this novel, a con artist appears in a series of guises to trick the patrons on a Mississippi riverboat. Melville used his own trip on the Mississippi River to furnish him with details. This publication marks the end of his professional career as a prose writer.

Melville spent the winter season of the next three years lecturing. In the years 1857 through 1860 he made a total of $1,273.50. (Ralph Waldo Emerson, by contrast, made about $1,700 in the single season of 1856.) Melville sent a collection of poetry, *Poems*, to be published in 1860 and left to accompany his brother Thomas as he circumnavigated the world. While he was gone, *Poems* was rejected, and upon arriving in San Francisco, Melville disembarked and headed home again, possibly because Thomas learned he had to stop his voyage and deliver cargo to England.

Melville sold Arrowhead to his brother Allan in 1863 and relocated to New York. Several factors converged to make this necessary: An accident left him unable to work the farm or even drive a sled in winter; Allan's wife wanted a summer home in the country; and Melville couldn't keep up with the payments he owed on the property. Melville's next commercial writing was *Battle-Pieces and Aspects of the War* (1866), a collection of poems tracking the American Civil War nearly from beginning to end. To research this work, he spent some time in the field in Virginia, where Confederate soldiers fired on him and his companions at least once.

Melville began work in the New York Customs House, for four dollars a day, in November 1866. In 1867 the Shaw family tried to get Elizabeth to leave Herman; it is unclear if she encouraged them, but in any case she never went through with it. In September of that year, Malcolm, their oldest son, shot himself at age eighteen. The inquest declared it an accidental death, though it may have been suicide.

Melville wrote a few more collections of poetry and paid for their publication himself. One, an epic poem called *Clarel: A Poem and Pilgrimage in the Holy Land*, he began in 1869 and published in 1876. It drew from his experience traveling in Jerusalem and the Near East. He left his last major prose work, *Billy Budd, Sailor* unfinished on his desk when he died on September 28, 1891.

Melville's reputation recovered a bit near the end of his life, though he never regained his earlier popularity. Many of his obituaries only referred to *Typee*. One called him Hiram Melville. Elizabeth received an inheritance, so Melville didn't die in penury, but his literary reputation seemed poverty-stricken. His friends and a new generation of readers extolled his virtues. His reputation grew up again through a slow groundswell in the early twentieth century. In 1921 Raymond Weaver wrote a biography of Melville titled simply, *Herman Melville*. In it he extolled the writer's virtues, and his opinion was picked up and expanded upon by other writers and critics, including D. H. Lawrence. These new and influential readers would, by the middle of the twentieth century, remake Melville's reputation, and America now considers Melville to be one of its greatest writers.

Works Cited

Freeman, John. *Herman Melville*. London: Macmillan, 1970.

Milder, Robert. "Herman Melville, 1819–1891: A Brief Biography." *A Historical Guide to Herman Melville*. Ed. Giles Gunn. New York: Oxford UP, 2005. 17–58.

Parker, Hershel. *Herman Melville: A Biography*. 2 vols. Baltimore: Johns Hopkins UP, 1996–2002.

Rollyson, Carl, Lisa Paddock, and April Gentry. *Critical Companion to Herman Melville: A Literary Reference to His Life and Work*. New York: Facts on File, 2007.

Rosenberry, Edward H. *Melville*. London: Routledge, 1979.

CRITICAL
CONTEXTS

Melville's America: The United States in the Mid-Nineteenth Century

John David Miles

There is a persistent myth about Herman Melville's artistic life, one that has a beleaguered and increasingly despondent Melville withdrawing from the world following the poor critical reception of *Moby-Dick* and the poor sales of *Pierre*. Rejected by the public he hoped to inspire, Melville turned inward and forged a life as a solitary artist, working silently away in his garret, ignored by and ignoring the world that swirled outside his doorstep. This version of Melville as the unappreciated genius has an attraction to it, drawing as it does on our notions of the romantic artist whose service to the transcendent Muse requires utter subservience to his or her art; the artist as the prophet of higher truths, a picture that accords with the autobiographical glimpses that we get in Melville's work. It is easy to imagine Melville as a tortured soul, an Ahab chasing his own white whale of inspirational art.

Like all good myths, this one has some truth to it, for Melville did indeed slow his literary output following the publication of *Pierre; or, The Ambiguities* in 1852, after which he concentrated less on novels and more on short stories and poetry. But Melville was never an artist who spurned the world around him in favor of the life of the mind, and while his art and life did shift during the 1850s, Melville remained an engaged—if never gregarious—mind throughout his career. Melville's work reflects this continual involvement, from his sensuous embrace of the culture of the South Pacific in his seafaring novels of the 1840s and '50s, through his contemplation of the changing middle class in 1853's "Bartleby, the Scrivener," to his 1866 poems about the Civil War, *Battle-Pieces and Aspects of the War*. Indeed, all of Melville's work grapples with his historical context, meditating on the world around him to produce an art that looked through the everyday to the eternal.

Melville did not want for provocative subjects: His long life (1819–91) coincided with the United States' transformation from a cultural backwater into an international economic and political power. Melville watched the nation grow from some ten million people distributed across twenty-three states—all of which were clumped east of the Mississippi River—to nearly sixty-three million people in forty-two states spreading from the Atlantic to the Pacific Ocean. More dramatic was the change in the nation's character: Born as the Revolutionary generation was dying, Melville lived to see the United States blossom into an industrial and capitalist nation with imperial longings. After spending much of his youth at sea, Melville settled in to watch these changes from his perch in the Northeast, his artist's gaze ranging widely, reflecting upon the changes to the nation and people around him.

During the height of Melville's productivity—roughly the twenty years from the publication of his first novel, *Typee*, in 1846 until *Battle-Pieces* in 1866—the nation was convulsed with questions about its identity, a process of self-definition on a national scale that found expression in Melville's writing. The full complexity of this period involves everything from the philosophical questions posed by the transcendentalists to the industrialization of urban centers. But Melville's writing winnows the many changes of the nation to focus on those events he saw as most important—or symbolic—for him and his peers. This essay focuses on the issues Melville addresses directly or indirectly in his work to explain how his literary excursions remained closely linked to the world about his feet. Whether it is his picture of the American afloat on the high seas in *Moby-Dick*, or his careful critique of the Civil War in *Battle-Pieces*, Melville's art shows a man engaging with and commenting upon an American society and culture adapting to its new global prominence.

America on the High Seas

The popular conception of Herman Melville today is tied closely to the sea, much as it was during his early literary career, and the image of the buff adventurer putting aside the harpoon for the pen is not far from the truth. What requires more explanation, however, is why such a career interested young Melville in the first place, as well as why the American public at large was hungry for tales of the sea.

The romance of the sea had been the subject of American writers since James Fenimore Cooper's novel *The Pilot: A Tale of the Sea* in 1824, which painted the exploits of the Revolutionary War naval hero John Paul Jones with a light fictional brush. While Cooper is now best known for his Leatherstocking Tales, a series of novels set on the American frontier and following the exploits of the backwoodsman Natty Bumppo, he wrote several novels and histories dealing with nautical subjects, and helped develop an American interest in both the sea and seafaring fiction. One young man who caught Cooper's sea-fever was Richard Henry Dana, Jr., a Harvard student whose 1840 memoir *Two Years before the Mast* detailed his experiences on a merchant ship sailing around the tip of South America from Boston to California, capturing horror and adventure in an almost ethnographic study of seafaring life. Melville, along with thousands of other Americans, devoured these and similar books, riding narrative ships around the world before making his own journeys.

Melville is most often associated with the whaling industry, but he first took to the sea in 1839 as a cabin boy aboard a merchant ship sailing between New York and Liverpool, England (Delbanco 27). With this first trip, Melville joined a stream of ships plying the waters from the United States to Europe, trade that continued to ferry raw materials east and finished goods west: Melville's first ship was laden with cotton from the South bound for the textile mills of England. The trip was no longer the terror- and malnutrition-inducing saga that it had been for the Pilgrims some two hundred years before, but neither was it simply a pleasure cruise: The journey lasted roughly six weeks, and was undoubtedly filled with both the mundane tasks of attending to the captain of a large merchant ship, as well as the threat of potentially fatal rough weather. Melville would later fictionalize these experiences in his novel *Redburn: His First Voyage*.

During the next few years the sea continued to call to Melville, as it did so many men: While certainly strenuous and always potentially dangerous, young men from around the country migrated to the ports of the Northeast to try their hand at the sail, tiller, or harpoon. The multimasted sailing vessels of the nineteenth century required enormous amounts of human labor, and what they charged in terms of life and limb they repaid in mobility, freedom, and sometimes fortune. Manning these ships was such a large task that shipping agents—essentially labor contractors—kept a constant supply of green and landlubbing young men flowing from the interior of the young nation to the ever-hungry ports on the coast (Moment 267). The ships were governed unquestionably by their captain-cum-dictator, and constant work was the norm: Sailing around the clock, the ships employed multiple crews who relieved one another in constantly trimming the sails, minding the rudder, and cleaning the deck. Each vessel was a world unto itself, with everything from a cook to a carpenter to a blacksmith on board. Once on land, the sailors made up for lost time: A worldwide network of ports serviced the needs of young men freed from the requirements of working on the ship and the moral pressures of home. At a time when an American farmer might never travel much farther than the nearest market, sailing represented the opportunity for a young man to see a world far beyond his own fields; whatever the risk, the sea's promise in terms of adventure and opportunity was great.

Melville's time as a cabin boy would have been relatively routine compared with his next journey, which began in 1841 aboard the whaling ship *Acushnet*, launching him into a more competitive and dangerous industry (Delbanco 37). Whaling was a major American business enterprise during the nineteenth century, representing both the development of domestic industry and the expansion of the nation's presence in international trade, not to mention international waters. From its humble beginnings on the Massachusetts coast, American whaling grew exponentially after the Revolutionary War, peaking in 1845–46 and dominating the profession worldwide throughout the nineteenth century (Moment 262; Davis, Gallman, and Hutchins 738). The Massachusetts towns of Nantucket and New Bedford anchored an industry that stretched far beyond the waters of New England, the United States, and even North America: one of the most striking aspects of American whaling was its reach, for while many whales were harvested locally, the majority came from seas thousands of miles away. Ships left the Massachusetts coast for journeys of up to four years, during which time they might hunt in waters literally around the world, dominating the seas they sailed: In the 1840s, American ships made up over 75 percent of the worldwide whaling fleet (Moment 263).

American whaling ships averaged from four to five hundred tons and carried between twenty and thirty-five sailors (Moment 264–69). They were usually captained by Americans, but crewed by sailors of various nationalities and ethnicities, including Americans recruited from the interior of the continent; like the waters they plied, the crews of American ships were truly international (Davis, Gallman, and Hutchins 739). While these ships were not strictly egalitarian in their division of labor and wages, they did represent a mixture of races and classes working and living intimately with one another (Craig and Fearn 126–27). Each ship carried between four and six longboats, which were dispatched when a whale had been sighted, to vie for the honor of being the first to harpoon the animal. In Melville's day the harpoons were still thrown manually, but soon after his journeys the whale bomb and harpoon gun grew into wider use, and by the 1850s these advances reduced the dangerous length of time that the longboats spent being dragged behind the whale. Once they were killed, the whales' carcasses were brought alongside the ship, where the crew harvested oil and blubber and packed it into casks to prevent spoilage on the long voyage home, a return that might be years in the future. While aboard, the men needed to be sailors, hunters, and butchers on these floating processing plants.

The men harvested different types of whales, but focused on the large, toothed, and potentially aggressive sperm whale (*Physeter macrocephalus*), which produces sperm oil: a pure, clean-burning oil whose fine nature also made it a good lubricant. Prior to the discovery of petroleum at Oil Creek, Pennsylvania in 1859, whale oil was the primary source of oil for home and industrial use in the United States, a level of demand that allowed a successful whaler to turn a considerable profit. A single large sperm whale could produce eighty-five barrels of oil with a value of up to three thousand dollars (Moment 265). Whalers also took right whales (family *Balaenidae*), which yielded a less pure whale oil that could be used as fuel or as cooking oil. Once on land, both sperm oil and whale oil were made into everything from candles to lamp oil to sewing-machine oil—this last a sign of just how important this oil was to the Industrial Revolution. Right whales and other baleen whales also offered lightweight whalebone to feed the Victorian desire for high-quality corsets: women around the world owed their undergarments in part to the fleet of hundreds of American whaling ships (Moment 266).

Manifest Destiny and the Mexican-American War

Writers like Cooper, Dana, and later Melville helped to ensure that, large though their economic impact was, the social aspects of whaling and seagoing more broadly were out of proportion with the number of men engaged in the industry. Just as the nation pushed west beyond the Mississippi River into the Great Plains, the extension of American ships around the world symbolized to the American public the grand potential of the nation. These spaces—marine and terrestrial—symbolized economic opportunity to a people bent on expansion. The free land of the North American interior and the free game of the sea made fortunes for many people, and simple, honest livings for even more. Of course the land of the West was not free—it was occupied by many different Native American nations, as well as being claimed by Mexico and England—and the whaling industry brought about a precipitous decline in whale populations throughout the world, but the American narrative of Manifest Destiny obscured these casualties. To a public who could ignore the slaughter of both buffalo and whales in the name of progress, the American march toward the horizon was an unquestionable good.

The term *manifest destiny* was coined in 1845 by the journalist and political writer John O'Sullivan to describe the inevitability of continued U.S. national expansion, though the belief that the United States should stretch from the Atlantic to the Pacific dates to at least the Louisiana Purchase of 1803 (Pratt 796). This idea pushed Americans out of the settled spaces in the East in search of what Daniel Boone famously called "elbow room" (Faragher 326). Melville's portrait of the ambitious American conquering the high seas was tonally similar, if geographically different, from books such as Washington Irving's *A Tour on the Prairies* (1835) and Francis Parkman's *The Oregon Trail* (1849), which celebrated Americans' expansion into open space. Moreover, Cooper's production of both seafaring and frontier novels makes it clear just how closely related these two movements were in both the popular and artistic consciousness of the nation. Following journalist Horace Greeley's advice to "go west, young man," in the early nineteenth century Americans carved out the states of Louisiana (1812), Missouri (1821), and Arkansas (1836) from the land west of the Mississippi.

Manifest Destiny was not a single, coherent, official governmental policy, but the ideas heavily influenced the annexation of Texas in 1845, and the subsequent Mexican-American War (1846–48). The Mexican-American War was clearly driven by the principles of Manifest Destiny and President James K. Polk's policy of expansion, with American troops staging a series of strikes from California—still a part of Mexico—to Texas, and eventually going so far as to capture Mexico City. There was some resistance on the part of American citizens who saw the war as unjustified, or primarily in the service of Southern slaveholders: Henry David Thoreau's imprisonment for refusing to pay his poll tax prompted his essay "Resistance to Civil Government" in 1849. Despite such dissent, the war was a clear military success: In the Treaty of Guadalupe Hidalgo, the United States paid Mexico fifteen million dollars for roughly half the southern nation's land (Zinn 169). The United States gained an enormous amount of territory, land that now comprises all of California, Nevada, and Utah, as well as parts of Arizona, New Mexico, Colorado, Texas, Oklahoma, and Wyoming: effectively one quarter of the continental United States.

When gold was discovered in 1848 at Sutter's Mill, California, the resulting flood of prospectors finished the Americanization process begun by the war. California entered the Union in 1850 as the thirty-first state, completing the work of the Mexican-American War: The nation now had organized states from the Atlantic to the Pacific. Whaling ships had been there first, cruising the fertile seas off Baja California, and with them was the gaze of writers such as Melville, who helped introduce Americans to the expansionist ethos that undergirded the rush to the West Coast and let them imagine a nation stretching from sea to shining sea.

New England Transcendentalism

While Americans marched toward California and the gold fields, Melville retired from the travels of his youth and settled into a life of domesticity. Having begun his career as a writer in New York, in the summer of 1850 Melville moved to Arrowhead, a farm in Pittsfield, Massachusetts. He lived in the Berkshires for the next thirteen years, dividing time between managing his farm and writing the remainder of his novels—from *Moby-Dick* in 1851 to *The Confidence-Man* in 1857—as well as numerous short stories and literary sketches.

This was more than simply a country retreat, however, for it was during this period that Melville became more intimate with transcendentalism, a philosophical movement centered outside Boston in Concord, Massachusetts. This was the most influential intellectual movement in the nation during the 1830s and 1840s, but it was highly localized, making Melville's northward migration all the more important. Transcendentalism is most closely linked with Ralph Waldo Emerson and a circle of his close friends and associates, many of whom worked with the journal *The Dial*, published in its first incarnation from 1840 to 1844. Emerson's 1836 essay "Nature" is the earliest coherent articulation of the group's philosophy, which rejected the intellectualism of the university and the complicated theology of the Unitarian Church for an unmediated experience between humans and the Oversoul— their name for the undivided Godhead. The transcendentalists rebelled against both the predestination asserted by their Puritan forebears and the empiricism of the Enlightenment, preferring a spirituality that offered a direct individual relationship with the divine, influenced by Eastern religions such as Hinduism and Buddhism (Howe 620).

In a famous passage from his oft-quoted essay "Nature," Emerson imagines moving beyond the physical to the immortal:

> Standing on the bare ground,—my head bathed by the blithe air, and uplifted into infinite space,—all mean egotism vanishes. I become a transparent eyeball; I am nothing; I see all; the currents of the Universal Being circulate through me; I am part or particle of God. The name of the nearest friend sounds then foreign and accidental: to be brothers, to be acquaintances, master or servant, is then a trifle and a disturbance. I am the lover of uncontained and immortal beauty. In the wilderness, I find something more dear and connate than in streets or villages. (Emerson 8)

For Emerson and his compatriots, the Trinity was replaced with the transcendent Oversoul, which flowed through all creation, contained by neither man nor religion. The transcendentalists likewise rejected the Christian doctrine of original sin, preferring instead to see children's innocence as the proper goal of the spiritual individual. One's individuality could itself be an impediment to the transcendental experience, for the ego—the product of a jaded adulthood—was a barrier to recognizing the spirit of the Oversoul flowing through all things. The beauty of the natural world was thus not coincidental, but an emanation of the spiritual truth that flowed through all things.

Transcendentalism was more of an intellectual force than it was the beginning of a new quasi-religion, and Emerson is often considered America's first great philosopher. The movement was heavily influenced by European romanticism—Emerson studied the romantics carefully, even meeting the British poets William Wordsworth and Samuel Taylor Coleridge on his trip to England in 1833—but added to these ideas an American individualism and social awareness that moved beyond its European counterpart (Reynolds 18–19). Emerson spent many years giving a popular series of lectures, many of which he published as essays, thus further spreading his ideas beyond Concord and the modest circulation of *The Dial*.

Not unlike a pebble dropped in a pond, the ideas of transcendentalism radiated out from Concord through the intellectual waters of the nation. One of the writers drawn into the circle was the young Nathaniel Hawthorne, who was so enamored with transcendentalist ideas that he briefly joined the commune at Brook Farm in Massachusetts. While he quickly grew disenchanted by the utopian community, going so far as to satirize it in his novel *The Blithedale Romance* (1852), Hawthorne continued to have an uneasy attraction to the ideas of transcendentalism (Howe 633). Importantly, Hawthorne's ability to discuss the democratic notions of Emersonian transcendentalism alongside the restrictive mores of his ancestral Puritanism made him a veritable test case for these conflicting strains of American thought.

Hawthorne carried these ideas with him while hiking in the Berkshires on August 5, 1850, when he met Melville; so began one of the most famous relationships in American literary history (Loving 262). The two were at once fast friends, and it is hard not to romanticize the friendship: At the time, they stood atop the American literary scene like two coequal giants, and their stature has only grown since that time. It is interesting to speculate on the full extent of their fireside chats, but at the least, Melville seems to have imbibed from Hawthorne both the ideas of transcendentalism and his discomfort with it, swallowing the critique with the substance: the spiritualism of Emerson's

Oversoul was all well and good, but what did one do when confronted with the monomania of Captain Ahab? Chillingsworth's drive for revenge? Neither author's work seems comfortable dispensing with the idea of evil, though both do seem willing to find god and salvation outside the walls of the church.

The men's relationship cooled after its initial burst of ardor, but Hawthorne continued to influence Melville's work: just as Hawthorne had satirized Brook Farm in *The Blithedale Romance*, Melville turned his pen against Emerson and his disciple Henry David Thoreau in his 1857 novel, *The Confidence-Man* (Oliver 61–72). Despite these portraits, throughout his life Melville's rebellious intellect and nontraditional spirituality showed hints of the iconoclasm of transcendentalism, hallmarks of his time in Massachusetts that lasted long after Arrowhead failed and he moved his family back to New York.

New York City and the American Publishing Industry

While Melville's time in Massachusetts was crucial to his artistic development, most of his adult years were spent in New York City. Melville settled in New York upon his return from the sea in the 1840s, and after his sojourn at Arrowhead returned to the city for good in the 1860s. During these years, New York grew into by far the largest and most important city in the United States. Its location at the mouth of the Hudson River made New York an important port for goods coming from upstate, but when the completion of the Erie Canal in the 1820s linked Albany and the Hudson River with Buffalo and Lake Erie, the city gained access to the Great Lakes, and by extension the booming Midwest (Howe 117–20). New York was soon unquestionably the most important port in the United States. Between 1824 and 1836 there was an almost fourfold increase in the number of ships in New York harbor; between 1820 and 1850 the population of the city ballooned from 125,000 to over 500,000 (Howe 120). Following this growth, the city crept slowly north up the small island of Manhattan. The city grew along an organized grid pattern adopted first in 1811 and modified throughout the nineteenth century, most notably with the inclusion of Central Park in 1859. In 1883, workmen finished the iconic and logistically important Brooklyn Bridge, spanning the East River to connect Manhattan with Long Island (Lankevich 117–20).

The ethnic makeup of the city changed as the population grew, and by 1850 a remarkable half of the city was foreign-born, with Irish immigrants leading the way (Lankevich 71). The population was young—in 1845 nearly a third were under the age of fifteen—and dominated by poor immigrants crowded into tenements (Delbanco 101). Most of the immigrants streamed into the city to find work in the growing manufacturing sector: millwork that employed men, women, and children, demanded long hours, and offered little pay. The result was an unsettled, heterogeneous population that sometimes seemed to share little more than their common geography. As the immigrants became Americans, they found common ground in their position as workers, and New York experienced a number of strikes and worker riots during the nineteenth century. Tensions were at their highest following the periodic panics, the most prominent of which were in 1837, 1857, and 1873 (Zinn 211–51).

Each of these panics represented a sudden and dramatic contraction of the economy, followed by as many as five years of general economic stagnation, a financial malaise that emanated from New York's Wall Street to infect all parts of the economy. During the nineteenth century, "Wall Street" came to signify not the actual street marking the boundary of the old Dutch settlement of New Amsterdam so much as the many financial firms that were located in and around this famous road; eventually the name became shorthand for all of the American financial industry. These institutions had their roots in an informal group of businessmen who began meeting on Wall Street underneath a buttonwood tree to trade securities in 1790. The group grew and eventually moved inside, and in 1817 a general stock exchange was formally founded (Lankevich 54). These firms proliferated throughout the nineteenth century and became a crucial part of the larger march of American capitalism. By mid-century the area around Wall Street became the province of men such as the narrator in Melville's "Bartelby, the Scrivener": business professionals whose highly specialized work drove the invisible hand of finance.

Alongside the immigrant worker and the top-hatted financier in New York walked the ambitious writers and editors of the American publishing industry: By the 1840s, New York had outstripped both Boston and Philadelphia in terms of sheer volume and the number of individual works printed (Charvat 25–27). The brothers Evert and George Duyckinck presided over the city's vibrant literary scene at mid-century, editing and financing a series of important periodicals, most prominently the *Democratic Review* and *Literary World*. Around the two men and their publications coalesced a nationalist and reformist circle that became known as Young America: "a national movement, of which the New York branch was loudest and largest, made up of brooders and glib talkers, ideologues and idealists; some were green, others were seasoned, but all had a scrappy, streetfighter style" (Delbanco 96).

The literary products of the Young Americans were diverse in their interests and subjects, but they were consistently national in their themes: The group forged a literary nationalism that sought to define American culture in the same way the Founding Fathers had done politically (Wald 109–26). Embracing an unapologetic Americanism in the face of (perceived) European elitism, the Young Americans set the agenda of the New York literati and the tenor of American publishing more broadly. Melville became attached to the group in both name and style, as his early works, especially, sought to voice a distinctly American viewpoint. Later, these associations led to his short stories appearing in the influential *Harper's Magazine* during the 1850s. But Melville was never a joiner, and just as he had satirized the leading lights of transcendentalism in *The Confidence-Man*, his ambivalence toward the Duyckincks' circle found its way into his novel *Pierre* in 1852. Eventually rejected by and rejecting these young lights, while at the same time still suffering under the financial exploitation of the publishing industry, Melville's later life as a customs officer was far removed from the white heat of the Young Americans, even as he continued to inhabit the same cosmopolitan city as the nation's more famous writers.

Slavery, Race, and the Civil War

More than anything else, however, one issue dominated the American consciousness during the mid-nineteenth century, peeking into Melville's retreat at Arrowhead and echoing down the alleys of New York City: Questions regarding slavery, and race more broadly, consumed the nation from the 1840s until at least the 1870s, if not later. Slavery was not simply a problem of the South and Southerners, but seemed to permeate every aspect of American life during this time, from political questions over the admission of new states to philosophical questions about the value of human life. Even from his relative remove in Massachusetts and New York, Melville would have seen a nation convulsed with the conflict among Southern slaveholders, Northern abolitionists, and a federal government seemingly bent on forestalling bloodshed, as well as a general populace that vacillated between ambivalence and passion.

Questions regarding the place of slavery in America stretched back to the colonial period, with the Puritan leader and Salem witch trial judge Samuel Sewall penning the first antislavery tract in Boston in 1700. Slavery also threatened to derail the Constitutional Convention of 1787, leading to the Three-Fifths Compromise, which valued African-American slaves as something less than a whole person, but still allowed their numbers to bolster Southern political influence. The debate over slavery seemed to subside for a time following the adoption of the Constitution, and many politicians believed that slavery would simply fade away as a vestige of feudalism antagonistic to the values of the new nation; slavery was being abolished in the North and it was conceivable that the South would follow. But after New York became the last Northern state to abolish slavery in 1804, no Southern states appeared likely to do the same.

Rather than fade into obscurity in the face of the rise of capitalism, Southern slavery exploded during the nineteenth century, growing from just half a million slaves in 1790 to four million in 1860 (Zinn 171). Eli Whitney's invention of the cotton gin in 1793 freed cotton producers from the laborious process of removing the seed from the cotton boll by hand, allowing the planters to move more land into the production of the cash crop, but also requiring more cheap labor. The importation of slaves was outlawed in 1808, but smugglers continued to bring Africans to the South to feed the seemingly insatiable need for field labor. Though not all slaves worked in cotton fields—some states concentrated on tobacco or sugar cane, and all regions employed slaves in household duties—as cotton production pushed from the southeast west into Alabama, Mississippi, and later Texas, the South became more and more dependent upon slave labor.

With a few exceptions—such as Nat Turner's slave revolt in 1831—the political crisis over slavery lay largely dormant until the 1840s, when Northern abolitionists such as William Lloyd Garrison pushed the issue to the fore. The Mexican-American War served as one flashpoint, with Northerners such as Thoreau viewing the war as a Southern campaign to protect the slaveholding state of Texas and further expand slavery in the Southwest. Garrison decried the war in his influential and stridently abolitionist newspaper the *Liberator*. Garrison was joined for a time at the paper by the escaped slave Frederick Douglass, whose impassioned pleas on the part of slaves came in the form of speeches, autobiographies, a novel, and later the newspaper the *North Star*. Other prominent activists included the freedwoman Sojourner Truth, who fought for the rights of African American women, and escaped slave Harriet Tubman, conductor on the Underground Railroad, as well as a network of religious and political figures linked and inspired by the outpouring of abolitionist literature.

The passage of the Fugitive Slave Act in 1850 helped abolitionists to make slavery the central issue in the nation's political debates. The act was a concession to Southern slaveholders angry over the admission of California as a free state following the Treaty of Guadalupe Hidalgo at the end of the Mexican-American War. The law set up a system to ensure the return of escaped slaves to the South, thus extending the legal reach of slaveholders by implicating Northern officials and financially incentivizing the return of escaped slaves. Even Melville's abolitionist father-in-law in Boston, Judge Lemuel Shaw, was compelled to enforce a law that he detested, an example of how the act forced even passive Northerners to confront their complicity with what was known as the "Slave Power" (Delbanco 153–54).

Antislavery sentiment in the North was further energized in 1852 by the publication of Harriet Beecher Stowe's unabashedly abolitionist novel *Uncle Tom's Cabin; or, Life Among the Lowly*. The cloying racism of Stowe's sentimental novel is at best distasteful today, but in the 1850s its promotion of abolition helped to lead toward the Civil War. Whether or not the story of Abraham Lincoln greeting Stowe by saying, "So you're the little woman who wrote the book that started this great war," is apocryphal, it accurately captures the public spirit regarding the novel's influence on mid-century America (Hendler 152).

In 1857, the Supreme Court issued a ruling in *Dred Scott v. Sanford* asserting that African Americans could not be citizens, regardless of whether or not they were slaves. The judgment was an affront not only to free African Americans, but also to anyone who took seriously the Declaration of Independence's claim that "all men are created equal." The case exposed the American legal system's inability to resolve the tension between a Constitution that allowed for slavery and the Declaration's yearning for equality, contradictions that had been allowed to fester through a combination of naïveté and willful ignorance. Written as the *Dred Scott* case made its way through the courts, Melville's story "Benito Cereno" (1855) portrays an American consciousness blinded by racism and unable to bring the law to bear on the atrocities of slavery.

The story leaves the reader as adrift as many in the country must have felt, powerless to control the seemingly inexorable creep toward war.

Incensed in part by the *Dred Scott* decision, in 1859 the radical abolitionist John Brown staged a dramatic but ill-fated raid on the federal arsenal in Harper's Ferry, Virginia, hoping to capture weapons to supply a slave rebellion. The raid failed miserably from a military standpoint, and Brown and his followers were tried for treason and hung. Publically, however, it offered another rallying point for Northern abolitionists in the form of the eccentric and uncompromising Brown, and served to embolden his admirers, pushing even the most reticent closer to a violent confrontation with the slave system (Zinn 185–86).

The 1860 election of Abraham Lincoln to the presidency did little to calm matters. Lincoln was himself lukewarm on the idea of immediate abolition, preferring instead a more gradual approach, but even this view was too radical for the slave-owning aristocracy in the South. As the first candidate from the abolitionist-minded Republican Party, Lincoln's presidency was anathema to Southerners, and states began to secede even before he was inaugurated. Fighting broke out at Fort Sumter in South Carolina in 1861, and the Civil War wracked the nation for the next four years. Lincoln trod a fine line, trying not to anger slaveholding states still in the Union, but his issue of the Emancipation Proclamation in 1863 gave a clear voice to what everyone understood: The war was first and foremost about the institution of slavery. By the time Confederate forces surrendered in April of 1865, 600,000 men were dead on both sides, representing roughly two percent of the population (Zinn 192). Dead along with the soldiers was Lincoln himself, assassinated by Southern sympathizer John Wilkes Booth as the president celebrated the close of the war.

It is hard to overstate the effects of the Civil War upon the United States. Whether it was the changed political landscape, or the sudden absorption of four million new citizens, the war seemed to change everything about the nation, all while reaffirming its dedication "to the proposition that all men are created equal," to quote Lincoln's

Gettysburg Address. Newspapers brought the war to Melville and the rest of the North in detailed accounts wired in from war correspondents around the country, offering heretofore-unseen access to the events on the front line. Melville puzzled over these reports alongside his comrades, eventually stitching together the simultaneously detailed and incomplete accounts of the far-flung reporters in his poetry collection *Battle-Pieces and Aspects of the War* (1866).

After the commercial failure of *Battle-Pieces*, Melville withdrew further from the literary circles in which he had once circulated. During the 1870s and 1880s, as he worked silently away in the Customs Office in New York, he most closely resembled the stereotype of the unknown artist alone with only his work. But even during these dark, declining years Melville was still writing and traveling, and embittered though he may have been, he never rejected the teeming city that surrounded his home, nor ignored the world that accompanied him on his daily commute down to the docks. Perhaps we need a better image of Melville at work, one to replace that of him alone at his attic desk: an image of Melville walking down to his job on the waterfront, an old sea cap perched on his head, making his way through the roiling streets of the cosmopolitan New York, buying a newspaper from an ex-slave and hailing an Irish-American policeman, while musing on the intersection of art and commerce. Here is a man in step with the contradictions and complications of the nineteenth century; here is an artist of and for an age.

Works Cited

Charvat, William. *Literary Publishing in America, 1790–1850*. Amherst: Massachusetts UP, 1993.

Craig, Lee A., and Robert M. Fearn. "Wage Discrimination and Occupational Crowding in a Competitive Industry: Evidence from the American Whaling Industry." *Journal of Economic History* 53.1 (1993): 123–38.

Davis, Lance E., Robert E. Gallman, and Teresa. D. Hutchins. "Technology, Productivity, and Profits: British-American Whaling Competition in the North Atlantic, 1816–1842. *Oxford Economic Papers* 39.4 (1987): 738–59.

Delbanco, Andrew. *Melville: His World and Work*. New York: Vintage, 2005.

Emerson, Ralph Waldo. *Nature*. Boston: Munroe, 1849.

Faragher, John Mack. *Daniel Boone: The Life and Legend of an American Pioneer*. New York: Holt, 1993.

Hendler, Glenn. "The Structure of Sentimental Experience." *Yale Journal of Criticism* 12.1 (1999): 145–53.

Howe, Daniel Walker. *What Hath God Wrought: The Transformation of America, 1815–1848*. New York: Oxford UP, 2007.

Lankevich, George J. *New York City: A Short History*. New York: New York UP, 2002.

Loving, Jerome M. "Melville's Pardonable Sin." *New England Quarterly* 47.2 (1974): 262–78.

Moment, David. "The Business of Whaling in America in the 1850s." *Business History Review* 31.3 (1957): 261–91.

Oliver, Egbert S. "Melville's Picture of Emerson and Thoreau in *The Confidence-Man*." *College English* 8.2 (1946): 61–72.

Pratt, Julius W. "The Origin of 'Manifest Destiny'." *American Historical Review* 32.4 (1927): 795–98.

Reynolds, David S. *Beneath the American Renaissance: The Subversive Imagination in the Age of Emerson and Melville*. New York: Oxford UP, 2011.

Vishneski, John S., III. "What the Court Decided in *Dred Scott v. Sandford*." *American Journal of Legal History* 32.4 (1988): 373–90.

Wald, Priscilla. *Constituting Americans: Cultural Anxiety and Narrative Form*. Durham, N.C.: Duke UP, 1995.

Zinn, Howard. *A People's History of the United States: 1492–Present*. New York: Perennial, 2001.

The Critical Response to Herman Melville _____

John Samson

The critical response to the works of Herman Melville has perhaps followed the most erratic path of any American author, for during his lifetime his works were lauded and disparaged, then largely forgotten. In the 1920s, thirty years after his death, his works were rediscovered and his reputation rehabilitated, so much so that he has been canonized by the critical establishment as one of the greatest American authors, and his *Moby-Dick* the greatest American novel, as a writer as great as William Faulkner has said. This essay will begin by discussing contemporary reviews, from the generally positive response to Melville's early novels to the increasingly negative reception of *Moby-Dick* through *Battle-Pieces*. Thereafter, Melville fell out of public and critical favor until the Melville revival in the twentieth century. From that time through 1945, criticism tended to go in two directions: New Critical assessments of the aesthetic qualities of Melville's fiction and historicist analysis of biographical, cultural, and literary influences. In the postwar period, these approaches continued and were joined by theory-based criticism, such as Marxist, psychoanalytical, phenomenological, deconstructionist, etc. These approaches also have in the past two decades generated several significant critical controversies, with critics discussing gender and sexuality in his work, as well as whether Melville's politics were liberal or conservative or some blend of the two. Finally, recent criticism has tended to expand the Melville canon to focus on those works previously labeled "minor" (his early works, his short fiction, his poetry), on his relation to the visual arts, and on his status as an international author.

Contemporary reviews, conveniently collected by Brian Higgins and Hershel Parker, trace the critical response during Melville's career. Melville's first two novels, *Typee* (1846) and *Omoo* (1847), were both popular and critical successes, as they were marketed as nonfiction and fed the contemporary interest in the South Seas that had begun with Louis de Bougainville's 1772 narrative describing the discovery of Tahiti. Reviews praised Melville for capturing the adventurous exploration of the exotic culture of the Polynesian paradise in detailed, evocative (even provocative) descriptions. However, considerable dissenting views were voiced by the religious press, which lamented Melville's criticism of missionaries and his celebration of what they considered a decadent, savage culture, and by those who saw Melville's criticism of imperialist expansion as opposing the spread of civilization. Finally, some critics voiced concerns about the books' veracity, since the events seemed too "romantic" and the prose too well-written to be the true events described by a sailor.

Melville's effort in his next novel, *Mardi* (1849), to move beyond the factual narrative genre provoked considerable critical puzzlement and censure, particularly from British reviewers: There seemed to them too much in the novel, too much philosophizing, too much social criticism, too much allegorizing, too much verbiage. American reviewers, caught up in the patriotic effort to define and promote a genuinely American literature not based on European models, were generally more positive, praising its style and its expansive subject matter, though many of the reviews noted the same faults that the British critics did. Melville returned to the personal narrative genre in *Redburn* (1849) and *White-Jacket* (1850), written in a period of four months and "done for money," as Melville confessed. Reviewers generally applauded his return to more straightforward, realistic narratives of nautical life, noting also that the two novels showed more interesting and accomplished writing than Melville's previous works. British reviewers, though, complained about *Redburn*'s depictions of poverty in Liverpool, while some from both sides of the Atlantic called *White-Jacket* less of a novel than an exposé of tyrannical practices in the American navy.

Similar to the responses to *Mardi*, reviews of *Moby-Dick* (1851), published in England as *The Whale*, were largely negative, with most critics expressing disappointment that Melville had again lapsed from the lively simplicity of the previous two books. Those positive reviews focused on the whaling passages and characterized the book as wild and adventurous, written in an accomplished and vigorous style. Others condemned the wildness, seeing the book as an odd mixture of romance and factuality, presented in a convoluted and incoherent style. Once more, Melville also ran afoul of the religious press, which censured his "blasphemous" philosophizing; many of those passages Melville's English publisher excised, as Higgins and Parker indicate, prompting generally better reviews in Britain. Melville's response to the criticism levied against *Moby-Dick* was to write an even more outrageous and controversial novel, *Pierre; or, The Ambiguities* (1852); in fact, Hershel Parker has argued that Melville's abrupt announcement, halfway into the novel, that Pierre is an author resulted from those reviews. The reviews of *Pierre* were even more broadly negative, even nasty, than those of the previous novel. Critics condemned virtually every aspect of the novel's subject matter and style.

Owing largely to the damage to his reputation from *Pierre*, there are considerably fewer and less extensive reviews of Melville's subsequent books. *Israel Potter* (1855) was seen as interesting and charming, but little more—reactions generally duplicated in reviews of the 1856 short-story collection *The Piazza Tales*. Some of the reviewers of *The Confidence-Man* (1857) voice the recurring wish that Melville had gone back to writing works like *Typee* and *Omoo* and left off the philosophizing and moralizing; others are simply puzzled by the book's oddity. Finally, Melville's poetry received increasingly fewer reviews and virtually no praise during his lifetime. Critics of the 1866 collection *Battle-Pieces and Aspects of the War* mainly point out the flaws in his poetry, a practice echoed in most of the reviews of the epic poem *Clarel* (1876) as well. And, but for a few scattered articles, the rest is silence until the Melville revival.

This renewed critical interest in Melville was sparked by the 1919 centenary of his birth, but also had its source in a major literary development in the first two decades of the century, the advent of American literary modernism; the modernists' emphasis on experimentation, on the destruction of literary forms, and on the revision of tradition found a significant predecessor in the Melville of those novels that nineteenth-century critics deplored. That Melville's works received the attention of the most significant critics of the day also helped launch the revival. Carl Van Doren mentioned Melville in his *The American Novel* (1921) and D. H. Lawrence included two chapters on Melville in *Studies in Classic American Literature* (1923), a book that placed Melville with such established writers as James Fenimore Cooper, Nathaniel Hawthorne, and Walt Whitman; Lawrence's assessment was later confirmed by F. O. Matthiessen's inclusion of Melville in his canon of writers in *American Renaissance: Art and Expression in the Age of Emerson and Whitman* (1941). Raymond Weaver (1921), John Freeman (1926), and Lewis Mumford (1929) wrote book-length studies devoted wholly to Melville. These works are both biographical and critical, attempting to recapture for the public the life and works largely lost since the 1850s and providing to varying degrees the application of the few available details from his life to the criticism of his works; of these, Mumford's account is the fullest and most satisfying. These efforts were supplemented by articles in a variety of established journals; in particular, *American Literature*, founded in 1929, would publish a number of articles on Melville in the 1930s. Interest focused not only on analyzing Melville's works but also in linking Melville, as Lawrence did implicitly, with other major literary figures, such as Homer, Dante, Spenser, Shakespeare, Emerson, and Whitman. Further contributing to interest in Melville was the first publication of *Billy Budd* (1924) and the republication of *Pierre* (1930). A recent (2001) commentary, interesting and eccentric, on the literary and political implications of the revival is Clare L. Spark's voluminous *Hunting Captain Ahab: Psychological Warfare and the Melville Revival*, in which she argues that early biographers and critics expressed their upper-class ideology by suppressing the centrality of Ahab and Ahabian values in the Melville canon.

The major aspect of the Melville revival was, as Spark's argument implies, the establishment of *Moby-Dick* as Melville's masterwork.

While earlier, H. S. Salt in England and Archibald MacMechan in Canada had praised *Moby-Dick*, Weaver and Lawrence in the 1920s began what would become a deluge of critical attention to the book. Essays by R. P. Blackmur and Walter Bezanson, as well as a book by W. S. Gleim, set the tone for consideration of *Moby-Dick*'s aesthetic qualities. A number of significant books devoted exclusively to *Moby-Dick* follow this path. In a 1953 study, C. L. R. James focuses on Ahab and sees the novel as a forecast of twentieth-century totalitarianism, while Charles Olson focuses on Ishmael and sees Shakespeare, particularly *King Lear*, as a source and inspiration. The continuing relevance and significance of Melville's masterwork for later twentieth- and early twenty-first-century culture and criticism is evident in the works applying recent critical theory. Edward Edinger follows a Jungian approach, and Paul Brodtkorb, Jr., Robert Zoellner, and Shawn Thomson interpret the novel from the perspective of phenomenology, which, like Jungian psychoanalysis, analyzes literature as it expresses the structures of the mind. Others use philosophical or poststructuralist approaches, which emphasize the breaking of traditional forms or structures to expose the artificial, constructed nature of literary texts. Melville's unconventional *Moby-Dick* thus seems an appropriate text for poststructuralist critics to examine. Therefore, Eyal Peretz reads the novel in terms of Antonin Artaud's theater of the future, David Dowling employs reader-response theory, K. L. Evans applies Wittgenstein, Bainard Cowan focuses on allegory, William Spanos uses Heideggerian and Foucauldian deconstruction, and Viola Sachs employs her own individualistic linguistic deconstruction.

The other general direction of *Moby-Dick* studies concerns identifying and applying Melville's sources. Howard P. Vincent's *The Trying-Out of* Moby-Dick (1949) is the most extensive early effort in this vein, but it is merely one of many articles and books. In notable articles, Howard C. Horsford relates the novel to Ralph Waldo Emerson; Millicent Bell relates it to Pierre Bayle; Richard Sewell to Shakespeare; James Barbour and Leon Howard to Thomas Carlyle;

Michael Hollister to Edgar Allen Poe; Gail Coffler to classicism; Gustaaf Van Cronphout to Faustian literature; Elizabeth Schultz to sentimental literature; Thomas Vargish to gnosticism; and Mukhtar Isani to Zoroastrianism. Bernhard Radloff uses Melville's philosophical sources as well as later philosophers such as Friedrich Nietzsche and Jacques Derrida to view the novel as a deconstruction of philosophical tradition. Book-length studies of *Moby-Dick*'s sources also deal with the novel's religious dimensions: H. Kulkarni sees the whale as a Hindu avatar, and Ibana Pardes discusses Melville's "bibles" from various cultures and religions, while, most significantly, T. Walter Herbert discusses the novel in light of Melville's Calvinist background. Finally, Tim Severin's *The Search for Moby Dick: The Quest for the White Whale* (2000) traces Melville's path through South Seas cultures and their legends about a white whale.

Including both critical analysis and source-study are collections of essays devoted to *Moby-Dick*. They include volumes edited by Tyrus Hillway and Luther S. Mansfield (1953), Milton R. Stern (1960), Richard Chase (1962), Howard P. Vincent (1969), Michael T. Gilmore (1977), Faith Pullin (1978), A. Robert Lee (1984), Harold Bloom (1986), John Gretchko (1992), and John Bryant, Mary K. Bercaw-Edwards, and Timothy Marr (2006). These volumes provide a convenient way of navigating through the vast number of articles and book chapters on *Moby-Dick* and also give a good overview of the shorter critical essays available to students of Melville's novel. Also helpful is Nick Selby's 1999 guide to the criticism of *Moby-Dick*.

A renewal of interest in Melville biography has occurred since 1950, spurred by Jay Leyda's *The Melville Log* (1951), itself not a biography but a collection, in chronological order, of biographical materials. Leyda shared this information with Leon Howard, whose biography remained the most balanced and accomplished account of Melville's life and works until the mid-1990s. Other biographies, by Newton Arvin (1950), Eleanor Melville Metcalf (1953), and Tyrus Hillway (1963), add little to Howard's work, though Metcalf does work from her more extensive knowledge of family documents. Three works approach Melville from the perspective of psychology: Richard Chase (1949) discusses Melville's works from a conventional psychological perspective, Edwin Haviland Miller (1975) offers a standard psychoanalytic view focusing on Melville's relationship with Hawthorne, while Philip Young (1993) speculates about the influence of "private" family details concerning Melville's father. Hershel Parker's monumental two-volume biography (1996, 2003) is easily the most meticulously researched, the fullest and most detailed account of Melville's life and career and should remain the definitive Melville biography. Two shorter biographies, by Laurie Robertson-Lorant (1996) and Andrew Delbanco (2005) are judicious, readable discussions of Melville's life and works. Other biographies focus on narrower periods of Melville's life: Wilson Heflin examines the whaling years, Merton M. Sealts, Jr., his years as lecturer, and Stanton Garner the Civil War years.

In addition to the biographies, Melville critics have available a wealth of research aids. The incomplete and often textually unreliable Hendricks House edition of Melville's works, does, however, include introductions by established critics of the time and copious endnotes identifying Melville's sources for particular allusions, images, and passages. Beginning in 1967, *The Writings of Herman Melville*, edited by Harrison Hayford, Alma A. MacDougall, Hershel Parker, and G. Thomas Tanselle and published by Northwestern University Press and the Newberry Library, has provided students of Melville with reliable texts approved by the Center for Editions of American Authors. Each volume of the Northwestern-Newberry edition contains a "Historical Note" on the composition and early reception and a "Note on the Text" containing emendations and variants. Essential to the study of Melville's sources is Merton M. Sealts's *Melville's Reading*, an authoritative listing of books Melville read, which has been supplemented by his *Pursuing Melville: 1940–1980* and by numerous notes by many Melville scholars in the *Melville Society Extracts,* the journal succeeded by *Leviathan: A Journal of Melville Studies*, published by the Melville Society, the academic group devoted to the study of Melville. Also of use are Mary K. Bercaw's *Melville's Sources*, Brian Higgins's *Herman Melville: A Reference Guide, 1931–1960*, G. Watson Branch's *Melville: The Critical Heritage*, Beatrice Ricks and Joseph D. Adams's *Herman Melville: A Reference Bibliography 1900–1972*, and John Bryant's *A Companion to Melville Studies*. The last is an extensive introduction to the criticism on Melville's life, works, and themes, with chapters by noted critics on these issues. Bryant also edited an annotated bibliography of Melville dissertations from 1924 to 1980. *American Literary Scholarship*, currently edited by David J. Nordloh and Gary Scharnhorst, is an annual that includes a chapter on Melville discussing notable publications and thus provides a good introduction to each year's criticism. More particular in scope are Gail Coffler's volumes summarizing Melville's classical and religious allusions and two recent guides, Robert L. Gale's *A Herman Melville Encyclopedia* and Carl Rollyson and Lisa Paddock's *Herman Melville: A to Z*, both of which summarize the works, identify characters, and provide background information. Finally, two recent studies provide sound, basic introductions to Melville's works: Christopher Sten's *The Weaver-God, He Weaves: Melville and the Poetics of the Novel* and Wyn Kelley's *Herman Melville: An Introduction*. For a more extensive critical introduction, see William B. Dillingham's four volumes, each centering on a particular period in Melville's career.

Students of Melville face a daunting and bewildering array of articles to consult; in the past two decades each year has produced over fifty articles, the totality giving perspectives on almost any imaginable topic and using every approach available to critics. However, since the late 1970s, many of the important recent articles are available in edited collections, most unrestricted by topic or approach. Such collections include those edited by Faith Pullin (1978), Louis J. Budd (1985), John Byrant and Robert Milder (1997), and Sanford E. Marovitz and A. C. Christodoulou (2001). Four works are introductory guides, by editors Robert S. Levine (1998), Giles Gunn (2005), Wyn Kelley, and Kevin J.

Hayes (2007). Milton R. Stern has edited a collection on *Typee* (1982), Brian Higgins and Hershel Parker on *Pierre* (1983), and both Robert Milder (1988) and Donald Yannella (2002) on *Billy Budd*, the latter a more recent and accomplished collection of four outstanding essays. Beyond these collections and the articles listed in bibliographies, students of Melville must rely on specific searches of the *MLA Bibliography* and the yearly Melville chapter in *American Literary Scholarship*.

As for books of Melville criticism, they, too, may seem overwhelming, so what follows is my attempt to classify them by theme and approach. As T. Walter Herbert's study of *Moby-Dick* indicates, religion was an important factor in Melville's life from the start, and it was often a nexus of conflict in his life and works. His mother was a staunch Calvinist and his father a more liberal Christian; moreover, Melville's experiences as a whaler and a sojourner among Pacific natives and his broad reading in writers such as the skeptic Montaigne and the French *philosophes* exposed him, perhaps more than any American, to religious alternatives to the dominant Protestantism of the day. Therefore, it is no surprise that religion and philosophy are some of the most important concerns of Melville's critics. William Braswell's seminal study in 1943 of Melville's religious thought was followed in 1949 by Nathalia Wright's more specific analysis of Melville's use of the Bible in his works. Lawrance Thompson, writing from a Calvinist perspective, indicts Melville's religious stance, which Thompson characterizes as a career-long quarrel with God. In contrast, Walter Donald Kring sees in Melville's career a continuing religious journey and places Melville in the context of nineteenth-century religious history. James Duban also uses this context to analyze Melville's major fiction but adds to religion its relation to politics and ideology in his excellent readings. Finally, Rowland A. Sherrill discusses Melville and belief, and H. Bruce Franklin, in a classic study, discusses Melville's use of comparative mythology and pagan religions.

Several important critical works focus on Melville's reading in and presentation of philosophy. In an important book from the 1950s, Milton R. Stern examines philosophical naturalism as a contrast to idealism in Melville's works, while in the 1960s Edgar Dryden shows Melville trying to maintain a distinction between art and truth as it changes throughout his career. John Seelye's 1970 book focuses on Melville's skepticism and uncertainty, expressed through his use of romantic irony. Three more recent studies further develop Melville's relation to philosophical issues. In an excellent and convincing argument, John Wenke discusses the forms of philosophical fiction in Melville and their relation to literary creation: Wenke shows Melville throughout his career engaged in a struggle to find fictional forms to express his moral imagination. Bernhard Radloff, in a companion volume to his book on *Moby-Dick*, uses historical philosophical sources and contemporary theory to discuss Melville's fiction from *Pierre* to *Billy Budd*. Most recently, Jamie Lorentzen compares Melville to the nineteenth-century philosopher and theologian Søren Kierkegaard, concentrating on the issues of tragic optimism and polarized worlds.

Less overtly philosophical are those critical works that deal with Melville, the mind, and art. Early works in this vein are William Ellery Sedgwick's *Herman Melville: The Tragedy of Mind* (1944) and Merlin Bowen's *The Long Encounter: Self and Experience in the Writings of Herman Melville* (1963). More recent criticism tends to be more particular and more valuable. As a sound introduction to these issues, students of Melville should turn to Robert Milder's *Exiled Royalties*, which discusses what Melville's texts reveal about his psychology. Neal L. Tolchin examines the topic of grief, which he sees stemming from the young Melville's observing his mother's bereavement over the loss of her husband. Bruce Grenberg focuses on the theme of quest and negation, Peter Bellis on identity and textual form, and Clark Davis on the head/heart conflict in the works following *Moby-Dick*. In an interesting pairing, Paul McCarthy examines the theme of madness and Daniel Paliwoda that of boredom. Three critics examine humor in Melville: Edward H. Rosenberry and Jane Mushabac offer fairly conventional readings, while John Bryant's *Melville and Repose* develops the full aesthetic implications of the rhetoric of Melville's humor. Finally, four books deal with one particular work each: John Bryant's textual study of *Typee*, novelist Dan McCall's reading of "Bartleby," Brian Higgins and Hershel Parker's analysis of Parker's "Kraken Edition" of *Pierre*, and Stanton Garner's discussion of narrative in *Billy Budd*.

Significant recent criticism has approached Melville's works from the perspective of cultural studies, though, as one might expect, works on this subject appeared in the mid-1960s and early 1970s, with John Bernstein writing on pacifism and rebellion in Melville, Nicholas Canaday on Melville and authority, and Ray B. Browne on Melville and humanism. In 1980 Carolyn Karcher published an influential book on Melville's relation to slavery, race, and violence, and in 1981 Joyce Sparer Adler wrote about the theme of war. Most interesting and influential, though, is Michael Paul Rogin's *Subversive Genealogy*, which uses Melville family politics, the American political situation of the 1840s and 1850s, and the writings of Marx to produce innovative reading of Melville's works. Wai-Chee Dimock, focusing on the poetics of individualism, also sees Melville's works echoing cultural paradigms such as Manifest Destiny. Nancy Fredricks relates democratic values to Melville's art in *Moby-Dick* and *Pierre*, which she sees as a diptych in which Ahab and Pierre are two sides of an erroneous response to the Kantian sublime. Two books focus on the profession of writing of the period: Sheila Post-Lauria discusses Melville's relation to the marketplace, forms of popular literature, and his audience, while John Evelev examines Melville and professionalism in New York. Wyn Kelley also concentrates on New York in her study of Melville and literary and urban form. Susan Weiner discusses Melville's fiction in the context of American law, while Harrison Hayford examines the motif of prisoners. Three 2009 books relate Melville's works to other cultures: Sterling Stuckey relates them to African culture, Dennis Berthold to Italian politics, and Robert T. Tally, Jr., to globalization and literary cartography.

Unsurprisingly, given Melville's travels and his early novels, one particular culture, that of the South Seas, has received perhaps the most sustained critical attention. Charles R. Anderson's seminal study, *Melville in the South Seas*, explores Melville's experiences, his reading in Pacific narratives, and their relation to the novels that are set there. James Baird's *Ishmael* examines the cultural symbolism involved in this subject, while T. Walter Herbert in *Marquesan Encounters*, narrowing and deepening Anderson's analysis, places Melville's work in the context of two South Seas narratives, by the naval captain David Porter and the missionary Charles Stewart. Foregrounding the cannibalism issue are Geoffrey Sanborn's theoretical and contextual *The Sign of the Cannibal*, which develops beyond Baird's thesis by showing Western culture's difficulty in dealing with the primitive, and Mary K. Bercaw-Edwards's historical *Cannibal Old Me*, which calls into question Melville's experiences among the Typees. Most recently, *"Whole Oceans Away": Melville and the Pacific*, edited by Jill Barnum, Wyn Kelley, and Christopher Sten, collects twenty-two essays on Melville and the Pacific, emphasizing his relation to postcolonialism.

Identifying Melville's sources and applying them to the analysis of his works has been a major component of Melville criticism. Early source studies, such as Anderson's, tended to focus on Melville's early novels. Merrell R. Davis examines *Mardi* and its sources (1952), William H. Gilman *Redburn* (1951), Howard P. Vincent *White-Jacket* (1970) and *Moby-Dick* (1948). More recent works have focused on particular influences. Dorothee Finkelstein analyzes Melville and the Orient, Sanford E. Marovitz discusses Melville and the Greeks, and Norwood Andrews, Jr., examines the influence of the Portuguese national poet, Camoens. Others explain the influence of British poets: of significance are Carol Moses on Spenser, Julian Markels on Shakespeare, Henry Pommer on Milton (supplemented by a special issue of *Leviathan: A Journal of Melville Studies* edited by Robin Grey), and Christopher S. Durer on the Romantics. Others look to the impact of American culture and writers. Kevin J. Hayes discusses Melville's folk roots, while John B. Williams links Melville with Emerson. Two recent works, a book by Robert K. Wallace and a collection edited by Robert

S. Levine and Samuel Otter, connect Melville to Frederick Douglass. It is Hawthorne, however, who had the greatest influence on the development of Melville's literary career in the early 1850s, as Melville indicated in his review-essay "Hawthorne and His Mosses" (1850). John P. McWilliams, Richard H. Brodhead, and Peter West have discussed their connection, the last with regard to the topic of information culture, while a special issue of *ESQ: A Journal of the American Renaissance* edited by Robert K. Martin and Leland S. Person and a collection by Jana L. Argersinger and Person develop various perspectives on the Hawthorne-Melville relationship.

Responding to the rise of literary theory in the 1960s, some recent Melville critics have applied the various methodologies of theory to their work. My work on what Melville referred to as his "narratives of facts" uses Mikhail Bakhtin's theories of the novel to discuss the dialogue of ideological discourses concerning native peoples, the missionary enterprise, capitalism, millennialism, and the American Revolution. Bryan C. Short employs rhetorical theory to good effect, while Samuel Otter effectively applies the rhetoric of the literary anatomy to discuss the body and race. Elizabeth Renker uses poststructuralist methods, psychoanalytic and deconstructionist, to discuss Melville's anxiety as he approaches the scene of writing, and, less interestingly and less successfully, Joseph Adamson provides a post-Freudian reading of Melville. Cesare Casarino uses poststructuralist theory to read *White-Jacket* and *Moby-Dick* in relation to Marx and Conrad. Carol Colatrella's Foucauldian reading discusses moral reform and discipline. William V. Spanos's sequel to his book on *Moby-Dick* concerns the fiction after it and uses the "New Americanist" approach, advocated by Donald Pease, to describe Melville as a precursor of poststructuralism. Gender-oriented approaches to Melville take one of two directions: seeing his works as they relate to or depict homosexuality and how they represent Melville's attitudes toward women. Robert K. Martin discusses homosexuality in Melville's fiction, particularly the sexual power structures within his society, while two works, James

Creech's *Closet Writing/Gay Reading* and Monika Mueller's *"This Infinite Fraternity of Feeling"*, discuss homosexuality in *Pierre*. Elizabeth Renker's 1994 article in *American Literature* alleging that Melville may have been a wife-beater (reprinted as a chapter in her *Strike through the Mask*) touched off a storm of controversy and raised the issue of Melville's relation to women. A less controversial counterpoint is a 2006 collection, *Melville and Women*, edited by Elizabeth Schultz and Haskell Springer, thirteen essays divided among the categories Melville's reading in women authors, women in *Pierre*, and women in other Melville works.

One particular development in Melville criticism, related to the interdisciplinary turn in literary theory, is an interest in the relation of Melville to the visual arts, a major interest throughout his travels and career. Christopher Sten's *Savage Eye* collects fourteen essays on Melville and architecture, painting, and sculpture, Douglas Robillard discusses Melville's interest in art and his allusions to it in his works, and Robert K. Wallace compares the work of Melville to one artist, J. M. W. Turner. Three recent works focus on *Moby-Dick* and the visual arts: Elizabeth A. Schultz's comprehensive *Unpainted to the Last* traces the influence and imagery of the novel in twentieth-century art; Robert K. Wallace presents Frank Stella's vast series of installations, each corresponding to a chapter from the novel; and artist Robert Del Tredici reproduces his own responses to Melville, along with an account of his engagement with the novel.

While the body of Melville criticism has been concerned with his novels, his short stories and poetry have also received critical attention. In the period from 1853 to 1856, Melville produced primarily short fiction, plus the short novel *Israel Potter*. "Bartleby, the Scrivener: A Tale of Wall Street" probably has generated the most criticism, and it is also the most frequently anthologized. Critics have discussed its religious emphasis on Christian responsibility and even seen Bartleby as a Christ-figure or a proto-existentialist, while others have emphasized the story as a critique of capitalism and working conditions in an increasingly urbanized and bureaucratized America. "Benito Cereno," also frequently anthologized, has been seen as one of the most cogent presentations of racial issues in antebellum America, particularly the limitations of white Americans' perceptions of blacks. "The Paradise of Bachelors and the Tartarus of Maids" has also garnered considerable critical notice, whether from feminist critics on the gender issues it treats or from social critics on class and working conditions. A few books are devoted exclusively to the study of Melville's short stories: Richard Harter Fogle initiated these with his 1960 New Critical study; R. Bruce Bickley, Jr. examines the methodology of Melville as short story writer; Marvin Fisher relates the stories to issues of 1850s America; William Dillingham provides a sound introduction to their themes; Mary-Madeleine Gina Riddle discusses the "prophetic vision" in them; and Lea Newman presents a valuable reader's guide to Melville's short stories. In the one book devoted to Melville's novel of the period, Alexander Keyssar examines *Israel Potter* and the American Dream.

While it began with R. P. Blackmur's 1946 article and Howard P. Vincent's 1947 anthology, on the whole, criticism of Melville's poetry has been a more recent phenomenon. William Bysshe Stein's *The Poetry of Melville's Late Years* (1970) and William H. Shurr's *The Mystery of Iniquity* (1972) begin the brief list of book-length studies by tracing themes and the increasing complexity and difficulty of Melville's poetic career. In *Melville and His Circle: The Last Years* (1996), William B. Dillingham discusses the intellectual influences on the poetry of Melville's late years. William C. Spengemann's 1999 *American Literary History* article sounded a challenging and significant note, arguing that Melville should be considered *primarily* a poet. Developing this idea more fully are Edgar A. Dryden, who in *Monumental Melville* (2007) chronicles Melville's turn from fiction to poetry, and Hershel Parker, who in *Melville: The Making of a Poet* (2008) discusses how Melville was a poet for a much longer time than he was a fiction writer; both offer extensive readings of Melville poems. In 2007, too, John

Bryant edited a special issue of *Leviathan* on "Melville the Poet." Significant study of Melville's very long epic of a group of pilgrims in the Holy Land, *Clarel*, begins with Walter Bezanson's introduction and extensive notes to his 1960 Hendricks House edition. Two other books deal exclusively with *Clarel*: Stan Goldman's *Melville's Protest Theism* (1993) and William Potter's *Melville's Clarel and the Intersympathy of Creeds* (2004).

Finally, the past twenty years have seen a number of what could be called quasi-critical works, novels which are a response to Melville's life and works. Ray Bradbury's *Green Shadows, White Whale* (1992) is a fictional account of Bradbury's experiences with the filming of John Huston's 1956 film adaptation of *Moby-Dick*, for which Bradbury wrote the screenplay. Frank Lentricchia's *Lucchesi and the Whale* (2001) includes his title character's extensive analysis of Melville's novel, while Sena Jeter Naslund's widely acclaimed *Ahab's Wife* (1999), as the title indicates, imagines the life of Melville's captain's wife. Three novels include Melville as a character: Larry Duberstein's *The Handsome Sailor* (1998), Frederick Busch's *The Night Inspector* (1999), and Jay Parini's *The Passages of Herman Melville* (2010). Through narration and journal entries, Duberstein presents his fictional Melville in incidents from 1850 to 1852, 1882 to 1883, and 1888; Busch's title character encounters Melville during his custom-house years; and Parini, in chapters alternating between first-person narrative by Melville's wife Lizzie and third-person narrative, covers the range of passages in Melville's life. These novels, though, had an interesting precursor in *Genoa: A Telling of Wonders* (1973), a novel by Paul Metcalf, Melville's great-grandson, who relates Melville to Columbus in an experimental fictional form combining letters, documentary, and imagination. All these works attest to the enduring inspiration Melville's works have been to critics and readers alike.

Works Cited

Adamson, Joseph. *Melville, Shame, and the Evil Eye: A Psychoanalytic Reading.* Albany: State U of New York P, 1997.

Adler, Joyce Sparer. *War in Melville's Imagination.* New York: New York UP, 1981.

Anderson, Charles R. *Melville in the South Seas.* New York: Columbia UP, 1939.

Andrews, Norwood, Jr. *Melville's Camoens.* Bonn: Bouvier Verlag, 1989.

Argersinger, Jana L., and Leland S. Person, eds. *Hawthorne and Melville: Writing a Relationship.* Athens: U of Georgia P, 2008.

Arvin, Newton. *Herman Melville.* New York: Sloan, 1950.

Baird, James. *Ishmael: A Study of the Symbolic Mode in Primitivism.* Baltimore: Johns Hopkins UP, 1958.

Barnum, Jill, Wynn Kelley, and Christopher Sten, eds. *"Whole Oceans Away": Melville and the Pacific.* Kent: Kent State UP, 2007.

Bellis, Peter. *No Mysteries Out of Ourselves: Identity and Textual Form in the Novels of Herman Melville.* Philadelphia: U of Pennsylvania P, 1990.

Bercaw, Mary K. *Melville's Sources.* Evanston: Northwestern UP, 1987.

Bercaw-Edwards, Mary K. *Cannibal Old Me: Spoken Sources in Melville's Early Works.* Kent: Kent State UP, 2009.

Bernstein, John. *Pacifism and Rebellion in the Writings of Herman Melville.* Hague: Mouton, 1964.

Berthold, Dennis. *American Risorgimento: Herman Melville and the Cultural Politics of Italy.* Columbus: Ohio State UP, 2009.

Bezanson, Walter, ed. *Clarel.* By Herman Melville. Chicago: Hendricks House, 1960.

_____. "*Moby-Dick*: Work of Art." Moby-Dick *Centennial Essays.* Ed. Tyrus Hillway and Luther S. Mansfield, eds. Dallas: Southern Methodist UP, 1953. 651–71.

Bloom Harold. *Herman Melville's* Moby-Dick. New York: Chelsea House, 1986.

Bowen, Merlin. *The Long Encounter: Self and Experience in the Writings of Herman Melville.* Chicago: U of Chicago P, 1963.

Bradbury, Ray. *Green Shadows, White Whale.* New York: Knopf, 1992.

Branch, Watson G., ed. *Melville: The Critical Heritage.* Boston: Routledge, 1974.

Braswell, William. *Melville's Religious Thought.* Durham: Duke UP, 1943.

Brodhead, Richard H. *Hawthorne, Melville, and the Novel.* Chicago: U of Chicago P, 1976.

Brodtkorb, Paul, Jr. *Ishmael's White World: A Phenomenological Reading of* Moby-Dick. New Haven: Yale UP, 1965.

Browne, Ray B. *Melville's Drive to Humanism.* Lafayette: Purdue UP, 1971.

Bryant, John. *Melville and Repose: The Rhetoric of Humor in the American Renaissance.* Oxford: Oxford UP, 1993.

_____. *Melville Unfolding: Sexuality, Politics, and the Verisons of* Typee: *A Fluid-Text Analysis.* Ann Arbor: U of Michigan P, 2008.

_____, ed. *Melville Dissertations, 1924–1980: An Annotated Bibliography and Subject Index.* Westport, Conn.: Greenwood, 1983.

_____, ed. *Melville the Poet.* Spec. issue of *Leviathan: A Journal of Melville Studies* 9.3 (2007).

Bryant, John, Mary K. Bercaw-Edwards, and Timothy Marr, eds. *Ungraspable Phantom: Essays on* Moby-Dick. Kent: Kent State UP, 2006.

Bryant, John, and Robert Milder, eds. *Evermoving Dawn: Essays in Celebration of the Melville Centennial*. Kent: Kent State UP, 1997.

Budd, Louis J. *On Melville: The Best from* American Literature. Durham: Duke UP, 1988.

Busch, Frederick. *The Night Inspector*. New York: Harmony, 1999.

Canaday, Nicholas. *Melville and Authority*. Gainesville: U of Florida P, 1968.

Casarino, Cesare. *Modernity at Sea: Melville, Marx, and Conrad in Crisis*. Minneapolis: U of Minnesota P, 2002.

Coffler, Gail. *Melville's Allusions to Religion: A Comprehensive Index and Glossary*. New York: Praeger, 2004.

_____. *Melville's Classical Allusions: A Comprehensive Index and Glossary*. Westport, Conn.: Greenwood, 1985.

_____. "*Moby-Dick*: Classicism in Melville's Style." *Essays in Arts and Sciences* 16 (1987): 73–84.

Colatrella, Carol. *Literature and Moral Reform: Melville and the Discipline of Reading*. Gainesville: U of Florida P, 2002.

Creech, James. *Closet Writing/Gay Reading: The Case of Melville's* Pierre. Chicago: U of Chicago P, 1993.

Davis, Clark. *After the Whale: Melville in the Wake of* Moby-Dick. Tuscaloosa: U of Alabama P, 1995.

Davis, Merrell R. *Melville's* Mardi: *A Chartless Voyage*. New Haven: Yale UP, 1952.

Delbanco, Andrew. *Melville: His World and Work*. New York: Knopf, 2005.

Del Tredici, Robert. *Floodgates of the Wonderworld: A* Moby-Dick *Pictorial*. Kent: Kent State UP, 2001.

Dillingham, William B. *An Artist in the Rigging: The Early Work of Herman Melville*. Athens: U of Georgia P, 1972.

_____. *Melville and His Circle: The Last Years*. Athens: U of Georgia P, 1996.

_____. *Melville's Later Novels*. Athens: U of Georgia P, 1986.

_____. *Melville's Short Fiction 1853–1856*. Athens: U of Georgia P, 1977.

Dimock, Wai-Chee. *Empire for Liberty: Melville and the Poetics of Individualism*. Princeton: Princeton UP, 1989.

Dowling, David. *Chasing the Whale: The* Moby-Dick *Marathon; or, What Melville Means Today*. Iowa City: U of Iowa P, 2010.

Duban, James. *Melville's Major Fiction: Politics, Theology, and Imagination*. DeKalb: Northern Illinois UP, 1983.

Duberstein, Larry. *The Handsome Sailor*. Sag Harbor, N.Y.: Permanent, 1998.

Durer, Christopher S. *Herman Melville, Romantic and Prophet: A Study of His Romantic Sensibility and His Relationship to European Romanticism*. Fredericton, N.B.: York, 1996.

Dryden, Edgar A. *Melville's Thematics of Form: The Great Art of Telling the Truth*. Baltimore: Johns Hopkins UP, 1968.

_____. *Monumental Melville: The Formation of a Literary Career*. Stanford: Stanford UP, 2007.

Edinger, Edward F. *Melville's* Moby-Dick: *An American Nekyia*. Toronto: Inner City, 1995.

Evans, K. L. *Whale!* Minneapolis: U of Minnesota P, 2003.

Evelev, John. *Tolerable Entertainment: Herman Melville and Professionalism in Antebellum New York*. Amherst: U of Massachusetts P, 2006.

Finkelstein, Dorothee. *Melville's Orienda*. New Haven: Yale UP, 1961.

Fogle, Richard Harter. *Melville's Shorter Tales*. Norman: U of Oklahoma P, 1960.

Franklin, H. Bruce. *The Wake of the Gods: Melville's Mythology*. Stanford: Stanford UP, 1963.

Fredricks, Nancy. *Melville's Art of Democracy*. Athens: U of Georgia P, 1995.

Freeman, John. *Herman Melville*. London and New York: Macmillan, 1926.

Gale, Robert L., ed. *A Herman Melville Encyclopedia*. Westport, Conn: Greenwood, 1995.

Garner, Stanton. *The Civil War World of Herman Melville*. Lawrence: U of Kansas P, 1993.

_____. *The Two Intertwined Narratives of Herman Melville's* Billy Budd: *A Study of an Author's Literary Method*. Lewiston, N.Y.: Mellen, 2010.

Gilman, William H. *Melville's Early Life and* Redburn. New York: New York UP, 1951.

Gleim, W. S. *The Meaning of* Moby-Dick. New York: Brick Row Bookshop, 1938.

Goldman, Stan. *Melville's Protest Theism: The Hidden and Silent God in* Clarel. DeKalb: Northern Illinois UP, 1993.

Grenberg, Bruce. *Some Other World to Find: Quest and Negation in the Works of Herman Melville*. Urbana: U. of Illinois P., 1989.

Gretchko, John M. *Melvillean Loomings: Essays on* Moby-Dick. Cleveland: Falk, 1992.

Grey, Robin, ed. *Melville and Milton*. Spec. issue of *Leviathan: A Journal of Melville Studies* 4.1–2 (2002).

Gunn, Giles, ed. *A Historical Guide to Herman Melville*. Oxford: Oxford UP, 2005.

Hayes, Kevin J. *The Cambridge Introduction to Herman Melville*. Cambridge: Cambridge UP, 2007.

_____. *Melville's Folk Roots*. Kent: Kent State UP, 1999.

Hayford, Harrison. *Melville's Prisoners*. Evanston: Northwestern UP, 2003.

Heflin, Wilson. *Melville's Whaling Years*. Ed. Mary K. Bercaw-Edwards and Thomas Farel Heffernan. Nashville: Vanderbilt UP, 2004.

Herbert, T. Walter. *Marquesan Encounters: Melville and the Meaning of Civilization*. Cambridge: Harvard UP, 1980.

Higgins, Brian. *Herman Melville: A Reference Guide, 1931–1960*. Boston: Hall, 1987.

Higgins, Brian, and Hershel Parker, eds. *Critical Essays on Herman Melville's* Pierre; or, The Ambiguities. Boston: Hall, 1983.

_____. *Reading Melville's* Pierre; or, The Ambiguities. Baton Rouge: Louisiana State UP, 2006.

_____. *Herman Melville: The Contemporary Reviews*. Cambridge: Cambridge UP, 1995.

Hillway, Tyrus. *Herman Melville*. New York: Twayne, 1963.

Hollister, Michael. "Melville's Gam with Poe in *Moby-Dick*: Bulkington and Pym." *Studies in the Novel* 21.3 (1989): 279–91.

Howard, Leon. *Herman Melville: A Biography*. Berkeley: U of California P, 1951.

James, C. L. R. *Mariners, Renegades, and Castaways: The Story of Herman Melville and the World We Live In*. London: Allison, 1953.

Karcher, Carolyn L. *Shadow Over the Promised Land: Slavery, Race, and Violence in Melville's America*. Baton Rouge: Louisiana State UP, 1980.

Kelley, Wyn, ed. *A Companion to Herman Melville*. Malden, Mass.: Blackwell, 2006.

_____. *Herman Melville: An Introduction*. Malden, Mass.: Blackwell, 2008.

_____. *Melville's City: Literary and Urban Form in Nineteenth-Century New York*. New York: Cambridge UP, 1996.

Keyssar, Alexander. *Melville's* Israel Potter: *Reflections of the American Dream*. Cambridge: Harvard UP, 1969.

Kring, Walter Donald. *Herman Melville's Religious Journey*. Raleigh, N.C.: Pentland, 1997.

Lawrence, D. H. *Studies in Classic American Literature*. New York: Seltzer, 1923.

Lentricchia, Frank. *Lucchesi and the Whale*. Durham: Duke UP, 2001.

Levine, Robert S. *The Cambridge Companion to Herman Melville*. Cambridge: Cambridge UP, 1998.

Levine, Robert S., and Samuel Otter, eds. *Frederick Douglass and Herman Melville: Essays in Relation*. Chapel Hill: U of North Carolina P, 2008.

Leyda, Jay, ed. *The Melville Log: A Documentary Life of Herman Melville, 1819–1891*. New York: Harcourt, 1951.

Lorentzen, Jamie. *Sober Cannibals, Drunken Christians: Melville, Kierkegaard, and Tragic Optimism in Polarized Worlds*. Macon: Mercer UP, 2010.

Markels, Julian. *Melville and the Politics of Identity: From* King Lear *to* Moby-Dick. Champaign: U of Illinois P, 1993.

Marovitz, Sanford E. *Humanizing the Ideal: Melville and the Greeks*. Kent: Kent State UP, 2001.

Marovitz, Sanford E., and A. C. Christodoulou, eds. *Melville "Among the Nations": Proceedings of an International Conference, Volos, Greece, July 2–6, 1997*. Kent: Kent State UP, 2001.

Martin, Robert K. *Hero, Captain, and Stranger: Male Friendship, Social Critique, and Literary Form in the Sea Novels of Herman Melville*. Chapel Hill: U of North Carolina P, 1987.

Martin, Robert K., and Leland S. Person, eds. *The Hawthorne-Melville Relationship*. Spec. issue of *ESQ: A Journal of the American Renaissance* 46.1–2 (2000).

McCall, Dan. *The Silence of Bartleby*. Ithaca: Cornell UP, 1989.

McCarthy, Paul. *"The Twisted Mind": Madness in Herman Melville's Fiction*. Iowa City: U of Iowa P, 1990.

McWilliams, John P. *Hawthorne, Melville, and the American Character: A Looking-Glass Business*. Cambridge: Cambridge UP, 1984.

Metcalf, Eleanor Melville. *Herman Melville: Cycle and Epicycle*. Cambridge: Harvard UP, 1953.

Metcalf, Paul. *Genoa: A Telling of Wonders*. Penland, N.C.: Jargon Society, 1973.

Milder, Robert, ed. *Critical Essays on Melville's* Billy Budd, Sailor. Boston: Hall, 1988.

_____. *Exiled Royalties: Melville and the Life We Imagine*. Oxford: Oxford UP, 2006.

Miller, Edwin Haviland. *Herman Melville: A Biography*. New York: Braziller, 1975.

Moses, Carole. *Melville's Use of Spenser*. New York: Lang, 1989.

Mueller, Monika. *"This Infinite Fraternity of Feeling": Gender, Genre, and Homoerotic Crisis in Hawthorne's* The Blithedale Romance *and Melville's* Pierre. Teaneck: Fairleigh Dickinson UP, 1996.

Mumford, Lewis. *Herman Melville*. New York: Harcourt, 1929.

Mushabac, Jane. *Melville's Humor: A Critical Study*. Hamden, Conn.: Archon, 1981.

Naslund, Sena Jeter. *Ahab's Wife, or, The Star-Gazer*. New York: Morrow, 1999.

Newman, Lea Bertani Vosar. *A Reader's Guide to the Short Stories of Herman Melville*. Boston: Hall, 1986.

Olson, Charles. *Call Me Ishmael*. New York: Reynall, 1947.

Otter, Samuel. *Melville's Anatomies*. Berkeley: U of California P, 1996.

Paliwoda, Daniel. *Melville and the Theme of Boredom*. Jefferson, N.C.: McFarland, 2010.

Pardes, Ibana. *Melville's Bibles*. Berkeley: U of California P, 2008.

Parini, Jay. *The Passages of Herman Melville*. New York: Doubleday, 2010.

Parker, Hershel. *Herman Melville: A Biography*. 2 vols. Baltimore: Johns Hopkins UP, 1996, 2003.

_____. *Melville: The Making of the Poet*. Evanston: Northwestern UP, 2008.

Peretz, Eyal. *Literature, Disaster, and the Enigma of Power: A Reading of* Moby-Dick. Stanford: Stanford UP, 2003.

Pommer, Henry F. *Milton and Melville*. Pittsburgh: U of Pittsburgh P, 1943.

Post-Lauria, Sheila. *Correspondent Colorings: Melville in the Marketplace*. Amherst: U of Massachusetts P, 1996.

Potter, William. *Melville's* Clarel *and the Intersympathy of Creeds*. Kent: Kent State UP, 2004.

Pullin, Faith, ed. *New Perspectives on Melville*. Kent: Kent State UP, 1978.

Radloff, Bernhard. *Cosmopolis and Truth: Melville's Critique of Modernity*. New York: Lang, 1997.

_____. *Will and Representation: The Philosophical Foundations of Melville's Theatrum Mundi*. New York: Lang, 1997.

Renker, Elizabeth. *Strike Through the Mask: Herman Melville and the Scene of Writing*. Baltimore: Johns Hopkins UP, 1996.

Ricks, Beatrice, and Joseph D. Adams, *Herman Melville: A Reference Bibliography 1900–1922*. Boston: Hall, 1973.

Riddle, Mary-Madeleine Gina. *Herman Melville's Piazza Tales: A Prophetic Vision*. Gothenburg: Acta Universitatis Gothoburgensis, 1985.

Robertson-Lorant, Laurie. *Melville: A Biography*. New York: Clarkson Potter, 1996.

Robillard, Douglas. *Melville and the Visual Arts: Ionian Form, Venetian Vision*. Kent: Kent State UP, 1997.

Rogin, Michael Paul. *Subversive Genealogy: The Politics and Art of Herman Melville*. New York: Knopf, 1983.

Rollyson, Carl, and Lisa Paddock, eds. *Herman Melville A to Z: The Essential Reference to His Life and Work*. New York: Checkmark, 2001.

Rosenberry, Edward H. *Melville and the Comic Spirit*. Cambridge: Harvard UP, 1955.

Samson, John. *White Lies: Melville's Narratives of Facts*. Ithaca: Cornell UP, 1989.

Sanborn, Geoffrey. *The Sign of the Cannibal: Melville and the Making of a Postcolonial Reader*. Durham: Duke UP, 1998.

Schultz, Elizabeth. "The Sentimental Subtext of Moby-Dick." *ESQ: A Journal of the American Renaissance* 42 (1996): 29–49.

_____. *Unpainted to the Last:* Moby-Dick *and Twentieth-Century American Art*. Lawrence: U of Kansas P, 1995.

Schultz, Elizabeth, and Haskell Springer, eds. *Melville and Women*. Kent: Kent State UP, 2006.

Sealts, Merton M., Jr. *Melville as Lecturer*. Cambridge: Harvard UP, 1957.

_____. *Melville's Reading: Revised and Enlarged*. Columbia: U of South Carolina P, 1988.

_____. *Pursuing Melville: 1940–1980*. Madison: U of Wisconsin P, 1982.

Sedgwick, William Ellery. *Herman Melville: The Tragedy of Mind*. Cambridge: Harvard UP, 1944.

Seelye, John. *Melville: The Ironic Diagram*. Evanston: Northwestern UP, 1970.

Selby, Nick. *Herman Melville:* Moby-Dick. New York: Columbia UP, 1999.

Severin, Tim. *In Search of Moby Dick: The Quest for the White Whale*. New York: Basic, 2000.

Sherrill, Rowland A. *The Prophetic Melville: Experience, Transcendence, and Tragedy*. Athens: U of Georgia P, 1979.

Short, Bryan C. *Cast by Means of Figures: Herman Melville's Rhetorical Development*. Amherst: U of Massachusetts P, 1992.

Shurr, William H. *The Mystery of Iniquity: Melville as Poet, 1857–1891*. Lexington: UP of Kentucky, 1972.

Spanos, William V. *The Errant Art of* Moby-Dick: *The Canon, the Cold War, and the Struggle for American Studies*. Durham: Duke UP, 1995.

_____. *Herman Melville and the American Calling: The Fiction After* Moby-Dick. Albany: State U of New York P, 2008.

Spark, Clare L. *Hunting Captain Ahab: Psychological Warfare and the Melville Revival*. Kent: Kent State UP, 2001.

Spengemann, William C. "Melville the Poet." *American Literary History* 11 (1999): 569–609.

Stein, William Bysshe. *The Poetry of Melville's Late Years: Time, History, Myth, and Religion*. Albany: State U of New York P, 1970.

Sten, Christopher, ed. *Savage Eye: Melville and the Visual Arts*. Kent: Kent State UP, 1991.

_____. *The Weaver-God, He Weaves: Melville and the Poetics of the Novel*. Kent: Kent State UP, 1996.

Stern, Milton R., ed. *Critical Essays on Herman Melville's* Typee. New York: Hall, 1982.

_____. *The Fine Hammered Steel of Herman Melville*. Urbana: U of Illinois P, 1968.

Stuckey, Sterling. *African Culture and Melville's Art: The Creative Process in* Benito Cereno *and* Moby-Dick. Oxford: Oxford UP, 2009.

Tally, Robert T., Jr. *Melville, Mapping, and Globalization: Literary Cartography in the American Baroque Writer*. New York: Continuum, 2009.

Thompson, Lawrance. *Melville's Quarrel with God*. Princeton: Princeton UP, 1952.

Thomson, Shawn. *The Romantic Architecture of* Moby-Dick. Cranbury: Fairleigh Dickinson UP, 2000.

Van Doren, Carl. *The American Novel*. New York: Macmillan, 1921.

Vincent, Howard P., ed. *The Collected Poems of Herman Melville*. Chicago: Hendricks House, 1947.

_____, ed. *The Merrill Studies in* Moby-Dick. Columbus, Ohio: Merrill, 1969.

_____. *The Tailoring of Melville's* White-Jacket. Evanston: Northwestern UP, 1970.

_____. *The Trying-Out of* Moby-Dick. Boston: Houghton, 1949.

Wallace, Robert K. *Douglass and Melville: Anchored Together in Neighborly Style*. New Bedford, Mass.: Spinner, 2005.

_____. *Frank Stella's* Moby-Dick: *Words and Shapes*. Ann Arbor: U of Michigan P, 2000.

_____. *Melville and Turner: Spheres of Love and Fright*. Athens: U of Georgia P, 1992.

Warren, Robert Penn. "Melville the Poet." *Kenyon Review* 8 (1946): 208–23.

Weaver, Raymond M. *Herman Melville: Mariner and Mystic*. New York: Doran, 1921.

Weiner, Susan. *Law in Art: Melville's Major Fiction and Nineteenth-Century American Law*. New York: Lang, 1992.

Wenke, John. *Melville's Muse: Literary Creation and the Forms of Philosophical Fiction*. Kent: Kent State UP, 1995.

West, Peter. *The Arbiters of Reality: Hawthorne, Melville, and the Rise of Mass Information Culture*. Columbus: Ohio State UP, 2008.

Williams, John B. *White Fire: The Influence of Emerson on Melville*. Long Beach: California State U Long Beach P, 1991.

Wright, Nathalia. *Melville's Use of the Bible*. Durham: Duke UP, 1949.

Yannella, Donald, ed. *New Essays on* Billy Budd. Cambridge: Cambridge UP, 2002.

Young, Philip. *The Private Melville*. University Park: Pennsylvania State UP, 1993.

Zoellner, Robert. *The Salt-Sea Mastodon: A Reading of* Moby-Dick. Berkeley: U of California P, 1973.

Melville and the Transcendentalists _____

Clark Davis

> Nay, I do not oscillate in Emerson's rainbow.
>
> > (Melville to Evert Duyckinck, 1849)
>
> But, every night, when the curtain falls, truth comes in with darkness.
>
> > (Melville, "The Piazza")

Herman Melville's 1853 story "Cock-A-Doodle-Doo!; or, The Crowing of the Noble Cock Beneventano" has one of the strangest endings in all of American fiction. The tale concerns a down-in-the-mouth narrator, depressed by debt and hounded by creditors, who one day hears a rooster crowing in the distance. "Hark! There again! Did ever such a blessed cock-crow so ring out over the earth before! Clear, shrill, full of pluck, full of fire, full of fun, full of glee. It plainly says—'*Never say die!*'" (Melville, *Piazza Tales* 271). Fired by the cheering sound of the bird, the debtor sets out across the countryside to locate the source of his sudden good mood. But after many inquiries and false trails, he inadvertently discovers that the cock belongs not to a rich and powerful landowner (as he had expected) but to the somber, poorly fed man who cuts his firewood. Merrymusk, as he's known, is an odd character: silent, tall and thin, "with a long saddish face, yet somehow latent joyous eye" (280). He seems cursed with bad luck but works hard to feed his sickly wife and four children. How is it that *he* owns this magnificent, golden rooster whose crowing lifts the soul and lightens the spirit? The narrator is both appalled by Merrymusk's poverty and puzzled by his claim to be a "rich man—a very rich man" because of the abundance of good feelings spread by the rooster. Not even death can weaken the sawyer's hopeful spirit. On his final visit to the woodcutter's shanty, the narrator witnesses the last moments of Merrymusk and his entire family as all expire in a moment of collective spiritual ecstasy inspired by the "musical, triumphant" crowing of the cock (287).

Most Melville scholars consider this story to be a satire, and though there have been disagreements over whether or not its author is attacking a specific contemporary (Thoreau and Wordsworth are the usual suspects), there is a general consensus on his wider target—optimism. The money-obsessed narrator may be wrong to equate wealth with happiness, but his attention to the sawyer highlights Merrymusk's questionable contention that mood can override reality. It may be possible, in other words, to be both poor and happy, but it's also true that too much optimism can cause neglect of the basic requirements of everyday life. Dying in a state of bliss may be desirable, but wouldn't it be better not to die at all by paying attention to your health? In the great majority of his writings, including his letters, Melville is consistently suspicious of attempts to cast a rosy light on what he considers the harder facts of life. In a well-known passage from a letter to Hawthorne in 1851, he complained about the German author Goethe's exhortation to "Live in the all": "That is to say, your separate identity is but a wretched one,—good; but get out of yourself, spread and expand yourself, and bring to yourself the tinglings of life that are felt in the flowers and the wood, that are felt in the planets Saturn and Venus, and the Fixed Stars. What nonsense! Here is a fellow with a raging toothache. 'My dear boy,' Goethe says to him, 'you are sorely afflicted with that tooth; but you must live in the all, and then you will be happy!'" (Melville, *Correspondence* 193). For Melville, nature may be benevolent and even glorious at times, but it is also threatening and painful, and no amount of positive thinking will change a cold hard fact.

Comments of this sort, as well as stories like "Cock-A-Doodle-Doo!," have led many commentators to classify Melville as an antitranscendentalist. A pedagogical commonplace lumps him in with Hawthorne and Poe as "dark romantics," or romantic skeptics who oppose the light-infused thinking of writers like Ralph Waldo Emerson, Henry David Thoreau, and Walt Whitman. The truth is somewhat more complicated. In the first place, Melville shared with the transcendentalists a generalized romanticism. Like Emerson, he considered nature—and particularly the relationship between the individual and nature—to be a topic of supreme importance in the era of early industrialization. The cultivation and discovery of the individual self was crucial to most thinkers of the period as a counterbalance to rapidly expanding technology and a response to moral and political questions raised by issues like slavery. Nature could be a refuge from the machine. The individual, alone in the woods, might be able to shed the distractions of the modern world and reach an inner divinity (or at least a stress-free authenticity) available to all—provided, of course, that nature was understood as benevolent and the intuitions of the self as godly. But what if nature wasn't inherently good? What if the individual, left to his or her own devices, turned out to be evil?

For Emerson, particularly early in this career, these critical questions caused little real anxiety. In his foundational essay "Nature," published in 1836, he established the spiritual agency of isolation in a non-urban environment: "In the woods too, a man casts off his years, as the snake his slough, and at what period soever of life, is always a child. In the woods, is perpetual youth. Within these plantations of God, a decorum and sanctity reign, a perennial festival is dressed, and the guest sees not how he should tire of them in a thousand years" (Emerson 1:10). Nature thus became a refuge from the distortions of civilization, an undeceiving mirror that revealed the modern individual's inner innocence, his childlike soul. And because uncorrupted nature was necessarily good, it followed that the intuitions of the natural self were simply the upwelling of this beneficent spirit. Explicitly opposing his Calvinist ancestors' doctrine of original sin, Emerson audaciously claimed that the untainted self could not produce evil impulses:

> On my saying, What have I to do with the sacredness of traditions, if I live wholly from within? my friend suggested,—"But these impulses may be from below, not from above." I replied, "They do not seem to me to be such; but if I am the Devil's child, I will live then from the Devil." No law can be sacred to me but that of my nature. Good and bad are but names

very readily transferable to that or this; the only right is what is after my constitution, the only wrong what is against it. (2: 30)

The question of morality for Emerson depended entirely upon the idea that civilization had corrupted the originally innocent self. Nature offered a restorative, a way to see our compromises and corruptions and return to the purity of our beginnings.

Though Melville shared a deep interest in these questions, the answers he found were both less certain and less hopeful than Emerson's. Throughout his career, from his first novel *Typee* to his final work of fiction, *Billy Budd*, he was fascinated by what he called "the mystery of iniquity." And though this phrase referred primarily to human personality, it could also apply to his understanding of nature. In *Typee* the narrator, Tommo, jumps ship in the Marquesas Islands in the South Pacific and with his fellow sailor Toby sets out to explore the interior of an island notorious for its cannibalistic natives. After much difficulty, the two sailors eventually penetrate the Typee valley, a seeming paradise, but despite the unspoiled beauty of this natural world, they can never be sure whether the people they meet there are good, evil, or somewhere in between. The Typees seem to live in an uncorrupted environment like the one Emerson describes, but are they originally innocent and therefore trustworthy or are they inherently wicked? Melville never completely answers these questions. His fictional method is complex enough to make us uncertain about Tommo's judgments, and what hints we find in the novel are shrouded in ambiguity.

In the novels and stories that follow *Typee*, nature is often a dominating presence, but its relationship to human values is rarely clear. In *Moby-Dick*, for instance, we often see moments of great beauty and tranquility that produce optimistic or even mystical moods in the narrator, Ishmael. And yet Melville rarely allows such perceptions to go unchallenged. He has a habit of thinking dialectically (that is, in terms of mutually opposing ideas), and this predilection for balance often leads him to undercut hopeful pictures of nature with a quick reminder of its cruelties. In a revealing passage from the first half of the book, Ishmael describes what it's like to serve as a lookout for nearby whales. He stands in the masthead, high above the deck, but the weather is so calm and the motion of the ship so hypnotizing that he almost falls into a trance: "There you stand, lost in the infinite series of the sea, with nothing ruffled but the waves. The tranced ship indolently rolls; the drowsy trade winds blow; everything resolves you into languor" (Melville, *Moby-Dick* 156). But rather than offer a simple scene of nautical laziness, Melville extends the description until it begins to sound very much like Emerson's account of the self in nature: "There is no life in thee, now, except that rocking life imparted by a gently rolling ship; by her, borrowed from the sea; by the sea, from the inscrutable tides of God" (159). Ishmael seems to achieve the kind of transcendental unity with nature that Emerson sometimes portrays as the way to reconnect with God. And yet, in an instant the scene changes, and wonder and oneness turn to terror: "But while this sleep, this dream is on ye, move your foot or hand an inch, slip your hold at all; and your identity comes back in horror. Over Descartian vortices you hover. And perhaps, at mid-day, in the fairest weather, with one half-throttled shriek you drop through that transparent air into the summer sea, no more to rise for ever" (159). Nature's beauty may be real, but its hazards and indifference to human life are no less real. To pretend otherwise, for Melville, is simply dangerous.

In this sense "the mystery of iniquity" could apply equally to nature and to people. A conception of the natural world as spiritually uplifting has to account, in Melville's view, for the presence of the shark. In chapter 66 of *Moby-Dick*, Ishmael describes the voraciousness of hoards of sharks as they rip into the carcass of a recently killed whale: "But it was not thus in the present case with the *Pequod*'s sharks; though, to be sure, any man unaccustomed to such sights, to have looked over her side that night, would have almost thought the whole round sea was one huge cheese, and those sharks the maggots in it" (302). Sharks regularly appear in Melville's work as representatives of the indifferent, violent energies of nature, what Melville sometimes calls the "universal cannibalism" of the ocean. They eat without conscience or consciousness and will even, in a wounded frenzy, consume themselves: "They viciously snapped, not only at each other's disembowelments, but like flexible bows, bent round, and bit their own; till those entrails seemed swallowed over and over again by the same mouth, to be oppositely voided by the gaping wound" (302). The sharks, like Moby-Dick himself, seem to Ishmael the agents of some malevolent deity, a sign that what you find in nature is not always a reflection of your own childlike innocence.

And if sharks are a product of nature, then what about shark-like people? In Melville's early novel *Redburn* (1849), he describes a sailor named Jackson, a sick-looking, pained little man with no hair and jaundiced skin, who combines intelligence with the suggestion of deep personal corruption: "And besides all this, it was quite plain, that he was by nature a marvelously clever, cunning man, though without education; and understood human nature to a kink, and well knew whom he had to deal with; and then, one glance of his squinting eye, was as good as a knock-down, for it was the most deep, subtle, infernal looking eye, that I ever saw lodged in a human head" (Melville, *Redburn* 57). Jackson is the first in a line of mysterious figures of strong natural will and moral blindness that includes Ahab and John Claggart, the sinister accuser of the title character in *Billy Budd*. A possible extension of Jackson, Claggart gives the appearance of education, perhaps even sophistication, but his deeper personality evokes Melville's fullest discussion of the idea of natural depravity. Though akin to Calvinism's doctrine of original sin, the definition of depravity Melville provides in *Billy Budd* seems closer to a description of psychosis, expanding on Edgar Allan Poe's sense of the "perverse": "Though the man's even temper and discreet bearing would seem to intimate a mind peculiarly subject to the law of reason, not the less in heart he would seem to riot in complete exemption from that law, having apparently little to do with reason further than to employ it as an ambidexter implement for effecting the irrational" (Melville, *Billy Budd* 76). This deceptive outer decorum masks "the mania of an evil nature, not engendered by vicious training or corrupting books or licentious living, but born with him and innate, in short 'a deprativity according to nature'" (76). As though explicitly to counter the transcendentalist claim that civilization corrupts the natural individual, Melville makes it clear that Claggart's particular kind of cruelty and perversity comes *from* nature, not in spite of it.

It may be that Melville simply lacked the temperament to accept the brighter gifts of Emersonian optimism, but it is abundantly clear that his experience, both of nature and of society, played a crucial role in the development of his critical take on transcendentalism. In *Moby-Dick*, Ishmael proudly claims that "a whale-ship was my Yale College and my Harvard" (112), suggesting not only that this is where he spent the formative years of early adulthood, but that life in the whaling fleet gave him his "higher education." The transcendentalists, on the other hand, *had* attended Harvard and were in fact deeply associated with its Unitarian tradition as well as its middle-class social milieu. The lessons learned on a whaling ship were harsh, to put it mildly, and the image of nature absorbed during bloody fights with enormous, enraged animals was unlikely to match that generated for frequenters of Walden Pond. In the plainest sense, the "nature" described by Emerson in his famous essay was essentially tame, a park-like expanse of neighboring woods that no longer contained dangerous animals or threatening natives. Melville's nature was the universally cannibalistic sea, beautiful and full of mystery but capable of stunning violence and ferocity. It may have occasionally elicited a feeling of oneness, but it also brought out the worst in the harsh men who worked on it. And if it was governed by a god, this deity was not the pleasant, all-encompassing pool of spirit that Emerson drew upon, but an inscrutable, Old Testament joker who plucked men from life as though he were picking berries.

The hardness of nature was matched for Melville by the pressures of economics in a way that seldom applied to most in the transcendentalist circle. The failure of the family business had led directly to the death of Melville's father when Herman was only twelve, and in the wake of that pivotal event the family struggled financially. Melville's turn to whaling in 1841 was a direct result of these poorer fortunes and the lack of job opportunities following the Panic of 1837. The experience of economic hard times made him acutely conscious of the relationship between money and ideas, and far more willing than many of his contemporaries to criticize the economic basis of idealistic thinking. He could be very suspicious, for instance, of what he saw as attempts to glorify poverty, a category that may have included Thoreau's experiment in personal thrift described in *Walden* (1854). In a story published that same year, entitled "Poor Man's Pudding," Melville offered a satirical account of a romantic poet named Blandmour who believes that "Nature is in all things beneficent" and so supplies the poor with substitutes for all of the things they can't afford (Melville, *Piazza Tales* 289). But when Blandmour is forced to take shelter in a dilapidated cottage and has to eat what he calls "poor man's pudding," he's disgusted by the taste and is forced for the first time to measure the strength of his optimism against the force of reality. For Melville, who had witnessed appalling poverty on his first voyage to Liverpool and had experienced enough of it himself to know what it felt like, it was irresponsible to make poverty sound desirable. Thoreau and other transcendentalists may have needed to reduce their property in order to freshen their staid, middle-class perceptions, but would they have developed these ideas if they hadn't already had a relatively comfortable standard of living?

This attention to the material basis of thought could also be detected in Melville's preference for testing ideas by pushing them to extremes. From *Moby-Dick* (1851) through the remainder of the 1850s, Melville created characters and situations in his fiction that often appear to follow early romantic or transcendentalist claims to their logical ends. For instance, some critics have found in Captain Ahab an extreme version of Emersonian self-reliance. Cut off from almost all human contact, following his own deepest intuitions, Ahab can be seen as a nightmare version of Emerson's naturalistic "devil's child." Not only does Ahab engage in demonic ceremonies, in Chapter 108 he jokingly orders the ship's carpenter to create an ideal man:

> Hold; while Prometheus is about it, I'll order a complete man after a desirable pattern. Imprimis, fifty feet high in his socks; then, chest modeled after the Thames Tunnel; then, legs with roots to 'em, brass forehead, and about a quarter of an acres of fine brains; and let me see—shall I order eyes to see outwards? No, but put a sky-light on top of his head to illuminate inwards. (470)

This self-obsessed giant may be a grotesque parody of the self-reliant American individual, with great power and intelligence but doomed to look only at itself rather than out at the world. Emerson may not have recognized such a bizarre creature and no doubt would have rejected the critical intent, but Melville seems to have caught a whiff of dangerous arrogance and ethical weakness in the famous lecturer's moral self-sufficiency. And once onto what he considered a flaw or false front, Melville could be ruthless in his attempts to expose its possible consequences.

This approach is perhaps nowhere clearer than in the 1853 story "Bartleby, the Scrivener." In this well-known "Tale of Wall Street," a lawyer tries ineffectually to help the increasingly silent copyist who works in his office. Ultimately cut off from all human interaction, Bartleby is certainly self-reliant, but his version of individualism is starkly empty. There appears to be no influx of divine spirit released by his inward attention. What would happen, Melville seems to be asking, if we turned to our instincts and found nothing there, that there was no "natural" source of goodness to feed our souls? In the world of Wall Street—that is, in the economic world of the mid-1850s—perhaps the faith of a well-to-do resident of Concord no longer has any validity. Would Bartleby be cured of his melancholy if he simply spent some time in the woods? The story suggests otherwise, positing a society where isolation has become an entrenched personal condition, and all that remains of the once divine self is Bartleby's quiet repetition of "I would prefer not to." The narrator too seems a victim of this erosion of human connection into a weak expression of petty willfulness. Though motivated in part by embarrassment, he works earnestly to help his disturbed employee, not realizing that Bartleby has placed himself beyond social interaction. In what can be seen as a brutal parody of Emerson's call to defer all relationships to the care of the self ("I shun father and mother and wife and brother, when my genius calls me." [Emerson 2:30]), Bartleby has shunned everyone to listen to an inner spirit that never speaks.

Once again, at the heart of Melville's criticism is a keen sense of the economic risk of some, particularly romantic, ideas. On his version of Wall Street, gestures of self-reliance are not only ineffectual but dangerous. Bartleby may be waiting for the "currents of the Universal Being" to flow through him (Emerson 1:10), but without the economic support of a comfortable life he is putting himself in the way of the unforgiving interests of society. It is hardly a surprise, then, that he ends up in jail, not as a criminal per se but as someone for whom this world has no use. His passivity may be admirable as a once-heroic refusal to conform, but by this point such a refusal to participate in the economic system comes closer to an empty radicalism, a kind of quiet anarchy. And Melville's world is too blunt and pitiless to make room for anyone who fails to understand the forces that drive it.

Melville may or may not have had Emerson explicitly in mind when he wrote "Bartleby," but most commentators agree that just months before, while finishing his novel *Pierre*, Melville did create an intentional portrait of the Sage of Concord. Melville had heard Emerson lecture in 1849 and was initially impressed. He wrote to his friend Evert Duyckinck, "Yet I think Emerson is more than a brilliant fellow. Be his stuff begged, borrowed, or stolen, or of his own domestic manufacture he is an uncommon man" (Melville, *Correspondence* 121). But upon reflection, he had begun to qualify his praise: "I could readily see in Emerson, notwithstanding his merit, a gaping flaw. It was, the insinuation, that had he lived in those days when the world was made, he might have offered some valuable suggestions. These men are all cracked right across the brow" (121). Though willing to grant Emerson's brilliance and charisma, Melville was suspicious of what he identified as his arrogance, even when not indulging in "transcendentalisms, myths & oracular gibberish" (121). Calling Emerson a "Plato who talks thro' his nose," he distrusted the public's preference for mysticism and therefore discounted the famous lecturer's trustworthiness as a self-reliant man: "The truth is that we are all sons, grandsons, or nephews or great-nephews of those who go before us. No one is his own sire" (121).

Pierre's Plotinus Plinlimmon (the first name referencing the well-known neo-Platonic philosopher, the second sounding like an unpleasant fruit) is a similarly charismatic leader of a group called the Apostles. The novel's title character sees Plinlimmon from a distance and is both attracted and disturbed by his look:

> The whole countenance of this man, the whole air, and look of this man, expressed a cheerful content. Cheerful is the adjective, for it was the contrary of gloom; content—perhaps acquiescence—is the substantive, for it was not Happiness or Delight. But while the personal look and air of this man were thus winning, there was still something latently visible in him which repelled. That something may best be characterized as non-Benevolence. Non-Benevolence seems the best word, for it was neither Malice nor Ill-will; but something passive. To crown all, a certain floating atmosphere seemed to invest and go along with this man. (Melville, *Pierre* 290)

As the leader of a philosophical cult, Plinlimmon is suspect both because he exempts himself from his own prescriptions and because he seems surrounded by an air of unquestioning worship. He appears to offer happiness but masks a creepy hostility, a passive indifference that undermines his supposed idealism. To the truly idealistic Pierre, Plinlimmon's "blue-eyed, mystic-mild face" (292) seems to urge nothing more than passive acceptance of all conditions, as though contentment could come from a hypocritical combination of inaction and attitude adjustment. Like Bartleby's, Plinlimmon's self-reliance seems not overtly hostile but not friendly either, and because he shows no sign of suffering from the loss of connection to others, he is more forbidding (that is, more inhuman) than the self-starved copyist. In the language of Melville's last novel published during his life, Plinlimmon is plainly a kind of intellectual confidence man. Whether he is literally deceiving people for monetary gain or just offering a marketable set of soothing ideas, he is a suspicious purveyor of a brand of hope unconnected to any verifiable reality.

That scholars have found another direct portrait of Emerson in *The Confidence-Man* (1857) is thus no surprise, though Mark Winsome, as the character is named, is less directly menacing than Plotinus Plinlimmon. Again, the portrait suggests a mixture of mysticism and Yankee shrewdness, but on this occasion Melville does more than merely describe the Emersonian figure from afar. In effect, he engages in a mock debate with transcendentalism by putting Winsome in conversation with the somewhat more skeptical and polemical figure called the "Cosmopolitan." Almost immediately the two find ground on which to disagree. Winsome calls his new companion a "beautiful soul—one full of all love and truth; for where beauty is, there must those be" (Melville, *Confidence-Man* 190); however, the Cosmopolitan quips back sarcastically that rattlesnakes are beautiful creatures and so must essentially be good as well. The conversation that follows pits Emerson's conception of nature's benevolence against Melville's unwillingness to ignore such obvious perils as poisonous reptiles. Winsome simultaneously offers hopeful conceptions of nature and friendship while exhibiting a contradictory hardness toward "a crazy beggar, asking alms under the form of peddling a rhapsodical tract" (194). Inconsistencies do not bother him; like Emerson, he pays no attention to changes of opinion because, "since nature is nearly all hill and dale, how can one keep naturally advancing in knowledge without submitting to the natural inequalities in the progress?" (193). And also like Emerson, he has a Thoreauvian disciple who has put into practice his mentor's "principles previously accounted as less adapted to life than the closet" (197).

Though critics have disagreed over who is or is not a confidence man in this dizzying collection of philosophical dialogues, there is a governing sense in the book that people and ideas are somewhat similar to money: Money depends upon faith for its exchange value, but if it is false, counterfeit, it ultimately has no value. In this respect, the wary individual in Melville's *The Confidence-Man* needs a "counterfeit detector," a way to separate the genuine from the fake, not only to keep from being scammed by thieves but to avoid investing in ideas that aren't firmly connected to reality. Transcendentalism may not have been the most personally vexing to Melville of such pre–Civil War enthusiasms, but its central tenets and major figures did suggest a kind of speculative bubble of belief that might prove hazardous without some prudent hedging of risk.

The ultimate difference between Melville and his transcendentalist contemporaries may boil down to conceptions of well-being or happiness. Seen from the perspective of the sailor's rougher experience, Emerson's prescriptions for self-improvement can appear to involve little more than shifts of perception. It is true that the self-reliant individual may go out into the world and change things for the better, but what if the conditions are not in place to allow him or her to spend quiet time in the woods in the first place? And what if a faith in nature yields not measurable social change but simply an acceptance of how things are? Pain, in Melville's view, cannot be wished away or converted into pleasure simply by means of a hopeful disposition. Nor can poverty be made palatable by a conviction that the poor live more authentic lives.

In the story Melville wrote to introduce his collection of short fiction, *The Piazza Tales*, he offered an encapsulated view of the attraction and cost of following what he considered to be illusory goodness. In "The Piazza," the narrator lives in an old country house and sits in the evenings on his porch (or piazza) gazing at the nearby mount Greylock. One day after a storm, he notices that one end of a rainbow is lighting up a "glen, or grotto" on the side of the mountain, turning it golden "like the Potosi mine" (Melville, *Piazza Tales* 5). Though a neighbor assures him that it's just an old barn, the narrator can't resist the temptation to seek out this "fairy-land" (6). But when he arrives at last he finds a tiny, overgrown house with a lonely young woman living in it. Her life is poor and miserable. The one thing that gives her hope is the thought that she might someday walk down to where the sun gilds a distant farm house: "Oh, if I could but once get to yonder house, and but look upon whoever the happy being is that lives there!" (12). The "happy being" is of course the unhappy narrator, who doesn't reveal to Marianna that the house is his or that he had hoped to find his fulfillment in the place she finds so desolate. He returns to his piazza, content to enjoy the illusion but unwilling to test it again. Light, it seems, may be pleasant, but its absence undeceives: "But, every night, when the curtain falls, truth comes in with darkness" (12). The image may not be hopeful or reassuring, but it does suggest that a reliable happiness has to be based on substantial goods and not an adjustment of vision. Otherwise, to look too hard at what nature seems to offer us is to court tragedy and despair.

Works Cited

Bohm, Arnd. "Wordsworth in Melville's 'Cock-A-Doodle-Doo!'" *Leviathan* 9.1 (2007): 25–41.

Emerson, Ralph Waldo. *The Collected Works of Ralph Waldo Emerson.* 9 vols. Cambridge: Belknap, 1971–2011.

Melville, Herman. *Billy Budd, Sailor (An Inside Narrative).* Ed. Harrison Hayford and Merton M. Sealts, Jr. Chicago: U of Chicago P, 1962.

_____. *The Confidence-Man: His Masquerade.* Ed. Harrison Hayford, Hershel Parker, and G. Thomas Tanselle. Evanston: Northwestern UP, 2002.

_____. *Correspondence.* Ed. Lynn Horth. Evanston: Northwestern UP, 1993.

_____. *Moby-Dick; or, The Whale.* Ed. Harrison Hayford, Hershel Parker, and G. Thomas Tanselle. Evanston: Northwestern UP, 1988.

_____. *The Piazza Tales and Other Prose Pieces, 1839–1860.* Ed. Harrison Hayford, Alma A. MacDougall, and G. Thomas Tanselle. Evanston: Northwestern UP, 1987.

_____. *Pierre; or, The Ambiguities.* Ed. Harrison Hayford, Hershel Parker, and G. Thomas Tanselle. Evanston: Northwestern UP, 1971.

_____. *Redburn: His First Voyage*. Ed. Harrison Hayford, Hershel Parker, and G. Thomas Tanselle. Evanston: Northwestern UP, 1969.

Miller, Perry. "Melville and Transcendentalism." *Virginia Quarterly Review* 29.4 (1953): 556–75.

Moss, Sidney P. "*'Cock-A-Doodle-Doo!'* and Some Legends in Melville Scholarship." *On Melville: The Best from American Literature.* Ed. Louis J. Budd and Edwin Cady. Durham: Duke UP, 1988. 116–34.

Oliver, Egbert S. "*'Cock-A-Doodle-Doo!'* and Transcendental Hocus-Pocus." *New England Quarterly* 21 (June 1948): 204–16.

Parker, Hershel. "Melville's Satire of Emerson and Thoreau: An Evaluation of the Evidence." *American Transcendental Quarterly* 7.2 (1970): 61–67.

Stein, William Bysshe. "Melville Roasts Thoreau's Cock." *Modern Language Notes* 74 (March 1959): 218–19.

Sten, Christopher W. "Bartleby the Transcendentalist: Melville's Dead Letter to Emerson." *Modern Language Quarterly* 35.1 (1974): 30–44.

Transgressing the Border: The Complexities of Colonial Critique in *Typee*_____

Nicole de Fee

In 1841, Herman Melville joined the crew of the whaler *Acushnet*, and found himself serving on the ship both as a whaleman then as a member of the U.S. Navy (Bryant xiii). He had been aboard the whaler for eighteen months when it docked in the Marquesas Islands in the South Pacific. Tired of conditions aboard the ship, Melville and another crew member, Richard Tobias Greene, deserted, fleeing into the interior of the island (xvi). Melville could not have known that his brief stay in the Marquesas with the indigenous Taipi (or "Typee"—a term for both the people and their land) would launch him into his career as an author. Nevertheless, an avid storyteller, Melville would need little convincing to turn his Pacific sojourn into a novel.

The end result of this compulsion to write was *Typee: A Peep at Polynesian Life* (1846). *Typee* was not merely the product of Melville's desire to tell a story of South Seas adventure: Melville biographer Laurie Robertson-Lorant explains that one of Melville's goals was political. Melville, she writes,

> wanted to express some strong political opinions. What he had seen of Western imperialism in the Pacific islands had shocked him. The "savages" he had met seemed much more civilized than the Americans and Europeans who were invading their lands. When he returned to find Democrats like his own brother supporting westward expansion in messianic terms, he knew he had found a debate into which he could pour his heart and soul. (135)

And so he did.

One striking aspect of *Typee* is the complexity of both its content and its structure. The complexity of the text gives Melville the freedom to engage the "debate into which he could pour his heart and soul." The text is novel, autobiography, travel narrative, anthropological study, and anti-imperialist polemic, as well as a text in which Melville manipulates rhetorical strategies to great effect (Bryant xi). While the text crosses genres in radical and transgressive ways for Melville's time, the genre to which it most closely adheres—the aspects of which provide Melville with the most freedom to explore the politics of colonialism and to critique the "civilization" such colonialism imposes on a native population—is the travel narrative. Through the conventions of the eighteenth- and nineteenth-century travel narrative, Melville is free to offer a penetrating critique of colonialism and explore the complexities and contradictions of Western colonization in the Pacific islands.

These complexities have fascinated Melville's audience since the first publication of *Typee*—"the capacity of [the] narrative to generate paradoxes" has been one of the text's enduring draws (Calder 27). For Alex Calder, the focal point of the novel's paradoxes can be found in the insider/outsider dichotomy Melville weaves into his travel narrative. The insider/outsider dichotomy is based on what Calder considers "the standard reading of *Typee*," one that focuses on "model making" and "metaphor making" (29). Model making is the meaning assigned to a particular culture from the perspective of a person outside the culture. One sees this process clearly, for example, in how Melville understands and reports elements of Typee "taboo" culture back to his readers. Metaphor making, on the other hand, describes the process through which cultural insiders assign meaning to their own culture. These meanings are derived and framed by their local customs and experiences, and the language they use in their metaphor making is motivated by a desire to try to relate these insider perspectives to *others*—often, but not always, others who are outsiders and thus do not share the native, insider set of cultural meanings, beliefs, and shared experiences.

Melville's narrator in *Typee*, Tommo, comes to his understanding of the process of colonization from firsthand experience, and his reporting of this process takes the form of model making rather than metaphor making, for the narrator is—as Melville had been—an outsider looking in on Typee culture. Melville did not like what he saw of the clash of cultures, according to Robertson-Lorant:

> Having retraced the steps of the so-called "march of civilization" by landing in unspoiled Polynesia, sailing from there to half-Westernized Tahiti, then spending some time in the "civilized" Sandwich Islands, Melville had come to believe colonization was a forced march to Hell that contradicted every principle on which America was founded. The "march of civilization" meant the destruction of native populations and the moral decay of the colonizers. (135)

If the focus of the "standard" reading of *Typee* is on paradox, then Melville's witness to the march of civilization through colonization illustrates this point precisely—civilization offers no improvement for anyone involved, the precise opposite of the ostensible goals of colonization efforts. The imperial and colonizing conquests that were defining America in the mid-1800s were, for Melville, actually un-American.

However, Melville's tale did appeal to the very American, in a sense, "secret fantasies of boundless sensuality and freedom," as well as the "social and economic idealism that had inspired the establishment of . . . communities like Brook Farm" (Robertston-Lorant 142). Melville's audience wanted to see the *exotic* juxtaposed with representations of the *self,* and wanted that self to emerge as the champion, and symbol, of freedom.

Melville highlights the twin characteristics of sensuality and freedom in his lush description of the landscape. In his discussion of the novel, Richard Ruland notes that the "Idyllic world of Typee has become part of the national legend, and nineteenth- and twentieth-century readers alike have shared Tommo's regret that the rest of the world cannot be more like Typee, that the purity of life there must give way to corrupting civilization" (312). Melville's readers wanted that escape, even if that idyllic paradise complicates Melville's colonial critique.

Melville's readers would have expected to read the island described as such. As Mary Louise Pratt agues, by the late 1700s, travel writers began to write the indigenous peoples out of the travel narrative by focusing on the landscape. While Pratt focuses her discussion on William Patterson, an English traveler who wrote in the decades before Melville, her critique of Patterson's landscape can be applied to Melville's landscape in *Typee*. Pratt writes,

> The landscape is written as uninhabited, unpossessed, unhistoricized, unoccupied even by the travelers themselves. The activity of describing geography and identifying flora and fauna structures an asocial narrative in which the human presence, European or African, is absolutely marginal, though it was, of course, a constant and essential aspect of the traveling itself. In the writing, people seem to disappear from the garden as Adam approaches—which, of course, is why he can walk around as he pleases and name things after himself and his friends back home. (51–52)

Likewise, Melville repeatedly writes the indigenous Typees out of his description of the island. After Tommo and his companion Toby successfully escape the *Dolly* (as Melville renamed the *Acushnet* in his book) and are a safe distance into the island's interior, they believe the land uninhabited: "As far as our vision extended, not a sign of life, nor anything that denoted even the transient residence of man, could be seen. The whole landscape seemed one unbroken solitude, the interior of the island having apparently been untenanted since the morning of the creation" (Melville 44). Neither human presence nor time, it seems, has penetrated the interior. When Tommo and Toby find a footprint, the discovery shocks them. Furthermore, not only is no human life imagined on the island, but neither is there fauna, only flora: "Over all the landscape there reigned the most hushed repose, which I almost feared to break lest, like the enchanted gardens in the fairy tale, a single syllable might dissolve the spell. . . . I remained gazing around me, hardly able to comprehend by what means I had thus suddenly been made a spectator of such a scene" (49). The interior is more than Edenic: It is magical, enchanting. Injured and near starvation, Tommo still imagines himself in a fairytale, only to break the enchanted spell in the hopes of being rescued.

Tommo and Toby are saved when they cross the border into what they assume is Happar territory, a rival tribe to the Typees. When they cross the border and make contact, the border becomes an important space for the text. The seemingly simple act of border crossing becomes a complex issue. Tommo and Toby believe they are crossing into Happar territory, but in reality, they find themselves in Typee territory and must quickly shift their imaginary allegiance from the Happars to the Typees. The border crossing and the shift in allegiance represents here what Mary Louise Pratt refers to as the "contact zone."

Pratt defines the "contact zone" as "the space of colonial encounters, the space in which peoples geographically and historically separated come into contact with each other and establish ongoing relations, usually involving conditions of coercion, radical inequality, and intractable conflict" (6). In the chapters preceding Tommo and Toby's presumed border crossing, Melville sets the stage for this kind of contact zone. When Tommo details the locations and histories of discovery of the islands in the area, he explains that for the most part they are "arbitrarily distinguished." Giving the details of the Washington Group of islands, Tommo elaborates: "The only reason why they were ever thus arbitrarily distinguished, may be attributed to the singular fact, that their existence was altogether unknown to the world until the year 1791, when they were discovered by Captain Ingraham, of Boston, Massachusetts, nearly two centuries after the discovery of the adjacent islands by the agent of the Spanish Viceroy" (11). Of course, the islanders already knew of their own existence, but as a long history of conquest and empire has taught us, that knowledge does not count for the conqueror.

Nukuheva (the island on which Melville landed, and where the book is set; the modern spelling is *Nuku Hiva*) is French occupied, and is by far the most enduring of the island contact zones. The island's beauty easily captivates Tommo: "Every moment open[ed] to the view some new and startling scene of beauty" to which no description could do justice (12). As the *Dolly* draws closer to the island, the French presence destroys Tommo's view: "That beauty was lost to me then, and I saw nothing but the tri-colored flag of France trailing over the stern of six vessels, whose black hulls and bristling broadsides proclaimed their warlike character. . . . The whole group of islands had just been taken possession of by Rear Admiral Du Petit Thouars, in the name of the invincible French nation" (12). Nukuheva's beaches then represent a contact zone in its purest sense—a foreign white nation stakes claim to a sovereign nonwhite nation, whose ongoing relation with the colonizer will be one of subjugation and coercion.

Melville's critical view of the Europeans' position in the contact zone is in a way its own contact zone. One the one hand, Melville has a very typical eighteenth- and nineteenth-century view of the islanders as exotic, placing him squarely in the Enlightenment travel tradition. On the other hand, critiquing the West's presence in the contact zone separates Melville from the traditional Enlightenment travel narrative. He depicts the French presence in Nukuheva as far from positive: His narrator observes that the island's "inhabitants have become somewhat corrupted, owing to their recent commerce with Europeans," and the tribes that have little contact with the Europeans remain uncorrupted (Melville 11). Corruption is not limited to just the French influence in the Marquesas Islands. Tommo informs us of a similar situation in the Sandwich Islands, where vice is prevalent and blessings few (198). No good comes from the "civilizing" European influence on the islands:

> Civilization does not engross all the virtues of humanity: she has not even her full share of them. They flourish in greater abundance and attain greater strength among many barbarous people. The hospitality of the wild Arab, the courage of the North American Indian, and the faithful friendships of some of the Polynesian nations, far surpass any thing of a similar kind among the polished communities of Europe. If truth and justice, and the

better principles of our nature, cannot exist unless enforced by the statute-book, how are we to account for the social condition of the Typees? (203)

Perhaps because the Europeans and other westerners have not pene-trated the Typee interior, we find they have none of the types of laws which govern the Western world, nor any of the crime. As far as Tom-mo can tell, in Typee there are no robberies, murders, rapes, abuses, or other problems that plague the "civilized" worlds of Europe and North America. Nor has Tommo witnessed the Typees fighting among them-selves. He attributes this phenomenon to both the lack of European presence and to the appearance of a strong sense of communal brother-hood among the Typees.

Because Tommo both idealizes the Typees and condemns the West's negative impact on indigenous cultures, his role, then, is not that of the narrative's heroic conqueror. Rather, he is the narrative's "anti-con-quest hero." The hero of the anti-conquest narrative positions himself as innocent of Western imperial/colonizing corruption. This position, however, does not leave him immune to "older imperialist rhetorics of conquest" that "assert European hegemony" (Pratt 7). Tommo offers a valid critique of empire, but in doing so he reinforces Western hege-monic ideals. Try as he might to maintain a complete criticism of the West, Tommo's identity, like Melville's, remains typically American. His leg injury represents an identity that embodies the predominant mid-nineteenth-century American identity that is its own contact zone. This is an identity wrapped in "Jacksonian imperialism and Jacksonian individualism, the building of an imperial nation and the making of a sovereign self" (Dimock 11). It presents conflict marked by lopsided control and coercion. Wai-chee Dimock argues that Melville himself wanted to create an empire out of his literature, but acknowledges the paradox, even irony, of this endeavor. Both the "empire for liberty" and the "anti-conquest" serve the same purpose—they position Mel-ville outside the corruption he sees as the result of the contact zone, colonialism, civilization, imperialism, and empire, while simultaneously exposing his grounding within those same spaces. Melville's very critique, like his identity, like Tommo's identity, and like the French presence in Nukuheva, is a contact zone.

Furthermore, Melville's reliance on Linnaean classifications reinforces these issues of the contact zone. In 1758, the Swedish biologist Carl Linnaeus introduced a classification system for plants and animals that would come to heavily influence the ways Americans and Europeans understood other peoples. Linnaeus had identified six classifications of "Man" in the century prior to *Typee*: the Wild Man, American, European, Asiatic, African, and Monster (Pratt 32). Of these classifications, Melville identifies three in *Typee*, the American, the European, and the Asiatic. The Polynesians and Arabs Melville describes would fit into the Asiatic category. For Linnaeus, the American is "governed by customs," the Asiatic is "governed by opinions," and the European "governed by laws" (qtd. in Pratt 32). Arguably, Linnaeus held the Europeans in the highest esteem because of their government by laws. Melville's audience would have recognized his Linnaean stereotypes when he calls attention to "the hospitality of the wild Arab, the courage of the North American Indian, and the faithful friendships of some of the Polynesian nations" (203). While Melville may rely on the emotional rather than the rational stereotypes of the Other, he privileges the emotional. And when Melville applies Linnaean standards of classification, he inverts the power structure. The Europeans' governance by laws and statutes does not suggest for Melville that they are more highly evolved than the "savages." Rather, Melville suggests the opposite—that civilization reflects devolution; people should not need to be governed by laws.

To drive his point home even further, Melville shows how civilization is less than civilized when Christianity is added to the colonizing narrative: "Ill-fated people! I shudder when I think of the change a few years will produce in their paradisiacal abode; and probably when the most destructive vices, and the worst attendances on civilization, shall have driven all peace and happiness from the valley, the magnanimous

French will proclaim to the world that the Marquesas Islands have been converted to Christianity! . . . Heaven help the 'Isles of the Sea!'" (195). Here civilization and Christianity are intimately linked, and when brought to "savage" lands in tandem, the destruction of the land is swift, powerful, and irreversible: "Among the islands of Polynesia, no sooner are the images overturned, the temples demolished, and the idolaters converted into *nominal* Christians, than disease, vice, and premature death make their appearance. The depopulated land is then recruited from the rapacious hordes of enlightened individuals who settle themselves with its borders, and clamorously announce the progress of the Truth" (195, emphasis in original).

Because of Melville's multiple roles as traveler, writer, anthropologist, and ethnographer, and because he also comes from an imperial Western nation, he writes from a "contact perspective." This is a "perspective [that] emphasizes how subjects are constituted in and by their relations to each other. It treats the relations among colonizers and colonized, or travelers and 'travelees,' not in terms of separateness or apartheid, but in terms of copresence, interaction, interlocking understandings and practices, often within radically asymmetrical relations of power" (Pratt 7). This makes it nearly impossible for Melville, or Tommo, to discuss the Typees without discussing them in the context of civilization or colonialism. In other words, Melville cannot talk about the "other" without discussing the "self." He cannot talk about the Typees as "Typees" without forcing them into a Linnaean system of classification. The Typees cannot exist outside empire. Melville cannot escape the anti-conquest or the dual Jacksonian drives (imperialism and individualism).

Even with all of this working against him, Melville successfully shifts the power structure of the contact zone. Melville makes Tommo vulnerable. He inverts the locations of the periphery and the center. The effect here is fourfold: First, it inverts the border, both literally and figuratively. Second, it eliminates Tommo's literal and figurative power. Third, it underscores Melville's critique of civilization/colonialism and Christianity. And fourth, it creates a space of "colonial difference." This is "the space where coloniality of power is enacted. . . . [It] is the space where *local* histories inventing and implementing global designs meet *local* histories, the space in which global designs have to be adapted, adopted, rejected, integrated, or ignored" (Mignolo ix). The contact zone itself helps us begin to understand the nuances of Melville's colonial critique. Examining the border itself in that contact zone illustrates the fourfold inverted power structure.

The border here, whether an actual physical border, a colonial border, or a metaphorical border, relies on an understanding of Walter Mignolo's *Local Histories/Global Designs: Coloniality, Subaltern Knowledges, and Border Thinking* (2000). What Mignolo successfully does in his book is to look at modernity/coloniality through subalternity and border thinking and border gnosis. This includes a theoretical exploration of the subaltern, Occidentalism, language, and the border (whether a physical or imaginary border—for Mignolo the imaginary border is just as real as the physical border, and the physical border is just as important as the figurative or imaginary border). While these issues in general are important for any discussion of Melville, the concept of the border here is the most useful. The border is the place where local histories, or experiences of culture, meet and clash. A significant aspect of this border space is what Mignolo defines as "border gnoseology," a "discourse about a colonial knowledge [that] is conceived at the conflictive intersection of the knowledge produced from the perspective of modern colonialisms (rhetoric, philosophy, science) and knowledge produced from the perspective of colonial modernities in Asia, Africa, and the Americas/Caribbean" (11). While Pratt's contact zone is a "space of colonial encounters . . . usually involving conditions of coercion, radical inequality, and intractable conflict" (Pratt 6), Mignolo's border is at the intersection of the conflict of knowledge, the place where the model makers and the metaphor makers meet. At that intersection is a frontier, the border between the two clashing cultures.

There are two types of knowledge gained in "border gnoseology," the interior and the exterior. The interior represents the "colonial world system," imperial conflicts and language barriers. The exterior is the space where the colonizer meets the cultures he seeks to colonize (Mignolo 11). Melville's inversion of the interior and the exterior borders disrupts the borders' spatial and temporal orders. This allows Melville to critique civilization and colonization simultaneously as an agent of and outsider to empire.

In *Typee*, the French have not been able to successfully push the Typee people to the margins of the island, either literally or figuratively. Nor has any country been able to successfully penetrate the interior of the island. Horror stories of cannibals and missing sailors and missionaries work as deterrents to internal exploration and serve as a defense against colonization. The island itself works to underscore the inversion of the center and the margin: Those who would want to lay claim to the Typees and their land are too frightened to venture into the interior. In the traditional colonial narrative, the colonizers lay claim to the center of a land marked out for colonization (in addition to the center of the colonial world system itself) as the stronghold and force the conquered to the margins. In the Marquesas Islands, the presumptive colonizers have power only on the islands' margins, while the Typees and Happars maintain control of the interior. In this colonial narrative, the Typees and Happars are in the position of power.

Given this colonial narrative then, one would assume that Tommo and Toby would occupy a position of power on the island's margins; but this is not the case. Melville portrays Tommo and Toby as powerless. On the *Dolly*, both men are assigned to the margins of the boat, literally. Their watches take place at the boat's edges. Those closer to the captain, who stays at the boat's center, are treated better. They are fed better, and they have more privileges. The boat serves as a microcosm of empire, something Melville returns to later in *Moby-Dick* on a much larger scale. If the *Dolly* were an empire, Tommo and Toby would be among the most vulnerable and marginalized. Additionally, Toby has a "naturally dark complexion," made darker after months of sailing in the tropics. He has a "mass of jetty locks clustered about his temples" and "large black eyes." He is "moody, fitful, and melancholy—at times almost morose" with a "quick and fiery temper . . . which when thoroughly roused, transported him into a state bordering delirium" (Melville 32). If we revisit Linnaeus's classifications of Man, Toby fits somewhere between the Asiatic and the African. What we know for sure is that Toby is a fiery, capricious, melancholy, and mysterious sailor. No one on the boat knows where he is from or who he really is. Tommo's companionship with Toby makes his own position even more vulnerable because of Toby's questionable background.

When Tommo and Toby flee the tyranny of the *Dolly*, thus also attempting to flee the tyranny of Western civilization, they do not find the security they seek in the island's interior. Tommo is literally powerless and even more vulnerable than when aboard the *Dolly*. What becomes an overarching metaphor for Tommo's underlying identity crisis in the text is the mysterious leg injury he incurs during the escape and subsequent trek through the jungle to the island's interior. Not only is Tommo's injury physically disabling, but it also completely "infantilizes him, forcing him to shift attention from dark Toby to the more fraternal Kory-Kory, who bears him like a child about the valley" (Bryant xix). For the majority of the text, Tommo relies completely on Kory-Kory, his indigenous servant, for mobility and basic needs like eating and bathing.

Tommo's leg injury becomes a site of "colonial difference." The injury represents the border where local histories clash, and where Tommo tries to reinvent his national identity as the Typees continue to challenge it. This is the site where "the physical as well as imaginary location [of the] coloniality of power is at work in the confrontation of two kinds of local histories" (Mignolo ix)—the Typee way and the Western way. Though Tommo may be in a vulnerable position, he still represents a colonial force or space. This space exposes his vulnerability, a vulnerability that continues to complicate the issues of colonialism, empire, and civilization in the text.

The "local histories" are in conflict with each other in Tommo's attempts to participate in Typee culture. He struggles to find a way to participate that allows him to remain "civilized," but only when it suits him. He says, "When at Rome do as the Romans do. . . . Being in Typee I made a point of doing as the Typee did" (Melville 209). He claims to eat poee-poee, a local food staple made from breadfruit, as the Typees do and claims to have adopted their sleeping habits and style of dress. Tommo's attire is an easily identifiable example of a challenge to his identity: He cannot wear a loin cloth like the men on the island; instead, he prefers a much more modest, presumably more civilized toga. The toga further marginalizes Tommo's power on the island, as his mode of dress aligns him visually with the women on Typee and not the men. However, he is much less of a prude when it comes to the island's culture of sexual freedom and promiscuity.

Eating raw fish, however, poses the greatest challenge to Tommo's delicate sensibilities up to this point in the narrative:

> I grieve to state so distressing a fact, but the inhabitants of Typee were in the habit of devouring fish much in the same way that a civilized being would eat a radish, and without any more previous preparation. They eat it raw; scales, bones, gills, and all the inside. The fish is held by the tail, and the head being introduced to the mouth, the animal disappears with a rapidity that would at first nearly lead one to imagine it had been launched bodily down the throat. (208)

As he must modify his attire, Tommo must also modify the way he consumes the raw fish. He must maintain his civility and eat the raw fish with a knife. Tommo is superficially willing to share his identity between the two cultures and revise both the Typee and Western identity to suit him. It is precisely this "border" position of identity that Tommo occupies that makes him a continued threat to the Typees and marks him as part of the colonial system he continually critiques. Tommo is Mignolo's "converso"—a reference to the term for Jewish or

Muslim converts to Christianity in early modern Catholic Spain—one who is "not so much a hybrid" but who occupies a place of "fear and passing, of lying and terror" (Mignolo 29).

Tommo fails to realize that he is a threat to the Typees. He also fails to realize that the Typees attempt to colonize and appropriate him through their hospitality. Tommo's position as a colonial agent may not be obvious through his actions, but his attitude reveals this position. He mistakenly believes that the chief befriends him because as a white, civilized westerner, he must therefore be superior. He believes that his whiteness bestows an inherent superiority. He cannot imagine any other reason why the Typees would treat him as they do. He receives a valet in Kory-Kory. He is "given" the most beautiful girl on the island. He is fed and sexed at will. Only after a couple of months have passed does Tommo begin to suspect there may be ulterior motives behind the Typee hospitality. He begins to believe that the Typees are enticing him to stay so that they may cannibalize him (they are trying to entice him, but not because they believe he will be a tasty morsel). However, Tommo is safe as long as he believes in his agency. When he is secure and feels safe in his imagined identity, the leg injury dissipates. After his encounter with Karky, a tattoo artist, he begins to question his safety and his identity, and the leg injury returns. Tommo then realizes that the Typee religion is tied to the mysterious tattoos of the Typees. What has Tommo terrified is not necessarily living life like a Typee, but the prospect of indigenous religious indoctrination. For all of Tommo's critique of the evils of Christianity, he cannot make the leap to the Typee religion as a valid alternative.

Tommo assumes at first that Karky wants to tattoo him because he has white skin: "I struggled to get away from [Karky], while Kory-Kory, turning traitor, stood by, and besought me to comply with the outrageous request. On my reiterated refusals the excited artist got half beside himself, and was overwhelmed with sorrow at losing so noble an opportunity of distinguishing himself in his profession" (218–19). Tommo has yet to realize that the tattoo is the Typees' final act of colonization/possession. Initially his concern is one of vanity: "The incident opened my eyes to a new danger; and now I felt convinced that in some luckless hour I should be disfigured in such a manner as never more to have the *face* to return to my countrymen, even should an opportunity offer" (219). Tommo cannot be marked Typee and be able to return to America.

He realizes that the tattoo would not only mark him as religiously and culturally Typee, but that it would also be a mark of Typee possession. This prompts the return of his leg injury "with symptoms as violent as ever" (232). Tommo realizes the complete lack of power he has in this situation. He finally realizes that his whiteness does not make him superior to the Typees.

Additionally, the return of the leg injury after Tommo's close call with his own colonization continues to complicate and underscore Melville's colonial critique. As Tommo now recommits himself to looking for a way to escape, he ironically becomes more dependent than ever on the Typees for his escape from them. And eventually he is able. Though Tommo's journey eventually ends and he returns home, Melville's journey is still incomplete. While Melville walks the frontiers between model maker and metaphor maker, insider and outsider, colonizer and colonized, his feelings toward colonization, imperialism, empire, and civilization become increasingly complex in the journey from *Typee* to *Moby-Dick*. What we see at the end of *Typee* with Tommo's return home (and Toby's, too, for that matter) is an odd sense of hope, that perhaps the West can learn something from contact zones and border traveling. As Tommo tells us his story, we can see on the one hand the contact zone's enduring effect on him, an effect that makes him critical of the West's imperial policies, and his desire not to take part in them. On the other hand, we see the fear he faces when his national identity is threatened; however, he does not seem to be worse for the wear. In the end, *Typee* occupies its own border frontier as a call against imperialism that cannot escape its own imperialist pull.

Works Cited

Bryant, John. Introduction. *Typee: A Peep at Polynesian Life*. By Herman Melville. New York: Penguin, 1996. ix–xxxvii.

Calder, Alex. "The Thrice Mysterious Taboo": Melville's *Typee* and the Perception of Culture." *Representations* 67 (1999): 27–43.

Dimock, Wai-chee. *Empire for Liberty: Melville and the Poetics of Individualism*. Princeton: Princeton UP, 1989.

Melville, Herman. *Typee: A Peep at Polynesian Life*. New York: Penguin, 1996.

Mignolo, Walter D. *Local Histories/Global Designs: Coloniality, Subaltern Knowledges, and Border Thinking*. Princeton: Princeton UP, 2000.

Pratt, Mary Louise. *Imperial Eyes: Travel Writing and Transculturation*. London: Routledge, 1992.

Robertson-Lorant, Laurie. *Melville: A Biography*. Amherst: U of Massachusetts P, 1998.

Ruland, Richard. "Melville and the Fortunate Fall: Typee as Eden." *Nineteenth-Century Fiction*. 23.3 (1968): 312–23.

CRITICAL READINGS

At the Axis of Reality: Melville's Aesthetic_____

David Dowling

Unusual sources for philosophical insight and lyrical beauty pervade Herman Melville's writing, as unlettered sailors populate his fictional worlds set aboard navy ships at war and merchant vessels engaged in the business of whaling, an enterprise as lucrative as it was dirty and dangerous. The technologies of whale lines, lances, and harpoons, and the processing of spermaceti into profitable oil provide the materials for a rugged aesthetic in his signature narrations. Melville frequently advocated this radical new aesthetic in the rhetoric of legal discourse, inspired by his older brother Gansevoort, an attorney and Melville's first literary agent. Melville was intimate with the effectiveness of the twin powers of skilled advocacy and the legal idiom, since his brother had successfully promoted his first novel *Typee* in 1846 to celebrity author Washington Irving, who became the key to its publication. In his fiction, poetry, and letters, Melville himself became an ardent publicist and even something of a defense attorney, persuasively advocating for a revolutionary American democratic aesthetic. Designed to suit the young democratic republic by treating contemporary antebellum subjects with the significance of classical mythology, Melville's aesthetic locates beauty in both kinetic embodied pursuits and in enigmas inscribed in the visual arts, living nature—particularly marine life—and human identity.

"Hawthorne and His Mosses" (1850) and "The Advocate," chapter 24 of *Moby-Dick* (1851), comprise Melville's most explicit arguments for his aesthetic theory. Both decry the negative connotations attached to American authors and their materials. In the former, Melville proposes that writers native to the United States can match and even top Shakespeare, particularly in the example of Nathaniel Hawthorne's short stories. America's real authors, not the "graceful" and "amiable" ones guilty of a "self-acknowledged imitation of a foreign model," are not desperate for patrons, for "it is the American author who now patronizes his country, and not his country him" (*Piazza Tales* 247). Placing the author in a new position of authority necessarily revolutionized aesthetic principles to suit the literary renaissance he envisioned. After writing *Moby-Dick*, Melville warned his neighbor Sarah Morewood, "Don't you read it," for it is not a fine piece of "silk—but is of the horrible texture of a fabric that should be woven of ships' cables and hausers" (*Correspondence* 206). The antithesis of a delicate and warm domestic novel, "a Polar wind blows through it, and birds of prey hover over it. Warn all gentle fastidious people from so much as peeping into the book," he advises with dry wit, "on risk of a lumbago and sciatics," among other neurological ailments (206). In the novel itself, Melville oppositely advises the reader, through Ishmael, "to go a whaling yourself" in order to "derive even a tolerable understanding of his living contour" (*Moby-Dick* 264). Ishmael's warning is nonetheless consistent with the one he delivers to Morewood, for in seeking the whale yourself, "you run no small risk of being eternally stove and sunk by him [and thus] had best not be too fastidious in your curiosity touching him" (264).

Thus, a pragmatic ruggedness is required to grasp the transcendent beauty of the whale, the largest mammal in the world, and a living work of art to Melville. His argument for the whale's universal significance was motivated by his belief in whaling as a quintessentially American literary subject. The dominance of the nation's whaling industry is visible in its capacity to transform a small New England port like New Bedford into the richest city per capita in the world. By 1846, the United States had built the largest whaling fleet in the world, boasting 735 of the 900 whale ships at sea (Dolin 206). More than a mere spilling of blood for profitable whale oil or an abhorrent "butchering sort of business," whaling should instead be mythologized in epic literature, according to Melville, to erase the claim that it "has no aesthetically noble associations with it" (*Moby-Dick* 111). Through Ishmael, he asserts that it brings "scores of anonymous captains" to "seas and archipelagoes which had no chart, where no Cook or Vancouver had ever sailed," placing romantic exploration at its heart (110).

Playing the pedant in increasingly strident tones, Ishmael imagines a series of objections to his argument, each of which he stridently dismisses with a historical example. "*Whaling not respectable?*" he asks, his voice rising with contrarian rebuke. "By old English statutory law, the whale is declared 'a royal fish,'" he retorts, adding that a Roman general's entrance into "the world's capital" prominently featured "the bones of a whale, brought all the way from the Syrian coast, [which] were the most conspicuous object in the cyballed procession" (111). The heavens even attest to the whale's dignity, as seen in the constellation of Cetus. For its heroes, he points to Queequeg, who "has taken over three hundred and fifty whales," a more honorable feat than the tsar of Russia, "who boasted of taking as many walled towns" (111).

If Ishmael appears determined and dogmatic to the point of self-parody in "The Advocate," it is not because Melville himself took the cause of a new revolutionary American aesthetic lightly. He took quite seriously the challenge of bringing American literature into the world spotlight in "Hawthorne and His Mosses." In it he applies the pugilistic, competitive spirit of "The Advocate" to the defense of his fellow native authors. His aesthetic specifically draws on William Shakespeare— "those deep far-away things in him; those occasional flashings-forth of the intuitive Truth in him; those short, quick probings at the very axis of reality"—as the standard for excellence in urging that "William of Stratford" is matched by our own "Nathaniel of Salem" (*Piazza Tales* 244). In touting "that blackness in Hawthorne" he himself had initially overlooked for "a pleasant writer with a pleasant style,—a sequestered, harmless man, from whom any deep and weighty thing would hardly be anticipated," Melville extolls the subtlety of "the dark half of his physical sphere" (242–43). Specifically, the element of chiaroscuro, the suggestive play of light and shadow that Melville admired in the nautical paintings of J. M. W. Turner, stood out in Hawthorne's embrace of "the great power of . . . a blackness, ten times black" (243).[1] In painterly terms, he describes his capacity to "avail himself of this mystical blackness as a means to the wondrous effects he makes it to produce in his lights and shades" (243). Indeed, "you may be witched by his sunlight," but "the skies he builds over you . . . play on the edges of thunder clouds" (243).

Melville makes clear in defining the ideal aesthetic for American literature that the power of dark themes—"Original Sin," mayhem, "the possibility of mad destruction"—resides in an artful restraint, a suggestiveness more effective than overt revelation. Melville calls this "the great Art of Telling the Truth,—even though be it covertly, and by snatches" (*Piazza Tales* 244). Shakespeare, he claims, was as great for "what he did do, as for what he did not do, or refrained from doing" (244). He similarly applauds the way Hawthorne "refrains from all the popularizing noise and show of broad farce, and blood-smeared tragedy; content with the still, rich utterances of a great intellect in repose" (245). Such repose and restraint[2] is well suited to the nature of truth, according to Melville, which "is forced to fly like a scared white doe in the woodlands" (244) much like the loon, a symbol of natural beauty that evades Henry David Thoreau's grasp in *Walden* (1854). Attaining truth in nature, furthermore, is a process in which artists (often unintentionally) seek themselves, like Narcissus reaching for "the ungraspable phantom of life; and this is the key to it all" (*Moby-Dick* 5). Melville shared the belief with such antebellum authors as Emily Dickinson that once truth is glimpsed, it is most effectively conveyed through subtle artistic expression. Dickinson's "Tell All Truth, But Tell It Slant," for example, urges that beauty's essence appears best through artfully circuitous renderings.

In discussing the oblique expression of truth, "Mosses" provides particularly useful insight into the core principles of repose and ambiguity in Melville's aesthetic.[3] In the absence of a coherent manifesto defining his theory of art, Melville's commentary on portraiture in "Mosses" and throughout his writings reveals essential elements of his aesthetic. Since photography was only beginning to be invented in the decades before the Civil War, painted portraits were the preferred medium to portray the mystery of human character. Portraiture appears throughout Melville's writings as a tool for characterization. "The true portrait painters," he urges, "in the multitude of likenesses to be sketched, do not invariably omit their own; and in all high instances, they paint them without any vanity" and even in self-deprecating toncs, as in Melville's literary self-portrait in 1952's *Pierre* (*Piazza Tales* 249). Where literary artists include themselves in their writings—as in Hawthorne's Holgrave in *The House of Seven Gables*—Melville loathed egotistical or vain self-portraits. Preferring suggestive shadowy lines exhibiting character on a moral continuum, Melville was repulsed by blunt garish self-portraits associated with commercial self-promotion. Character in painting and in creative writing, he believed, should allude to, without making too explicit, the essence of identity in "a lurking something, that would take several pages to define" (249). That lurking something beyond words and brush strokes appears in the portrait of Pierre's father in *Pierre*. In the portrait, Melville's aesthetic of artful restraint is calculated for dramatic effect as a key to the novel. Pierre initially does not see the darkness in his father's persona, just as Melville confesses to having been blind to the darkness of Hawthorne's short stories. He compares his prior failure to apprehend Hawthorne's "landscape of the soul" to the way "a man may travel along a country road, and yet miss the grandest, or sweetest of prospects, by reason of an intervening hedge, so like all other hedges, as in no way to hint of the wide landscape beyond" (240).

Melville was acutely sensitive to the limitations of physical vision, from its liability to random obstruction and interference, to its capacity to apprehend objects only from a singular perspective one moment at a time. Specifically, he regarded this issue of restricted and limited vision as an aesthetic problem inherent in conventional portraiture. "Leviathan has never fairly floated himself for his portrait," he notes; but even when captured on deck, "isolated angles of perception fail to render his magnificent bulk" (*Moby-Dick* 263). Ironically, direct eyewitness of the whale—which Ishmael recommends as far preferable to the distorted glimpses provided by the compromised artistic portrayals he describes in the chapter "Of the Monstrous Pictures of Whales"—leaves one with a sublime experience of simultaneously seeing everything and nothing. Since "there is no earthly way of finding out precisely what the whale really looks like," and since "one portrait may hit the mark nearer than another, but none can hit it with any considerable degree of exactness," verisimilitude must be felt as an accumulation of visual evidence, and more metaphysically, an aura to be felt only in his presence (264). Thus, although the sperm whale appears totally faceless and blank "in the full front view of the brow," with its eyes set wide on each side of his head and mouth tucked underneath, Ishmael is overwhelmed with the "high and mighty god-like dignity" inherent in it (347). Though he sees "no one point precisely" because it appears to have "no nose, eye, ears, or mouth; no face; he has none proper," the sublime—an aesthetic mix of beauty and terror, magnificence and vulnerability in response to tremendous powers of nature—makes "you feel the Deity and the dread powers more forcibly than in beholding any other object in living nature" (347). The whale's own range of perception is equally mystifying, and indeed outdoes our own. His capacity to hold two complete and discrete fields of vision in his mind at once endows him with a powerfully subtle awareness of his surroundings. Ishmael points out that his brain is tiny compared to the bulk of his body. However small, the whale's brain is profoundly "more comprehensive, combining, and subtle than man's" since he "can at the same moment in time attentively examine two distinct prospects, one on one side of him, and the other in an exactly opposite direction," the functional equivalent of performing "two distinct problems in Euclid," he quips (331). "Why then do you try to 'enlarge' your mind? Subtilize it," Ishmael concludes in an apt signature of Melville's aesthetic of multiperspectivism (331).

Multiperspectivism feeds Melville's aesthetic of the indistinct. To hold multiple images in the mind at once indeed subtilizes perception and requires an agile imagination. Despite blind spots and limitations, Melville continues searching beyond the obstructing hedgerow to gain another and potentially better angle on the object. Thus, if external representations of the world—its truth, its beauty, its terror—resist representation on a two-dimensional canvas or in language, then what can art do to compensate? It can capture an essence by alluding, through artful restraint, to what is not there, and giving a sense of its shape without rendering it in its full multidimensional anatomical glory. If one cannot capture the true essence of Leviathan, who ultimately "remains unpainted to the last," the futility of art seems to support an abandonment of the pursuit of truth (*Moby-Dick* 264). But Melville never surrenders. The closer we inspect reality in Melville's world, the more it complicates. "The more I consider this mighty tail, the more do I deplore my inability to express it," Ishmael confesses (378). The whale's tail is embodied, kinetic, and dynamic, a true art form, truer even than the human capacity to express it.

The power of Ishmael's language, however, lies in its ability to suggest the nature of his subject without pretending to have the last word on it. He does not want to become an encyclopedia; he even mocks the inconsistency of whale data in the chapter "Cetology." But he continues to gather perspectives, copiously recording and annotating them for a closer glimpse at the fluid dynamism of his subjects, whether broad, as in the whaling and nautical worlds, or minute, as in the anatomical wonder of a whale tail. Robert K. Wallace has called this Melville's "exploratory aesthetic," an intellectual pursuit of knowledge in an uncertain condition (*Melville and Turner* 357). However provisional and incomplete, Melville values such exploration as a token of a growing organic form rather than a fixed, picturesque, and thus reified art object. In this way, "Incompleteness for Ishmael, like indistinctness for Turner, is at once his fault and forte" (*Melville and Turner* 357). Especially relevant to Melville's questing and dynamic sense of the artistic process that avoids totalizing closure is Elizabeth Schultz's observation that, "although he might *attempt* to create a manuscript about whales, as creator rather than Creator, he knew the limitations of his knowledge and his abilities," as well as that of the provisional nature of both scientific and aesthetic knowledge itself (Schultz 317).

Melville demonstrates the dynamic nature of knowledge by dramatizing shifts in the observer's perspective over time. Pierre's understanding of his father's portrait, for example, shifts from an innocuous "free-templed head [that] is sideways turned, with a peculiarly bright, and care-free, morning expression" to the horrifying revelation of adultery and its implications for Pierre's own acts of incest when he views it again (*Pierre* 72). After suspecting his own ruinous fate prophesied by his father's misdeeds, he sees in the portrait a full confession of the patriarch's sins and his own complicity with them. "In strange relativeness," Melville puns on Pierre's filial connection to his father and his perspective on the portrait, "reciprocalness, and transmittedness, between the long-dead father's portrait, and the living daughter's face, Pierre might have seemed to see reflected to him, by visible and uncontrollable symbols, the tyranny of Time and Fate" (197). Paternity is revealed, as with Sophocles's Oedipus, in an ungraspable phantom of himself, like Narcissus reflected in the water toward which all humanity seems drawn. We reach for our own identities in those indistinct portraits, Melville suggests, reflected in water on canvas, or on the broad blank brow of the White Whale himself.

The portrait cannot function as conclusive factual evidence against Pierre's father, since it was "painted before the daughter was conceived or born" (*Pierre* 197). But "like a dumb seer, the portrait still seemed leveling its prophetic finger at that empty air," clearly indicating Pierre's father's inevitable capacity for evil, "from which Isabel [his illegitimate daughter and Pierre's lover] did finally emerge" (197). Such gesturing toward the invisible yet totally incontrovertible truth is precisely the aesthetic of the indistinct that Melville also appreciated in Hawthorne's best work. "There seemed to lurk some mystical intelligence and vitality in the picture; because, since in his own memory of his father, Pierre could not recall any distinct lineament transmitted to Isabel, but vaguely," and indeed indistinctly, "saw such in the portrait"

(197). Thus, the "portrait's painted self seemed the real father of Isabel" so much that it leads him to burn the painting in haste, his fingers trembling with compulsion to destroy the evidence and keep his public memory inviolate (197). The flame burns the string that tied it, and the portrait eerily unrolls in the blaze affording the smoldering patriarch one last accusing glare at his son: "the upwrithing portrait tormentedly stared at him in beseeching horror," and in a flare of "oily fire, disappeared forever" (198).

Even the moment of Pierre's father's disappearance in the oily fire speaks to a presentiment, a powerful aesthetic of the indistinct and a withholding of a potent unexpressed gesture. We, of course, know that Pierre feels the picture torments him, but its ambiguities achingly remain. Has he invented his father's dark past as a way of justifying his own forbidden romance? If he ascribes his transgressions to fate, of course, he releases himself from such liability. An essential part of Melville's aesthetic, especially over the course of a broad narrative sweep like *Pierre*, is the role ambiguity plays in building tension toward climactic action. Pierre will explode at the end of the novel in a fatal raging attack on his former patron and dandy rival Glen Stanly, just as Moby Dick and Ahab will finally clash after a lengthy circumnavigation of the globe in anticipation of their long overdue meeting. Melville typically delights in the spectacle of figures grappling with ambiguity toward such climatic action.

The aesthetic of the indistinct thus is linked in Melville's fiction to an intense compulsion to break violently through ambiguity—figured in Ahab's hatred of the pasteboard mask his shell of a life represents to him, and in Glen Stanly's superficial genteel graces—to arrive at meaning. Ishmael does not resort to such drastic measures, however, despite being tantalized by partial and cryptic puzzles and prophecies that beg for him to produce a solution. Just as the hazy ill-defined figures in the Spouter Inn painting rivet Ishmael, a pamphlet Pierre finds, a kind of philosophical roadmap or guidebook of one Plotinus Plinlimmon, similarly challenges him: "The more he read and re-read, the more [his] interest deepened, but still the more likewise did his failure to comprehend the writer increase" (*Pierre* 209). Also drawn to an ambiguous work that is tantalizingly inscrutable, Ishmael is as compelled as he is confused by the painting before him. He finds "a sort of infinite, half-attained, unimaginable sublimity about it that fairly froze you to it, till you involuntarily took an oath yourself to find out what the marvelous painting meant" (*Moby-Dick* 12). Just as Plinlimmon's work is not fine philosophy, for he is the mere "writer of a sleazy rag pamphlet," the artwork adorning the entryway of the cheapest hotel in New Bedford is far from a nautical masterpiece. The youthful protagonist of *Redburn* clutches his father's guidebook to England as his lifebuoy upon landing there, only to realize it is riddled with factual errors and inauthentic descriptions of the landscape. Like the portrait of Pierre's father, the guidebook corrodes his faith in his father, so "as the authority of the book goes, so goes the authority of the father," as Cindy Weinstein notes (379).

But semantic collapse is not always the inevitable result of documents bearing misleading significance. The preponderance of inscrutable or unreliable texts in Melville points to the profound significance that can inhere in unlikely subjects, from shadowy and smudged kitsch art to a torn pamphlet discarded at the floor of a carriage with half its pages missing. In the least likely places, perhaps the keys to our future reside, Melville muses, particularly though the eyes of the young and overzealous ravenous for signs of their fate, like Pierre and Ishmael. Chris Sten's comment that Ishmael has a "fixation on the question of what distinguishes a true picture from a false one" equally applies to Pierre (Sten 176). Art, even of this lowly variety, can point beyond personal fate toward larger understandings of the forces of good and evil in "a general life-theory and practical course of life," as Pierre describes the Plinlimmon pamphlet (*Pierre* 215). Part of the torture of life, according to the moral ramifications of Melville's aesthetic, is that we chase white whales; we pursue the ideal despite being trapped in a murky ambiguous real world. In regard to this condition, Plinlimmon's last comment before his writing abruptly disappears after the tear offers "consolation to the earnest man, who, among all his human frailties, is still agonizingly conscious of the beauty of chronometrical [i.e., ideal] excellence" (215).

In chiding Ishmael and Pierre's attempts to read their fortunes, Melville parodies the guesswork of interpretation as a way of increasing narrative tension. This art of concealment that Melville found so potent in Hawthorne is his way of staving off his eventual plunge into the sublime, an aesthetic state in which the observer neither physiologically relaxes in a warm bath of pleasure nor chills in intense fear. This middle-way at the heart of Melville's aesthetic occurs when, as John Bryant aptly explains, "the emotion aroused is neither pleasure nor pain but 'curiosity,'" like Ishmael and Pierre's, "and the artistic elements that naturally arouse this sensation are roughness and sudden variation joined with irregularity" (Bryant 17). Ishmael's curiosity indeed occupies the intervals between intermittent gliding serenity and the jarring tumult of the *Pequod*'s journey. Ambiguity, in this sense, directly arises from this state of what Bryant calls an aesthetic of repose, and that ambiguity in turn arouses intellectual curiosity. The silence of the whale and Bartleby also lends itself to this aesthetic, not as emptiness in itself, but as "artful evocations of silence either in symbols of whiteness and circularity, walled-in characters, or, oddly enough, in voluble speakers poised before a nonspeaking world" (Bryant 10).

In the chapter "Less Erroneous Pictures of Whales" in *Moby-Dick*, Melville delights in artistic impressions of precisely this poised and efficacious moment. After skewering countless paintings for inaccurate depictions of whaling and whales—one makes the unpardonable blunder of depicting a whale with horizontal flukes!—he comes to a series of French artists whom he celebrates for their favorable representations of the trade. Interestingly, Melville does not champion the verisimilitude of detail in these works as one might expect, given his harsh criticism of errors in others. Instead, he praises them for capturing moments of poise prior to abrupt action, the sort Melville movingly dramatizes in Billy Budd's struggle to defend himself verbally when confronted with Claggart's accusation. Gathering momentum into "that one single incomputable flash of time," one particular painting depicts "an oarsman, half shrouded by the incensed boiling spout of the whale, and in the act of leaping, as if from a precipice" (*Moby-Dick* 266). Ishmael remarks that "the action of the whole thing is wonderfully good and true," revealing an essential tenet of Melville's aesthetic: Terrifying beauty lies in the contrasting chaos and control of tumult and repose between "raging commotion" and "the inert mass of a dead whale, a conquered fortress, with the flag of capture lazily hanging from the whale-pole inserted into his spout hole" (266). This aesthetic is also captured in a whale warrior like Queequeg, who is "as cool as an icicle" (30) amid the chaotic clamor of the Spouter Inn, and rendered in "the hardy fishermen under one of their few aspects of oriental repose" (267). Tellingly, the whale in the Spouter Inn painting is not impaled upon the masts of the ship, but is in the air above it, poised to commit "the enormous act of impaling himself upon the three mast-heads" in yet another "incomputable flash of time" (266).

Another figure illustrative of the aesthetic of the calm before the storm—like the whale's tail rising up beautifully prior to lowering its thunderous bulk and shattering a chase boat—is Laocoon, a mythological character cast in a Roman statue Melville described in his 1857 lecture. The figure, surrounded by serpents sent by the gods to devour him, is not screaming in terror, but in a much more aesthetically powerful way Melville admired, is rendered in an eerie moment of stillness just prior to his scream as "the symbol of human misfortune" (*Piazza Tales* 404). The statue of Laocoon exudes meaning prior to expression, like the silence before the breach, the calm as Moby Dick swims under the chase boat, a marvel of serene beauty gliding amid destruction and butchery. The sublime inheres in such moments by way of anticipation through the suggestion of action before it actually takes place.

In addition to this anticipation of dramatic action, Melville's sublime tends to emphasize gothic effects. Ishmael's ponderings of the meaning of the Spouter Inn painting reveal that his own excuses for the work's sublimity are more extraordinary than what is on the canvas itself. More than the content of the painting itself, smoke, smudges, bad lighting, and defacement all create and condition Ishmael's experience of the painting. Ishmael thus spends time elaborating on the conditions shaping his interpretation of the painting and "describing his reactions to the picture rather than the art object itself," as Douglas Robillard observes (72). The gothic in this case is comic, a snapshot of a greenhorn whaleman fantasizing with half fear and half desire about the adventure upon which he will soon embark, reaching for clues as to the nature of the experience that will soon overwhelm him. But in a chapter like "The Chart," Melville is deadly serious with his sublime aesthetic, manipulating the atmosphere to enhance the gothic effect of the scene's central object of Ahab's map. His chart becomes something of a work of art, equally sacred and profane. The sinister swinging "heavy pewter lamp suspended in chains over his head" provides the shadowy light for the madman at work plotting the course of his pursuit (*Moby-Dick* 198). He takes on a mad scientist's persona, figured here as part cartographer and part sketch artist in this gothic light that threw "shifting gleams and shadows of lines upon his wrinkled brow, till it almost seemed that while he himself was marking out lines and courses on the wrinkled charts, some invisible pencil was also tracing lines and courses upon the deeply marked chart of his forehead" (198). Here, Melville again sets the tone of the chapter with a visual art metaphor as he had toward the beginning of the novel with the painting in the Spouter Inn. In both cases, evil portents loom. Ishmael's struggle to decipher the Spouter Inn seascape is matched by Ahab's struggle to compose, as if he were an author or sketch artist, Moby Dick's capture. His charts are a daily ritual, for "almost every night some pencil marks were effaced, and others were substituted" in his attempt to weave the nets through "all four oceans" by "threading a maze of currents and eddies, with a view to the more certain accomplishment of that monomaniac thought of his soul," an obsessive process that interestingly echoes Ishmael's vow to find meaning in the painting he ponders (199). Ahab's monomania thus appears to be an expression of an aesthetic state of irresistible compulsion and even obsession for the art object's essential meaning. The new meaning Melville discovers in Hawthorne's fiction similarly transfixes him in "Hawthorne and His Mosses." This aesthetic experience of intuitive obsession in an isolated subject that seems to select the viewer stems from the English romantic poets, beginning with William Wordsworth and extending through Mary Shelly's *Frankenstein* (1818), a work that Melville himself read aloud to his family near the time of his composition of *Moby-Dick* (Robillard 109).

The artistry of Ahab's chase is visible on his charts as well as the lines on his face, pointing toward Melville's larger aesthetic principle regarding the profound impact of art on human identity. The art we create, pursue, and consume shapes our identities, according to Melville. Ahab's scar, for example, runs from "crown to sole," causing him to appear as a man "with a crucifixion in his face" (*Moby-Dick* 124). It weaves the full length of his body just as the lines of his chart span the full extent of the globe in an elaborate cartographic net designed to capture the White Whale. His self-destructive art woven into his chart is contiguous with his scar. Upon his first appearance before the crew, Ahab himself appears a work of art—however mutilated, dismembered, gloomy, and gothic—much in the way Queequeg does with his "unearthly tattoings" that stun Ishmael into another interpretive quagmire (49).[4] Later in the novel, we learn that the designs Queequeg carves into his coffin directly correspond with the elaborate tattoos that cover his body and face. His artistry is the functional equivalent of Ahab's—only sacred and life-preserving rather than profane and destructive—in that it corresponds directly to his own identity and the belief system to which it is wedded. While Queequeg's tattoos represent "a complete theory of the heavens and earth, and a mystical treatise on the art of attainting the truth," Ahab has created in his charts of the earth's oceans, including its currents and winds, an equally elaborate worldview (480). His, however, is expressly designed for the destruction of Moby Dick, the object of his revenge at the center of his universe.

Such symbols of the art of attaining the truth and its impact on human identity were deeply self-reflexive of Melville's own authorial circumstances. While surging with creativity that appeared unstoppable— "Give me a condor's quill! Give me Vesuvius' crater for an inkstand! Friends, hold my arms!" shouts Ishmael in *Moby-Dick*—Melville also acutely strained at the limitations of his readership. He lamented in a letter to Hawthorne that "Truth is ridiculous to men. . . . Try to get a living by telling the Truth and go to the Soup Societies" (*Correspondence* 191). Complicating the creative process was the real literary market threatening Melville's idealistic vision of a sudden universally acknowledged burst of artistic accomplishment. This vision appears in "Mosses" and in a key letter to Hawthorne in which he posits that "genius, all over the world stands hand in hand, and one shock of recognition runs the whole circle round" (*Correspondence* 249). Like the narrator in "I and My Chimney" who clings fast to his sacred object of meditation and philosophy despite the forces of the market (his wife and Mr. Scribe) that conspire to remove it, Melville would not relinquish his art of attaining the truth according to his monumental vision. The struggle could be daunting, causing him "to write a little bluely" on his creative process (*Correspondence* 191). Although the cost to his career was great, exerting colossal powers of creativity and working with a subject bearing "a comprehensiveness of sweep, as if to include the whole circle of sciences, and all the generations of whales, and men, and mastodons, past, present, and to come" paid the dividend of personal growth, for "we expand to its bulk" (*Moby-Dick* 456). This audacious authorial disposition led him to appreciate Hawthorne's bold social criticism of Puritanical morality in the *Scarlet Letter* and legacies of oppression in New England family histories in *The House of the Seven Gables*. Melville extolled the subversive undercurrent of Hawthorne's ironic distance from rigid monolithic doctrine to which "he says NO! in thunder; but the Devil himself cannot make him say *yes*" (*Correspondence* 186). Hawthorne's sharp critiques proved more discreetly hidden than Melville's and thus his career enjoyed greater commercial success.

Melville's sense of the creative process, however resolute and determined, at times fell to moments of doubt. Spiritually, Melville was a questing agnostic, described by Hawthorne as a condition in which "he can neither believe, nor be comfortable in his unbelief; and he is too honest and courageous not to try to do one or the other" (Hawthorne 163). Although driven by the physical and pragmatic world, as seen in Ishmael's constant discovery of peace and tranquility while working aboard the *Pequod*, Melville still embraced a romantic sensibility rooted in intuition, a fundamental feature of American authors of the antebellum era. This spirituality that everywhere shapes his aesthetic even prompted Hawthorne to suggest that "if he were a religious man, he would be one of the most truly religious and reverential; he has a very high and noble nature and better worth immortality than the rest of us" (163). Hawthorne realized that Melville invested his nondoctrinaire faith in individuals rather than formal religious or political institutions. "Knowing you," Melville wrote to Hawthorne, "persuades me more than the Bible of our immortality" (*Correspondence* 213).

This yearning for immortality appears in the baby whale's blind gaze toward its mother and the heavens in "The Grand Armada" chapter of *Moby-Dick*. A similar intuitive and instinctual beauty appears in the character of Billy Budd, whose natural fitness for heaven makes him the embodiment of Adam before the fall. Billy is thus wholly incongruous with the depraved condition of war in which he finds himself. His beauty is not just physical, although he is compared to Michelangelo's *David*. As Gail Coffler has demonstrated, "in accordance with the Greek belief that a man's exterior reflects his inner nature, Billy's moral goodness matches his outward beauty" (267). Melville thus draws from ancient Greece and the Italian Renaissance to forge Billy's peculiar and potent beauty. His beauty lies in his capacity to love and forgive, convincing Captain Vere, the crew, and even the malignant Claggart (whose conspiracy against him is eventually fatal for both) of the manifest power of human compassion as the true source of immortality. The dogma of the ship's chaplain and the newspaper reports of Billy's death all miss the mark: The beauty of Billy is in his innocence, so deeply internatlized by Captain Vere that he utters the boy's name in his dying breath.

Melville's aesthetic vision was not entirely bleak, but instead maintained a buoyant and irreverent sense of humor, as well as a pragmatic foundation. In his poem "Art," Melville posits that such unlike things as "Sad patience—joyous energies; / Humility—yet pride and scorn; / Instinct and study; love and hate; / Audacity—reverence" all "must meet and mate" (*Published Poems* 280). Such an aesthetic requires a large canvas, or "plenty of sea room to tell the truth in" as Melville described it (*Piazza Tales* 246). At his best, Melville's writing takes classical subjects and makes them familiar and colloquial, or conversely works common and unsung subjects into the stuff of epic poetry. During his Mediterranean voyages in 1856 and 1857, he was acutely aware of the interplay between the exalted and the common. As Wallace aptly observes, he "was intrigued not only by the sanctity of St. Sophia but by the water taxis to the Scutari. In Egypt he was attracted not only to the Pyramids but to the 'donkey boys' who resourcefully plied the tourist trade," exhibiting the nature of the unique aesthetic fusion of the colloquial with the universal, the immediate with the classical, and the contemporary with the timeless ("Unlike Things" 352). The statue of Socrates, for example, strikes him "more like that of a bacchanal or the debauchee of a carnival than of a sober and decorous philosopher," and "reminds one of the broad and rubicund phiz of an Irish comedian." However, "a closer observer would see" characteristics that aptly describe Melville's aesthetics of repose in a "cool, sarcastic, ironical cast indicative of his true character" (*Piazza Tales* 400). Seneca strikes him as a "disappointed pawnbroker," while Nero seems "a genteelly dissipated youth" (401).[5]

These descriptions reveal the principled inconsistency with which Melville formed his own fictional characters. Otherwise mad with vengeance, Ahab's humanities surface in "The Symphony," for example, when he drops a tear into the ocean for his wife and child. A similar roundness of character is visible in Captain Vere, whose inner conscience painfully protests the steely resolve of his decision to execute Billy in strict adherence to military necessity. Melville even inveighed against the use of artificially consistent characters in a chapter of *The Confidence-Man* dedicated to the defense of "that author who draws a character, even though to common view incongruous in part," because he "may yet in so doing be not false but faithful to facts" (*Confidence-Man* 69). Since "no writer has produced such inconsistent characters as nature herself has," he argues that the diverse and contrary forces listed in his poem "Art" adhere to essentials in human nature that "are the same to-day as they were a thousand years ago. The only variability in them is in expression, not in feature" (*Confidence-Man* 70–71).

Melville's comments on the Roman statue of Apollo express precisely the aesthetic range illustrated in his poem "Art." In the presence of the statue, "few speak or even whisper, when they enter the cabinet where it stands. It is not a mere work of art that one gazes on, for there is a kind of divinity in it that lifts the imagination of the beholder" to a heightened aesthetic consciousness that "makes ordinary criticism impossible" (*Piazza Tales* 402). Melville sees in the statue a realized Platonic ideal through its "visible response to that class of human aspirations of beauty and perfection that, according to Faith, cannot be truly gratified except in another world" (402). Melville admired how "to the Greeks nature had no brute. Everything was a being with a soul" (406).

Rugged, pragmatic, and audaciously bold on the one hand, Melville's aesthetic held a high appreciation for idealized beauty as well, but one not to be confused with Ralph Waldo Emerson's more abstract and disembodied sense of nature's perfection. Unlike Emerson, Melville's aesthetic was earthy and embodied, sinewy like the tapestry of muscle fibers that artfully enmesh the whale's mighty tail, the epitome of how power and beauty can be mutually reinforcing. Beauty to Melville was also much more than physical: It was a matter of faith in the perfection toward which the greatest art points, for "it is with fiction as with religion," as he wrote in *The Confidence-Man*, "it should present another world, yet one to which we feel the tie" (158).

Notes

1. Wallace explains the influence of Turner's art on Melville's "aesthetic of the indistinct" in *Melville and Turner* 19–70. A broader view of the art world's impact on the formation of Melville's aesthetic of restraint, ambiguity, and multiperspectivism, particularly in *Moby-Dick* and *Pierre*, is featured in Robillard 70–122.

2. For a thorough and subtle definition of Melville's use of repose in his aesthetic, especially as a way of negotiating between the sublime and the picturesque, see Bryant 8–27.

3. A complete overview of scholarly research on Melville's aesthetic through 1986 appears in Dettlaff 625–65. The most recent work on Melville and the visual arts is in Kelley, specifically Robert K. Wallace's "'Unlike Things Must Meet and Mate': Melville and the Visual Arts," 342–62; Cindy Weinstein's "Artist at Work: *Redburn, White-Jacket, Moby-Dick*, and *Pierre*," 378–92; and Elizabeth Schultz's "Creating Icons: Melville in Visual Media and Popular Culture," 532–52.

4. Reynolds 523–44 provides a useful account of Melville's appropriation of popular antebellum gothic tropes and political debates for his aesthetic. For an analysis of Ishmael's reading of Queequeg as an epistemological challenge in deciphering foreign ethnicity, see Dowling 43–69.

5. Bryant 109–128 treats Melville's penchant for characters who are genial misanthropes exuding qualities like those he finds in Nero's statue.

Works Cited

Bryant, John. *Melville and Repose: The Rhetoric of Humor in the American Renaissance*. Oxford: Oxford UP, 1993.

Coffler, Gail. "Classical Iconography in the Aesthetics of *Billy Budd, Sailor*." *Savage Eye: Melville and the Visual Arts*. Ed. Christopher Sten. Kent: Kent State UP, 1991. 257–76.

Dettlaff, Shirley M. "Melville's Aesthetic." *A Companion to Melville Studies*. Ed. John Bryant. New York: Greenwood, 1986. 625–65.

Dolin, Eric Jay. *Leviathan: The History of Whaling in America*. New York: Norton, 2007.

Dowling, David. *Chasing the White Whale: The Moby-Dick Marathon; or, What Melville Means Today*. Iowa City: U of Iowa P, 2009.

Hawthorne, Nathaniel. *The English Notebooks, 1856–1860*. Ed. Thomas Woodson and Bill Ellis. Columbus: Ohio State UP, 1977. Vol. 12 of *The Works of Nathaniel Hawthorne*.

Kelley, Wyn, ed. *A Companion to Herman Melville*. Malden, Mass.: Blackwell, 2006.

Melville, Herman. *The Confidence-Man*. Ed. Harrison Hayford et al. Evanston and Chicago: Northwestern-Newberry, 1984. Vol. 10 of *The Writings of Herman Melville*.

_____. *Correspondence*. Ed. Lynn Horth. Evanston and Chicago: Northwestern-Newberry, 1993. Vol. 14 of *The Writings of Herman Melville*.

_____. *Moby-Dick*. Ed. Harrison Hayford et al. Evanston and Chicago: Northwestern-Newberry, 1988. Vol. 6 of *The Writings of Herman Melville*.

_____. *The Piazza Tales and Other Prose Pieces, 1839–1860*. Ed. Harrison Hayford et al. Evanston and Chicago: Northwestern-Newberry, 1987. Vol. 9 of *The Writings of Herman Melville*.

_____. *Pierre, or The Ambiguities*. Ed. Harrison Hayford et al. Evanston and Chicago: Northwestern-Newberry, 1971. Vol. 7 of *The Writings of Herman Melville*.

_____. *Published Poems*. Ed. Robert C. Ryan et al. Evanston and Chicago: Northwestern-Newberry, 2009. Vol. 11 of *The Writings of Herman Melville*.

Reynolds, David S. "'Its Wood Could Only Be American!': Moby Dick and Antebellum Popular Culture." *Critical Essays on Herman Melville's Moby-Dick*. Ed. Brian Higgins and Hershel Parker. New York: Hall, 1992. 523–44.

Robillard, Douglas. *Melville and the Visual Arts: Ionian Form, Venetian Tint*. Kent: Kent State UP, 1997.

Schultz, Elizabeth. *Unpainted to the Last: Moby-Dick and Twentieth-Century American Art*. Lawrence: UP of Kansas, 1995.

Sten, Christopher. *The Weaver-God, He Weaves: Melville and the Poetics of the Novel*. Kent: Kent State UP, 1996.

Wallace, Robert K. *Melville and Turner: Spheres of Love and Fright*. Athens: U of Georgia P, 1992.

_____. "'Unlike Things Must Meet and Mate': Melville and the Visual Arts." *A Companion to Herman Melville*. Ed. Wyn Kelley. Malden, Mass.: Blackwell, 2006. 342–61.

Weinstein, Cindy. "Artist at Work: *Redburn, White-Jacket, Moby-Dick*, and *Pierre*." *A Companion to Herman Melville*. Ed. Wyn Kelley. Malden, Mass.: Blackwell, 2006. 378–92.

Melville and the Gothic Romance_____

Gale Temple

I. The Gothic Uncanny

It seems relatively straightforward to rehearse a "gothic" lineage in British fiction, and to establish a constellation of loosely defined parameters that give substance to the form. Beginning with Horace Walpole's *Castle of Otranto* (1764) and continuing through such works as Ann Radcliffe's *Mysteries of Udolpho* (1794), Matthew Lewis's *The Monk* (1796), perhaps finding its most famous incarnation in such works as Mary Shelley's *Frankenstein* (1818) or even later in Bram Stoker's *Dracula* (1897), the British gothic form is characterized, broadly speaking, by such themes as corrupt ancient aristocracies, haunted castles, mysterious murders, innocent victims, hidden corpses, dark winding passageways, and supernatural events—all rendered through a kind of frenetic, sensationalized prose. As Peter Kafer notes, such early examples of the gothic all "share a continental Roman Catholic frame, and all thereby exploit priests and monks, perverse nuns, corrupt/libertine French and Italian aristocrats," as well as probing England's own "corrupt and useless aristocrats" and their "social and political privileges" (xv).

Such tropes, however, while certainly relevant to the ancient cultural legacy of Western Europe, do not necessarily apply to the early America of Charles Brockden Brown or, even later, Herman Melville, for America had no centuries-old noble legacies, much less haunted castles to house them. Perhaps more significantly, one of the most abiding myths about "American" culture since the time of the Puritans is that it *has* no past—or at least it willfully rejects its own cultural precedents in favor of a perpetually future-oriented social, political, and economic optimism. This deliberately forward-looking ethic is what sustains the myth of American innocence; as Thomas Jefferson put it in a 1789 letter to James Madison, "I set out on this ground, which I suppose to be self evident, that the earth belongs in usufruct to the living; that the dead have neither powers nor rights over it" (959); or, as Emerson perhaps more optimistically phrased it, "why should we grope among the dry bones of the past, or put the living generation into masquerade out of its faded wardrobe? The sun shines to-day also" (27). In other words, live in the now, for the past holds no real lessons for those with sufficient moxy to make their own path, and what's more, it tends to cloud optimistic visions of the future with pesky forms of historical guilt.

Perhaps, though, it is this very notion of a nation without a history, a culture perpetually seeking the horizon without turning back to witness and reflect on the ethical ramifications of that pursuit, that makes the literary field of the *American* gothic so fertile. As Kafer and others have suggested, the ancient estates of English or Italian noblemen are in many ways no more haunted by the past than the American wilderness, or even the superficially benign farmhouses of the early frontier, the "virgin" status of which was, of course, achieved through the bilking and genocide of countless American Indian tribes, and whose agrarian and industrial prosperity was often achieved on the backs of enslaved Africans. In other words, for the twin myths of American innocence and exceptionalism to maintain their ideological purchase, the crimes and injustices of the past, as well as the desires that inspired them, must be collectively repressed. The resonance of American gothic fiction is that it stages in eerie and haunting ways the return of the repressed guilt of history—and perhaps more importantly, it encourages us as readers to recognize our complicity both in those various forms of historical repression, and in the uncanny ways repression's return affects us psychologically and emotionally.

Readers familiar with the legacy of psychoanalysis will recognize in my formulation of American gothic Sigmund Freud's notion of "the return of the repressed." Broadly conceived, this notion suggested that the desires of the primal self (the "id") clash with the imperatives of the normative social contract (the "superego"). Consequently, in order to create viable, healthy cultural identities, we must repress primal desire, banishing it into the unconscious. Desire is a notoriously restless thing, however, and according to Freud it returns in various ways—literature, art, dreams, verbal slip-ups, that can be inspired and productive, but more often are haunting and unsettling.

What I want to explore in this essay is how Melville dramatizes this process of collective repression and return in three of his works: *Typee* (1846), *Redburn* (1849), and *Pierre* (1852). For Melville, repressed forms of individual and collective guilt, desire, anxiety, and so on, return in the form of what Freud would have called the "unheim-lich," or the "uncanny," which Freud defines as "something repressed which recurs" (241). According to Freud, uncanny elements of a story, a dream, or even everyday life remind us—often in unconscious or sickening ways—of those elements of the id, particularly sexual taboos, that we have repressed. This theme of the return of the repressed as a constitutive element of American gothic is articulated even more forcefully by Robert K. Martin and Eric Savoy, who argue that if the gothic form in its American incarnation has any unifying element at all, it is in its "situation of the reader at the border of symbolic dissolution" (vii); that dissolution, Savoy further argues, is driven by the "monstrous and unthinkable," which takes form through its invocation of the Freudian "uncanny." And, as Savoy writes, "the writing of the uncanny is the field—or, more precisely, the multivalent tendency—of American gothic, an imaginative requirement by which, as Leslie Fielder pointed out, 'the past, even dead, *especially* dead, could continue to work harm'" (4).

Theresa Goddu takes the Freudian formulation of gothic fiction even further, giving it a specific political resonance in its American incarnation. Goddu writes:

American gothic literature criticizes America's national myth of new-world innocence by voicing the cultural contradictions that undermine the nation's claim to purity and equality. Showing how these contradictions contest and constitute national identity even as they are denied, the gothic tells of the historical horrors that make national identity possible yet must be repressed in order to sustain it. . . . By resurrecting what these narratives repress, the gothic disrupts the dream world of national myth with the nightmares of history. (10)

In other words, the purity and optimism of America are predicated on the suppression of "historical horrors," which as Goddu suggests return symbolically in gothic fiction, disrupting in often unsettling, even violent ways the ostensibly benevolent arc of American progress.

So how, specifically, are the three novels I will analyze in this essay—*Typee*, *Redburn*, and *Pierre*—gothic? In *Typee*, I will argue, Tommo's confusion about the cultural and culinary practices of the supposedly cannibalistic Typee people masks his sexual unease with his radically free island "captors," whose way of life threatens to evoke in uncanny ways those elements of himself that he has had to repress as a Victorian American male. In *Redburn*, Wellingborough Redburn's experiences with the opaque and darkly mysterious Harry Bolton lead him not to a greater awareness of his own sexual and experiential possibilities, but rather to the same stultifying antebellum moral codes he has left behind at the beginning of his voyage. And finally, in *Pierre*, Melville explores what it might mean to live in concert with, rather than in opposition to, illicit desire—seemingly, as several critics have argued, to "queer" conventional social and sexual mores.

As Kafer effectively puts it, perhaps the most powerful motif in fiction is the idea that in order to discover and uproot evil we must first look within ourselves. While this chapter will not explicitly mine Melville's treatment of evil, it will explore the way Melville challenges his readers to look within the labyrinth of their own psyches in order to rethink the often oppressive and ideologically confining nature of everyday life.

II. *Typee*: A Peep at Polyvalent Sexuality

Typee may not seem like the first place one would begin an analysis of Melville's treatment of the gothic romance. Far better, perhaps, to explore the gothic themes of, say, *Moby-Dick*, which Robert Hume has called "perhaps the greatest of gothic novels, and an almost perfect example of the form," for, in Hume's view, it "ends in moral ambiguity; there is no message, no moral, no final statement of right and wrong" (287). For Hume, effective gothic writing leaves us in a kind of ethical abyss, forced to confront the inadequacy of religious faith or reason to definitively solve the problem of evil in the world, or "to make comprehensible the paradoxes of human existence" (289).

I want to begin with an analysis of the gothic in *Typee*, though, because I believe it represents a trenchant critique of how a form of what we might think of as gothicized cross-cultural ignorance leads not to enlightenment and a shared sense of common humanity between the binary categories "American/civilized" and "savage/native," but instead to a seemingly willful ignorance of, and ultimate flight from, those aspects of the primal self that threaten Tommo's Americanized antebellum superego.

Typee (1846) begins with a despondent Tommo longing to escape the oppressive whaling ship *Dolly*, which he informs us is captained by a heartless tyrant and destined for an interminable voyage ("More than three years have elapsed," Melville tells us, "since I left this same identical vessel," and "she still continues in the Pacific" [23].)

Subtitled *A Peep at Polynesian Life*, Melville's first novel does indeed represent a sort of antebellum literary peep show. As Tommo and his enigmatic, charismatic friend Toby ("as smart a looking sailor as ever stepped upon a deck" [32]) consummate their flight into the depths of the jungle on one of the Marquesas Islands, making their way through sublime cataracts and seemingly insurmountable precipices—a route inland that certainly invokes the disorientation and geographical confusion characteristic of the gothic form—they ultimately find themselves confronted by a sort of curtain into the past in the form of one last barrier of tropical foliage. Tommo pulls aside the final vestiges of the jungle, and there before them lies the surpassingly beautiful valley of either the Typee or the Happar people. Shaking off the delirium of hunger and the unremitting pain of a mysterious injury to his leg, Tommo writes:

> I chanced to push aside a branch, and by so doing suddenly disclosed to my view a scene which even now I can recall with all the vividness of the first impression. Had a glimpse of the gardens of Paradise been revealed to me I could scarcely have been more ravished with the sight. . . . Over all the landscape there reigned the most hushed repose, which I almost feared to break lest, like the enchanted gardens in the fairy tale, a single syllable might dissolve the spell. For a long time, forgetful alike of my own situation, and the vicinity of my still slumbering companion, I remained gazing around me, hardly able to comprehend by what means I had thus suddenly been made a spectator of such a scene. (49)

One of the allures of reading *Typee*, both in Melville's day and our own, is that it stages for us the fantasy of a return to a prelapsarian world, free from the competition, materialism, and pressures of life under capitalism. Melville well knew that the world could be insufferably cruel, as the bankruptcy and eventual death of his father Alan exemplified on a personal level, and such events as the economic panic of 1837, with its attendant bank foreclosures, poverty, hunger, and rampant homelessness demonstrated in a broader cultural way.

At the same time, however, *Typee* is a deeply conflicted narrative. On the one hand Melville wants to titillate with stories of semi-clothed "whihenies"—indigenous maidens—flocking to the ship once it is in port, with portrayals of a limitlessly abundant and seductive landscape that invites one to do absolutely nothing all day, and with portrayals of quirky natives who both welcome and serve Tommo as if he is a privileged member of their communal group. *Typee*, in this sense, idealizes the ease and harmony of a more pastoral life, deliciously seasoned with sexual freedoms unimaginable in Victorian American culture. Melville frequently rails against the inroads of modern life, particularly its evangelical strain, defending the "savages" and excoriating the supposed Christians who have exploited their erstwhile primal innocence for economic and imperial gain. Put differently, a world before modern time, of which readers are afforded a vicarious "peep," is enormously appealing for the sailor who is in many ways escaping from the dual repressions of shipboard discipline and nineteenth-century American socio-sexual mores.

That allure, however, is throughout the narrative darkly shadowed—we might even say gothically haunted—in two ways. First, in order for Tommo to fully revel in the abandonment of the society he has come from, he must literally evacuate his former self. The culture of the Typee, which Tommo repeatedly claims not to understand, their language and customs frequently signifying for him so much primordial gibberish, threatens to undermine a number of carefully constructed identity categories—sexual, economic, religious—whose "return" from the depths of Tommo's unconscious he ultimately cannot tolerate without the risk of psychological breakdown.

The second threat, of course, is the primary tension that drives Tommo's interaction with the Typee, which is the possibility not just that he is living with actual cannibals, but that he might, wittingly or unwittingly, actually have to eat a person himself. Despite the initially friendly reception of the Typee, for example, Tommo nevertheless wonders if "these fair appearances" might conceal "some perfidious design, and that their friendly reception of us might only precede some horrible catastrophe" (77).

These dual threats—of a kind of existence without moral or institutional boundaries, and of cannibalism—work together to produce a wildly schizophrenic narrative. Tommo incessantly vacillates between praising what he sees as the native guilelessness and sexual freedom of the Typee on the one hand, and condemning their lurid, opaque savagery on the other. His description of a typical day among the Typee, for example, seems to exemplify the liberating antithesis of the strictures of the whale ship he has just escaped from, or the mind-numbing pressures of life amidst a developing capitalist economy. Tommo writes:

> Nothing can be more uniform and undiversified than the life of the Typees; one tranquil day of ease and happiness follows another in quiet succession; and with these unsophisticated savages the history of a day is the history of a life. . . . In truth these innocent people seemed to be at no loss for something to occupy their time; and it would be no light task to enumerate all their employments, or rather pleasures. (149)

The Typee as Tommo describes them are in no hurry to meet deadlines, under no financial pressures, no risk of bankruptcy or debtor's prison. Instead, they follow what Marx might call the imperatives of "sensuous human activity"—they live for the pleasure of living, not for the more fleeting and empty distinctions that come from the accumulation of material wealth (Marx 143).

Later, however, as Tommo feels the boundaries of his American self begin to dissolve, and in particular as the threat represented by Karky's desire to tattoo Tommo looms ever more ominously (more on this below), he takes a very different tone. He begins to panic. While he says that his servant Kory-Kory is as devoted as ever, he nevertheless "had now been three months in their valley, as nearly as I could estimate; I had grown familiar with the narrow limits to which my wanderings had been confined; and I began bitterly to feel the state of captivity in which I was held" (231). Rather than reveling in the freedom of a life without clocks and poverty and competitive individualism, Tommo now feels "bitter" at his "captivity," a sentiment that we might view as symbolic of his fears of the potential other that exists within his own psyche. In other words, Tommo's bounded self is threatened by the potential eruption of the "primitive" desires it has repressed. To fully cross over into a Marquesan identity is terrifying for Tommo, for the very nature of his "civilized" status is premised on the repression of the "savage" within his own psyche, and on the creation of a clear "other" whose barbarism will throw his civilized self into relief. In so doing, Tommo enacts what Louis S. Gross refers to as one "common thread" of American gothic, which is the demarcation of "the singularity and monstrosity of the Other: what the dominant culture cannot incorporate within itself, it must project outward onto this hated/desired figure" (90). Tommo both desires and hates the Typee, for while they represent the antithesis of his staid Victorian self, they also symbolize the uncanny return of all that he and his culture have repressed in order to maintain their status as progressive, civilized, and moral.

If Tommo simultaneously fears and desires the freedom of the Typee, he is even more conflicted about what seems to be their far more liberated forms of sexual expression. It becomes almost a trope in the novel that Tommo initially dazzles readers with portrayals of scantily clad and innocently inviting natives, only to follow such portrayals by inveighing against their violations of sexual propriety. About the semi-nude whihenies, for example, who shimmy up the ropes of the Dolly in order to preen and frolic on its decks, Tommo writes: "What a sight for us bachelor sailors! . . . Their appearance perfectly amazed me; their extreme youth, the light clear brown of their complexions, their delicate features, and inexpressibly graceful figures, their softly moulded limbs, and free unstudied action, seemed as strange as beautiful" (15). Tommo doesn't luxuriate long, however, in this scene, for ultimately, he says, "Our ship was now wholly given up to every species of riot and debauchery. Not the feeblest barrier was interposed between the unholy passions of the crew and their unlimited gratification. The grossest licentiousness and the most shameful inebriety prevailed, with occasional and but short lived interruptions, through the whole period of her stay" (15). Again, when Tommo and Toby first arrive in the valley, a bevy of apparently nubile Marquesan girls flock to them, examining intimately their complexions, bodies, facial hair, and so on. "Long and minute was the investigation with which they honored us, and so uproarious their mirth, that I felt infinitely sheepish; and Toby was immeasurable outraged at their familiarity. . . . My feelings of propriety were exceedingly shocked, for I could not but consider them as having overstepped the due limits of female decorum" (77). Even in his portrayal of Fayaway, the seeming love interest in Melville's tropical island romance, Tommo steers what seems to be an initial sense of titillating sexual desire into a more conventional and proper Victorian romance. For example, whereas early on he describes Fayaway as "the very perfection of female grace and beauty," particularly as she habitually wears only "the primitive and summer garb of Eden" (85), by the end of the novel she merely looks on sadly as he makes his escape, a devoted admirer whose love for Tommo will forever remain (seemingly) unconsummated.

While both the vocational and sexual freedoms of the Typee present a conflicting allure for Tommo, the most significant threat to his integrated self is that he will either be eaten, or will be forced to eat another human being. This is the unbridgeable gulf between civilized and savage, self and other, and it is the most squarely gothic theme in all of *Typee*. It is this threat, which is more hypothetical than actual, that forces Tommo to flee from his tropical paradise back to the confines of the stultifying society he had so desperately longed to escape, for it ineluctably marks the Typee as savagely other, the repressed, uncanny, gothic nightmare that symbolizes the buried foundation of his civilized self.

Throughout *Typee*, Tommo is repeatedly presented with either a mysterious ceremony that he fears may result in cannibalism, or with some form of mystery meat that may, he thinks, have come from a dead member of the rival Happar tribe. Each time, however, the looming threat of cannibalism is deflated by the realization that the meat is familiar—"puarkee" (pork), for example. One of the most comedic of such scenes occurs during one of the numerous ceremonies that neither Toby nor Tommo understands in the least. As they are taken to the "Hoolah Hoolah" ground, which seems to be a sort of boys' club from which women are prohibited because of the pervasive and elaborate "taboo" system on the island, the two Americans fear that they're either about to be eaten themselves, or that some other cannibalistic rite is about to occur. Tommo awakens from a nap, as he puts it, "apprehensive of some evil" (93), they are hailed by familiar voices, and soon presented with a "wooden trencher" filled with some sort of "steaming meat." The two Americans are horrified at the prospect that they're being encouraged to eat "baked baby," "mouthfuls from a dead Happar's carcass," Toby avers, "as sure as you live, and no mistake!" (95). Their fears are allayed, however, when Kory Kory tells them that it's merely a young pig, killed and cooked for their especial gratification: "'Puarkee!' exclaimed Kory-Kory, looking complacently at the dish" (95).

Not all such encounters, however, are as benign and humorous. Toward the end of the novel, just as Tommo feels strongly the threat of Karky's desire to tattoo him, he makes an unexpected entrance into the house of another Typee, Marheyo, and finds that the mysterious packages he had seen hanging from the roof contain embalmed human heads. One of them, he thinks, might be that of Toby, who hasn't returned from an outing. "Was the same doom reserved for me? Was I destined to perish like him—like him, perhaps, to be devoured and my head to be preserved as a fearful monument of the event? My imagination ran riot in these horrid speculations, and I felt certain that the worst possible evils would befall me" (233). Tommo's fears about the cannibalism of the Typee are, of course, confirmed, he thinks, later in the novel when, after a skirmish with the Happar and a lengthy nighttime ceremony from which he is barred, he confronts "a curiously carved vessel of wood . . . with a cover placed over it." He cannot resist, and despite panicked exclamations from chiefs telling him that to open the container is "taboo," he boldly peers inside to see "the disordered members of a human skeleton, the bones still fresh with moisture, and with particles of flesh clinging to them here and there!" (238). Despite Kory-Kory's frantic attempts to mollify Tommo by telling him he's merely seen the remnants of a recently eaten "puarkee," Tommo has his evidence, and from that point on the boundaries between "civilized" and "savage" become ineluctably unbridgeable for Tommo.

As Samuel Otter has noted, however, the threat of cannibalism is given added piquancy once Tommo begins to feel pressure from the Marquesan tattoo artist Karky, who begins increasingly to want to ply his trade on Tommo's virgin face. Tommo's anxiety, as Otter suggests, is that his face will become literally marked, and as such he will lose his privileged interiority, becoming instead a racially marked and therefore readable "other." "Marquesan tattooing," Otter writes, "threatens to hatch and crosshatch the observer's body with so many lines that they will alter and confound his complexion," thus blurring the lines between the civilized white observer and the racialized, readable savage (45). "Tommo sees himself," Otter continues, "in the stippled flesh of Karky's subjects" (49). Otter's formulation is richly suggestive for a gothic reading of *Typee*. While the threat of anthropophagy is indeed horrific to Tommo, it becomes even more pronounced when he sees *himself*—or perhaps his future self—in the flesh-eating savages whom he has heretofore in the narrative described from the distanced perspective of the anthropologist. In other words, when the allure of cannibalism moves from the merely sensational—which it certainly was for Melville's antebellum readership—to the literal, the repressed threatens to return in horrifying, self-annihilating ways. To risk the mark of Karky's ink, then, threatens to blur the lines between Tommo and the Typee, which extends to other forms of savagery that Tommo's superego simply cannot withstand.

Tommo at last makes his escape in what can only be described as a harrowing rescue by members of an Australian whaling ship, aided by a "tabooed" islander who is a member of her crew. As he makes his escape, Tommo all but abandons calling his erstwhile captors by their proper names, referring to them instead repeatedly as bloodthirsty and vengeful "savages," whose success in "intercepting us" would prove "fatal" as they "grapple the oars, and seizing hold of the gunwhale, capsize the boat," leaving Tommo and his helpless shipmates "entirely at their mercy" (*Typee* 252). Tommo does, in fact, make it safely to the ship, which had originally stopped at the Marquesas in the hope of augmenting its depleted crew (did they desert, as Tommo originally did, in order to attain a modicum of freedom?)

The abruptness with which Tommo reverts from reverential admiration of the lives of the Typee to portraying them as the essence of violent and grotesque otherness is a function, I would suggest, of Tommo's revulsion at the idea that he may not be so different from the Typee after all. To be devoured is not just a literal fear of Tommo's: He also dreads at a subconscious level being consumed by the culture that both promises to release him from the shackles he has fled (symbolized by the discipline, rigor, and never-ending Sisyphean labors of the *Dolly*), but that also threatens to undermine the very self that has been created by his Americanized superego. Tommo "escapes" back into confines almost identical to the ones he had earlier in the narrative sought to flee, exchanging in the process metaphorical confinement among the Typee to literal confinement on an Australian whale ship, and this to him seems like a return, a relief.

Despite his best intentions, then, Tommo/Melville reveals to his readers all that they shut out as a result of rigid subscriptions to a confining nineteenth-century ideological framework. He also shows how the breakdown between self and other is a very gothic journey indeed. The "other" returns not just as an erstwhile form of longing, but as a savage cannibal, ready both literally and metaphorically to devour the infinitely fragile, tenuously integrated identity.

III. *Redburn's* Gothic Disavowal

If *Typee* deploys elements of the gothic romance in order to defamiliarize, or make "uncanny" many of the sexual and ideological strictures of nineteenth-century American society, *Redburn's* gothic scenes interrogate the taboo nature of intimacy between men in antebellum America—intimacy that must be disavowed in favor of the necessary forms of competitive individualism between men that formed the bedrock of the capitalist market.

There are any number of characters and scenes in *Redburn* that might qualify as "gothic": the vile misanthrope Jackson and his maniacal leer; the impressed corpse that spontaneously combusts below deck just after they sail; another impressed sailor who awakens aboard ship with delirium tremens and promptly heaves himself overboard and drowns; the mother and child who starve to death in the sewers of Liverpool while the heartless police turn a blind eye; the pedophile in the salt ship who invites a naïve Redburn to sleep with him after plying him with beer, and so on. But perhaps no episode in the novel falls so squarely within the realm of the gothic as Redburn's visit to a mystery mansion in London, a sort of hybrid brothel/casino, with Harry Bolton, the neophyte swindler/quasi-gentleman/hustler whom Redburn befriends during his sojourn in Liverpool.

The gothic confusion that suffuses *Redburn* is driven, in part, by the absence of a father figure for the young man, who initially clings to and then sadly abandons the guidebook to Liverpool once owned by his father:

> It was a sad, a solemn, and a most melancholy thought. The book on which I had so much relied, the book in the old morocco cover; the book with the cocked-hat corners; the book full of fine old family associations; the book with seventeen plates, executed in the highest style of art; this precious book was next to useless. Yes, the thing that had guided the father, could not guide the son. And I sat down on a shop step, and gave loose to meditation. (224)

Redburn's realization that his father's map to Liverpool can no longer serve him illustrates what Anne Williams refers to as one of the fundamental tropes of gothic fiction, which is a profound sense of disorientation, what she calls "the fragility of our usual systems of making sense of the world" (70). "In short," Williams writes, "an extraordinary number of gothic conventions, including certain narrative techniques, plots, and characters, imply disorder in the relations of signifiers and signifieds that are taken for granted in our ordinary conception of 'reality'" (71). Williams is referring here to the dreamlike and supernatural sequences in much Continental gothic fiction, but the same formula might well be applied to Redburn's experiences as a sailor, and in his travels throughout London and Liverpool. The city he had imagined he would encounter, bequeathed to him by his beloved but now deceased father, only corresponds loosely to his symbolic conception of it; Liverpool represents a kind of uncanny, entropic vision of what he believed he had clearly mapped out and could therefore control and navigate.

Without a reliable "guidebook," then, Redburn is in many ways little more than a helpless bumpkin in the bustling seaport metropolis of Liverpool, and then even more egregiously when he visits London. He is thus more easily taken in by Harry Bolton, of whose claims to wealth and status Redburn seems dimly incredulous, but nevertheless ultimately accepts. Harry, whom Redburn describes as "one of those small, but perfectly formed beings, with curling hair, and silken muscles," and "large, black, and womanly" eyes (294), tells Redburn what seems to be a fabricated story about being raised by a maiden aunt in Bury St. Edmonds, losing his inheritance through gambling, resolving to join the merchant service (making several trips to Bombay in the East India service), and then finally resolving to sail to America, ideally to make (or remake) his fortune. "With this object in view," Melville's narrator tells us, "he packed his trunks, and took the first train for Liverpool. . . . There was a dash of romance in it; a taking abandonment; and a scorn of fine coats, which exactly harmonized with his reckless contempt, at the time, for all past conventionalities" (396).

If ever there were a literary example of the "uncanny," Harry Bolton is it. His ostensibly superior upbringing, his scorn for the niceties of refined life, his reckless naïveté, and (despite his romanticization of its charms) his hopeless ignorance about actual life on a real ship, virtually mirror Redburn's at the outset of the novel. The one key difference, of course, between Redburn and Harry is that Harry has about him an element of reckless, illicit sexuality. In a sense, it is the open secret about Harry that readers share but of which Redburn seems ignorant—and that sense of sexual experience renders Harry a kind of exotic, prurient complement to Redburn's ostensible innocence.

That sense of explicit sexual lawlessness is epitomized in the scene where Harry takes Redburn to an infamous "semi-public place of opulent entertainment" in London that "far surpassed anything of the kind I had ever seen before" (306). The house seems to be some combination of casino and brothel, and despite the fact that Melville leaves whatever secret obligation Harry has there deliberately ambiguous, it seems to leave him deeply scarred, revealing Harry's ultimate vulnerability despite his exterior bravado.

Melville's descriptions of the house seem deliberately to invoke gothic tropes. There are hidden passageways, spring-loaded trap doors, statues that can hear, "russet hued" marble floors that echo hollowly "as if all the Paris catacombs were underneath," mysterious waiters who pass knowing looks, walls painted "so as to deceive the eye with interminable colonnades; and groups of columns of the finest Scagliola work of variegated marbles," and so on (307). Harry, of course, leaves Redburn in an opulent room for virtually the entire night, and whether he gambles away his money or prostitutes himself to some mystery guest, he returns to Redburn virtually inconsolable, drinks brandy until the morning while Redburn sleeps, and then finally resolves to return to America with Redburn as a sailor—a role at which he is beyond useless.

Although the exact nature of the house they visit—and the specific activities that so dismay Harry therein—remain something of a mystery, Harry attempts to soothe Redburn with what seems to be a significant, albeit ironic platitude about the illicit nature of the place. "'Sit down, Wellingborough,' said Harry; 'don't be frightened, we are at home" (310). The idea that the overdetermined splendor and prurience of the brothel-casino would constitute "home," I would argue, represents the essence of the gothic form. On the surface, of course, the place the two young men visit is the antithesis of home: It is alienating, rife with criminally illicit sexuality and financial recklessness, and its glittering exterior opulence masks myriad forms of what, for Redburn at least, are unimaginable forms of vice. At the same time, however, it also does symbolize a metaphorical "home" for the various prurient and at times uncontrollable vices that constitute male adulthood. The subtitle of *Redburn* is *His First Voyage*, and in many ways the novel represents a coming-of-age story for the young, naïve, and impressionable Wellingborough Redburn. In a very real sense, the integrated and nurturing home of his boyhood is forever closed for him as he enters into adult life, and what now awaits him is the dark underside of that erstwhile ideal of domestic bliss. The world of Harry Bolton, in other words, is now shared by Redburn, whether he likes it or not, and whether he can live in and tolerate and whitewash that new world will in some way hinge on the extent to which he chooses to embrace Harry and help him to succeed in the world, or instead shun him in favor of his own self-interest.

Redburn's choice, of course, is finally to shun Harry. After they arrive again in New York after what turns out to be a nightmarish voyage for Harry (a better way to describe it might be "hazing"), Redburn tells him that they must now, inexplicably, part ways. "Take my advice," Redburn tells Harry, "and while I am gone, keep up a stout heart; never despair, and all will be well" (403). All, of course, does not turn out well. Years later, while serving on a whale ship, Redburn hears of Harry's fate from another whaleman, who tells Redburn that Harry has died, crushed between a ship and a freshly caught whale. "Poor fellow," the sailor tells Redburn, "he had a hard time of it, from the beginning; he was a gentleman's son, and when you could coax him to it, he sang like a bird" (406). As he tells Redburn Harry's fate, a horrible realization seems to dawn on the sailor: "'Harry Bolton was not your brother?' cried the stranger, starting" (406). Redburn refuses to answer, and the novel closes with the unsatisfactory and abrupt statement that "I, Wellingborough Redburn, chance to survive, after having passed through far more perilous scenes than any narrated in this, My First Voyage—which here I end" (406).

From a gothic standpoint, I would argue that Harry Bolton is more than Redburn's brother: he is his uncanny other, whose explicit sexual allure, combined with a form of impractical naïveté, Redburn chooses to repress or shun rather than embrace. Put differently, Redburn does not just fail to assist Harry Bolton, abandoning him to his own devices soon after they arrive in New York. Rather, symbolically, Redburn represses his own "uncanny" doppelganger—whose egregious naïveté, ambiguous sexuality, and explicit knowledge of the prurient underside of civilized life threaten to vitiate Redburn's quest for respectable American selfhood. Redburn's failure to recognize and embrace Harry dramatizes yet again what Peter Kafer describes as perhaps the most pronounced message of American gothic fiction: That is, if we want to plumb the depths of evil, we need not look to ancient castles or paranormal mysteries or corrupt noblemen, but rather within the labyrinthine passageways of our own inner psyches. Safely on the shores of familiar territory once again, Redburn makes the choice to repress the Harry Bolton within, and in so doing paves the way for his own potential staid middle-class success.

IV. *Pierre* and the Liberated Uncanny

While there is not nearly enough space here to address in detail all the thematic intricacies of *Pierre*, which I take to be one of Melville's most sophisticated deployments of the gothic form, I would nevertheless like to conclude by gesturing toward what I view as *Pierre*'s deliberate exploration of what it might mean to live with or even celebrate the ambiguous or uncanny elements of the human psyche. To revel in one's taboo impulses, Pierre suggests, can be both inspiring and liberating, even if such desires are ultimately untenable.

If the gothic form is primarily about how the sins of the ancestral fathers continue to haunt the houses of the living, then *Pierre* certainly fits the formula. While the novel opens with deliberately saccharine portrayals of Pierre's impending domestic bliss with his betrothed, Lucy Tartan, carefully supervised by his haughtily overprotective mother, such heavenly prospects are soon shattered when Pierre learns that his now deceased father may have fathered a child with a French immigrant. Because Pierre believes that his family background has been forever vitiated, he chooses to reject, rather than repress, his own historical legacy, and concocts what Wyn Kelley calls a "warped utopian alternative" to typical nineteenth-century narratives of domestic harmony (93). He will abdicate his birthright, abandon his fiancé, and live with Isabel, his purported sister, under the guise that the two are married. This arrangement, thinks Pierre, will somehow rectify the wrongs of his father, making right again the sexually illicit crimes of the past.

Rather than make amends for past injustice, what Pierre creates instead is a surreal, richly suggestive dream world in his new tenement at "the Apostles," a kind of bohemian artists' community, where he lives not just with his half sister, but eventually with Lucy as well, who will attempt to paint while Pierre labors as a writer. Of course, the arrangement creates a meshwork of thinly repressed sexual tension between Pierre, Lucy, and Isabel. However, Pierre's domestic arrangement also throws into relief the desires of the id, and how such sexual taboos can unleash themselves in inspired forms of creative, artistic energy. In one of the novel's most-discussed passages, after Pierre and Lucy and Isabel have been living for a while with the open secret that Pierre and Lucy were once lovers and that Pierre and Isabel are, if not brother and sister, at least not all they seem, Pierre's tensions erupt in a kind of creative manifesto of moral negation. He addresses Isabel:

> "Hark thee to thy furthest inland soul"—thrilled Pierre in a steeled and quivering voice. "Call me brother no more! How knowest thou I am thy brother? Did my mother tell thee? Did my father say so to me?—I am Pierre, and thou Isabel, wide brother and sister in the common humanity,—no more. For the rest, let the gods look after their own combustibles.

If they have put powder-casks in me—let them look to it! let them look to it! Ah! now I catch glimpses, and seem to half-see, somehow, that the uttermost ideal of moral perfection in man is wide of the mark. The demi-gods trample on trash, and Virtue and Vice are trash! Isabel, I will write such things—I will gospelize the world anew, and show them deeper secrets than the Apocalypse!—I will write it, I will write it!" (273)

This avowal precedes in the novel Melville's most explicit description of what may or may not be an act of incestuous consummation between Pierre and Isabel ("How can one sin in a dream?" Pierre asks Isabel as he clasps her in his arms [274]), as if once he has renounced one social taboo, all others fall spectacularly in succession. Pierre will write! He will speak "truth to the face of falsehood," as Father Mapple might have it! He will transcend the strictures of mortal law and in so doing, become a kind of god, or at least a prophet, "gospelizing the world anew"! Read from a gothic perspective, one might well read this scene as a psychological meditation on the limiting nature of the repressive superego, and how desire's emergence for an artist can lead not to sickening or enervating forms of uncanny self-loathing, but rather to inspired artistic insights. Melville implies, then, that to be a writer of great truths, one must in some ways move beyond the gothic form into a new artistic space, one neither hampered by arbitrary taboos, nor afraid to explore (and even celebrate) those taboos when they return from the dark recesses of the unconscious.

Whether one reads *Pierre*, as such scholars as James Creech have suggested, as an encrypted exploration of anormative forms of queer intimacy, or, like Wyn Kelley, as a meditation on the limitations of domestic fiction, it seems clear from passages such as these that by this time in his authorial career, Melville was capable of embracing—even reveling in—those aspects of his culture whose ambiguities threatened a univalent, normative worldview. We might think of Melville as attempting (in spectacularly unsuccessful fashion, at least from a commercial standpoint) to unmask the gothic uncanny and "write it!" head

on. And while critics famously panned the novel, perhaps it nevertheless allowed Melville a satisfying artistic rebellion in a culture that was
both fascinated and repulsed by its own uncannily repressed perversity, the eruptive potential of which could only be hidden behind the
thinnest of psychological veneers.

Works Cited

Emerson, Ralph Waldo. "Nature." 1836. *Emerson's Prose and Poetry*. Ed. Joel Porte
and Saundra Morris. New York: Norton, 2001.

Freud, Sigmund. "The Uncanny." *The Standard Edition of the Complete Psychological Works of Sigmund Freud*. Trans. James Strachey et al. Vol. 112. London: Hog-
arth, 1955. 219–52.

Goddu, Theresa. *Gothic America: Narrative, History, and Nation*. New York: Columbia UP, 1997.

Gross, Louis S. *Redefining the American Gothic: From Wieland to Day of the Dead*.
Ann Arbor: UMI Research P, 1989.

Hume, Robert D. "Gothic Versus Romantic: A Revaluation of the Gothic Novel."
PMLA 84.2 (1969): 282–90.

Jefferson, Thomas. *Writings*. New York: Library of America, 1984.

Kafer, Peter. *Charles Brockden Brown's Revolution and the Birth of American Gothic*.
Philadelphia: U of Pennsylvania P, 2004.

Kelley, Wyn. "Pierre's Domestic Ambiguities." *The Cambridge Companion to Herman Melville*. Ed. Robert Levine. Cambridge: Cambridge UP, 1998.

Martin, Robert K., and Eric Savoy. *American Gothic: New Interventions in a National
Narrative*. Iowa City: U of Iowa P, 1998.

Marx, Karl. "Theses on Feuerbach." *The Marx-Engels Reader*. Ed. Robert C. Tucker.
New York: Norton, 1978.

Melville, Herman. *Pierre: or, The Ambiguities*. 1852. New York: Penguin, 1996.

_____. *Redburn: His First Voyage*. 1849. New York: Penguin, 1976.

_____. *Typee: A Peep at Polynesian Life*. 1846. New York: Penguin, 1996.

Otter, Samuel. *Melville's Anatomies*. Berkeley: U of California P, 1999.

Williams, Anne. *Art of Darkness: A Poetics of Gothic*. Chicago: U of Chicago P, 1995.

The Many Masks of Melville's God[1]

John Wenke

> O God (I prayed), come through
> The cloud; hard task Thou settest man
> To know Thee.
>
> —*Clarel* 2.18.133–35

I. "A Pondering Man"

On Sunday, December 9, 1849, when considering what awaited him in "this antiquated gable-ended old town" in Germany, Herman Melville scribbled an off-handed self-portrait. He was not thinking of himself as a world traveler or a famous author. Instead, in the privacy of his journal he simply anticipated that Cologne would offer "much to interest a pondering man like me" (*Journals* 35). Sophia Hawthorne, Nathaniel's wife, experienced firsthand the epistolary and conversational energy of this "pondering man." In a letter to her sister Elizabeth Palmer Peabody, Mrs. Hawthorne copied "a very remarkable quotation" from the mid-April 1851 letter Melville had written to Hawthorne describing the tragic reach of *The House of the Seven Gables*. She also described her pleasure in listening to "this growing man dash his tumultuous waves of thought up against Mr. Hawthorne's great, genial, comprehending silences." In this high tide of discourse, Melville "speaks his innermost about GOD, the Devil & Life" (qtd. in Leyda 926; uppercase in original).

Melville's letters to Hawthorne also contain "tumultuous waves of thought" that he did not always control: "I could rip an hour. You see, I began with a little criticism . . . and here I have landed in Africa" (*Correspondence* 187). In the process of praising Hawthorne's novel, Melville discusses "the visable [*sic*] truth," "the absolute condition of present things," and the deification of the "sovereign" self (186). In a surprising passage, he announces that "the Problem of the Universe" is really not so mysterious after all. But then he complicates matters:

We incline to think that God cannot explain His own secrets, and that He would like a little information upon certain points Himself. We mortals astonish Him as much as He us. But it is this *Being* of the matter; there lies the knot with which we choke ourselves. As soon as you say *Me*, a *God*, a *Nature*, so soon you jump off from your stool and hang from the beam. Yes, that word is the hangman. Take God out of the dictionary, and you would have Him in the street. (186; italics in original)[2]

What Melville actually means here—is he decrying the danger that comes with limiting one's understanding of God to a dictionary definition?—is of less import to the present discussion than recognizing that any mention of "the Problem of the Universe" could not be dissociated from the continually reconceived problem of God and the attending relationship between physical and spiritual, phenomenal and numinous realms of existence.[3]

Melville rejected what he took to be the pedestrian achievements of *Typee* (1846) and *Omoo* (1847), his first two books, in favor of exploring what he calls in *Mardi* (1849) "the world of mind" (557). By embarking on a lifelong literary voyage replete with theological intensities, Melville takes "God out of the dictionary" and pursues Him across the widening expanse of many written pages. This chapter will explore how Melville dramatizes the nature and agency of various deific entities. In such works as *Mardi*, *Moby-Dick* (1851), and *Pierre; or, The Ambiguities* (1852), he generates a conflicting range of reference that includes highly conventional figurations of the orthodox Judeo-Christian God; comedic, often profane, delineations of pagan gods; iconoclastic, even blasphemous, interrogations of a frightening, unknowable God; allusions to a pantheon of mythic gods; a multitude of incidental rhetorical tropes referencing God and the gods; and even the paradoxical notion that God's "Voice" is "profound Silence" (*Pierre* 208). God and the gods are at once attentive to human affairs and indifferent to human affairs. God is a companionate presence immanent within human beings, at times even a beneficent, democratizing muse; God is a tyrannical oppressor of human beings, at times the deaf progenitor of indifferent natural forces. In *Moby-Dick* and *Pierre*, Melville advances this endeavor by creating narrators who reveal the workings of their minds in the activity of thinking, a version of the seemingly spontaneous process that animated his conversational and epistolary interactions with Hawthorne. Indeed, Sophia Hawthorne noted the tireless energies Melville expended to "get at the Truth . . . having settled nothing as yet" (Leyda 926). The many masks of Melville's God give shifting, provisional form to whatever transcendent divinity exists beyond the verbal reach of narrators and characters. Melville's approach to writing about God was continually exploratory and open-ended rather than fixed and doctrinal. He never settled anything. He was concerned more with dramatizing circumstances faced by narrators and characters in their unfolding, experiential moments than with adumbrating the intricacies of theological dogma.

II. Orthodox and Heterodox

On August 19, 1819, Herman Melvill (as the name was originally spelled) was baptized into the Dutch Reformed Church. He was raised in a household steeped in the Bible-centered Reformation Protestantism that found the fallen human being helpless to attain salvation without God's freely bestowed irresistible grace. The more dire, damnation-tinged implications of the Dutch Reformed mindset were softened by an insistent faith in the nurturing, restorative agency of Divine Providence, the belief that a watchful, merciful God authors the unfolding human story.[4]

Allan Melvill, Herman's father, was a highly conventional religious man whose liberal Unitarian sensibilities seemed to balance his wife's more stringent Dutch Reformed convictions (Sherrill 488). Allan Melvill was prone to administering pietistic advice. For example, in his letter of October 27, 1824, to his nephew Guert Gansevoort, who was about to take his first voyage as a midshipman, Melvill offers the sort of pieties he later served his children—Gansevoort, Helen, and Herman—once they were old enough to understand him: "But above all, my little sailor Boy, let me conjure you, *forget not your* Creator in the dawn of youth . . . neglect not the *Bible*, regard it as *your polar star*, its religious precepts & moral doctrines are alike pure & sublime" (Leyda 19; italics in original). Although his father died in 1832, when Herman was twelve years old, Allan's voice continued to resonate within his imagination. Hershel Parker describes the ineradicable influence Allan Melvill had on his loving and devoted eldest children: "No matter that his pronouncements were conventional opinions elegantly couched, they sounded in his children's ears as if they were products of his unique hard-won philosophical comprehension of the workings of the universe"(60). Only later would Melville perceive such utterances not as determinate conclusions of a magisterial order, but as materials to adapt to specific narrative purposes. Indeed, his parents' religious traditions served Melville as fertile resources for the many deeply felt orthodox dramatizations that appear throughout four and a half decades of literary activity.

Following the publication of *Typee* and *Omoo*, Melville became a target of religious conservatives for his scathing, polemical attacks on Christian missionaries in sunny Polynesia (*Typee* 124–27, 195–99; *Omoo* 122–26, 172–76, 184–92). Melville's special focus was the hegemonic imperatives that led these missionaries to colonize and debase indigenous populations. In *Mardi*, Melville turned his polemical impulses to the service of religious satire. Melville's narrator parodies those decidedly mortal beings that turn themselves into cartoonish demigods. The narrator himself adopts the self-serving fiction that he is "some gentle demi-god" (140). In fact, many islands of Mardi's archipelago are cluttered with a proliferating retinue of self-ordained "strolling divinities" (166). During his travels on Maramma, the narrator also satirizes the luxurious excesses of Roman Catholicism. While criticizing the perversions of organized Christianity in *Typee* and *Omoo* and mocking them in *Mardi*, Melville does not attack the Judeo-Christian God. However much he excoriated the missionaries and their conquering, codependent military operatives, he remained fully capable of separating the specific rhetorical demands of polemics and satire from narrative occasions that called for powerful, celebratory depictions of a conventional Judeo-Christian God. This God, whether existing as a rhetorical trope or as an article of belief, remained a touchstone presence throughout his creative life. For example, Melville's narrator demonstrates nothing but reverence for Oro, Mardi's sovereign God above all other gods. A distant and mysterious being, Oro remains beyond the reach of satire and parody. He is one version of Melville's true God, and Alma is his Christ-like son. In fact, when the philosopher Babbalanja renounces his wayward, self-defeating skepticism, he humbly accepts epistemological limitation: "Some things there are, we must not think of. Beyond one obvious mark, all human lore is vain. . . . All I have said ere this, that wars with Alma's precepts, I here recant. Here I kneel, and own great Oro and his sovereign son" (630).

The point is not that Melville himself ever sees religious orthodoxy as a final resolution to "the universal problem of all things" (*Moby-Dick* 293), but that he recognizes the abiding power of Christian orthodoxy to give legitimate shape and value to select passages in the human story. At the very least, the orthodox God of Melville's childhood remains a readily available source for a kind of in-text pulpit oratory. In *White-Jacket* (1850), when discussing Jesus' admonition "to turn the left cheek if the right be smitten," the narrator contends, "That passage embodies the soul and substance of the Christian faith. . . . And that passage will yet, by the blessing of God, turn the world" (321). Near the end of *White-Jacket*, the narrator evokes the Christian God to establish a determinate macrocosmic metaphor of the world-ship built and commanded by God: "We mortals are all on board a fast-sailing, neversinking world-frigate, of which God was the shipwright; and she is but one craft in a Milky-Way fleet of which God is the Lord High Admiral" (398).

Such highly charged affirmations provide foundational points of departure for Ishmael's wide-ranging, divided interrogations of the nature and meaning of disparate divine entities. Within *Moby-Dick*, Ishmael appears both as a tyro actor in the reconstructed past-tense narrative and as the present-tense composer of the unfolding text. Ishmael's narrative voice comes into being through the emergent energies of his expansive, often digressive, compositional process.[5] The exigencies of any given situation create conditions to which Ishmael responds. Any affirmation of the orthodox God, therefore, becomes contextually true, or applicable, to the specific moment, rather than ultimately true, or applicable, for the entire text. In considering *Moby-Dick*'s complicated narrative form, one must recognize how the professed truth of one moment might contradict or displace the professed truth of a subsequent moment. A foolish consistency, to borrow Emerson's phrase, is not only the hobgoblin of little minds: In *Moby-Dick*, a search for mere consistency imposes arbitrary criteria on the protean adaptations of Ishmael's present-tense narrative. For example, Ishmael celebrates the pulpit as a synecdoche for the primacy of Christian orthodoxy: "The pulpit leads the world. From thence it is the storm of God's quick wrath is first descried, and the bow must bear the earliest brunt. From thence it is the God of breezes fair or foul is first invoked for favorable winds. Yes, the world's a ship on its passage out, and not a voyage complete; and the pulpit is its prow" (40).

These heartfelt sentiments prepare the reader for one of the great set pieces in *Moby-Dick*. Father Mapple's sermon redacts in a sailor's vernacular the biblical tale of Jonah and the whale.[6] In the sermon, Jonah's whale behaves as a completely subservient instrument of God's vengeance. Mapple's assertion that "God is everywhere" reflects his abiding faith in the ubiquitous presence of Divine Providence (47). The whale swallows Jonah whole, and, following the wayward prophet's repentance, releases Jonah to actualize God's purpose—"to preach the Truth in the face of Falsehood!" (48). Ishmael presents the Mapple sermon without postscript commentary, although Mapple's warning to the "pilot of the Living God" (47) might well serve as an implicit countertext and possible corrective to Captain Ahab's heterodox, insurrectionist repudiations of the moral rectitude of Jonah's God. Mapple's sermon remains an iconic delineation of one man's faith in "this sure Keel of the Ages" (48). Like Jonah's whale, the figure of Moby Dick that appears in Ishmael's retelling of the *Town Ho*'s story operates as an instrument of Divine vengeance—a circumstance that makes the White Whale subservient here to God's interruptive divine plan. The resolution of the conflict between Steelkilt and Radney "seemed obscurely to involve with the whale a certain wondrous, inverted visitation of one of those so called judgments of God which at times are said to overtake some men" (242). Indeed, as Ishmael notes, "Heaven itself seemed" to commission the whale to slaughter Radney and thus prevent Steelkilt from enacting "the damning thing he would have done" (255–56).

In these instances, Ishmael depicts the power of the sovereign Christian God, but he is by no means confined by a single creed. The same Ishmael who proclaims the pulpit as the center of the Christian faith soon gets down on his knees to worship cannibal Queequeg's wooden idol Yojo. Using a mock-syllogism to justify a blatantly blasphemous act, Ishmael satirizes his own capacity for self-serving rationalization: "Do you suppose now, Ishmael, that the magnanimous God of heaven and earth—pagans and all included—can possibly be jealous of an insignificant bit of black wood? . . . Ergo, I must turn idolator" (52). By having Ishmael identify himself as a good Presbyterian, Melville overtly baits the righteous avengers of the Presbyterian press. Not for too little did Melville earn the ire of reviewers, who had not forgotten his caustic treatment of Christianity's holy mission in the South Seas. Their Presbyterian God could never be construed as a "magnanimous God," and these Cromwellian reviewers did not spare the ax.[7] Through the irreverent power of comic burlesque, Melville decenters the reigning ideology of Christian orthodoxy. By celebrating the humanity of pagan Queequeg, Melville embraces the radical principle of cultural and theological relativism. In a similar vein, Ishmael mocks "the grand Programme of Providence" (7) and later uses Queequeg's "great confidence in the excellence of Yojo's judgment" to satirize this "rather good sort of god, who . . . in all cases did not succeed in his benevolent designs" (68).

In a more serious vein, Melville recognizes that the concept of Providence can be contorted into the very human attempt to construe one's own behavior as reflecting providential approbation. In his story "Benito Cereno," for example, the captain of a Spanish slave ship marvels at how the American captain Amasa Delano "had the Prince of Heaven's safe conduct through all ambuscades"; with complacent self-congratulation, Delano professes that "all is owing to Providence" (115). In his smug way, Delano cannot see that his "Providence" is nothing more than a self-generated fiction justifying slavery, colonial domination, and an imperial legal system that exacts a savage brand of justice.

These contrastive moments constitute interpretive acts that are true to the demands of their respective narrative situations, but they do not possess hermeneutical priority. Indeed, they do not offer anything like a single paradigmatic expression of Melville's view of God. In another passage seemingly designed to inflame Christian conservatives, Ishmael affects the tone of oratorical self-righteousness and rejects the supremacy of *any* single theological system: "I say, we good Presbyterian Christians should be charitable in these things, and not fancy ourselves so vastly superior to other mortals, pagans and what not, because of their half-crazy conceits on these subjects. . . . And Heaven have mercy on us all—Presbyterians and Pagans alike—for we are all somehow dreadfully cracked about the head and sadly need mending" (81). Like Melville, Ishmael is "a pondering man" of expansive, flexible, accommodating sensibility. Ishmael does not approach the mysterious, masked deity convinced of the unassailable correctness of any creed, but through open-minded speculations regarding the putative efficacy of none, some or all of these "half-crazy conceits." As a narrator, Ishmael presents himself through the ever accumulating sum of dialectically divergent points of view. Even the heterodox Ahab, a "grand, ungodly god-like man" (79), has his rare moments of orthodox expression. Holding the musket to Starbuck, Ahab exclaims, "There is one God that is Lord over the earth, and one Captain that is lord over the Pequod.—On deck!" (474). Like Ishmael, Ahab articulates an expansive range of deific figures, from the most conventional to the most profane and blasphemous. As Captain Peleg notes, "Ahab's been in colleges, as well as 'mong the cannibals" (79). Like Ishmael, Ahab's deific tropes are frequently products of specific intellectual or emotional responses. Ishmael dramatizes Ahab as he lives through many moods.

Melville applies conventional delineations of the God image not only to matters of theology and cultural ideology, but also to very distinct, celebratory political purposes. In *White-Jacket*, for example, the narrator launches a chauvinistic affirmation of America as the redeemer nation fueled by the determinate principle of Manifest Destiny. In fervent tropes reflective of contemporary political oratory, the narrator proclaims, "And we Americans are the peculiar, chosen people—the Israel of our time. . . . God has given to us, for a future inheritance, the broad domains of the political pagans. . . . God has predestinated, mankind expects, great things from our race" (151). In this case, a conventional God supports the most conventional of political platitudes. In *Moby-Dick*, Ishmael applies a politically motivated deific figuration to a more complex celebration of the workers' democratic world. Ishmael adapts the hyperbolic tones of contemporary political oratory to describe a God who sanctions and sustains the egalitarian world of work. Gone is *Mardi*'s distant, sovereign Oro or Father Mapple's jealous, exacting Jehovah. Arrived is an Everyman's God who rejects the aristocratic privilege of "robed investiture" in favor of "that democratic dignity which, on all hands, radiates without end from God; Himself! The great God absolute! The centre and circumference of all democracy! His omnipresence, our divine equality!" (117). Ishmael taps into energies that animate the contemporary transcendentalist insistence on the divinity of man. In fact, this democratic God sanctifies Ishmael's unfolding creative venture. He calls on God—"Thou just Spirit of Equality"—to infuse his literary performance and thus connect him with such predecessors as John Bunyon, Miguel de Cervantes, and Andrew Jackson. This paean reinvents the Puritan God as a populist advocate of the "kingly commons" (117).

III. Ishmael, Ahab, and Pierre: "The Interlinked Terrors and Wonders of God"

Ishmael's evocations of God and the gods often erupt as sudden rhetorical tropes. One finds an abundance of cautionary moments—"God keep thee! Push not off from that isle, thou canst never return!" (*Moby-Dick* 274)—as well as numerous iconoclastic displacements of orthodox Christianity—"Long exile from Christendom and civilization inevitably restores a man to that condition in which God placed him, i.e., what is called savagery" (222). The deity might make a cameo appearance as Ishmael's companionate muse of artistic incompletion: "God keep me from ever completing anything" (145). The reign of Providence covers "the inscrutable tides of God" (159) and extends to the migratory patterns of sperm whales: "Besides, when making a passage from one feeding-ground to another, the sperm whales, guided by infallible instinct—nay, rather, secret intelligence from the Deity—mostly swim in *veins*" (199; italics in original). Ishmael writes of "sea-gods" (303), "the hands of [Queequeg's] gods" (321), Pip's "big white God" (178), and those "gods [who] shipwrecked [Captain Pollard] again upon unknown rocks and breakers" (206).

Besides such frequent deific irruptions, Ishmael mounts extended explorations of the nature and agency of God and the gods that propel the reader far beyond the narrow contours of orthodox Christian theology. Ishmael exemplifies how the human mind, rather than remaining imprisoned within unrelieved servitude, can stand in a defiant state of intellectual rebellion. In "The Lee Shore" chapter, Ishmael describes an intransigent conflict between the liberating powers of human thought and the conspiratorial antagonism of natural and deific forces: "Glimpses do ye seem to see of that mortally intolerable truth; that all deep, earnest thinking is but the intrepid effort of the soul to keep the open independence of her sea, while the wildest winds of heaven and earth conspire to cast her on the treacherous, slavish shore?" (107). For Ishmael, Ahab, and Pierre, to pursue freedom of mind and soul is to stand as Promethean figures—defiant romantic rebels who wish to usurp the proprietary exclusion of the God realm. Empowered by intellectual energies uncontained by orthodoxy, Ishmael depicts how the most august and powerful aspects of the natural world—in this case, the sperm whale's "vast tail"—provide "comprehensible" metaphorical and symbolic forms that permit him to reach *toward* a distant, incomprehensible, and terrifying God: "For what are the comprehensible terrors of man compared with the interlinked terrors and wonders of God!" (109). Ishmael's whale is not simply a magnificent "god-like" (346) being, but he is also an inscrutable object that evokes without containing or specifying the dreadful mysteries of God's hidden nature. The brow of the whale constitutes a fit emblem of how surfaces might suggest the teasing presence of indecipherable forms: "Human or animal, the mystical brow is as that great golden seal affixed by the German emperors to their decrees. It signifies—'God: done this day by my hand'. . . . But in the great Sperm Whale, this high and mighty god-like dignity inherent in the brow is so immensely amplified, that gazing on it . . . you feel the Deity and the dread powers more forcibly than in beholding any other object in living nature" (346). The brow of the whale, unreadable and overwhelming though it remains, is a living sign of the transcendent God's displaced grandeur and mystery.

The divine attributes of any sperm whale are only intensified when Ishmael ponders the specific godlike attributes of the "ubiquitous" Moby Dick (183). In "The Whiteness of the Whale" chapter, Ishmael reads the divine intimations stirred by the whale's pallor. The language of orthodox Christianity is simply not adequate to express the expansiveness and terror of this God. He incorporates references to disparate religious mythologies—Zoroastrian, Hellenic, Native American—and thereby suggests that a fit conception of God can be achieved not within any specific doctrine per se, but only by accumulating an ever expanding range of eclectic configurations:

Though even in the higher mysteries of the most august religions [whiteness] has been made the symbol of divine spotlessness and power; by the Persian fire-worshippers, the white-forked flame being held the holiest on the altar; and in the Greek mythologies, Great Jove himself being made incarnate in the snow-white bull, and though to the noble Iroquois, the midwinter sacrifice of the sacred White Dog was by far the holiest festival of their theology. . . . Yet for all these accumulated associations, with whatever is sweet and honorable, and sublime, there yet lurks an elusive something in the innermost idea of this hue, which strikes more of panic to the soul than that redness which affrights in blood. (189)

"The Whiteness of the Whale" constitutes Ishmael's most penetrating attempt to suggest the doubleness that exists in nature and the absolute. God seems pure love; God seems terrifying; God seems enticing and beneficent; God seems frightening and malevolent. Indeed, in an image that depicts natural force as a compressed symbol of the beauty and horror of the displaced divinity, Ishmael concludes that "all deified Nature absolutely paints like the harlot, whose allurements cover nothing but the charnel-house within" (195).

Only by plunging through the quotidian forms of social existence can one look behind the masks of God and achieve a direct vision of the deity's vexing doubleness—a vision that ironically excludes one from the company of sane, reasonable mortals. The cabin boy Pip experiences just such a transit. When abandoned by Stubb in the midst of the sea's "heartless immensity," Pip undergoes a traumatic transfiguration and thereby attains a privileged view of creation: His soul, while "not drowned entirely" is "carried down alive to wondrous depths." He visits "the unwarped primal world" and there sees "God's foot on the treadle of the loom, and spoke it; and therefore his shipmates called him mad. So man's insanity is heaven's sense; and wandering from all mortal reason, man comes at last to that celestial thought, which, to reason, is absurd and frantic; and weal or woe, feels then uncompromised, indifferent as his God" (414). In this extreme formulation, the human realm of normative, rational consciousness remains inimical to the supernatural order of an "indifferent God." To see and speak the ways of this God is to be seen and understood as mad. Ishmael posits an irreconcilable split between earthly and divine spheres—a position later developed in *Pierre*. Plotinus Plinlimmon's pamphlet argues for the complete incompatibility of earthly, or "horological," wisdom, and heavenly, or "chronometrical," wisdom (*Pierre* 210–15).[8] In describing Pip, Ishmael has moved well beyond those conventional depictions of the providential God in favor of a silent God detached from the realm of human affairs. Indeed, shortly thereafter, Ishmael paints a portrait of a deaf and distant God: "The weaver-god, he weaves; and by that weaving is he deafened, that he hears no mortal voice" (450). Ishmael not only tries to contain God within the language of conventional religious orthodoxy, but he also delineates the dialectical counterpoint to this endeavor when suggesting that God remains implacably beyond the contextual world of human beings and their tenuous semiotic constructs.

Ahab and Pierre resist the notion that God is distant and unreachable. In the fiery monomania that fuels his complicated, purposeful vengeance, Ahab depicts how the indigent human self can act and speak in terms of Promethean, God-assaulting defiance. In "The Quarter-deck" chapter, Ahab's "pasteboard masks" speech offers *the* foundational paradigm expressing the theological basis animating Ahab's quest. He is not interested, as Starbuck claims, in inflicting "vengeance on a dumb brute . . . that simply smote [Ahab] from blindest instinct" (163–64). Ahab rejects Starbuck's premise and proceeds with his crucial "little lower layer" of explanation. To Ahab, all things are infused with the divine purpose:

> All visible objects, man, are but as pasteboard masks. But in each event— in the living act, the undoubted deed—there, some unknown but still reasoning thing puts forth the mouldings of its features from behind the unreasoning mask. If man will strike, strike through the mask! How can the

prisoner reach outside except by thrusting through the wall? To me, the white whale is that wall, shoved near to me. (164)[9]

Ahab reverses the Platonic and transcendental insistence on the absolute benevolence of Divine forms and forces and replaces it with a God that orchestrates the "inscrutable malice" of Moby Dick (164). According to Ahab, there may be "naught beyond" the "pasteboard masks" of material forms; there may be nothing other than a blank, godless realm of spiritual nullity and physical force, but for Ahab, the thought of defeating God's purposeful evil is "enough" (164). Ahab hates a God-ordained cosmology that perpetuates and condones willful evil. Ahab, therefore, anoints himself a Promethean antagonist of these malign entities. Essentially, Ahab blames God for the consequences of the fall and sees Providence as a tyrannical force tormenting indigent mortals.

At the center of Ahab's antagonism to the God realm resides his compensatory, self-deifying rhetoric. He would "strike the sun if it insulted [him]" (164). Through his fevered tropes, Ahab attempts to make the absent gods assume vicarious presence. His words attempt to bring the gods down to fighting size: "Now, then, be the prophet and the fulfiller one. That's more than ye, ye great gods, ever were. I laugh and hoot at ye, ye cricket-players, ye pugilists, ye deaf Burkes and blinded Bendigoes! . . . Come forth from behind your cotton bags! I have no long gun to reach ye" (143). Repeatedly, Ahab deprecates the God-realm. Pip's madness especially infuriates Ahab: "There can be no hearts above the snow-line. Oh, ye frozen heavens! look down here. Ye did beget this luckless child, and have abandoned him, ye creative libertines" (522). What Starbuck calls Ahab's "heaven-insulting purpose" (169) extends to Ahab's attitude toward pagan and mythic divinities. "The Candles" chapter presents an extreme manifestation of Ahab's self-empowering rhetoric. He is Prometheus tortured and chained to a rock, but remaining the unrepentant, and highly vocal, rebel: "Oh, thou clear spirit of clear fire, whom on these seas I as Persian once did worship, till in the sacramental act so burned by thee, that to this hour I bear the scar; I now know thee, thou clear spirit, and I now know that thy right worship is defiance. . . . I own thy speechless, placeless power; but to the last gasp of my earthquake life will dispute its unconditional, unintegral mastery in me. In the midst of the personified impersonal, a personality stands here" (507).[10]

However frenzied, blasphemous, and self-defeating Ahab's rhetoric may be, he nevertheless retains what Captain Peleg calls "his humanities" (79). When he speaks with Starbuck in "The Symphony" chapter, Ahab presents himself as a chastened tragic figure burdened by the weight of impossible tasks:

> I feel deadly faint, bowed, and humped, as though I were Adam, staggering beneath the piled centuries since Paradise. God! God! God!—crack my heart!—stave my brain!—mockery! mockery! bitter, biting mockery of grey hairs, have I lived enough joy to wear ye; and seem and feel thus intolerably old? Close! stand close to me, Starbuck; let me look into a human eye; it is better than to gaze into sea or sky; better than to gaze upon God (544).

This climactic moment celebrates human federation and fealty, even as it directly precipitates Ahab's final rejection of the contextual, nurturing sphere of human felicity. Ultimately, Ahab is no match for "the glorified White Whale as he so divinely swam" (548). Indeed, Moby Dick's divine attributes surpass Jupiter and Jove. When Moby Dick finally appears within the dramatic action and initiates the sequence that ends with the *Pequod*'s destruction, Ishmael tears away the masks of God and simply notes that "the grand god revealed himself, sounded, and went out of sight" (549).

Like Ahab, Pierre is another self-anointed Promethean figure who can only fail to contain, comprehend, or conquer God. As Melville repeatedly dramatizes, when human beings believe they can *be* and *act* like God, they court, and eventually achieve, disaster for themselves and others. In *Mardi*, the demigod Taji, with "eternity . . . in his eye," renounces the contextual world of social forms and dooms himself to seek the Absolute even as he flees indefatigable, vengeful pursuers "over an endless sea" (654). In *Moby-Dick*, Ahab's God-obsession destroys the ship of the world. Whereas Ahab remains a man of heroic stature and tragic majesty, Pierre becomes little more than an overreaching fool who wrestles the "ambiguities" surrounding his putative half-sister Isabel into a fiction of divine warrant. With a mocking voice, the third person narrator prescripts the inevitable failure of Pierre's quest to actualize what he feels are those "divine commands upon him to befriend and champion Isabel, through all conceivable contingencies of Time and Chance" (106). Early in the text, the narrator's sarcasm foreshadows Pierre's inevitable doom: "We shall yet see . . . whether Fate hath not just a little bit of a word or two to say in this world; we shall see whether this wee scrap of latinity be very far out of the way—*Nemo contra Deum nisi Deus ipse*" (14; italics in original). This "wee scrap" literally translates as "No one against God but God himself," or more liberally as "Only God can oppose God." In his foolish innocence and cloying self-righteousness, Pierre is no god. He assumes the existence of his own deific attributes and expresses them through fiercely overheated declamations. He sets conditions for God and the gods, "ye Invisibles," and proclaims that regardless of whether these divine lights forsake him he will "declare [himself] an equal power with [God and man]" (107). Although voicing the hyperbolic tropes of the self-deifying Prometheus, Pierre remains a "thing" of clay, a human being incapable of containing divine power: "But Pierre, though charged with the fire of all divineness, his containing thing was made of clay. Ah, muskets the gods have made to carry infinite combustions, and yet made them of clay!" (107). *Nemo contra Deum nisi Deus ipse*.

Once again, Melville dramatizes the incompatibility of human and divine realms of existence. Pierre finds nothing but mystery, failure, and the detritus that comes with an obsessively willed self-destruction. According to the narrator, Pierre believes that the unknowable mysteries of life are derived from the unknowable mysteries of God: "He saw that human life doth truly come from that, which all men are agreed to call by the name of *God*; and that it partakes of the unravelable inscrutableness of God" (141). Thus Pierre casts himself within an impossibly contradictory role. Because Isabel's mysteries come from God, these mysteries are beyond resolution. By loving Isabel and destroying his social past, he marries confusion and cross-purposes. Pierre is so completely identified as a force of rhetorical self-invention that he implicitly places himself in diametrical opposition to the paradoxical "Voice" of a silent God. The narrator remarks, "Silence is the general consecration of the universe. Silence is the invisible laying on of the Divine Pontiff's hands upon the world. Silence is at once the most harmless and the most awful thing in all nature. It speaks of the Reserved Forces of Fate. Silence is the only Voice of our God" (204). The extreme declamations of Ahab and Pierre have little effect on the ineffable silence of the remote, utterly transcendent God.

IV. "Pyramidical Silence"

With his ten-year career as a fiction writer in a tattered state, Melville left the United States on October 11, 1856, for a protracted tour of Europe, the Middle East, and the Holy Land. In a very real sense, the second half of Melville's life was beginning. Cut loose from the demands of domesticity and the self-induced weight of commercial failure—a condition that would reach its terminus following the April Fool's Day publication of *The Confidence-Man: His Masquerade* (1857)—Melville had the world all before him and nowhere he had to be. He made a point to visit Hawthorne in Southport, England. On November 12, 1856, the two friends took a walk on the beach and engaged in one of their standard sessions of "ontological heroics" (*Correspondence* 196). What Melville describes merely as "good talk" (*Journals* 51) receives an expansive account in Hawthorne's notebook: "Melville, as he always does, began to reason of Providence and futurity, and of everything that lies beyond human ken, and informed me that he had 'pretty much made up his mind to be annihilated'; but still he does not seem to rest in that anticipation; and, I think, will never rest until he gets hold of a definite belief." In a penetrating assessment of Melville's life as "a pondering man," Hawthorne concludes that his friend "can neither believe, nor be comfortable in his unbelief; and he is too honest and courageous not to try to do one or the other" (qtd. in Leyda 529). The desire to reach beyond what any human can know fueled Melville's imagination and informed the creation of his literary works.

His travels did not result in popular literary success, but laid building blocks for Melville's truncated career as a lecturer and his long career as a poet. His travels in the Holy Land and his journal notes were primary sources for the monumental *Clarel* (1876). His time in the Middle East continually brought him to ponder the origin of things—the origin of Christianity; the origin of biblical events; the origin of Jehovah. In *Moby-Dick*, Ishmael writes of the sperm whale's "pyramidical silence" (347), but when Melville finally found himself inside an Egyptian pyramid, he experienced not silence but a stifled sense of incipient panic, "[a] feeling of awe & terror," a dread of "ancient Egyptians. It was in these pyramids that was conceived the idea of Jehovah" (*Journals* 75). Melville suggests that the figure of Jehovah was indeed a creation of "terrible inventors, those Egyptian wise men" (*Journals* 78). God *is* whatever God may *be*, but it is the office of ancient Egyptian holy men and Promethean literary artists to conjure representations that dare to reflect ostensible aspects of God's infinite and unknowable identity. From "out of the crude forms of the natural earth," the Egyptians raised pyramids and thereby "rear[ed] the transcendent conception of a God" (*Journals* 78). The pyramids reflect the unresolved nature of Melville's ongoing search for God. In this process the artist employs available forms, whether stones or words, to "evoke by art" (78) projected images of an always elusive, always masked divine essence.

Notes

1. Dedicated to Thomas A. Werge and Milton R. Stern: The Greatest of Teachers.

2. See Marovitz for an expansive discussion of this passage and its relation to the influence of such writers as Sir Thomas Browne on Melville's philosophical development.

3. "The Problem of the Universe" is a recurrent phrase in Melville's letters (*Correspondence* 180, 185, 186, and 452) and *Moby-Dick* (158 and 293). For discussions of Melville's exploration of the relation of the phenomenal and numinous realm of existence, see Stern 1–28; Sealts; and Wenke 112–63.

4. For discussions of Melville's relation to the religious traditions that influenced his life and work, see Goldman; Herbert; Obenzinger; Sherrill, "Melville and Religion" and *The Prophetic Melville*; Thompson; and Werge, "Luther and Melville" and "*Moby-Dick* and the Calvinist Tradition." In *The Prophetic Melville*, Sherrill discusses Melville's relation to the tradition of the hidden God: "The point here is that the encounter with the hidden God does not automatically lead to skepticism or pessimism. Another more deeply committed alternative . . . was to explore the dimensions of the presence of this hidden God in order to calculate its significance for an understanding of human experience" (251).

5. For discussions of Ishmael as narrator, see Brodtkorb; and Wenke 114–31.

6. For Melville's use of biblical materials, see Hutchins; Pardes; and Wright. Hutchins argues, "By writing his wicked book, Melville re-inscribes the Bible, producing a third testament whose form corresponds to that of the Old and New Testaments and whose content provides its readers with a new iteration of and a commentary on the salvific narratives found in those texts" (18). For a seminal discussion of Melville's use of Jonah, see Wright 82–93.

7. For a large selection of contemporary reviews of *Moby-Dick*, see Higgins and Parker 351–416. For a discussion of the harsh treatment Melville received from Christian reviewers prior to the publication of *Moby-Dick*, see Hayford and Parker 57 n. 4 and 465–509. For a sample vitriolic review of *Moby-Dick*, see the piece published by "H." in the New York *Independent* on November 20, 1851, attacking Melville's "primitive formation of profanity and indecency": "The Judgment day will hold [Melville] liable for not turning his talents to better account, when, too, both authors and publishers of injurious books will be conjointly answerable for the influence of those books upon a wide circle of immortal minds on which they have written their mark. The book-maker and the book-publisher had better do their work with a view to the trial it must undergo at the bar of God" (Hayford and Parker 605).

8. For interpretations of Plinlimmon's pamphlet, see Stern 189–95; Higgins and Parker, *Reading Melville's Pierre* 113–19.

9. For a discussion of Martin Luther's possible influence on this passage, see Werge, "Luther and Melville."

10. For discussions of Melville's relation to exotic theologies, see Finkelstein; and Vargish.

Works Cited

Brodtkorb, Paul, Jr. *Ishmael's White World: A Phenomenological Reading of* Moby-Dick. New Haven: Yale UP, 1965.

Finkelstein, Dorothee Metlitsky. *Melville's Orienda.* New Haven: Yale UP, 1961.

Goldman, Stan. *Melville's Protest Theism: The Hidden and Silent God in* Clarel. DeKalb: Northern Illinois UP, 1993.

Hayford, Harrison, and Hershel Parker, eds. "Before *Moby-Dick*: International Controversy over Melville." *Moby-Dick; or, The Whale.* By Herman Melville. New York: Norton, 2002. 465–519.

Herbert, T. Walter, Jr. Moby-Dick *and Calvinism: A World Dismantled.* New Brunswick, N.J.: Rutgers UP, 1977.

Higgins, Brian, and Hershel Parker, eds. *Herman Melville: The Contemporary Reviews.* New York: Cambridge UP, 1995.

_____. *Reading Melville's* Pierre, or, The Ambiguities. Baton Rouge: Louisiana State UP, 2006.

Hutchins, Zachary. "*Moby-Dick* as Third Testament: A Novel 'Not Come to Destroy But to Fulfill' the Bible." *Leviathan: A Journal of Melville Studies* 13.2 (2011): 18–37.

Leyda, Jay. *The Melville Log: A Documentary Life of Herman Melville, 1819–1891.* 2 vols. New York: Gordian, 1969.

Marovitz, Sanford A. "Melville's Problematic 'Being.'" *ESQ: A Journal of the American Renaissance* 28.1 (1982): 11–23.

Melville, Herman. "Benito Cereno." *The Piazza Tales and Other Prose Pieces: 1839–1860.* Ed. Harrison Hayford et al. Evanston and Chicago: Northwestern-Newberry, 1987. 46–117. Vol. 9 of *The Writings of Herman Melville.*

_____. *Clarel: A Poem and Pilgrimage in the Holy Land.* Ed. Harrison Hayford et al. Evanston and Chicago: Northwestern-Newberry, 1991. Vol. 12 of *The Writings of Herman Melville.*

_____. *Correspondence.* Ed. Lynn Horth. Evanston and Chicago: Northwestern-Newberry, 1993. Vol. 14 of *The Writings of Herman Melville.*

_____. *Journals.* Ed. Howard C. Horsford with Lynn Horth. Evanston and Chicago: Northwestern-Newberry, 1989. Vol. 15 of *The Writings of Herman Melville.*

_____. *Mardi, and a Voyage Thither.* Ed. Harrison Hayford et al. Evanston and Chicago: Northwestern-Newberry, 1970. Vol. 3 of *The Writings of Herman Melville.*

_____. *Moby-Dick; or, The Whale.* Ed. Harrison Hayford et al. Evanston and Chicago: Northwestern-Newberry, 1988. Vol. 6 of *The Writings of Herman Melville.*

_____. *Omoo: A Narrative of Adventures in the South Seas.* Ed. Harrison Hayford et al. Evanston and Chicago: Northwestern-Newberry, 1968. Vol. 2 of *The Writings of Herman Melville.*

_____. *Pierre; or, The Ambiguities.* Ed. Harrison Hayford et al. Evanston and Chicago: Northwestern-Newberry, 1971. Vol. 7 of *The Writings of Herman Melville.*

_____. *Typee: A Peep at Polynesian Life.* Ed. Harrison Hayford et al. Evanston and Chicago: Northwestern-Newberry, 1968. Vol. 1 of *The Writings of Herman Melville.*

_____. *White-Jacket; or, The World in a Man-of-War*. Ed. Harrison Hayford et al. Evanston and Chicago: Northwestern-Newberry, 1970. Vol. 5 of *The Writings of Herman Melville*.

Obenzinger, Hilton. " 'Wicked Books': Melville and Religion." *A Companion to Herman Melville*. Ed. Wyn Kelley. Malden, Mass.: Blackwell, 2006. 181–96.

Pardes, Ilana. *Melville's Bibles*. Berkeley: U of California P, 2008.

Parker, Hershel. *Herman Melville: A Biography: 1819–1851*. Vol. 2. Baltimore and London: Johns Hopkins UP, 1996.

Sealts, Merton M., Jr. "Melville and the Platonic Tradition." *Pursuing Melville, 1940–1980*. Madison: U of Wisconsin P, 1982. 278–336.

Sherrill, Rowland A. "Melville and Religion." *A Companion to Melville Studies*. Ed. John Bryant. New York: Greenwood, 1986. 481–513.

_____. *The Prophetic Melville: Experience, Transcendence, and Tragedy*. Athens: U of Georgia P, 1979.

Stern, Milton R. *The Fine Hammered Steel of Herman Melville*. Urbana: U of Illinois P, 1957.

Thompson, Lawrance R. *Melville's Quarrel with God*. Princeton: Princeton UP, 1952.

Vargish, Thomas. "Gnostick Mythos in *Moby-Dick*." *PMLA* 81 (June 1966): 272–77.

Wenke, John. *Melville's Muse: Literary Creation and the Forms of Philosophical Fiction*. Kent: Kent State UP, 1995.

Werge, Thomas A. "Luther and Melville on the Masks of God." *Melville Society Extracts* 22 (May 1975): 6–7.

_____. "*Moby-Dick* and the Calvinist Tradition." *Studies in the Novel* 1 (Winter 1969): 484–506.

Wright, Nathalia. *Melville's Use of the Bible*. Durham: Duke UP, 1949.

Melville's Democratic America _____

Shelby Crosby

In the mid-nineteenth century, the United States was a rapidly changing and growing nation. The development of railroads, a key component of the already swift industrialization process, made the distribu-
tion of goods and services easier and faster. Americans were moving
from rural to urban spaces, slavery was being hotly debated, gender
equality was becoming a growing issue with the Seneca Falls Convention of 1848, and economic progress was becoming the top priority
of the growing nation. Economic progress was determined, in large
measure, by an agreeable relationship between what had become the
"free" North and the "slave" South. The North greatly benefited from
the agrarian South and needed its products to fuel the growing Industrial Revolution; conversely, the agrarian South needed the industrial
North to process its raw goods.

While the North/South relationship was essential to the economic
health of the nation, it was not always a friendly one. The Fugitive
Slave Act of 1850 was unsettling to many Northerners because it le-
gally required that Northern citizens turn any known fugitive slaves
over to officials to be returned to their owners in the South. Thus, the
North became complicit in the "peculiar institution" of slavery and the
federal government further sanctioned the constitutionality of it. Moreover, as the abolitionist movement increased pressure on the federal
government to abolish slavery, American women began to demand
civic equality through enfranchisement. As the United States faced a
Civil War that would redefine the nation, a suffragist movement that
would demand that women be given the right to vote, and rapid industrialization that would change the face of the American city, American
authors set about creating an American literary tradition that looked to
the country's future while meditating on its past.

Celebrated nineteenth-century author Herman Melville saw America as a nation with "boundless ambition, civilized in externals but a

savage at heart" (qtd. in Reynolds 300). Melville's canon reflects this portrait of America, addressing in compelling ways the nation's most disturbing social issues: racial inequities, gender disparities, and the growing distance between the socioeconomic classes brought about by industrial capitalism. Therefore, this chapter will examine Melville's commentary on racial, gendered, and economic structures in *Redburn: His First Voyage*, "Bartleby, the Scrivener," "Benito Cereno," and "The Paradise of Bachelors and the Tartarus of Maids." Unlike many political reform writers of the nineteenth century, Melville does not present easy answers; his texts are ambiguous explorations of America's systemic problems.

Redburn and the Estranged Children of Adam

On June 5, 1849, in a letter to his publisher, Richard Bentley, Herman Melville discusses his latest project, *Redburn: His First Voyage*:

> I have now in preparation a thing of a widely different cast from "Mardi":— a plain, straightforward, amusing narrative of personal experience—the son of a gentleman on his first voyage to sea as a sailor—no metaphysics, no conic-sections, nothing but cakes and ale. I have shifted my ground from the South Seas to a different quarter of the globe—near home—and what I write I have almost wholly picked up by my own observations under comical circumstances. (qtd. in Reynolds 285)

This highly autobiographical novel is a return to a more commercial form of writing, a style of writing that Melville had abandoned with his third novel, *Mardi*, which was a commercial failure. Unlike *Mardi*, *Redburn* became one of Melville's most popular and commercially successful novels. The novel is the coming-of-age tale of Wellingborough Redburn, an impoverished gentleman's son setting sail on his first sea voyage. Told by a mature Redburn, the story is one of disillusionment. The young Redburn comes face to face with the social injustices brought about by the institutions of man, and, unfortunately, discovers that his naïve acceptance of the status quo and identification with the upper classes cannot continue because of the social evils he sees perpetrated upon the masses in the name of authority. Melville's Redburn is raised to be a good, God-fearing, temperance-following boy, yet his time aboard the *Highlander*, under the reign of Captain Riga, moves him "from a naïve reverence for the fathers into a shocking and finally enervating realization of the social evil behind or beneath" the authority he once revered (Bell 561). Redburn's reverence for authority is challenged by Riga's treatment of the crew, and this challenge is reinforced upon landing in Liverpool, England, and his exposure to the urban poor.

Upon his arrival in Liverpool, Redburn is confronted with visions of poverty, disease, and, most importantly, wanton disregard for those in need. While walking through a narrow street called Launcelott's-Hey, Redburn sees a woman and her two children living below the streets:

> At last I advanced to an opening which communicated downward with deep tiers of cellars beneath a crumbling old warehouse; and there, some fifteen feet below the walk, crouching in nameless squalor, with her head bowed over, was the figure of what had been a woman. Her blue arms folded to her livid bosom two shrunken things like children, that leaned toward her, one on each side. At first, I knew not whether they were alive or dead. They made no sign; they did not move or stir; but from the vault came that soul-sickening wail. (199)

Once Redburn sees their plight he tries to find out who they are and why no one is helping them. He speaks to police officers, but to no avail. The poor have no rights and no one can help them. Redburn is forced to accept that this woman and her children were going to die beneath the streets and there was nothing he could do to help them. His naïve belief in authority is dispelled in this moment and he recognizes that "authority is in fact built upon a system of social inequality and oppression" (Bell 561).

Melville does not stop here; he also incorporates the urban poor as steerage passengers on Redburn's return voyage to America. Therefore, Redburn cannot escape contrasting the steerage passengers' experience with the cabin passengers' experience. Moreover, he cannot forgive the blatant disregard the cabin passengers have for the steerage passengers' well-being. He begins to hate the cabin passengers: "I will let nature have her own way for once; and here declare roundly that, however it was, I cherished a feeling toward these cabin-passengers, akin to contempt. Not because they happened to be cabin-passengers: not at all: but only because they seemed the most finical, miserly, mean men and women, that ever stepped over the Atlantic" (Melville 286). While Redburn insists that in America "there is a future which shall see the estranged children of Adam restored as to the old hearth-stone in Eden" (185), the microcosm of America presented on board the *Highlander* is one that foreshadows the urban, capitalist America that Melville would explore in "Bartleby, the Scrivener." Redburn returns to an America that callously disregards the poor, the Native American, and the African, an America that cruelly uses power to maintain power.

Bartleby and the Old Adam of Resentment

Originally published in *Putnam's* magazine in its November/December 1853 issue and later reprinted in the short story collection *The Piazza Tales* in 1856, "Bartleby, the Scrivener: A Story of Wall Street" has become one of Melville's most popular and baffling works. It is the story of a young copyist who, once hired, refuses to do any work; in fact, he answers every request with one statement: "I would prefer not to." Literary critics have read the story primarily as an allegory for Melville's own failure in the publishing marketplace; as a story about the psychological effects of capitalism brought about by the economic separation between the rich and the poor, which dramatically increased in mid-nineteenth-century America; and as a philosophical exploration of the human conditions of alienation, passivity, and resistance. Although the story is titled "Bartleby, the Scrivener," it is in large measure about the narrator's responses to Bartleby, and as such it is also a tale about charity, compassion, and the dehumanizing effects of a world dominated by economics.

The narrator, an unnamed lawyer, employs Bartleby in his law office as a scrivener, or copyist. The story begins with the lawyer noting that he is an "elderly man" who has employed an "interesting and somewhat singular set of men, of whom as yet nothing that I know of has ever been written:—I mean the law-copyists or scriveners" (*Piazza Tales* 13). Yet, of the many scriveners he has employed, one stands out as "the strangest I ever saw or heard of," Bartleby. He was "one of those beings of whom nothing is ascertainable, except from the original sources, and in his case those are very small. What my own astonished eyes saw of Bartleby, that is all I know of him, except, indeed, one vague report which will appear in the sequel" (13). For the lawyer, Bartleby represents a puzzle, a problem that he cannot understand or solve. His other workers—Turkey, Nippers, and Ginger Nut—have all been decoded and categorized. In fact, rather than give readers their real names, the narrator presents only their nicknames, defining each worker by his behavior and appearance in the workplace rather than getting to know him on any personal level, which serves as its own kind of commentary on the increasing separation between the socioeconomic classes. Through his characterizations in the story, Melville points out that the "period's growing social stratification is everywhere obvious, from the spectacularly rich John Jacob Astor, whom the lawyer proudly served, to the upper-middle-class lawyer himself, and down to his lowly paid employees" (Kuebrich 385). Moreover, it is the unnamed social stratification that haunts the story; the lawyer is unable to see that his responses to his workers, while on the surface kindly, do not actually afford them any subjectivity. They are defined solely by his observations of them in the workplace, a space that alienates them from nature and one another. Even the lawyer is not given a name; thus, despite his authority, even he can be replaced with any other lawyer. Despite his socioeconomic class he, too, is just another nameless lawyer trying to secure his place in the financial world, name-dropping to show his importance: "The late John Jacob Astor, a personage little given to poetic enthusiasm, had no hesitation in pronouncing my first grand point to be prudence; my next, method" (14). Mentioning Astor, a German-American business man who made his fortune in real estate, stocks, and fur trading, as one of his mentors gives the lawyer business clout and respectability.

Significantly, the lawyer continues to participate in the dehuman-izing effects of the socioeconomic system by presenting each worker to readers prior to beginning his reminiscences of Bartleby. What he presents reflects how each worker copes with the alienation of the workplace. Turkey drinks heavily at lunch to deal with the depressive work environment: "In the morning, one might say, his face was of a fine florid hue, but after twelve o'clock, meridian—his dinner hour—it blazed like a grate full of Christmas coals; and continued blazing" (15). Nippers is irritable and cranky; according to the lawyer, he is "the victim of two evil powers—ambition and indigestion. . . . The indiges-tion seemed betokened in an occasional nervous testiness and grin-ning irritability" (16). And, finally, there is Ginger Nut, a young boy of twelve years of age, "sent by his father to be a student at law, errand boy, and cleaner and sweeper" (18). Ginger Nut's father was a carman "ambitious of seeing his son on the bench instead of a cart, before he died" (18). Clearly, this man hopes that his child will be able to move up the socioeconomic ladder by working for the lawyer, but one has to wonder if that is feasible considering that the lawyer does not present readers with even his birth name.

Once hired, Bartleby is placed next to a window that is three feet away from the building next door, effectively putting Bartleby up against a wall. He works steadily and quietly for a couple of days, but on the third day, when asked to edit a document with the lawyer, his resistance begins:

In my haste and natural expectancy of instant compliance, I sat with my head bent over the original on my desk, and my right hand sideways, and somewhat nervously extended with the copy. . . . In this very attitude did I sit when I called him, rapidly stating what it was I wanted him to do—namely, to examine a small paper with me. Imagine my surprise, nay, my consternation, when without moving from his privacy, Bartleby in a singularly mild, firm voice, replied, "I would prefer not to." (20)

The lawyer is shocked by Bartleby's noncompliance with his request but decides to deal with it at another time, and a few days later requests his help again. Again he is refused. At first the narrator is shocked, outraged, and angry; however, as with his other employees, he attempts to work with Bartleby's eccentricities. Bartleby, however, is different from the others: "The passiveness of Bartleby sometimes irritated me. I felt strangely goaded on to encounter him in new opposition, to elicit some angry spark from him answerable to my own" (24). It is Bartleby's inexplicable passiveness that confuses, angers, and surprises both the narrator and readers alike. If Bartleby had responded with anger, then the lawyer might have felt justified in firing him, but he evinces no anger, just a desire to be left alone. At first, this is precisely how the lawyer handles the situation; he surrenders to Bartleby's will and his work is edited by the other scriveners. However, the lawyer's attitude changes once he realizes that Bartleby is living in the offices.

Ironically, the lawyer discovers Bartleby's living arrangements while on his way to church one Sunday morning, and he responds with Christian charity: "What I saw that morning persuaded me that the scrivener was the victim of innate and incurable disorder. I might give alms to his body; but his body did not pain him; it was his soul that suffered, and his soul I could not reach" (29). Yet, within a day or two, Bartleby decides to give up copying and do nothing, which the lawyer cannot understand or tolerate, so he attempts to fire him. "Attempt" is the key word here—Bartleby, as we have seen, has a mind of his own and does not do anything unless he chooses: "The time has come; you must quit this place; I am sorry for you; here is money; but you must go," and, of course, Bartleby responds: "I would prefer not to" (33).

Once again, the narrator cannot understand such a response and convinces himself that Bartleby will be gone in the morning.

Bartleby does not leave the premises, and the lawyer does not know how to respond. He is simultaneously filled with resentment and pity: "But when this old Adam of resentment rose in me and tempted me concerning Bartleby, I grappled him and threw him. How? Why, simply by recalling the divine injunction: 'A new commandment give I unto you, that ye love one another.' Yes, this it was that saved me. Aside from higher considerations, charity often operates as a vastly wise and prudent principle—a great safeguard to its possessor" (36). Unfortunately, the lawyer is unable to maintain this attitude; his business colleagues do not understand his compassion and he is mocked for a fool. There is obviously no room for compassion and charity in the business world of Wall Street. In response to such censure, the lawyer decides he will quit the premises and rid himself of Bartleby that way; however, his grand plan does not work. While he may have quit the premises, Bartleby has not and does not seem to have any plans to relocate.

The lawyer's attempts at kindness are not effective because he and Bartleby are part of a larger social structure that does not allow for such charity and compassion. America's rapidly changing financial structures and urban industrialization further alienate people from one another and nature. Bartleby starves himself to death after he is imprisoned; his death, like his life, is a quiet one. He falls asleep under a tree in the prison yard and passes away. The lawyer concludes the story with a bit of information about Bartleby; sometime prior to coming to work for the narrator, Bartleby has worked as a postal clerk and was suddenly removed from his post by an administrative shift in government. The narrator is left to wonder how such a depressing job changed Bartleby, turning him into a quiet, sad human being. Yet it seems more complicated than that. The closing line of the story—"Ah Bartleby! Ah Humanity!"—implicates not just Bartleby for his personal response to a depressing job, but also society for having no way to deal with him. Are we not our brother's keepers?

"Benito Cereno," Race, and Seeing without Seeing

Published six years prior to the start of the Civil War, "Benito Cereno" is Melville's only story that is overtly about American slavery. Although not a clear manifesto against slavery, it is not a clear pro-slavery story either. Rather, it is a complicated exploration of the racial tensions that existed in mid-nineteenth-century America. Choosing to publish "Benito Cereno" serially in October, November, and December of 1855 in *Putnam's* was a significant political decision for Melville because its new editor, Frederick Law Olmstead, pushed the magazine forward with an outspoken antislavery stance. Melville later included a slightly revised version of the story in his collection *The Piazza Tales* in 1856.

Melville adapted Amasa Delano's *Narrative of Voyages and Travels, in the Northern and Southern Hemispheres* to create "Benito Cereno." Although written in the third person, the story is told primarily through the eyes of Captain Delano; moreover, the novella is filtered through his perceptions as a nineteenth-century American man, particularly a Northerner from one of the most liberal states in the union, Massachusetts. A tale of slave insurrection aboard a slave ship, the story challenged contemporary readers' preconceived notion that Africans are savage barbarians lacking the ability or intelligence to take care of themselves. Melville's choice to rename the slave ship *San Dominick*, rather than keep its actual name *Tryal*, suggests that he is referencing the black revolution in Santo Domingo (Haiti) in 1791. The Haitian Revolution stunned the eighteenth-century world and defied its racial stereotypes. Santo Domingo, a French colony, reacted to the spirit of revolution that swept across France in 1789 by demanding its freedom in August of 1791, after it became apparent that the predominately black population was not considered free and equal. The revolution lasted ten bloody years and resulted in the full emancipation of all slaves, the abolition of slavery, and the establishment of one of the first black republics, Haiti. Obviously, Melville was aware of the revolution and it seems clear he chose to highlight it in the naming of the slave ship. It was no doubt an effective strategy, for the name *San Dominick* would likely inspire contemporary white readers to recall tales of the bloody coup related by white refugees from Haiti who had settled in the United States. This allusion would not only increase sales, it would guarantee the readers' engagement with the text because it reflected a contemporary issue in the Americas: slave insurrections.

As the central figure in this complex drama, Captain Delano examines the sociopolitical relationships between blacks and whites in a country divided by the question of slavery. Like the lawyer in "Bartleby, the Scrivener," Captain Delano is a contemplative and somewhat passive character. Rather than react to the odd and somewhat sinister behavior that he sees aboard the *San Dominick*—a ship captained by Benito Cereno, and which Delano has stopped to help—he remains condescendingly passive because he does not believe that a group of Africans could possibly organize a revolt or set up a ruse to keep him from finding out about such a revolt while aboard ship. Captain Delano's response would be that of contemporary nineteenth-century readers; moreover, these racialized ideas are rooted in the founding of the United States. Thomas Jefferson, the third U.S. president and author of the Declaration of Independence, believed that Africans were by nature inferior to Caucasians:

> Besides those of colour, figure, and hair, there are other physical distinctions proving a difference in race. . . . Comparing them by their faculties of memory, reason, and imagination, it appears to me, as I think one could scarcely be found capable of tracing and comprehending the investigations of Euclid; and that in imagination they are dull, tasteless, and anomalous. (Jefferson 145–46)

Even the father of democracy sees Africans as savages incapable of intelligent thought and ideas. Jefferson's view is the predominant one throughout much of eighteenth- and nineteenth-century America. Thus, a black character like Babo, Cereno's servant, is a challenge for

Captain Delano and the story's readers. At first meeting, he fulfills all the assumptions about a good slave: He is subservient, caring, and docile. Melville carefully and subtly crafts Babo to appear the perfect slave; it is only in retrospect that readers understand the implications of Babo's behavior, turning every perception on its ear and forcing readers to examine critically those initial misperceptions.

For example, Melville introduces his themes through the layering of perceptions, as can be seen in Captain Delano's reaction to Babo's reaction to Cereno's fainting spells: "'Faithful fellow!' cried Capt. Delano. 'Don Benito, I envy you such a friend; slave I cannot call him.' As master and man stood before him, the black upholding the white, Captain Delano could not but bethink him of the beauty of that relationship which could present such a spectacle of fidelity on the one hand and confidence on the other" (*Piazza Tales* 57). Captain Delano's response reflects contemporary American attitudes regarding race; moreover, he romanticizes the master/slave relationship in such a way that he elides servant and friend, which is even more ironic given the real relationship between Cereno and Babo. Melville purposefully inverts the master/slave relationship to "illustrate how when the master/slave, ruler/ruled roles are inverted, each side reveals characteristics of the other. . . . Slaves whose lives have been regulated by violence perpetuate that violence when in command" (Lock 59).

For example, when the occupants of the *San Dominick* run out of water and wind, they kill the only mate capable of navigating the boat and enslave the rest of the crew: "That on the fifth day of the calm, all on board suffering much from the heat, and want of water, and five having died in fits, and mad, the negroes became irritable, and for a chance gesture, which they deemed suspicious—though it was harmless—made by the mate, Raneds, to the deponent, in the act of handing a quadrant, they killed him" (*Piazza Tales* 108). This savagery, rather than a reflection of their blackness, is really a product of the system that raised them, slavery; thus, "both Babo and Benito Cereno are trapped within the two terms of the paradox, whether that be read as the slave mutiny or as slavery itself. Both are destroyed by it, which suggests that the false binaries that have been imposed on them bear the responsibility for this destruction" (Lock 60). Therefore, Melville is critiquing the system rather than the men perpetrating the act; thus, Captain Delano, Babo, and Benito Cereno are victims of a violent system (slavery and racism) that trains them to be callous and violent toward one another. Like the lawyer and Bartleby, Babo, Cereno, and Delano are all implicated in a larger political and racial system that they are not necessarily even aware of; moreover, Melville challenges both characters and readers to see the system because if we see it, per-haps—we can change it.

Paradise, Tartarus, and Nineteenth-Century Sexual Economics

Melville's attention to large systemic structures continues in "The Para-dise of Bachelors and the Tartarus of Maids." One of his paired sketch-es, published in *Harper's New Monthly Magazine* in 1855, the story describes a visit to a temple of self-indulgent British lawyers and an-other to an American paper mill operated primarily by young unmarried women. While at first glance these two worlds seem to have nothing in common, in presenting them together Melville sets them up as a cohe-sive unit that reveals the interdependence of each world on the other:

> In fact, the critical term used to describe the pair of stories, a "diptych," suggests much more about the stories' construction than the use of a sim-ple narrative technique that joins both halves. It is possible to see Mel-ville's stories as interdependent portraits, hinged together like medieval diptychs, which are locked in a dialectical relationship that maintains nar-rative control while it questions its own authority. (Serlin 81)

The narrator of the tales negotiates the space between these two gen-dered worlds, always remaining a visitor in both; thus, his point of view changes throughout the story. Melville creates a narrator who is able to see past the bachelors' indulgences to the gender disparities that allow their paradise to exist, thereby exposing the dialectical and damaging relationship between masculinity and femininity in mid-nineteenth-century America.

He first introduces readers to the Paradise of Bachelors, which is "found in the stony heart of stunning London. In mild meditation pace the cloisters; take your pleasure, sip your leisure, in the garden water-ward; go linger in the ancient library; go worship in the sculptured chapel" (*Piazza Tales* 316). This beautiful, tranquil space in the heart of London serves as the backdrop of Melville's first sketch. The bachelors of the story are descendents of the Knights Templar, one of the most famous medieval Christian military orders. It is significant to note that the Knights Templar fell out of popularity with the Catholic Church, and many of its members were excommunicated or hung. Yet at the height of their power they controlled much of the financial world of the Middle Ages. In Melville's telling, the Templar of yesteryear is "to-day a Lawyer"; "like many others tumbled from proud glory's height—like the apple, hard on the bough but mellow on the ground—the Templar's fall has but made him all the finer fellow" (318). The narrator enjoys all the fine fellows at the bachelors' dinner, seeing their Paradise as an oasis where a man can relax and "give the whole care-worn world the slip" (316). The dinner, a sumptuous multicourse affair, leads to good conversation, good port, and wonderful stories of the diners' past lives:

It was the very perfection of quiet absorption of good living, good drinking, good feeling, and good talk. We were a band of brothers. Comfort—fraternal, household comfort, was the grand trait of the affair. Also, you could plainly see that these easy-hearted men had no wives or children to give an anxious thought. Almost all of them were travelers, too; for bachelors alone can travel freely, and without any twinges of their consciences touching desertion of the fire-side. (322)

The narrator cannot imagine a better life than the ones led by the bachelors; a world of good food, wine, manner, conversation, and no mention of the world's pain: "Pain! Trouble! As well talk of Catholic miracles. No such thing.—Pass the sherry, Sir—Pooh, pooh! Can't be!—The port, Sir, if you please. Nonsense; don't tell me so.—The decanter stops with you, Sir, I believe" (322). This, according to the narrator, is indeed paradise.

The Tartarus of Maids is far removed from this paradise; in fact, in Greek mythology Tartarus is an underworld where inhabitants are tortured and true suffering exists. The paper factory of Melville's story, located in a hollow known locally as "the Devil's Dungeon," is filled with silent, blank women who radiate misery. Upon first arriving at the factory, the narrator encounters a young woman with "a face pale with work, and blue with cold; an eye supernatural with unrelated misery" (*Piazza Tales* 327). He continues his tour and sees "rows of blank-looking girls, with blank, white folders in their blank hands, all blankly folding blank paper" (328). This haunting and disturbing image reflects the women's position under a patriarchal system. They are blank and filled with misery. Not only were these women blank, they were silent as well: "Not a syllable was breathed. Nothing was heard but the low, steady, overruling hum of iron animals. The human voice was banished from the spot" (328). Despite the noise of the machines, silence pervades the factory. These blank women are not allowed to speak while working, and their voices are effectively cut off from the rest of the world. Wavering between emotion and rationality, the narrator is appalled by the working conditions in the factory. It is in this moment that he begins to recognize that while both the "bachelors and maids are defined by the essential relationship to male power," it is the maids who are "enslaved by a male-controlled labor system" (Serlin 80). Thus, the women of Devil's Dungeon are slaves to the intertwining relationship between industrialism and patriarchy.

The rise of industrialism led to the birth of places like the Devil's Dungeon, towns that were designed to be beautiful and productive;

however, greed ruins the Eden-like work existence. Mill towns, instead, bred hazardous working conditions, long hours with little pay, and an expendable workforce with rapidly deteriorating health. These women were treated little better than slaves: "Machinery—that vaunted slave of humanity—here stood menially served by human beings, who served mutely and cringingly as the slave serves the Sultan" (328). Melville specifically used Carson's Mill in Dalton, Massachusetts, as a model when writing the short story. At first, these mill towns and factories were designed to avoid the rampant poverty and filth of European factory towns; however, industrialization is clearly incompatible with democratic ideals. In the mid-nineteenth century, the United States believed it could bridge the gap between industrialization and democracy; that, in fact, democracy could flourish alongside rapid industrialization. However, in reality, industrialization increases economic division, more clearly demarcating the boundaries between the privileged and working classes. Moreover, in Melville's tale it is the young, unmarried maids who are most affected by industrialization. As mid-nineteenth-century American women, they would have held very little economic or social power (women did not gain the right to vote until 1920); thus, they become the victims of an inhumane industrial system that supports the bachelors' male privileges and indulgences.

Melville structures the story as a diptych to expose and explore the fissure between American men and women. As in "Bartleby" and "Benito Cereno," he is not making a definitive statement; he is just exposing the larger structure for all to see. In "The Paradise of Bachelors and the Tartarus of Maids," Melville displays gender disparities that have arisen through the economic gaps of industrialized America. While the bachelors are enjoying seven-course meals, good conversation, and comfort, the mill girls are cold, hungry, and eerily silent. Even the narrator notes that the mill town is the "very counterpart of the Paradise of Bachelors, but snowed upon, and frost-painted to a sepulchre" (327). These women will die in the factories; the factories have become their tombs. And the narrator, for good or bad, is the only person "who can absorb the Maids' silence and give voice to their exploited position" (Serlin 83).

Although Melville's two worlds are geographically far from one another, they are intricately intertwined. Without the mill girls' labor and sacrifice, the bachelors' paradise could not exist; the factory produces paper so that "all sorts of writings would be writ on those now vacant things—sermons, lawyer's briefs, physicians' prescriptions, love-letters, marriage certificates, bills of divorce, registers of births, death-warrants, and so on, without end" (333). Women's labor, therefore, makes male labor possible. Indeed, "all social discourse will be written on the blank pages of female labor" (Wiegman 746). Thus, the bachelors obtain paradise by the sacrifice of the maids.

Interestingly, it is not until the end of the story that the narrator thinks to ask why the women are always referred to as "girls." Their male supervisor is stunned at the question, but replies readily enough that the women who worked in such towns were generally unmarried and young because factory owners "will not have married women; they are apt to be off-and-on too much. We want none but steady workers; twelve hours a day, day after day, through the three hundred and sixty-five days, excepting Sundays, Thanksgiving, and Fast-days. That's our rule" (334). The girls must only be married to their machines, as a husband and family would interrupt the factory and the industrialization process. The narrator becomes emotional when he realizes that all these women are maids; that they will never marry and have children. The "girls" sacrifice their womanhood and families so that the bachelors may have their privilege and their paradise. The story ends shortly thereafter, and the closing lines reflect the narrator's realization that the bachelor's life comes at a steep cost to the maids: "Oh! Paradise of Bachelors! and oh! Tartarus of Maids!" (335).

Melville's America was rapidly growing, shifting, and changing. His celebrated literary canon reflects the contemporary political and social issues facing nineteenth-century Americans. From *Redburn: His First Voyage* to "The Paradise of Bachelors and the Tartarus of Maids,"

Melville challenges readers to ponder how the nation's brisk economic growth affected the individual American; moreover, his literature questions whether America, a nation with "boundless ambition," could maintain its democratic ideals in the face of dehumanizing industrialism, gender inequities, and slavery. Like the lawyer in "Bartleby, the Scrivener," one cannot help but sigh after reading Melville and think: "Ah Bartleby! Ah humanity!"

Works Cited

Bell, Michael Davitt. "Melville's Redburn: Initiation and Authority." *New England Quarterly* 46.4 (1983): 558–72.

Jefferson, Thomas J. *Notes on the State of Virginia.* 1785. New York: Penguin Books, 1999.

Kuebrich, David. "Melville's Doctrine of Assumptions: The Hidden Ideology of Capitalist Production in 'Bartleby.'" *New England Quarterly* 69.3 (1996): 381–405.

Lock, Helen. "The Paradox of Slave Mutiny in Herman Melville, Charles Johnson, and Frederick Douglass." *College Literature* 30.4 (2003): 54–70.

Melville, Herman. *The Piazza Tales and Other Prose Pieces, 1839–1860.* Ed. Harrison Hayford, Alma A. MacDougall, and G. Thomas Tanselle. Evanston and Chicago: Northwestern-Newberry, 1987.

_____. *Redburn, White-Jacket, Moby-Dick.* Ed. G. Thomas Tanselle. New York: Literary Classics, 1983.

Reynolds, David S. *Beneath the American Renaissance. The Subversive Imagination in the Age of Emerson and Melville.* Cambridge: Harvard UP, 1988.

Serlin, David Harley. "The Dialogue of Gender in Melville's 'The Paradise of Bachelors and the Tartarus of Maids.'" *Modern Language Studies* 25.2 (1995): 80–87.

Wiegman, Robyn. "Melville's Geography of Gender." *American Literary History* 1.4 (1989): 735–53.

Typee and the Myth of Paradise_____

Jonathan A. Cook

In a June 1851 letter to Nathaniel Hawthorne, Herman Melville meditated on the vanity of literary fame as he completed the composition of *Moby-Dick*: "All Fame is patronage. Let me be infamous: there is no patronage in that. What 'reputation' H.M. has is horrible. Think of it! To go down to posterity is bad enough, any way; but to go down as a 'man who lived among the cannibals'!" (*Correspondence* 193). Melville's fear of going down to posterity only as a chronicler of Polynesian cannibals—his role in his first book, *Typee*—is ironic on several counts. We should first note that Melville's whimsical prediction was ironically fulfilled, for in his lifetime *Typee* was reprinted more often than any of his other books and was the work most often cited as the kind of work the author should be producing instead of his later, more philosophically challenging fiction. The stigma of being only known to posterity as the author of *Typee* was also ironic in that one of the main reasons for his fleeing the Typee Valley as recounted in that book was the fear of being forever identified with the tribe by receiving their tattooing; yet his book would ineluctably mark him in a comparable manner. It was also ironic to be exclusively associated with the Polynesian cannibals of *Typee* because after the book was first published, both his publishers and reviewers cast doubt about whether Melville had actually experienced everything recounted in the narrative—or even whether he had ever been in the Typee Valley. (Such doubts continued even after the unexpected reappearance in Buffalo, New York, of Toby, Melville's lost companion in the narrative, a few months after the book was published in 1846.) And it was ironic for posterity to think of *Typee* as Melville's supreme achievement because in that work he had been forced by his American publisher, Wiley and Putnam, to expurgate significant portions of the text in its revised edition because of the offense they caused to the nation's religious establishment, this being the edition that was reprinted in America throughout Melville's lifetime.[1]

Yet the final irony with regard to *Typee* as an index of Melville's literary achievement is that it is in fact a work for which Melville had little to be ashamed. For *Typee* continues to attract readers and critics who are drawn to the narrative's stylistic grace, youthful exuberance, exotic appeal, and engaging combination of dramatic and discursive components in its semi-autobiographical evocation of Melville's "captivity" among the Typees on the island of Nukuheva in the Marquesas Islands sometime within a period of four weeks—July 9 to August 9, 1842—that Melville stretched out to four months in the narrative. Modern commentators on *Typee* have explored a variety of critical approaches relating to questions of genre, biography, literary sources, primitivism (i.e., the "noble savage"), sexuality, ethnography, colonialism, and imperialism, among others. Yet another likely reason for the work's continued appeal is also doubtless its imaginative incorporation of mythic elements; in this case, the archetypal Western myth of paradise, the Garden of Eden, and the Fall. Much of Melville's later fiction and poetry would show a masterful handling of mythic paradigms, and we may track the beginnings of this process in his first book. In *Typee*, Melville dramatizes the dominant Western myth of human origins and moral transgression, but he also critiques, satirizes, and ironically reshapes it, in the process revealing both the complexity of such myths and their continuing relevance for the modern world.[2]

The Judeo-Christian myth of paradise is based on the biblical story recounted in Genesis 1–3, which has had an immeasurable influence on Western history and culture.[3] Familiar as the story may be, we must still provide a basic outline in order to frame the following discussion. The biblical paradise ("enclosure"), or Eden ("delight"), was a garden of beautiful trees providing attractive fruit with a branching river running through it. Having been created by God from the soil, Adam was designated as keeper of the garden and instructed not to eat the fruit of the tree of good and evil on pain of death; he was then provided with a female helper, Eve. Unashamed of their nakedness, Adam and Eve enjoyed their garden until the "subtle" serpent tempted Eve by claiming that by eating the forbidden fruit, "your eyes shall be opened, and ye shall be as gods, knowing good and evil" (Gen. 3:5). Eating the attractive fruit, Eve shared it with Adam, but they were quickly caught by God while hiding among the trees, newly ashamed of their nakedness after hearing God's voice. Despite Adam's attempt to blame Eve for his actions, they both faced penalties for their transgression, namely, pain in childbirth for Eve and forced labor for Adam: "In the sweat of thy face shalt thou eat bread" (Gen. 3:19). The serpent would also be punished by experiencing eternal enmity with the human race. Exiled from paradise for their transgression, a guilty Adam and Eve forever abandoned their blissful garden.

Thus was enacted the divine curse of "original sin" that, according to Christian tradition, has permanently tainted humanity. The key creator of this doctrine was St. Paul, who traced humanity's collective guilt, as manifested in sin and death, to the Fall of Adam (Rom. 5:12). This mythic doctrine was in turn reinterpreted for medieval Catholicism by St. Augustine and for Protestantism by John Calvin, whose punitive theology was bequeathed to the New England Puritans and their doctrinal successors. One of the major interpretations of the paradise myth was that the loss of innocence was a "fortunate fall" because it allowed for the redemptive mission of Christ (as depicted in John Milton's *Paradise Lost*), or that it catalyzed the moral growth of Adam and Eve (as symbolically represented in some of Nathaniel Hawthorne's fiction). It should be noted that from its very beginnings, the Judeo-Christian myth of paradise incorporated elements from cognate Greco-Roman traditions of the Golden Age, the Elysian Fields, the Happy Isles, and Arcadia, in which primordial or posthumous human life was characterized by peace, harmony, ease, and natural abundance. Such mythic ideas were found in the writings of Hesiod, Homer, Plato, Theocritus, Virgil, Ovid, and others. The Western paradise myth thus forms a composite tradition with a variety of features beyond the biblical story. Christianity theorized that, although paradise was a permanently forbidden realm, it might still exist somewhere in the world, and medieval and Renaissance writers and map-makers accordingly located it some-where to the east in a variety of locations including Palestine, Mesopotamia, and India. Writers in the era of global exploration also associated paradise with various primitive peoples who allegedly revealed human nature in its original goodness, as embodied in the "noble savage" living in a state of nature. As an imaginative construct, then, the myth of paradise has shaped the Western imagination as an archetypal parable of lost innocence and simplicity, and a sign of discontent with the mixed blessings of civilization.

In *Typee*, Melville plays multiple variations on this myth, for the Typees manifestly live in a Polynesian Eden, yet it is an ambiguously pre- and postlapsarian paradise whose ultimate moral identity remains ambiguous. Tommo is thus an American Adam who eagerly explores this exotic Eden while showing its consistent superiority to modern Western culture; but he must eventually flee the Typee Valley in a quest for moral freedom even as his flight inadvertently causes a symbolic Fall for the Typee. As a romantic rebel against the oppressive powers of Christian dogma and Western cultural chauvinism, moreover, Melville is also an outspoken critic in *Typee* of contemporary missionary Christianity and European imperialism; for it is missionaries and their commercial and political coadjutors who will ultimately precipitate the larger Fall of the inhabitants of the Typee Valley, the Marquesas, and the islands of Polynesia generally.

Typee begins with the narrator's evocation of weariness at being at sea on an American whaler for half a year with an abusive captain and rough crew. In this condition his yearning for land becomes a kind of acute sensory deprivation, as he longs "for a refreshing glimpse of one blade of grass—for a snuff at the fragrance of a handful of the loamy earth!" (3). The general longing for land in this case coincides with the ship's proximity to the Marquesas Islands, which in the contemporary civilized world were still identified by sensationalistic clichés about its primitive inhabitants, including such features as "Naked houris," "cannibal banquets," and "heathenish rites and human sacrifices" (5).

While evoking the exotic appeal of the Marquesas as a South Sea island paradise, however, the narrator quickly deflates the alien identity of this culture by revealing the familiar presence of American, British, and French interests in the area, as well as recounting a series of comic vignettes on the ostensible nature of their primitivism; for these involve nothing more than minor violations of Western codes of etiquette in the natives' disrobing of a missionary's wife and the indiscretion of a Marquesan queen in revealing the tattoo on her backside.

Having established a ribald tone suitable for a novel of nautical picaresque, the narrator also quickly establishes himself as an informed commentator on the island of Nukuheva, where his ship is headed for provisioning and where the French navy has only recently claimed the island as a French colony. In Western traditions of paradise, the paradisiacal island is a persistent feature, and it proves so again in the sheer natural beauty of the harbor and the greeting that the natives of Nukuheva give to the narrator's ship, the *Dolly*. For coming into the island's chief bay, the ship is quickly surrounded by a flotilla of canoes, floating cocoanuts, and naked young women who board the ship and offer the narrator a first glimpse of the beauties that the island has to offer: "Their appearance perfectly amazed me; their extreme youth, the light clear brown of their complexions, their delicate features, and inexpressibly graceful figures, their softly moulded limbs, and free unstudied action, seemed as strange as beautiful" (15). The young women are in fact there to give the sailors an exuberant erotic welcome, in keeping with the mores of their native religion and its celebration of sexuality (which the missionaries considered a symptom of their pagan depravity). There ensues a scene of "riot and debauchery" in which the narrator blames the "unholy passions of the crew" (15) for the drunken orgy—with likely transmission of venereal disease—that takes place, thereby establishing a motif of native innocence and European-American corruption that will continue throughout the narrative and color its depiction of Marquesan life.

Once the *Dolly* has arrived in port, the narrator is determined to jump ship, citing as his excuse the limited terms of his contracted services and the tyrannical behavior of the captain in prolonging the ship's cruises and inflicting violence on the crew. The allure of the island of Nukuheva is evident from the ship, with a shoreline of "deep and romantic glens" (24), each with cascades and waterfalls, backed by towering mountain peaks. The geography of the island has created a series of isolated valleys, the one closest to the bay being occupied by the tribe of friendly Happars and the next valley by the much-feared, allegedly cannibalistic Typee who, the narrator notes, had fought the American naval captain David Porter about three decades earlier; indeed, the latter's scorched-earth campaign in the Typee Valley at that time had turned the tribe into fierce enemies of the white man. Already beginning to dispel the myth of innate depravity in this tribe, the narrator notes that it is the invading whites who have been guilty of poisoning the native goodness of the islanders, whose initial friendly welcome (like the earlier naked young "houris" in the harbor) makes them "fold to their bosoms the vipers whose sting is destined to poison all their joys; and the instinctive feeling of love within their breasts is soon converted into the bitterest hate" (26). Western intruders are thus the stinging serpent in the Eden of Polynesia.

The narrator's plan in jumping ship is to climb to the mountainous heights above the bay until his ship departs, avoiding all contact with the natives who might want to capture him for a ransom, or in the case of the Typee, might want to consume him—although the latter seems a remote possibility at this point. Finding a fellow crewman named Toby who is equally dissatisfied with conditions on the ship, the narrator and his companion decide to abscond together and are soon able to execute their escape during their official shore leave. The narrator and Toby's ensuing five-day ordeal into the interior of the island reveals the geographical ignorance and seriocomic naïveté of the adventurous young sailors, whose exhausting trek provides an archetypal sense of remoteness and inaccessibility to the paradise that they eventually discover in the Typee Valley. Appropriately enough, the uninhabited region be-hind the mountain they have climbed suggests a mythical antiquity, "the interior of the island having apparently been untenanted since the morning of the creation" (44). Moreover, on a symbolic level Tommo (as he is later identified) and Toby are obliquely compared to the Satan of Milton's *Paradise Lost*, whose approach to the newly created realm of paradise bears similarities to Tommo's description of their approach to the Typee Valley.

Early in their flight, Tommo and Toby had thus resorted to crawl-ing along the ground to remain unseen, "screened from observation by the grass through which we glided, much in the fashion of a couple of serpents" (39). Then, in the process of Tommo and Toby's challenging climb through the interior landscape of the island, we first hear about Tommo's leg injury, which critics have viewed as serving a variety of symbolic functions. Following their first wet night out in the open, Tommo begins to experience shivering and fever, and notices another symptom of illness: "One of my legs was swelled to such a degree, and pained me so acutely, that I half-suspected I had been bitten by some venomous reptile, the congenial inhabitant of the chasm from which we had lately emerged" (48). The mention of a snake as the hypotheti-cal (but incorrect) source for Tommo's leg injury, seen within the larg-er context of the novel's archetypal symbolism, hints that he will carry the Judeo-Christian legacy of original sin as he approaches the borders of the Typee paradise. Tommo's leg injury may thus evoke the divine curse on the serpent in the Eden narrative, for the latter creature would allegedly "bruise" the "heel" of the descendents of Adam and Eve in their eternal enmity (Gen. 3:15). Yet another relevant biblical source here is St. Paul's assertion that all human "members" were captive to sin; for besides the law of God, "I see another law in my members, warring against the law of my mind, and bringing me into captivity to the law of sin which is in my members" (Rom. 7:23; see also 6:19, 7:5). In Tommo's case, his sinful "member" is a diseased leg that will pain and incapacitate him during part of his stay with the Typee, providing a psychosomatic index to his initiation into their seemingly prelapsarian way of life.

Having reached an elevated prospect on their long trek, Tommo and Toby gain a distant view of the Typee Valley that they will eventually reach, without knowing who its inhabitants are. Tommo now pulls back the curtain, as it were, on the Edenic beauty of the valley: "I chanced to push aside a branch, and by so doing suddenly disclosed to my view a scene which even now I can recall with all the vividness of the first impression. Had a glimpse of the gardens of Paradise been revealed to me I could scarcely have been more ravished with the sight" (49). Tommo thus sees the "palmetto-thatched houses" of the native inhabitants, as well as the stunning natural landscape; for the "crowning beauty of the prospect was its universal verdure" (49). The valley is similarly distinguished by numerous "silent cascades, whose slender threads of water, after leaping down the steep cliffs, were lost amidst the rich herbage of the valley" (49). In its proliferation of trees and fresh water, the Typee Valley clearly evokes the landscape of Eden, where "out of the ground made the Lord God to grow every tree that is pleasant to the sight, and good for food" and where the river flowing out of Eden is divided into four abundant streams (Gen. 2:9–10). At this point, the valley exists in a "hushed repose" that Tommo is fearful to break "lest, like the enchanted gardens in the fairy tale, a single syllable might dissolve the spell" (49). The Typee Valley will in fact prove to be an Edenic "enchanted garden" where Tommo will assume the role of Adam and a single word, "cannibal," will threaten to dissolve the garden's spell.

Although Tommo and Toby have gained a view of a paradisiacal realm, they still don't know whether it is inhabited by friendly Happar or fierce Typee, so they forge ahead on their journey across the challenging landscape. In his feverish condition, Tommo has a raging thirst, but when he drinks from a stream at the foot of a gorge, he experiences a shock reminiscent of the fallen angels in Pandemonium who have been transformed into serpents in Milton's *Paradise Lost* and who then enact a grotesque version of Satan's recent temptation of Eve by biting into ashen apples (X.547–71). As Tommo now notes, "Had the apples of Sodom turned to ashes in my mouth, I could not have felt a more startling revulsion. A single drop of cold fluid seemed to freeze every drop of blood in my body" (53). Tommo and Toby are clearly not fallen angels, but their journey through the chaotic landscape of sharp ridges and deep chasms highlights their status as alien intruders traveling through a seemingly primordial realm of creation; indeed, their final dramatic descent into the valley is a "fall" of sorts, involving clambering down hanging vines and then jumping into a palm tree top.

True to the valley's underlying mythic identity, the first inhabitants that Tommo and Toby meet are a youthful Adam-and-Eve-like couple, "slender and graceful, and completely naked, with the exception of a slight girdle of bark" (68). Though fearful, the young couple mischievously proceed to mislead the two sailors about the identity of the valley, affirming it to be Happar, and then take them down to their community. It is only by chance that Tommo, under the impassive scrutiny of the chief Mehevi, correctly answers the chief's query whether the tribe is Happar or Typee, and the two are forthwith welcomed into the Typee community, as consummated by their exchange of names.[4] Despite the fact that some of the imagery of their journey has depicted Tommo and Toby as quasi-Satanic interlopers into a seemingly unspoiled Eden, the duplicity of the young couple and the chief's immediate mention of hatred of the Happar both demonstrate that the Typee are not total moral innocents; indeed, the ensuing interplay of pre- and postlapsarian motifs among Tommo, the Marquesans, and their European colonizers gives the narrative its complex thematic texture.

With their fortuitous identification of the tribe as Typee, Tommo and Toby are henceforth part of the community, as Tommo is given ineffectual medical treatment by the local medicine man and introduced to a surrogate family of Marheyo (a kindly father figure), Tinor (his industrious wife), Kory-Kory (Tommo's body servant), and Fayaway (his female companion). He also begins his explorations, with Kory-Kory's help, of the setting of the tribal community, including the Taboo

Groves of consecrated bread-fruit trees, the Hoolah-Hoolah Ground (devoted to religious rituals), and the Ti (dedicated to male sociability and feasting). Although Tommo's situation is almost luxurious in its many enjoyments, he remains anxious and depressed about his ultimate fate, still unsure what his alleged cannibal hosts ultimately mean to do with him. This anxiety is exploited for comic purposes when Tommo and Toby wake up in the Ti one midnight shortly after their arrival and see the wild celebrations of a feast taking place, and Toby mordantly jokes that the natives are getting ready to consume their new visitors. When it turns out that they are merely being invited to join the feast, Toby again jokes that the meat they are given to eat is a "baked baby" (94), but it is pork from the island's wild pigs.

The exotic locale where he now resides is clearly alien and at times overwhelming to Tommo, but as he increasingly takes on the role of amateur ethnographer, he gains perspective on the natives' culture by occasionally providing incongruous comic comparisons between Typee life and the familiar domestic worlds of Western civilization. Thus, when presenting Tommo "some outlandish kind of savage sweetmeat or pastry," Tinor is said to resemble "a doting mother petting a sickly urchin with tarts and sugar-plums" (85). When preparing to carry the disabled Tommo, Kory-Kory looks like "a porter in readiness to shoulder a trunk" (89). And when Tommo is returning with the remains of his first feast to his new domicile with a group of followers, "the superannuated warrior [Marheyo] did the honors of his mansion with all the warmth of hospitality evinced by an English squire when he regales his friends at some fine old patrimonial mansion" (96). Such incongruous comparisons bridge the gap between primitive and modern cultures, creating a sense of a universal human community.

Throughout his prolonged residence in the Typee Valley, and especially after Toby's departure in chapter 14, Tommo observes that virtually every aspect of the life of the natives—their physical appearance, natural environment, social relations, laws and institutions—evokes various aspects of the paradise tradition in the West. One of the first things that strikes Tommo about the Typees is their impressive physical beauty, which resembles that of the first mythical humans. (In Milton's epic, Adam and Eve before the Fall are accordingly "Godlike erect, with native Honor clad / In naked Majesty seem'd Lords of all" [*Paradise Lost*, IV.289–90].) Thus, the morning after their arrival in the Typee Valley, Tommo and Toby are visited by the chief, Mehevi, who, "from the excellence of his physical proportions, might certainly have been regarded as one of Nature's noblemen" (78). Among his Typee surrogate family, Tommo notes that Marheyo "was a native of gigantic frame" (83), while Kory-Kory, though covered with unsightly tattooing, was "about six feet in height, robust, and well made" (83). Most captivating of all was Fayaway, a "beauteous nymph" whose "free pliant figure was the very perfection of female grace and beauty" including a "rich and mantling" olive complexion, oval face, full lips, brown hair, soulful eyes, soft hands, small feet, and beautiful oiled skin (85–86). In Tommo's catalogue of physical attributes, we see a traditional Petrarchan "blazon" of female beauty; moreover, Fayaway's "soft and delicate" hands and "diminutive" feet compare favorably to those found in aristocratic and genteel women of the West. In a deliberately provocative image, Tommo notes that Fayaway "for the most part clung to the primitive and summer garb of Eden. But how becoming the costume!" (87). Typee corporeal beauty, with its echoes of paradise, is thus epitomized by Tommo's Eve-like companion. Not surprisingly, Fayaway and the other young Typee women wear a rich variety of flowers for ornament, using them for necklaces, chaplets, bracelets and anklets; for "the maidens of the island were passionately fond of flowers, and never wearied of decorating their persons with them" (87).

Tommo later adds to this portrait of personal beauty among the Typee who in "beauty of form surpassed anything I had ever seen"; indeed, "nearly every individual of their number might have been taken for a sculptor's model" (180). The contrast between such "naked simplicity of nature" (180) in the natives and contemporary European gentlemen and dandies would show the hidden artifice that creates the latter's visual appeal: "Stripped of the cunning artifices of the tailor, and standing forth in the garb of Eden,—what a sorry set of round-shouldered, spindle-shanked, crane-necked varlets would civilized men appear!" (181). With the ironic gusto of a Thomas Carlyle, Melville strips civilized man of his sartorial deceits, revealing the grotesque form beneath. In addition, the Typee all have flawless white teeth due to "the pure vegetable diet of these people, and the uninterrupted healthfulness of their natural mode of life" (181); for as Tommo subsequently mentions with rhetorical indirection, the venereal disease ("one of the most dreadful curses under which humanity labors") introduced by the West to Polynesia has not affected the Typee, hence their physical health remains intact.

Mention of the "garb of Eden" worn by many of the Typee women raises the question of sexuality in the valley, and it is here that Melville necessarily walks a fine line between truth and fiction in his narrative. In most evocations of paradise over the last two millennia, physical relations between Adam and Eve are depicted as chastely innocent; for example, the sexual relations in Milton's epic are only delicately hinted, as Adam and Eve perform "the Rite / Mysterious of connubial love" (*Paradise Lost*, IV.743–43). Among the Marquesans, however, the whole culture was devoted to a celebration of sexual relations, which were allegedly pleasing to their gods. Young men and women sought to enhance the appeal of their sexual organs and were authorized to spend their adolescent years in unbridled sexual activity. We will never know whether Melville enjoyed any of this sexual freedom during his stay in the Typee Valley; for in *Typee* he maintains a strategic decorum. Tommo's dalliance with Fayaway is thus largely free of signs of eroticism, being instead defined by the conventions of pastoral romance. Tommo's infected leg would seem to put a damper on any sexual activities during much of his residence; indeed, his most suggestive erotic scene is a quasi-Byronic picture of therapeutic massage when Fayaway and other young women rub down Tommo's various "limbs" with fragrant oil: "And most refreshing and agreeable are the juices of the 'aka,' when applied to one's limbs by the soft palms of sweet nymphs, whose bright eyes are beaming upon you with kindness; and I used to hail with delight the daily recurrence of this luxurious operation" (110).[5]

The erotic potential of this scene is more fully expressed by the immediately ensuing description of Kory-Kory's energetic routine in starting a fire to light Tommo's pipe by rubbing a stick against a grooved log, which he mounts like a horse. As numerous commentators have noted, the description here doubles as a disguised version of male sexual arousal and orgasm. A brief excerpt from the detailed description conveys Melville's ribald analogy: "As he [Kory-Kory] approaches the climax of his effort, he pants and gasps for breath, and his eyes almost start from his sockets with the violence of his exertions. . . . The next moment a delicate wreath of smoke curls spirally into the air, the heap of dusty particles glows with fire, and Kory-Kory almost breathless, dismounts from his steed" (111). In the Eden of Typee, "the most laborious species of work" (111) thus seems to be lighting a fire to be able to smoke a pipe, an activity that covertly doubles as a male sexual performance. In this subversive parody of the curse in Genesis, Kory-Kory only works hard to light a fire (or have an orgasm), unlike the oppressed Adam who must labor in the sweat of his face to feed his family (Gen. 3:19).

One of Tommo's favorite activities once his leg has improved is to swim among the young women in a lake in the valley, or go boating in a canoe with Fayaway after she has been exempted from the general taboo on women in boats. (Significantly, a lake is a feature of Milton's Eden [*Paradise Lost*, IV.261–63] but not the geographical Typee Valley.) It is in the latter activity that Fayaway famously shows her artless ingenuity by making her tappa robe into a sail, after which Tommo asserts, in the incongruous accents of genteel courtship, that he is now the "declared admirer of Miss Fayaway" (134). Despite his regular exposure to Fayaway's full frontal nudity, Tommo's romantic vocabulary remains chastely conventional.

Not only do the beauty and nudity of the Typee natives convey an Edenic impression, but their physical environment is also suggestive of the realm of paradise. Thus, there are no seasons—a traditional sign of the Fall—in the Typee Valley; for "there day follows day in one unvarying round of summer and sunshine, and the whole year is one long tropical month of June just melting into July" (213). In fact, an aura of timelessness seems to hang over the valley, for "the history of a day is the history of a life" (149). Following his companion Toby's departure to help secure his release, Tommo accordingly begins to lose "all knowledge of the regular recurrence of the days of the week" (123). Another key feature of the biblical Eden and paradise tradition is the flourishing condition of the natural world, including the harmony of all living creatures and the lack of predation. So, too, in the realm of the Typee, the "birds and lizards of the valley show their confidence in the kindness of man" (212). Tommo describes "a beautiful golden-hued species of lizard" that "at all hours of the day showed their glittering sides as they ran frolicking between the spears of grass or raced in troops up and down the tall shafts of the cocoa-nut trees" and were "perfectly tame and insensible to fear" (211). In like manner, "frisking play'd / All Beasts of th' Earth" in Milton's prelapsarian Eden (*Paradise Lost*, IV.340–41). Among the Typee, the solitudes are "unbroken by the roar of beasts of prey" and there are "no venomous reptiles; and no snakes of any description to be found in any of the valleys" (212). On a comic note, Tommo remarks that even the native flies are remarkably—and annoyingly—tame (212). In addition, there are innumerable "bright and beautiful birds" flying through the valley with variegated plumage of "purple and azure, crimson and white, black and gold; with bills of every tint:—bright bloody-red, jet black, and ivory white" (215). Another required feature of paradise is the presence of majestic fruit-bearing trees, and this is true as well of the Typee valley, where the bread fruit and coconut palm nourish and otherwise contribute to the health and welfare of the natives.

The paradisiacal aura of the Typee valley can be viewed ironically with regard to the natives' religious beliefs; for instead of a jealously restrictive Judeo-Christian god overseeing the activities of Eden, we find a set of grotesque-looking idols seemingly powerless to control their human subjects. Indeed, the latter manipulate them for their own mysterious ends. Thus Tommo is surprised that the supreme Typee god Moa-Artua carried by the warrior-priest Kolory is a diminutive figure wrapped in white tappa cloth with a human head at the top that looks like a "mere pigmy in tatters" (175). In a bizarre ritual, Kolory first caresses the god like a baby but then yells at it, hits it, and strips off its clothing before putting it away in a trough; and the process is then repeated until the god allegedly speaks a message to the priest. With irreverent humor, Tommo expresses mystification as to why this peculiar little figure is the chief god: "Moa Artua was certainly a precocious little fellow if he said all that was imputed to him; but for what reason this poor devil of a deity, thus cuffed about, cajoled and shut up in a box, was held in greater estimation than the full-grown and dignified personages of the Taboo Groves, I cannot divine" (176–77). The comic anthropomorphizing of the god here is subversively ironic, as is the possible analogy with the two chief gods (Jesus and Yahweh) of the Christian world. All of this allegedly shows that the Typee, as a free people living in a perfected social state, "were not to be brow-beaten by chiefs, priests, idols, or devils" (177). The Typee irreverence toward their gods is also seen when Tommo and Kory-Kory encounter a decayed wooden idol leaning against a bamboo temple. When Kory-Kory attempts to prop it upright, it unexpectedly falls on his back, causing him furiously to beat and yell at it in a way that makes Tommo "shocked at Kory-Kory's impiety" (179). In this ironic reversal of Western archetypal history, it is the gods, not their human creations, who "fall" and are punished in the Typee Eden.

In chapter 17, following Tommo's earlier feeling of despair at his evident "captivity" among the Typee—which is probably based on the tribe's recognition of him as a bargaining chip for future exchanges with whites—Tommo's leg seems to heal and he experiences a greater "elasticity of mind" (123). This enables him to survey Typee society more carefully, leading to an outspoken representation of the Typee as morally superior to Europeans due to their closer approximation to the condition of traditional ideas of paradise. Partly drawing on the notion of the "noble savage," the narrator offers a defense of the simple life of the Typee: "In a primitive state of society, the enjoyments of life, though few and simple, are spread over a great extent, and are unalloyed; but Civilization, for every advantage she imparts, holds a hundred evils in reserve" (124). Even the worst moral depravity of the Typee, their alleged cannibalism, pales in comparison with the Western barbarities of drawing and quartering, a form of capital punishment only recently made illegal in England, and the relentless development of military technology among all civilized nations which, in a judgment worthy of Jonathan Swift—as in Lemuel Gulliver's proposal of giving gunpowder to the King of Brobdingnag—reveals "white civilized man as the most ferocious animal on the face of the earth" (125). The narrator's ensuing notion that "so far as the relative wickedness of the parties is concerned, four or five Marquesan Islanders sent to the United States as Missionaries might be quite as useful as an equal number of Americans dispatched to the Islands in a similar capacity" (125–26). Such a suggestion looks back to Swift's depiction of Gulliver meditating on the civilizing possibilities of sending some Houyhnhnms to England to teach the latter some of their virtues, in a process of reverse colonization.[6]

Tommo goes on to note that the Typee, with a "perpetual hilarity reigning through the whole extent of the vale" (126), are instinctively happier than civilized Europeans; and he enumerates an extended list of the many features of European life that are missing in the Typee Valley: "There were none of those thousand sources of irritation that the ingenuity of civilized man has created to mar his own felicity. There were no foreclosures of mortgages, no protested notes, no bills payable, no debts of honor in Typee. . . . No beggars; no debtors' prisons;

no proud and hard-hearted nabobs in Typee; or to sum up all in one word—no Money! That 'root of all evil' was not to be found in the valley" (126). Such a roster of the missing items of civilized life in a paradisiacal society has a long pedigree, going back to such works as Hesiod's *Works and Days*, Ovid's *Metamorphoses*, Montaigne's "Of the Cannibals," Shakespeare's *The Tempest*, and Swift's *Gulliver's Travels*. The shaping power of the paradise tradition can be seen, too, in the conclusion that the primitive innocence and happiness of Typee society stems from the absence of money, the love of which is the supposed "root of all evil" according to the New Testament (2 Tim. 6:10). The innocence of the Typee thus originates with a lack of the basic features of modern commercial society, including the latter's pervasive signs of misery and oppression.

The depiction of the happy simplicities of Typee society continues in chapter 27. Here again we read about the nonexistent evils of the Typee, now in relation to their absence of any formal legal code, made possible by "an inherent principle of honesty and charity towards each other. They seemed to be governed by that sort of tacit common-sense law which, say what they will of the inborn lawlessness of the human race, has its precepts graven on every breast. The grand principles of virtue and honor, however they may be distorted by arbitrary codes, are the same all the world over" (201). In this invocation of instinctive laws governing the human race, Melville draws on St. Paul's address to a group of early Christians who embody the "Spirit of the living God; not in tables of stone, but in the fleshly tables of the heart" (2 Cor. 3:3). Having Christian virtues without Christianity, the Typee possess a "universally diffused perception of what is *just* and *noble*" (201), so that they don't fear acts of theft or murder, despite the existence of personal property among them: "Each islander reposed beneath his own palmetto thatching, or sat under his own bread-fruit-tree, with none to molest or alarm him" (201). The evocation of Typee security here draws on the well-known depiction in the Old Testament prophet Micah of a future blessed age when men wouldn't "learn war any more.

/ But they shall sit every man under his vine and fig tree: and none shall make them afraid" (Micah 4:3–4). Again, the Typees instinctively possess the virtues of Christianity without needing its flawed version brought by the Western missionaries.

As earlier in chapter 17, Melville again provides a sharp contrast between civilization and "savagery," reiterating that the former "does not engross all the virtues of humanity" (202). Indeed, Typee social relations are so exemplary that Tommo marvels on their possession of virtues that compare favorably to those in the West who formally study morality and repeat the Lord's prayer every night. Among other virtues, the Typee exhibit an extraordinary "unanimity of feeling" (203) and spirit of cooperation in their actions. Their women are respected and not overburdened with work, and they exhibit a generalized form of social love like that preached by Paul in early Christianity: "The natives appeared to form one household whose members were bound together by the ties of strong affection. The love of kindred I did not so much perceive, for it seemed blended in the general love; and where all were treated as brothers and sisters, it was hard to tell who were actually related to each other by blood" (204). Again showing themselves as belonging to the kind of peaceful society found in the paradise tradition, the Typee outdo the virtues of nominal Christians of the West, who were instructed by Jesus to "love one another" (John 15:1).

One of Melville's polemical purposes in the creation of an Edenic aura around the Typee Valley was to critique the actions of Westerners in despoiling the primitive innocence and pristine beauty of comparable Polynesian Edens. Indeed, one of his most outspoken passages juxtaposes the paradisiacal circumstances of the Typee with the relentless encroachment of Western civilization, which has been spearheaded by the missionaries and is now virtually assured by the recent French annexation of the Marquesas. The passage begins with an ironic dismissal of the divine curse of hard labor:

The penalty of the Fall presses very lightly upon the valley of Typee; for, with the one solitary exception of striking a light, I scarcely saw any piece of work performed there which caused the sweat to stand upon a single brow. As for digging and delving for a livelihood, the thing is altogether unknown. Nature has planted the bread-fruit and the banana, and in her own good time she brings them to maturity, when the idle savage stretches forth his hand, and satisfies his appetite.

Ill-fated people! I shudder when I think of the change a few years will produce in their paradisiacal abode; and probably when the most destructive vices, and the worst attendances on civilization, shall have driven all peace and happiness from the valley, the magnanimous French will proclaim to the world that the Marquesas Islands have been converted to Christianity! and this the Catholic world will doubtless consider as a glorious event. Heaven help the "Isles of the Sea!" [see Isaiah 24:15]— The sympathy which Christendom feels for them has, alas! in too many instances proved their bane.

How little do some of these poor islanders comprehend when they look around them, that no inconsiderable part of their disasters originate in certain tea-party excitements, under the influence of which benevolent-looking gentlemen in white cravats solicit alms, and old ladies in spectacles, and young ladies in sober russet low gowns, contribute sixpences towards the creation of a fund, the object of which is to ameliorate the spiritual condition of the Polynesians, but whose end has almost invariably been to accomplish their temporal destruction! (195)

We see here how Melville's projection of the likely future of the Marquesas, based on his observation of the more advanced decline of native cultures on the islands of Tahiti and Hawaii, posits the "destructive vices" and general influence of "civilization" as the cause of the future Fall of Marquesan native society. Moreover, in a grotesque irony, it is the naïvely ignorant agents of Christian charity, in the comfortable setting of secure bourgeois parlors in America and England, who are the ultimate perpetrators of this evil because they have led the field in collecting money for missionary enterprises.

Melville's outspoken indictment continues with a recital of the unholy alliance of Christianity and civilization in the eradication of paganism from the face of the earth along with the pagans themselves, while pointing out the similarities between the fates of the American Indians—referring to the era of Indian removal in the 1830s—and the Polynesians in the process of genocide: "Let the savages be civilized, but civilize them with benefits, and not with evils; and let heathenism be destroyed, but not by destroying the heathen. The Anglo-Saxon hive have extirpated Paganism from the greater part of the North American continent; but with it they have likewise extirpated the greater portion of the Red race" (195). The same process is now happening to the "pagan" inhabitants of Polynesia: "Among the islands of Polynesia, no sooner are the images overturned, the temples demolished, and the idolaters converted into *nominal* Christians, than disease, vice, and premature death make their appearance" (195). The principal consequences of the Fall—hard labor, sin, and death—are thus inadvertently inflicted on the Polynesians by the missionary and commercial invaders from the West; and the inhabitants of paradise must now sweat for their daily bread because their natural resources have been requisitioned by the invaders.

Even though Melville is a fierce defender of the Polynesians against Western religious, commercial, and political depredations, Tommo is ultimately ambivalent about his extended residence among the Typee, for he is never totally comfortable in the valley, given his anxieties about his captivity and the absence of Toby's companionship. As commentators have noted, one of Tommo's underlying reasons for wanting to leave the Typee Valley is the regressive, infantilized condition he is forced to assume there, as well as the childlike quality of life among the Typee generally. Significantly, both these conditions confirm a common interpretation of the Eden myth as an allegory of childhood maturation. Constantly carried around the valley like a child by his faithful attendant (and implicit jailer) Kory-Kory, Tommo is fed regularly and sleeps a good part of the day and night like the other natives who "pass a large portion of their time in the arms of Somnus" (152). Tommo is also treated like a child by the Typee; for example, when he is first having his leg painfully pounded by the tribe's medicine man: "Mehevi, upon the same principle which prompts an affectionate mother to hold a struggling child in a dentist's chair, restrained me in his powerful grip" (80). So, too, when Tommo is first given Kory-Kory as his valet, the latter, "as if I were an infant, insisted upon feeding me with his own hands" (88).

Yet it is not only that the Typee treat Tommo like a child; for they themselves in many respects live in a juvenile world. Tommo notes, for example, that after a brief skirmish with the neighboring Happar, he hears only "some straggling shouts from the hillside, something like the halloos of a parcel of truant boys who had lost themselves in the woods" (129). In his chapter describing their religion, Tommo notes that "in the celebration of many of their strange rites, they appeared merely to seek a sort of childish amusement" (174). So, too, in their acts of devotion to their gods, the Typee looked like "a parcel of children playing with dolls and baby houses" (176). Tommo's perception of the Typees' child-like behavior is again on display when he improvises a popgun out of a three-foot length of bamboo for a child with whom he was playing. He was then besieged by others of all ages, clamoring for the same toy gun. After making several more, he delegates this job to a helper and soon the whole community is playing with these guns, and "green guavas, seeds, and berries were flying about in every direction" (145).

As in other literary depictions of paradisiacal societies, the "uniform and undiversified" (149) life of the Typees is also problematic to an outsider like Tommo, whose recurrent desire for knowledge about Typee life reveals that his view of the world is conditioned by Western traditions of intellectual inquiry and aspiration, as opposed to the contented insularity and stasis of Typee society. The contrast is perhaps best observed in the scene when Tommo and Kory-Kory observe the bamboo mausoleum of the dead warrior chief. In a seven-foot coffin canoe, the effigy of a deceased chief is seen strenuously rowing "as if eager to hurry on his voyage" (172), but facing him in the canoe is the *memento mori* of a human skull. After Kory-Kory explains that the chief is "paddling his way to the realms of bliss, and bread-fruit—the Polynesian heaven" (172), Tommo asks him whether he would like to accompany the chief there. He tellingly replies that he is happy living in the Typee Valley as it is, on the prudent principle that "a bird in the hand is worth two in the bush" (173). Tommo, on the other hand, is haunted by the image of the dead chief, which he often visits, viewing it as embodying a model for human aspiration after the unknown; and he accordingly addresses it in the allegorical accents of John Bunyan's *Pilgrim's Progress*: "Paddle away, brave chieftain, to the land of spirits! To the material eye thou makest but little progress; but with the eye of faith, I see thy canoe cleaving the bright waves, which die away on those dimly looming shores of Paradise" (173). In sum, Kory-Kory and the other inhabits of the Edenic Typee Valley see life with a contented material eye, whereas Tommo sees it as a ceaseless journey towards a posthumous paradise; hence it is not surprising that a few chapters later he himself is headed back to sea on the next phase of his journey.

The first event that causes Tommo actively to seek release from his benign captivity in the Typee Valley occurs when it becomes evident that to remain within the tribe he must receive their tattooing, an overt sign of giving up his individuality and becoming permanently identified with a "savage" society. Although the depiction of the tattoo artist Karky is initially comic in its conflation of Western traditions of the fine arts with this local creator of epidermal designs using mallet and shark's tooth (Karky is humorously seen "touching up the works of some of the old masters of the Typee school" [218]), the pressure on Tommo to be tattooed becomes more serious when the chief Mehevi supports it; and when it becomes clear that nothing less than his face must be so disfigured, he is increasingly horrified by the possibility. Thinking that the tattoo was connected with making a religious "convert" of him (220),

Tommo realizes that receiving such tattooing would cause a fundamental change in his Western identity. Tattooing thus becomes a reminder of Tommo's status as an alien within the Polynesian Eden; but this is not nearly as anxiety-inducing as his discovery of the archetypal evil of cannibalism among the Typee.

Tommo's ultimate exposure to this sensationalized Polynesian practice occurs in chapter 32 in an obligatory climax that looks back to comparable scenes in Daniel Defoe's *Robinson Crusoe* and the writings of Pacific explorers such as James Cook, G. H. von Langsdorff, David Porter, and Charles Wilkes. At this point in Melville's narrative, the pain in Tommo's leg has mysteriously returned, indicating that the infection might be permanently disabling unless outside medical attention is sought; it may also indicate that the anxieties newly aroused by the Typees' desire to see him tattooed include a reminder of his alien Western heritage of having potentially sinful bodily "members." Even more upsetting, Tommo's eye-opening witness of Typee depravity occurs in two phases, both of which may be obliquely associated with the Fall.

The first event that causes Tommo alarm is his discovery that three mysterious packages wrapped in tappa hanging over his head from the ridge pole of Marheyo's house were in fact preserved human heads. Tommo had earlier noted without comment that "heads of enemies killed in battle are invariably preserved and hung up as trophies in the house of the conqueror" (194). In the past, Tommo had asked to see the three packages that hung over his head but had been refused, even though he had previously been allowed to see some of the natives examining the contents of other suspended packages. On this occasion, Tommo forces his way into the circle examining the three packages and fleetingly sees three preserved human heads—one of which is "that of a white man" (233)—before the natives cover them up, explaining that these were Happar warriors slain in battle. It should be noted here that it is Tommo's irrepressible, Adam-like *libido sciendi*, or desire for knowledge, that leads to his discovery of the heads, which hang from the ridge pole of Marheyo's house like the fruit of the tree of good and evil (ironically, this "fruit," unlike the fruit in Eden, is utterly repulsive to the sight). The discovery of the white man's head causes Tommo's imagination to run rampant with speculation about Toby's—or his own—possible murder and subjection to cannibalism, even though the Typee have treated him kindly and vowed they never ate human flesh.

Not having seen any evidence of cannibalism in the valley so far, Tommo hopes that if it exists at all, it happens on rare occasions and that he will never see direct evidence of it. Yet only a week after his discovery of the three heads, Tommo makes an even more shattering discovery of signs of cannibalism among the Typees. While lounging in the Ti, Tommo hears a war-alarm, followed by an engagement against invading Happars. The bodies of three slain enemy wrapped in leaves and suspended from a pole carried by two men then appear. Tommo is encouraged by Kory-Kory to leave the scene, but he wants to remain; however, the ferocious-looking and now wounded warrior Mow-Mow insists that he immediately depart. The next day Tommo hears drumming and learns that a feast is taking place, but only for the chiefs and priests of the valley. On the third day, everything seems to have returned to normal, although Tommo's suspicions have been aroused and as he walks in the Ti he "observed a curiously carved vessel of wood, of considerable size, with a cover placed over it, of the same material" (238). This carved tree trunk, like the tree of the knowledge of good and evil in Eden, yields the ultimate revelation when Tommo looks under the cover and sees "the disordered members of a human skeleton, the bones still fresh with moisture, and with particles of flesh clinging to them here and there!" (238). Told that this is the remains of a pig, Tommo pretends to acquiesce, but his discovery confirms his previous suspicions and his determination to leave this newly fallen paradise.

Following his failure to secretly slip out of his residence at night in order to escape to a neighboring valley, Tommo is eventually excited by the news that Toby has possibly returned to the Typee Valley by sea, and he is allowed to be carried a few miles towards the coast. Yet even though the rumor turns out to be false, Tommo in desperation painfully hobbles part of the remaining distance towards the beach before his surrogate father, Marheyo, sympathetically pronouncing the words "home" and "mother," which Tommo has taught him, tells his son to carry his charge. At the beach, he discovers an English whaleboat manned by Polynesians, including a Hawaiian whom he recognizes from the *Dolly*'s first arrival at Nukuheva and who is prepared to barter for Tommo's release—with cotton cloth, gunpowder, and a musket—in order to augment the crew of a nearby Australian whaler. In a dramatic scene worthy of James Fenimore Cooper's Leatherstocking novels, Tommo then narrates his harrowing escape from the "savages." In keeping with his initial symbolic identity as a Miltonic serpent entering the Typee Valley, moreover, Tommo's violent exit is effectuated by actions that suggest he is inflicting his own symbolic Fall on the Typees. Thus, the divided opinion among the tribe regarding his fate results in fierce arguments and then open violence ("blows were struck, wounds were given, and blood flowed" [250]), an anomalous breakdown of the normally peaceful tribal relations that Tommo had previously noted. Then, after Tommo is able to make his way through the water into the waiting whaleboat, the latter is threatened by a group of Typee warriors who throw their spears at the departing boat and then swim out to intercept it. Only the one-eyed warrior Mow-Mow gets close enough to threaten the boat, and Tommo attacks him with the boat-hook, which "struck him just below the throat, and forced him downwards" (252), suggesting that Tommo has killed the most ferocious of Typee warriors. Even as a sympathetic Westerner, a complicit Tommo inadvertently brings sin and death to the inhabitants of the Typee paradise.

We have seen, then, that the paradise myth in *Typee* works on several levels. On the most basic, the Typee are depicted by the narrator as living in a secluded Polynesian Eden characterized by abundance, ease, beauty, and harmony. However, though an admirer of the Typee world, Tommo is also represented as an inadvertent violator of its primitive sanctity even as his experience there reveals the intellectual and moral limits of Typee life. Yet the narrator is also a fierce defender of the Polynesian "savage" against the depredations of Western commerce and Christianity, which have revealed the West to be the relentless Satanic despoiler of this vulnerable Edenic world, inadvertently bringing about its tragic, and even genocidal, Fall. In Melville's intricate interweaving of various motifs of the Western paradise myth, we find many of the features that make *Typee*, and the astute young "man who lived among the cannibals," worthy of our closest critical attention.

Notes

1. The text used for the authoritative Northwestern-Newberry edition of *Typee*, which will be the edition cited in the present essay, is based on the second English edition, which kept the passages that were expurgated in the revised American edition and added "The Story of Toby" as a sequel. *Typee* is unique among Melville's novels in that a substantial, thirty-two-page portion of the manuscript has survived, discovered in 1983 in a trunk of Melville family papers in Gansevoort, New York. For a full analysis of the manuscript and the composition of the novel, see Bryant. On Melville's life in relation to the composition and publication of *Typee*, see Parker chapters 11, 18–22; see also the "Historical Note" in *Typee* 277–301. It is traditional to refer to *Typee* as a novel even though its generic makeup is a combination of travel writing and romance.

2. For a selection of critical writings on the novel up to the early 1980s, see Stern; see also Weidman. Thompson's Introduction to *Melville in the Marquesas* provides a selective review of criticism from 1985 through 2005. For more recent approaches, see the essays on *Typee* in Barnum, Kelley, and Sten. On *Typee* as a form of travel literature, see Giltrow. On the continuing controversy over how much of *Typee* is true to the author's experience on Nukuheva, see the essays in Thompson. On Melville's sources in *Typee*, see Anderson chapters 5–8 and Bryant chapters 14 and 15. On the idea of the noble savage in the narrative, see Beauchamp and Scorza. On Marquesan sexuality and *Typee*, see Heath. On *Typee* and contemporary American ethnographic writing, see Herbert and Elliott. On *Typee* and Western colonialism and imperialism, see Harvey, Blair, Rowe, and Calder. For other studies examining the theme of paradise in *Typee*, see Stanton, Miller, Ruland, Babin, Young, and Gollin.

3. On the history of the Eden and paradise myth in Western culture, see Delumeau; on paradise motifs in European and American literature, see Daemmrich.

4. The narrator's assumed name of Tom—which he changes to Tommo for ease of Polynesian pronunciation—is a possible tribute to Melville's deceased cousin Thomas W. Melvill (1806–1844), who briefly visited the Typee Valley as a midshipman in the U.S. Navy in 1829 and was later buried on Lahaina, Hawaii,

following his early death as a crewman on a whaler. See Parker 70, 74–75, 80, 141, 208, 350, 381. Melville's youngest brother, eleven years his junior, was also named Thomas.

5. In the manuscript version of this passage, Melville deleted allusions to the Ottoman sultan and Sardanapalus (i.e., Assur-danin-pal, a ninth-century BCE mythical king of Assyrian) that more closely identify the scene with the writings of Lord Byron, whose poetic romances set in the Near East frequently refer to the Ottoman Turks and who wrote a well-known play on the life of Sardanapalus. See the transcription of the manuscript in Bryant 420–23.

6. "But instead of Proposals for conquering that magnanimous Nation [i.e., the Houyhnhnms], I rather wish they were in a Capacity or Disposition to send a sufficient Number of their Inhabitants for civilizing *Europe*, by teaching us the first Principles of Honour, Justice, Truth, Temperance, public Spirit, Fortitude, Chastity, Friendship, Benevolence, and Fidelity" (Swift 274).

Works Cited

Anderson, Charles Roberts. *Melville in the South Seas*. New York: Columbia UP, 1939.

Babin, James L. "Melville and the Deformation of Being: From *Typee* to Leviathan." *Southern Review* 7 (Winter 1971): 89–114.

Barnum, Jill, Wyn Kelley, and Christopher Sten, eds. *"Whole Oceans Away": Melville and the Pacific*. Kent: Kent State UP, 2007.

Beauchamp, Gorman. "Montaigne, Melville, and the Cannibals." *Arizona Quarterly* 37 (Winter 1981): 293–309.

Blair, Ruth. Introduction. *Typee: A Peep at Polynesian Life*. By Herman Melville. New York: Oxford UP, 1996.

Bryant, John. *Melville Unfolding: Sexuality, Politics, and the Versions of Typee*. Ann Arbor: U of Michigan P, 2008.

Calder, Alex. "Pacific Paradises." *A Companion to Herman Melville*. Ed. Wyn Kelley. New York: Blackwell, 2006.

Daemmrich, Ingrid G. *Enigmatic Bliss: The Paradise Motif in Literature*. New York: Lang, 1997.

Delumeau, Jean. *History of Paradise: The Garden of Eden in Myth and Tradition*. Trans. Matthew O'Connell. New York: Continuum, 1995.

Elliott, Michael A. "Other Times: Herman Melville, Lewis Henry Morgan, and Ethnographic Writing in the Antebellum United States." *Criticism* 49 (Fall 2007): 481–503.

Giltrow, Janet. "Speaking Out: Travel and Structure in Herman Melville's Early Narratives." *American Literature* 52 (March 1980): 18–32.

Gollin, Rita K. "The Forbidden Fruit of *Typee*." *Modern Language Studies* 5 (Autumn 1975): 31–34.

Harvey, Bruce A. "'Precepts Graven on Every Breast': Melville's *Typee* and the Forms of the Law." *American Quarterly* 45 (September 1993): 394–425.

Heath, William. "Melville and Marquesan Eroticism." *Massachusetts Review* 29 (Spring 1988): 43–65.

Herbert, T. Walter. *Marquesan Encounters: Melville and the Meaning of Civilization.* Cambridge: Harvard UP, 1980.

Melville, Herman. *Correspondence.* Ed. Lynn Horth. Evanston and Chicago: Northwestern-Newberry, 1993. Vol. 14 of *The Writings of Herman Melville.*

———. *Typee: A Peep at Polynesian Life.* Ed. Harrison Hayford, Hershel Parker, and G. Thomas Tanselle. Evanston: Northwestern UP; Chicago: Newberry Library, 1968. Vol. 1 of *The Writings of Herman Melville.*

Miller, James E., Jr. "*Typee* and *Omoo*: The Quest for the Garden." *A Reader's Guide to Herman Melville.* New York: Farrar, 1962.

Milton, John. *Paradise Lost.* Ed. Philip Pullman. New York: Oxford UP, 2005.

Parker, Hershel. *Herman Melville: A Biography. Volume 1, 1819–1851.* Baltimore: John Hopkins UP, 1996.

Rowe, John Carlos. *Literary Culture and U.S. Imperialism: From the Revolution to World War II.* New York: Oxford UP, 2000.

Ruland, Richard. "Melville and the Fortunate Fall: *Typee* as Eden." *Nineteenth-Century Fiction* 23 (December 1968): 312–23.

Scorza, Thomas J. "Tragedy in a State of Nature: Melville's *Typee*." *Interpretation* 8 (January 1979): 103–20.

Stanton, Robert. "*Typee* and Milton: Paradise Well Lost." *Modern Language Notes* 74 (May 1959): 407–11.

Stern, Milton, ed. *Critical Essays on Melville's* Typee. Boston: Hall, 1982.

Swift, Jonathan. *Gulliver's Travels.* Ed. Claude Rawson. New York: Oxford UP, 2005.

Thompson, G. R., ed. "Melville in the Marquesas: Actuality of Place in *Typee* and Other Island Writings." *ESQ* 51.1–3 (2005).

Weidman, Bette S. "*Typee* and *Omoo*: A Diverging Pair." *Companion to Melville Studies.* Ed. John Bryant. Westport: Greenwood, 1986.

Young, Philip. "Melville's Eden, or *Typee* Recharted." *Three Bags Full: Essays in American Fiction.* New York: Harcourt, 1973. Rpt. in *Critical Assessments: Herman Melville.* Ed. A. Robert Lee. Vol. 2. Mountfield: Helm Information, 2001.

Mardi: Melville's Search for Narrative_____

Anna Krauthammer

Mardi was not much of a commercial or critical success when it was published in 1849. Even today, many critics refer to the novel's unwieldy mixture of romance, allegory, satire, travelogue, philosophy, and social commentary, and differ in their interpretation of the novel's themes and purpose. Newton Arvin, in his essay *"Mardi, Redburn*, and *White Jacket,"* proposes: *"Mardi* has several centers, and the result is not a balanced design. There is an emotional center, an intellectual center, a social and political center; and though they are by no means utterly unrelated to one another, they do not occupy the same point in space" (21). But when analyzed in the context of Melville's body of work, it is clear that *Mardi*'s themes and narrative structure are shaped by those of earlier novels, especially *Typee* (1846). Furthermore, Melville refined many narrative elements of *Mardi* when structuring his later works, specifically *Moby-Dick* (1851), "Benito Cereno" (1855) and *The Confidence-Man* (1857). Richard Brodhead, in *"Mardi*: Creating the Creative," referring to the novel's link to *Moby Dick,* states: "Many more examples could be added to images that are introduced in *Mardi,* but only fully realized in Melville's later books; indeed almost every image central to his major work is presented here in embryonic form" (149).

The novel begins with the escape of the narrator (an unnamed seaman) from his ship, the *Arcturion*, and continues with his encounter with—and abduction of—a mysterious white-skinned woman, Yillah, and his murder of the priest Aleema who was keeping her captive. The balance of the work describes his subsequent journey to various islands in the South Seas accompanied by four companions, all of whom search for Yillah after she mysteriously disappears. Ostensibly an account of the narrator's encounters with the native people of the islands, the story is metaphorically one of Melville's journey as a writer discovering and flexing his own voice. For Melville, the process of writing *Mardi* was a process of experimenting with various forms of narrative: "His central problem as a writer was to find a fictional style in which there would be a particular kind of dynamic balance between fact and form, between concept and symbol, between the general and the particular" (Arvin 25). The appropriate end to this search, however, occurs in his later works, after he refined his use of different narrative modes.

In *Mardi,* Melville uses an extraordinary number of literary, philosophical, historical, scientific, and biblical sources to provide narrative complexity.[1] They are embedded in the novel, and are often referenced by the main characters: Media, Mohi, Yoomy, Babbalanja, Taji, and the narrator, each of whom also create their own narratives. Therefore, the narrator's quest to find Yillah (and what she may symbolize) is the quest of storytellers whose narratives complement and compete with each other.

The novel is a kind of metaphorical "work in progress" in which Melville embraces his freedom to experiment with different types of narratives, including allegory, and puts narrative to a variety of uses. *Mardi*, therefore, constantly evolves and has no definitive end, at least for the narrator, who on the last page embarks on an ongoing journey of escape in which he will be pursued by Aleema's sons. This journey seems as chartless as his original escape and his subsequent search for Yillah. Furthermore, there is a suggestion at the end of the novel that this chase of pursuers and pursued will go on indefinitely. This ending, while consistent with one of the novel's themes—the random quality of human existence—is also indicative of a type of narrative exhaustion, of a story that must be, if not finished, then truncated, because both the adventure narrative and the allegorical narrative can continue indefinitely, framed by a perpetual chase. This lack of narrative closure may be one consequence of what Wai-chee Dimock, in *Empire for Liberty*, refers to as authorial sovereignty. He speaks of *Mardi* as "an attempt to elevate the author from a mere writer to a sovereign creator . . . someone who, thanks to his freedom and invention, is able to reign . . . in his fictive domain: reign supreme and reign alone" (44). Dimock then connects Melville's authorial sovereignty with the creation of allegory: "Aside from its obvious political allegory . . . what makes *Mardi* more subtly allegorical is a process of signifying appropriation—a process that enables the author continually to produce his characters as signs, harness them to his scheme of reference, make them carry his meaning. In this manner, he constitutes the entire textual field as a field of 'authorial significance'" (54).

In one of his most beautiful chapters, "Dreams," Melville illustrates this imperiousness. He is omnipresent and omnipotent, encompassing all, the creator of an ever-expanding text: "Dreams! Dreams! golden dreams: endless, and golden, . . . And like a frigate, I am full with a thousand souls. . . . In me, many worthies recline, and converse. . . . I walk a world that is mine; and enter many nations" (366–68). Melville, in the voice of the narrator, clearly references the limitlessness not only of his experience, but also of his wide range of reading; the chapter is packed with a myriad of biblical and classical references. He also states his declaration of his freedom and responsibility to express this limitlessness: "As he writes, Melville is articulating his own mental world" (Brodhead 150). In *The American Novel and Its Tradition*, Richard Chase states: "Melville thought of art as a process, as an emergent, ever creative, but never completed metaphor" (95). In *Mardi*, Melville is in love with language and different sounds, striving for an ever-expanding inventory of names, places, and terms. Moreover, his fictive world is physical as well as metaphysical, as illustrated in his descriptions of different kinds of sea life in chapter 13.

In chapter 180, Babbalanja, who functions as Melville's surrogate, describes Lombardo's creation of a written work called the Koztanza, embodying Melville's reflections on his own creative process. Melville (through Babbalanja) sees writing as a slow, almost painful, careful process: "More conduits than one to drain off the soul's overflowings. Besides, the greatest fullnesses overflow not spontaneously; and, even when decanted, like rich syrups, slowly ooze; whereas, poor fluids glibly flow, wide-spreading" (593). Melville also believed in the connection of the present to the past, and he viewed time as cyclical rather than linear. He believed that the past created unlimited possibilities for the present; it was a creative force. Babbalanja continues: "We are full of ghosts and spirits: we are as grave-yards full of the buried dead, that start to life before us. And all our dead sires, verily, are in us; *that* is their immortality. . . . Every thought's a soul of some past poet, hero, sage. We are fuller than a city" (593–94).

Therefore, it is no accident that in many of his descriptions of the island kingdoms he visits, the narrator relates parts of their histories. Babbalanja also mentions the emotional source of creativity: "We need fiery baptisms in the fiercest flames of our own bosoms. We must feel our hearts hot—hissing in us" (594). This echoes the narrator in "Dreams": "Fire flames on my tongue . . . my cheek blanches white while I write; I start at the scratch of my pen; my own mad brood of eagles devours me" (368). Melville saw himself as driven by his creative urge, and recognized an emotional and intellectual source of inspiration that was intuitive and almost unconscious. Babbalanja continues: "When Lombardo set about his work, he knew not what it would become. . . . It was a sort of sleepwalking of the mind" (595–96). Babbalanja also echoes Melville's belief in contradictions in the act of creation: "There are things infinite in the finite; and dualities in unities" (597). This acknowledgment of dualities is reflected in Melville's ambivalence about the major social issues he examines in *Mardi*.

Babbalanja's description of Lombardo's writing process is expressed in the construction of the novel. Melville allows *Mardi* to flow freely into different narrative forms while weaving in his own meditations on his creative process. Edgar Dryden, referencing Charles Feidelson, suggests that "*Mardi* is both structurally and thematically a voyage from fact to fiction, from object to subject, a voyage to the very center of the writer's creative imagination. It is with the process and implications of inhabiting this mental world that the book is centrally concerned" (47). For Melville, then, this is a matter not only of imperiousness, but also of trust in his own powers as a writer. Each of the characters accompanying Taji on his quest to regain Yillah represents a different source of Melville's creative process: poetry, history, philosophy.

Melville's strongest and most passionate defense of his creative process in chapter 180 is his attack on critics, probably due to his understanding of (and contempt for) the marketplace culture in which commercial success was furnished by popular opinion and publishers who controlled public consumption of books: "They are fools. In their eyes, bindings not brains make books. . . . He is the great author, think they, who drives the best bargain with his wares. . . . They are men who would not be men, had they no books. . . . Critics?—Asses!" (599). But Babbalanja also adds a disclaimer: "Lombardo never presumed to criticize true critics; who are more rare than true poets" (600). Melville is quite direct in his disdain for his detractors, but he is careful not to insult those he needs and those who can understand his work and are willing to defend it. This is the pragmatic side of Melville, the writer who recognizes his dependence on critics and publishers.

Melville introduces and eliminates characters at will, as they serve his allegorical purposes; this accounts for the lack of narrative continuity and lack of character development: "When Jarl's death is reported, Melville has transformed *Mardi* from a narrative of action to a narrative of discourse" (Dimock 55). There is a shift from a predominantly action narrative to a narrative focused on discussions by Media, Yoomy, Mohi, and Taji as they search for Yillah. Therefore, each of the other main characters accompanying the narrator on his quest to find Yillah are also resources for Melville's process of creating this narrative of discourse. Similarly, events and places that form the romance and travelogue narratives are introduced without any clear reason for their sequence, except for the ongoing search for Yillah. The narrator's journey seems, indeed, chartless.

However, embedded in these narratives are also the seeds of the allegorical elements of the novel. There is a dreamlike quality in the narrator's early descriptions of his journey immediately after his escape.

In the chapter "A Calm," the narrator describes the impact of calm upon the sailor: "At first he is taken by surprise, never having dreamt of a state of existence where existence itself seems suspended. . . . To his alarmed fancy, parallels and meridians become emphatically what they are merely designated as being: imaginary lines drawn round the earth's surface . . . The stillness of the calm is awful. . . . But more than all else is the consciousness of his utter helplessness" (9–10). In "They Are Becalmed," the narrator continues: "But that morning, two gray firmaments of sky and water seemed collapsed into a vague ellipsis. And alike, the Chamois seemed drifting in the atmosphere as in the sea. Every thing was fused into the calm: sky, air, water, and all. Not a fish was to be seen. The silence was that of a vacuum. . . . And this inert blending and brooding of all things seemed gray chaos in conception" (48). There is peace yet threat in the calm. It is a contradiction in nature, which is a recurring theme in Melville's novels.

These chapters reveal Melville's view of the power and mystery of nature and the powerlessness of man as he confronts nature. The conflicting human feelings of attraction and comfort and repulsion and fear toward nature repeat in his sea novels.[2] They are negotiated fictively through the tropes of sea, ships, and journey: On the water, boundaries are erased; aboard ship, men who sail can form a separate society of their own (often more democratic than those on land); a journey becomes a process in which men do not need a specific destination. The sea becomes a separate world and a ship a separate society in which all men are equal and interdependent. Men depend on the sea, but need to protect themselves against it. To Melville, the sea is a great equalizer, albeit completely amoral; the sea is beautiful but also terrible.

Mardi represents the world, and the narrator's descriptions of the various islands he visits in search of Yillah represent Melville's comments on the governments and cultures of different countries; furthermore, his comments reference a number of historical events that significantly changed these countries. Merrell Davis, in *Melville's* Mardi: *A Chartless Voyage*, writes: "The incidents in *Mardi* which are based on historical events include: first, the chapter on Franko (France) and Porpheero (Europe) which describes the effects of the 1848 revolutions; second, the chapters on Dominara (England) which describe the Chartists' abortive march on Parliament in 1848; third, the chapter concerned with the reception in Vivenza (the United States) of the news of the 1848 revolutions . . . as well as the gold rush in California" (81–82). However, Melville's comments on the United States are the most specific, and reflect the major cultural, economic and political issues of Melville's time. His work clearly conforms to his political views. Lucy Maddox, in *Removals*, writes:

> Melville, therefore, helps to define for us certain constraints within which the American writer was working . . . during much of the nineteenth century. He also helps us to recognize the complex and problematic relationship between the writing that was being produced in New England and the writing that was being generated on the American frontiers. The definition of that relationship was, as Melville seems to have known, deeply political in its nature, and of critical importance to both the writer and the ordinary citizen, since it had everything to do with the larger definition of America as a nation and as a culture with claims to legitimacy. (12)

Anne C. Rose, in *Voices of the Marketplace*, discusses the changes capitalism wrought in America from 1830 to 1860. It reshaped American society, and Melville was quite aware of its impact. For example, in "Bartleby, the Scrivener," Melville clearly describes a society in which people die or thrive in a capitalistic environment. Rose writes: "Melville worried about the social and moral consequences of the nation's enterprising spirit" (125). But what was troubling to him was the duality of the reform goal. Perhaps this accounts for the ambivalence he demonstrates when discussing social issues. David Reynolds, in *Beneath the American Renaissance*, writes: "*Mardi* also marks a deepening in Melville's reflection upon debated social realities such as class divisions, Roman Catholicism, and slavery. . . . Although, like many popular authors, Melville finds in good deeds and social work some relief for troublesome issues, one issue he cannot fully resolve is slavery" (143). Reynolds continues:

> So Melville in *Mardi*, his first truly "Melvillian" novel, could air many radical views relating to slaves and the poor but at the same time could include arguments for the reactionary side as well. . . . The rather frenetic, kaleidescopic texture of *Mardi,* which always drives forward without truly confronting the moral questions it raises, is the natural result of a novelist who is now freely riding the reform impulse instead of pretending to advocate any single reform. (144)

That may be why the novel ends inconclusively. Carolyn Karcher also refers to Melville's ambivalence on the slavery issue: "Melville seems to have been a refractory conformist and a reluctant rebel" (qtd. in Krauthammer 12). And Marius Brewly writes: "What paradoxically confronted him was not a polarity between good and evil . . . but a tragic confusion in which good and evil were indistinguishable" (qtd. in Krauthammer 13). While these questions are examined more closely in "Benito Cereno" and *The Confidence-Man*, they are also introduced and explored in *Mardi*, although Melville's position is not as specific or forceful as it is in the later works. However, the urgency for solutions to these issues became more apparent as the United States drifted toward civil war, propelled by the slavery issue, and this urgency was reflected by Melville's more focused later works.

Imperialism was a major feature of the nineteenth-century world. In *Typee*, his first novel, Melville directly and graphically indicts the behavior of seamen representing the various colonizing countries. Not so in *Mardi*. However, Taji, by committing murder, motivated primarily by his desire to possess Yillah, is acting out his own imperialist fantasies of dominance. He invents a demigod identity for himself, and strives to create his own world, with Yillah at the center. Moreover, even the narrator sees other characters egocentrically, through a lens of cultural superiority. So while Melville does not express direct criticism of their behavior and attitudes, Taji and the narrator actually practice a type of cultural imperialism. Furthermore, although Taji may be seen by many critics as a wanderer or a seeker, he is also a criminal, and is no better than Aleema. According to Lawrance Thompson, in *Melville's Quarrel with God*: "The priest has held the chaste and innocent Yillah captive and has deceived her in order to subvert her to his own diabolical ritual; the hero also holds Yillah captive and deceives her in order to subvert her to his own fleshly ritual of lovemaking"(60). The price Taji pays for his crime is his sense of guilt and the transformation of his search for Yillah into a constant attempt to escape the pursuit of Aleema's sons.

In *Mardi*, Melville shows no realistic view of South Seas life; instead, he creates a fictional vehicle in which to explore his own beliefs and questions. That is, facts were not as important to him as his desire to create a work that was reflective of his creative process. Furthermore, in *Mardi*, Melville did not romanticize, vilify, or sentimentalize his non-European characters, as many of his contemporary novelists did. However, Melville was aware of these literary representations of non-European others, and so in his later works he focused on the treatment of African American and Indians fictively, as well as politically and socially. "Benito Cereno" and *The Confidence-Man* describe the hypocrisy and racism of these representations. These later works also show that Melville understood how literary representation of the non-European other—even nature—was a key element of the Euro-American struggle to forge a unique identity on the new continent.[3] But because Melville's work had to compete with sensational, sentimental, and romantic novels, which enjoyed tremendous popularity, he melded these elements into *Mardi*'s action narrative, yet also focused on revealing his moral and religious dilemmas and his reform stances.

The focus of Melville's social commentary is on the United States (Vivenza). He begins his political discourse in chapter 146 with a description of the country as young, strong, free, arrogant and expanding: "Yet, the men of Vivenza were no dastards; not to lie, coming from lion-like loins, they were a lion-loined race. Did not their bards pronounce them a fresh start in the Mardian species, requiring a new world for their full development? . . . Vivenza was a noble land. Like a young tropic tree she stood, laden down with greenness, myriad blossoms, and the ripened fruit thick hanging from one bough" (472). The description is Edenic and similar to earlier American visions of the New World as a garden. It also echoes the nineteenth-century literary representations of the United States as a vigorous, growing republic. But Melville also points out America's cultural legacy from Dominara (England) and describes their relationship as like that of a father and son (519). In chapter 161, Melville introduces his subtext of the importance of the past. He weaves through his description of the United States a repeated emphasis on the country's youth and its disregard of the past, which leads to a broader consideration of time and its cyclical nature, saying pointedly (using a young, unnamed youth as surrogate throughout the chapter) of the United States: "You are free, partly, because you are young" (526). This statement, made in a political context, also echoes Melville's earlier comment that youth has its drawbacks: "But childhood reeks of no future, and knows no past; hence, its present passes in a vapor" (484). Therefore, the youth of the United States will have its drawbacks as well.

The lessons of history and the cyclical nature of time are subtexts that run throughout the novel. In chapter 161, they are combined with a consideration of the state of the United States and a projection of its possible future, and forms the body of Melville's position on American political, social, and cultural development. This chapter combines his general views of the nature of men and governments, which he more specifically applies to the evolution of the United States as a political, economic, and cultural entity. But Melville also suggests, through Babbalanja in chapter 157, that growth carries within it the seeds of its own destruction: "The East peoples the West, the West peoples the East; flux and reflux. And time may come, after the rise and fall of nations yet unborn, that, risen from its future ashes, Porpheero shall be the promised land" (512). However, in chapter 161, the unidentified youth reads from a scroll to harangue the inhabitants of Vivenza. It is clear that part of the text is a warning against the transient nature of governments and countries: "Time is made up of various ages; and each thinks its own a novelty. . . . So every age thinks its erections will forever endure. But as your forests grow apace . . . overrunning the tumuli in your western vales, so, while deriving their substance from the past, succeeding generations overgrow it, but in time themselves decay" (525). For Melville, time is cyclical; decay is inevitable. The youth continues: "Throughout all eternity, the parts of the past are but parts of the future reversed. . . . And though crimson republics may rise in constellations . . . yet down must they sink at last, and leave the old sultan-sun in the sky, in time again to be deposed" (527). Chapter 161 ends with both Media and Babbalanja accusing each other of authoring the anonymous scroll. The narrator's opinion is, "Indeed the settlement of this question must be left to the commentators on Mardi, some four or five hundred centuries hence" (530). For Melville, the universe is constantly evolving and unfolding; the narrative itself will continue to inspire and confound future critics. Time is the test of longevity in countries and in art. In an earlier discourse, Babbalanja summarizes the lessons of history and encapsulates Melville's stance on the importance of the past: "The past is a prophet" (520).

Chapter 161 is notable for Melville's cynicism as well as his reluctance to endorse armed revolution against injustice. Here Melville questions the nature of the promise of America as a democracy, given the political reality of the time, which included marginalization of blacks and Native Americans. He mentions the hypocrisy of the oppressed becoming the oppressors (526). But he stops short from endorsing the remedy of revolt, the inevitability of which must have become apparent to him: "Now, though far and wide, to keep equal pace with the times, great reforms of a verity be needed; nowhere are bloody revolutions required. Though it must be the most certain of remedies, no prudent invalid opens his veins, to let out his disease with his life. And though all evils may be assuaged; all evils cannot be done away. For evil is the chronic malady of the universe; and checked in one place, breaks forth in another" (529). In this chapter, he also suggests not all monarchies are evil. For Melville, political questions are also moral questions.

In chapter 157, Melville points out the contradiction of United States democracy as revealed in a large inscription and a smaller one beneath it: "In-this-re-pub-li-can-land all-men-are-born-free-and-equal . . . Except-the-tribe-of-Hamo" (512). Later, in chapter 162, Melville zeroes in on the issue of slavery. What follows in this chapter is a wrenching description of the what the travelers see, the brutal and dehumanizing aspects of Southern slavery: "It was a great plain where we landed; and there, under a burning sun, hundreds of collared men were toiling in trenches, filled with the taro plant . . . Standing grimly over these, were men unlike them; armed with long thongs, which descended upon the toilers, and made wounds" (531–32). Although the narrator refers to the workers as serfs, it is clear that Melville is really describing slaves picking cotton and the brutality of their overseers. Babbalanja turns to Mohi and questions the humanity of the slaves, reflecting a major aspect of the political discourses that framed pro- and antislavery arguments. Mohi only asks what Babbalanja means and does not reply to the question. Babbalanja then approaches Nulli, who is an overseer, and asks if the slaves have souls. Nulli replies: "Their ancestors may have had; but their souls have been bred out of their descendants" (532). Babbalanja next approaches one of the slaves directly and asks him to define himself as to his feelings, morality, and faith. The slave replies: "Speak not of my Maker to me. Under the lash, I believe my masters, and account myself a brute; but in my dreams, bethink myself an angel. But I am bond; and my little ones;—their mother's milk is gall" (532). While Yoomy refers to slavery as a sin and as "a blot foul as the crater pool of Hell" (534), stating that all humanity cries against it, Media cautions that the United States must decide a course for itself.

Melville also confronts other issues related to slavery: the argument that some slaves are content, the specter of civil war as destroying the Union, a call not to judge so harshly the culture of the South, the futility of revolt by the slaves. Yoomy appeals to Oro for intervention and the passage of time rather than direct human intervention. So while the chapter spells out the deleterious effects of slavery and the political and cultural issues emanating from it, Melville cannot commit to a speedy and, if need be, bloody end to it.

The allegorical narrative centers around Taji, Yillah, and Hautia and involves four stages: Taji's capture of Yillah, her disappearance and his search for her, his temptation by Hautia, and his escape pursued by Aleema's sons. In the chapter "The Tent Entered," Taji describes his first encounter with Yillah: "Did I dream?—A snow-white skin; blue, firmament eyes; Golconda locks. For an instant spell-bound I stood. . . . Crossing my hands before me, I now stood without speaking. . . . At length she slowly chanted to herself several musical words . . . but though I knew not what they meant, they vaguely seemed familiar" (136–37). He is transfixed by her. He kills Aleema, and takes Yillah with him; she disappears, and he searches for her in vain among the various islands of Mardi. However, in reading Taji's search for Yillah as an allegory, critics have posed several different interpretations. Thompson ascribes Taji's search for Yillah as an allegory of Melville's quest for a universal truth (68). But Donna Partridge Mitchell in "*Mardi, Moby Dick*, and *Pierre*: A Survey of Allegorical Interpretations"[4] states of Merrell Davis: "Davis agrees with Stone that since Taji's quest through Mardi is a literary device used to hold the book together, any attempt to find a perfectly consistent allegory is fruitless. Melville was not concerned with a precise meaning for the quest" (34).

Babbalanja and Taji are traveling together in search of Yillah. But Babbalanja, the philosopher, is more than a companion to Taji; he is also a seeker of meaning. This is obvious not only in his description of Lombardo's creative process, but also when he tells Taji why he has decided to stay in Serenia. In chapter 188, Babbalanja describes his dream to indicate his final understanding that truth may not be absolute. He also reveals his understanding of Taji's quest. He relates what his dream guide told him: "Loved one, love on! But know, that heaven hath no roof. To know all is to be all. Beatitude is there none. And your only Mardian happiness is but exemption from great woes—no more. Great love is sad; and heaven is love. Sadness makes the silence throughout the realm of space; sadness is universal and eternal; but sadness is tranquility; tranquility the most that souls can hope for" (636). He continues in chapter 189 with an admonition to Taji based on his understanding:

My voyage is ended. Not because what we sought is found; but that I now possess all of which may be had of what I sought in Mardi. Here, I tarry to grow wiser still:—then I am Alma's and the world's. Taji! for Yillah thou wilt hunt in vain; she is a phantom that but mocks thee; and while for her thou madly huntest, the sin thou didst cries out, and its avengers still will follow. But here they may not come: nor those, who, tempting, may track thy path. Wise counsels take. Within our hearts is all we seek; though in that search many need a prompter. Him I have found in blessed Alma. Then rove no more. Gain now, in flush of youth, that last wise thought, too often purchased, by a life of woe. Be wise: be wise. (637)

He drives his last warning home again: "Be sure thy Yillah never will be found; or found, will not avail thee. Yet search, if so thou wilt; more isles, thou say'st, are still unvisited; and when all is seen, return and find thy Yillah here" (638). But Taji responds: "I am the hunter, that never rests! the hunter without a home! She I seek, still flies before; and I will follow, though she lead me beyond the reef; through sunless seas; and into night and death. Her, will I seek, through all the isles and stars; and find her, whate'er betide!" (638). Babbalanja has found peace, although not the truth he seeks. Taji will never rest; his restlessness is that of a perpetual seeker on a possibly futile journey. Both Taji and Babbalanja are seekers, but they encounter different resolutions. Babbalanja remains in Serenia; Taji continues searching.

Prior to leaving Mardi entirely, Taji encounters Hautia, who represents desires of the flesh, and tempts him thus: "Come let us sin and be merry. . . . Lo! Taji; all these may be had for the diving; and Beauty, Health, Wealth, Long Life and the Last Hope of Man. But through me alone, may these be had" (651). This refers to the trading of the soul for desire, and the possible descent into Hell, and are obviously biblical in origin. But Taji rejects her, saying: "Show me that which I seek, and I will dive with thee, straight through the world, till we come up in oceans unknown." But she replies: "Nay, Nay; but join hands, and I will take thee, where thy Past shall be forgotten; where thou wilt soon learn to love the living, not the dead" (651). He rejects the temptation that includes forgetfulness of his quest and replies, "Better to me, O Hautia! all the bitterness of my buried dead, than all the sweets of the life thou canst bestow; even, were it eternal" (651). This exchange prefigures Taji's final voyage, his escape. It also illustrates his assertion of his quest, his willingness to risk all, and his lack of acceptance of the understanding and peace Serenia might offer him. As he prepares to escape from Mardi, leaving his companions behind, he asserts his will, his sovereignty over his own destiny: "Let me then be the unreturning wanderer. . . . By Oro I will steer my own fate" (654). The last image the narrator shares with his readers is that of the pursuit of Aleema's sons, arrows poised, and the chase that ensues "over an endless sea" (654).

Mitchell states: "*Mardi* is considered an experiment or exercise which led to greater things" (95). However, it is clear from the analysis in her thesis, and in the majority of other criticism, that there is allegory in *Mardi,* and while it may not be fully developed, it contains the moral and religious questions and doubts that can be found in all of Melville's work. *Mardi* is also partly an allegory about the creative process. In commenting on Babbalanja's description of Lombardo's writing process, Brodhead states: "Where in 'Sailing On' he implied that there is some connection between chartless voyaging and coming upon new worlds of mind, Melville sees much more clearly here how writing and discovery are linked, and he is able to specify much more

precisely what the world of mind consists of" (144). When Babbalanja states that Lombardo said he was "creating the creative," it was
Melville's view of his creation of the various narrative modes he was
experimenting with in *Mardi*.

Finally, *Mardi* is also an expression of Melville's stances on the major social, political, and cultural issues of his day. He was able to pin-
point fundamental and troubling moral contradictions in the country's
democratic ideals. In *Mardi*, Melville examines slavery, the marginalization of nonwhite others, the country's struggle for a national identity, the cultural separation of North and South, U.S. relationships with
foreign powers, and the impact of growing capitalism. All the while,
Melville the writer and the individual, like Babbalanja, wrestled with
his own doubts about the elusive nature of goodness and the universal-
ity of evil.

Notes

1. See Davis for a comprehensive look at the various sources, biographical background, and historical issues pertaining to *Mardi*.
2. See Lawrence, *Selected Literary Criticism*, for several discussions of the Western attraction to the primitive.
3. For discussions on the representation of the savage other in nineteenth-century
   American literary and political discourses and the connection to identity, see
   Krauthammer, and Pearce.
4. Mitchell's work is especially useful as a survey of major, older criticism of *Mardi*, separately, and in comparison to *Redburn* and *Pierre*, and serves as a short
   history of traditional criticism of the novel.

Works Cited

Arvin, Newton. "*Mardi, Redburn*, and *White Jacket*." *Melville: A Collection of Critical Essays*. Ed. Richard Chase. Englewood Cliffs: Prentice, 1962. 21–38.

Brodhead, Richard. "*Mardi*: Creating the Creative." *Herman Melville*. Ed. Harold
Bloom. New York: Chelsea House, 1986.

Chase, Richard. *The American Novel and Its Tradition*. Baltimore: Johns Hopkins
UP, 1957.

Davis, Merrell. *Melville's* Mardi: *A Chartless Voyage*. New Haven: Yale UP, 1962.

Dimock, Wai-chee. *Empire for Liberty*. Princeton: Princeton UP, 1989.

Dryden, Edgar A. *Melville's Thematics of Form*. Baltimore: Johns Hopkins UP, 1968.

Krauthammer, Anna. *The Representation of the Savage in James Fenimore Cooper and Herman Melville*. New York: Lang, 2008.

Lawrence, D. H. "*Typee* and *Omoo*." *D. H. Lawrence: Selected Literary Criticism*. Ed. Anthony Beal. New York: Viking, 1966.

Maddox, Lucy. *Removals: Nineteenth-Century American Literature and the Politics of Indian Affairs*. New York: Oxford UP, 1991.

Melville, Herman. *Mardi, and a Voyage Thither.* Evanston: Northwestern UP, 1970.

Mitchell, Donna Partridge. "*Mardi, Moby Dick*, and *Pierre*: A Survey of Allegorical Interpretations." MA Thesis. Texas Tech University, 1969.

Pearce, Roy Harvey. *Savagism and Civilization.* University of California Press, 1988.

Reynolds, David. *Beneath the American Renaissance*. Cambridge: Harvard UP, 1988.

Rose, Anne C. *Voices of the Marketplace: American Thought and Culture, 1830–1860*. New York: Twayne, 1996.

Thompson, Lawrance. *Melville's Quarrel with God*. Princeton: Princeton UP, 1952.

Moby-Dick and Metaphysics_____

Steven Frye

Herman Melville stood on the edge of an intellectual precipice, in a time of unprecedented change in European and American culture. As Andrew Delbanco notes in his recent biography *Melville: His World and Work*, when Melville was born in New York City in 1819, the provincial town that was to become the nation's greatest metropolis was a relatively small community more medieval than modern. But by the time he died in 1891, New York was fully urban, organized around technologies such as electricity and telephones, and people traveled using the Brooklyn Bridge and the Second Avenue Elevated Railway (Delbanco 3). The same cataclysmic transformation took place in the intellectual culture of the West, and in this sense, Herman Melville was America's great Victorian, preoccupied with the issues and concerns of his contemporaries, who were trying to sort out the social and intellectual complexities of the age.[1] Central to these concerns was the relationship between science and traditional religion, and questions related to metaphysics were increasingly placed within the framework of the scientific sensibility. Metaphysics is an important issue in *Moby-Dick,* and Melville's search for truth leads to a distinctly Melvillean skepticism, predicated on a profound sense of the sublime, a heartfelt and subjective apprehension of realms that transcend human understanding.

The mid- to late nineteenth century was a time when the term "skepticism" took on a particular meaning. *Moby-Dick* was published in 1851, but the religious and metaphysical questions the book raises were current before and after its composition, crystallizing in one instance in the "Great Debate" between biologist Thomas Henry Huxley and Bishop Samuel Wilberforce at Oxford University in 1860. The argument centered on the issue of biblical authority with respect to creation in light of the new theories of evolution. In *Agnosticism and Christianity*, Huxley later laid out his position in writing, claiming that "it is wrong for a man to say that he is certain of the objective proof of any proposition unless he can produce evidence which logically justifies that certainty" (1567). In this context, Huxley coined the term "agnosticism" and associated it with the scientific mindset, with the assumption that all that can be claimed as knowledge must emerge from scientific inquiry and experimentation. In common parlance today, "skepticism" is often seen precisely in these terms.

Huxley's assertions are typical of an intellectual position in the nineteenth century and beyond. In *Without God, Without Creed: The Origins of Unbelief in America*, James Turner explores the evolving line of thinking that made both atheism and agnosticism reasonable options for intellectuals in the late nineteenth century. He explores how the scientific revolution and the Enlightenment changed the mindset of many within Western intellectual culture. The objective and scientific modes of inquiry presented by thinkers such as Huxley came to define the academic world, and even religious intellectuals began to concur that metaphysical propositions such as the existence of God should be subject to scientific inquiry. The discipline of natural theology, on which Charles Darwin's *Origin of Species* (1859) draws in part, is built on the notion that evidence of God's existence may be derived from an "argument from design." Darwin was trained as a theologian, and many of his earliest mentors were natural theologians. *Origin of Species* is a revolutionary work of science that retains much of the language and the sensibility of theology. But his work also suggests that, in essence, many religious intellectuals yielded the field to scientists, allowing them not just to define the rules of the game but to design the game itself. Scientists and natural theologians alike generally came to agree that scientific methods can and should be the primary epistemological approach.[2] The result was an inexorable shift away from religious ways of knowing—which are frequently subjective, aesthetic, and personal—and toward empirical methods based on objective inquiry into the natural world. Though Melville became critical of many traditional Christian orthodoxies, *Moby-Dick* represents perhaps the greatest challenge to the exclusive dominance of the scientific sensibility. Melvillean skepticism, then, is broader and more radical, pointing to the limitations of any system that takes as its task the discovery of complete and ultimate knowledge, particularly as it relates to metaphysical questions.

Any inquiry into Melville's conception of the metaphysical in *Moby-Dick*, however, must be considered in the context of his tortured Victorian ambivalence about religion and religiosity. His lifelong contemplation of the metaphysical is complex and varying. In a letter written to his friend Nathanial Hawthorne in 1851 (the year *Moby-Dick* was published), he writes, "The reason the mass of men fear God, and *at bottom dislike Him*, is because they rather distrust His heart, and fancy Him all brain like a watch" (*Correspondence* 192). Here Melville demonstrates his antipathy to the watchmaker God of scientific deism, but he also implicitly questions the religious perspective he was exposed to during childhood. Lawrance Thompson places these concerns within the Protestant tradition, arguing that Melville came to reject the more harsh conception of God that this tradition tended to emphasize (6). William Braswell points to the pervasive influence of Presbyterian Calvinism and argues that Melville came to reject the form of Christianity that expressed itself in, among other things, the missionary projects in the South Seas (74–76). Jenny Franchot sheds light on these conflicts as she observes in Melville a malleability of conception with respect to the divine, figured in the trope of the "traveling God," in which "the dead body of Christianity is remobilized . . . as metaphor by Melville's circular procedure of return and departure" (157). From Franchot's perspective, Melville is a spiritual traveler who moves continually between the realms of belief and unbelief and back again.

Melville's continued metaphysical quest takes place in the context of an age in which purely mythological conceptions of the divine were seemingly untenable, but secular scientific concepts of reality were bereft of transcendent meaning. Somewhat later, Melville reflects these concerns in his Palestine journal, written on a trip to the Holy Land. He laments the absence of enchantment brought on by the modern intellectual climate. Upon traveling through many sacred places, he finds himself "sadly and suggestively affected" by the indifference of nature and man to all that suggests transcendence, making special reference to the "great curse of modern skepticism." Referring to two influential European scholars, historian Barthold Georg Niebuhr and modernist theologian David Friedrich Strauss, he laments, "When my eyes rested on the arid heighth [*sic*], spirit partook of barrenness.—Heartily wish Niebuhr and Strauss to the dogs.—The deuce take their penetration and acumen. They have robbed us of the bloom" (*Correspondence* 97). Melville felt out of place in the modern world. He seemed unable to reject the potential of scientific explanation, yet he has a deep sense of its inadequacy, its inability to enchant, and its failure to penetrate the deepest human truths that perhaps find their origin in the divine, however inadequately understood.

It is in this sense that Melville's preoccupation with the metaphysical, expressed most fully in *Moby-Dick*, is distinctly modern. *Moby-Dick* is deeply imbued with certain essential questions. It is a book built on biblical allusion and language, and in that context it asks: If a sacred text such as the Bible cannot be trusted for its historical veracity, from where do we derive our spiritual heritage? If the mystery and magic that imbues the Bible with meaning is no longer tenable to the modern mind, how do we contend with our disenchantment? If we remain convinced at our deepest levels that we are in some way connected to the divine, how do we find an intellectual and historical grounding for our spiritual leanings?

It is here that one must remember that Melville was first and foremost an artist, and this becomes the most essential fact bearing upon the role of metaphysics in *Moby-Dick*. In an age in which truth and empirical knowledge were often seen as synonymous, the role of subjective and personal religious experience as a means of attaining truth had become highly questionable. But so had the epistemic content of art, particularly literature. As religious intellectuals were increasingly marginalized in the intellectual culture, so too were the artists and the scholars who studied them. But it was a central feature of the romantic movement (of which Melville was a part) that the most essential human truths were the product of insight, intuition, and imagination, resulting in great works of art that inspire an apprehension that science cannot provide. The subjective knowledge that is achieved through these experiences is similar to that which is acquired through religious experience. From this romantic perspective, a kind of truth emerges from both religious and aesthetic experience. This knowledge is not objective, in that it cannot be tested through the scientific method, but for those who experience this form of understanding, it remains profound and deeply meaningful. The religious and the aesthetic are thus intimately related with respect to epistemology.

James Turner points out that the terms "belief" and "faith" had come to have distinct meanings in the nineteenth century, the former having to do with definable scientific propositions based on evidence, the latter referring to the personal apprehension of truths that cannot be proven. Struggling in a manner similar to Melville with the particular form of religious apprehension he was experiencing, the Catholic novelist Graham Greene said he often had less "belief" but more "faith." In his book-length interview titled *The Other Man: Conversations with Graham Greene*, the author expresses his position: "There is a difference between belief and faith. . . . Faith is above belief. . . . Belief is founded on reason. On the whole I keep my faith while experiencing long periods of disbelief" (162–63). This deep sense that reason is a powerful and essential tool but cannot yield all is at the heart of the metaphysical themes that appear in *Moby-Dick*. As a work of art, the book engages these questions without positing singular conclusions. But through it, Melville writes one of the greatest quest novels of all time.

The book begins with perhaps the most famous opening sentence in American literature: "Call me Ishmael." From its first line, Melville establishes his practice of literary allusion, and the balance of the work will involve an elaborate system of symbols, metaphors, and complex literary devices. The reference to the biblical Ishmael is potent with meaning in the context of the metaphysical questions dealt with in the book. Ishmael is the wanderer, the first son of Abraham, loved by God but destined to leave his homeland to establish a new and indeterminate future kingdom. He is not the cursed wanderer Cain, who is exiled for his guilt, but an everyman figure bound to the peculiar travails of the metaphysical and epistemological quest.

Melville's Ishmael recalls his feelings upon leaving home, the near suicidal depression that led him to sea, and he struggles emotionally to maintain his right state of mind as he ventures forth, the sea and all it contains becoming the grand metaphor for the universe in all its mystery. In that impenetrable sea is the image of "the ungraspable phantom of life" that is "the key to it all" (*Moby-Dick* 20). From a metaphysical point of view, Ishmael ponders "the grand programme of Providence that was drawn up a long time ago" and questions the effect of his own "discriminating judgment" in the seemingly preordained plan that took him to sea and set him against the great white whale (22). He is capable of rationalizing his experience in empirical terms, acknowledging that appearances suggest he went to sea by choice. Objectively, he knows this is possible, that "belief" affirms choice and human volition, but a deep conviction emerges from the recesses of "faith" that indicates otherwise. He anticipates something preordained and extraordinary, and he feels it at the deepest and most subjective level, as "the great flood-gates of the wonder-world swung open" and "two and two there floated into my inmost soul, endless processions of the whale, and, midmost of them all, one grand hooded phantom, like a snow hill in the air" (22).

Thus he alludes to the mystery of the metaphysical absolute, the albino whale that will evoke a vast array of symbolic associations: sublimity, horror, nature in its destructive power and indescribable beauty, and the mystery of the divine. It is a quest that compels him with a kind of heroic urgency, which he describes later in "The Lee Shore" chapter, in a metaphor in which the entirety of the human experience is described as a storm. In this analogy, the individual is the storm-tossed ship that must strike out into the "howling infinite" of a sea that is "shoreless, indefinite as God" (97). It is the existential condition of the seeker to quest for the infinite, to transcend all intellectual boundaries and limitations—scientific, religious, or otherwise—in a perilous quest for the metaphysical unknown: "Glimpses do ye seem to see of that mortally intolerable truth; that all deep, earnest thinking is but the intrepid effort of the soul to keep the open independence of her sea; while the wildest winds of heaven and earth conspire to cast her on the treacherous, slavish, shore?" (97). Placing this dramatic claim in the context of Melville's time, the conventions that restrict are religious, but they are also scientific and secular. They are at times the conventions of "belief," of the empirically demonstrable propositions of science that work to deny the generative possibilities of the soul, of the personal and subjective quest for metaphysical truth.

It is in this context that the intellectually rebellious character of the book is often misinterpreted, as "convention" is too often associated exclusively with religion. Perhaps because of the negative reaction of Christian conservatives in Melville's time, some of whom characterized the book as blasphemous, *Moby-Dick* has sometimes been seen as hostile to religion and metaphysics. Some critics have referred to the book as, among other things, a document of atheism. With some horror, Ishmael does contemplate this possibility. In "The Whiteness of the Whale," he ponders the symbolic import of the color white, and in that color "there yet lurks an elusive something in the innermost idea of this hue, which strikes more of panic to the soul than the redness which affrights in blood" (160). Though he acknowledges that human beings have always associated whiteness with the supernatural, he concludes with the possibility that the white whale itself is a grand and horrific symbol of nothingness: "Is it that by its indefiniteness it shadows forth the heartless voids and immensities of the universe, and thus stabs us from behind with the thought of annihilation," that whiteness in fact suggests "a colorless, all-color of atheism from which we shrink?" (165). In the context of Melville's time, this speculation was not uncommon, but what is notable is Ishmael's reaction: He is not passive and indifferent to the potential absence of God; he is horrified by the prospect. The book is by no means a unified document of atheism, much less a manifesto.

On the contrary, in "The Chapel," Ishmael contemplates the opposite. As he looks on at the memorials to the many whalers who have died at sea, he is inspired into a kind of poetic reverie, an aesthetic and quasi-religious response to what he is experiencing as he rests in the chapel and ponders the lives that have been lost. It is here that "faith, like a jackal, feeds among the tombs, and even from these dead doubts she gathers her most vital hope" (45). He uses the term "faith" in the same terms as identified by Turner and Greene, reflecting the distinction between "belief" and "faith" that was emerging during the time. This becomes evident as he extrapolates in passionate terms a subjective and personal truth:

> Methinks we have hugely mistaken this matter of Life and Death. Methinks that what they call my shadow here on earth is my true substance. Methinks that in looking at things spiritual, we are too much like oysters observing the sun though the water, and thinking that thick water the thinnest of air. Methinks my body is but the lees of my better being. In fact take my body who will, take it I say, it is not me. . . . And come a stove boat and stove body when they will, for stave my soul, Jove himself cannot (45).

Clearly an affirmation of the soul's transcendence, at this moment the spiritual traveler Ishmael contemplates realms beyond the physical. The passage alludes to both Christian and classical roots, echoing St. Paul's analogy of seeing though a glass darkly in 1 Corinthians 13:12. More directly, it reflects Plato's allegory of the cave in the *Republic*. Certainly one of the most seminal thinkers in the tradition of Western transcendental philosophy, Plato imagines physical existence as a distorted reflection of an ideal that transcends the material world, a realm to which the philosopher and intellectual seeker may in time ascend. Early in the book, through Ishmael, Melville introduces ideas that stand at the heart of both related metaphysical traditions; as the story evolves, the intellectual journey that leads to a greater if incomplete understanding involves an intense and sometimes tortured contemplation of the sublime, a personal experience of "faith" that stands outside propositions and empirical truth claims, one that becomes most dramatically evident in the great white whale.

The process by which Ishmael and other characters, particularly Captain Ahab, contend with the meaning of the whale is primarily personal, subjective, aesthetic, and by implication religious. Melville's respect for science is evident, but he is programmatic in articulating the limitations of empiricism. This becomes most clear in the "Cetology" chapter. This section draws from the tradition of nineteenth-century natural philosophy, what was in essence eighteenth- and nineteenth-century physical science, some of its most notable practitioners being Thomas Malthus, William Paley, and Charles Darwin. *Moby-Dick* as a whole is an attempt to understand the meaning of the whale, but in this chapter Melville's method for discovering meaning is empirical. Somewhat playfully, he begins by miming the language and mindset of the scientist: "It is some systematized exhibition of the whale in his broad genera, that I would now fain put before you. Yet it is no easy task. The classification of the constituents of a chaos, nothing less here is essayed. Listen to what the best and latest authorities have laid down" (115). He then goes on to define the various species and subspecies of whale in what some might consider excruciating detail.

The chapter in many ways represents one of the great challenges of the book because it involves the most obvious digression from the story and is written in a style that diverges from what one expects from imaginative literature. It is the language of science and the mentality of the scientist that is presented and mildly parodied. Even in the previous passage, when he refers to "the constituents of a chaos," he anticipates the failure of the scientist to unlock the deeper secret implied by the whales. Melville attempts to demonstrate both the value and limitations of the scientific enterprise. Readers are encouraged to apprehend the descriptive power of the natural philosopher's project. But after his lengthy attempt at complete definition, he acknowledges failure: "Finally: It was stated at the outset, that this system would not be here, and at once, perfected. You cannot but plainly see that I have kept my word. But now I leave my cetological system standing thus unfinished, even as the great Cathedral of Cologne was left" (125).

He comes to the conclusion that the real meaning of the whale, the sublime mystery it connotes, cannot be understood through the empirical method. There is something to the whale, especially the great white whale Moby-Dick, that cannot be understood by any method. In this sense, he acknowledges that the failure of "Cetology" is the failure of *Moby-Dick* itself: "God keep me from ever completing anything. This whole book is but a draught—nay, but the draught of a draught. Oh, Time, Strength, Cash, and Patience!" (125). But if *Moby-Dick* is a failure, it is a glorious one that Melville intends from the beginning. There can be no end to the quest of the seeker for the absolute, no "completion" to the wanderer who casts out from the lee shore into the vast infinite expanse of the sea. Melville's embrace of faith over belief appears as he builds the book around the most powerful method for discovering the subjective, quasi-religious, and aesthetic truths around which individuals live their lives: the language of symbol.

There are many theories that attempt to come to terms with the role of symbol in works such as *Moby-Dick*. But here it is reasonable to note that Melville dedicated the book to his friend Nathaniel Hawthorne. Melville had a great admiration for Hawthorne, and although a letter from Hawthorne that expresses his reaction to reading *Moby-Dick* is lost, we know from Melville's enthusiastic response to the letter that Hawthorne admired the book. In his "Custom-House Introductory to *The Scarlet Letter*," Hawthorne establishes a theory of symbolism that seems to apply to *Moby-Dick,* which can be affirmed because the whale as symbol functions in much the same way as the scarlet letter in Hawthorne's romance. In fact, while writing *Moby-Dick*, Melville published a glowing and ecstatic review of Hawthorne's short story collection *Mosses from an Old Manse* (1846), and this suggests that Hawthorne's use of symbolism was much in Melville's mind at the time.

In referring to his purported though not actual discovery of the scarlet letter in the custom house, Hawthorne writes: "My eyes fastened themselves on the old scarlet letter, and would not be turned aside. Certainly, there was some deep meaning in it, most worthy of interpretation, and which, as it were, streamed forth from the mystic symbol, subtly communicating itself to my sensibilities, but evading the analysis of my mind" (25). What emerges here is what might be deemed a "conservative" theory of symbolism. On the one hand, symbols contain meaning that cannot be fully understood by the probing rational intellect, by the scientist or philosopher perhaps. But on the other hand, they *do* contain meaning, and that meaning is not imposed upon the object by the observer. Again, "there was *some deep meaning in it, most worthy of interpretation*" (emphasis added). The scarlet letter streams forth with meaning, and though its content may be complex and varied, it is by no means infinite or peculiar to the observer alone.

Some postmodern readings of the symbolism in *Moby-Dick* emphasize the multiplicity of symbolic interpretation as seen through various characters, and in doing so, these critics attempt to void symbols of inherent content. This is a presentist reading that ignores the manner in which figurative language functions in Melville and Hawthorne. In their works, the experience of symbolic interpretation is again subjective, personal, aesthetic, and quasi-religious, and there are multiple possibilities, but meaning in symbolic suggestion is not relativistic and therefore less than real. Ishmael himself asserts the resonating power of symbols themselves, even in their mystery and multiplicity. At the conclusion of "The Whiteness of the Whale," after pondering the meaning of color, the whale and its whiteness are too powerful and overwhelming to be mere objects upon which psychological states are imposed:

"And of all these things the Albino whale was the symbol. Wonder ye then at the fiery hunt?" (165). Meaning, truth, the object of the metaphysical and epistemological quest, involves the pursuit and contemplation of symbols replete with genuine meaning, and this is the heart of *Moby-Dick*, as the symbol of the great white whale revolves primarily though not exclusively around the question of the metaphysical.

Moby Dick becomes a symbol for many characters. To Ishmael in "The Whiteness of the Whale," it is a horrifying emblem of annihilation. But in other chapters it takes on other possibilities for him, variously suggesting the beauty and sublime indomitability of nature as well as the sustaining force that defines all living things. In "The Grand Armada," whales in general suggest even familial love and community, and in "The Spirit-Spout," the spray of the whale's breath against the night sky lends a preternatural quality to the creature and its environment. But the white whale as symbol is most compelling and direct from the perspective of the monomaniacal Captain Ahab. In a previous encounter, Moby Dick has taken Ahab's leg, and Ahab has become obsessed with killing the whale. Melville is careful to make certain readers understand that Ahab's reaction is not typical or necessary. Ahab's tortured mind antedates his injury, and the whale becomes a symbol of a godhead that stands against all the hopes and aspirations of the human race. Ahab will not accept this fate and vows to destroy the potentially metaphysical source of human suffering represented by the whale. In a conversation with his first mate Starbuck, who reasonably attempts to convince Ahab to abandon his mad quest, Ahab is clear about the symbolic dimension of the whale:

> Hark ye yet again,—the little lower layer. All visible objects, man, are but as pasteboard masks. But in each event—in the living act, the undoubted deed—there, some unknown but still reasoning thing puts forth the mouldings of its features from behind the unreasoning mask. If man will strike, strike through the mask! How can the prisoner reach outside except by thrusting through the wall? To me, the white whale is that wall, shoved

near to me. Sometimes I think there's naught beyond. But 'tis enough. He tasks me; he heaps me; I see in him outrageous strength, with an inscrutable malice sinewing it. That inscrutable thing is chiefly what I hate; and be the white whale agent, or be the white whale principal, I will wreak that hate upon him. Talk not to me of blasphemy, man; I'd strike the sun if it insulted me. (140)

For Ahab, all physical things possess a symbolic import, and to think deeply is to read the layers of meaning implied in a world that is itself an elaborate system of figurative emblems suggesting realms that transcend. The nature of those realms is uncertain, but the search for them is in some ways necessary, at least for the mad captain.

While he acknowledges the possibility that there is nothing beyond the whale, that it may be a "principal," the ultimate source of his suffering, Ahab seems to believe more strongly otherwise: The white whale is an "agent" of the divine. Unlike other characters, however, Ahab has come to believe, as Lawrance Thompson argues, that Moby Dick is the agent of an evil metaphysically constituted and absolute. Starbuck has argued that the whale is merely a "dumb brute" that "smote thee from blindest instinct" rather than a symbol of a malevolent deity, and if Ahab could believe this he might abandon his monomaniacal quest (139). But he cannot. He will strike out at all that stands against human aspiration and hope, wreaking his hate against the malevolence that appears to degrade and cruelly diminish human beings. In a strange and unconventional sense, Ahab possesses the deepest kind of "faith," a capacity to read symbols and the meanings that stream forth from them, a meaning that evades analysis and demands only a forthright and oddly heroic action. However, Thompson argues that Ahab's perspective regarding the malevolent nature of divinity is the dominant view of the novel, implying in fact that it is Melville's own view. This is a significant overstatement, as the numerous other symbolic meanings of the whale would suggest otherwise. Ahab's quest is destructive. He displays a kind of heroic majesty, but by any standard he is out of balance. Faith leads him to intuit the divine, but in the larger context of the book he distorts its nature, reducing the symbol to a single meaning and ignoring its multiplicity. The whale is much more, and the metaphysical realities the creature implies, though real rather than relative, are more complex and varied.

But in spite of his apparent error, it is through the character of Ahab that readers apprehend most fully the manner in which faith in subjectively constituted truths can influence human beings living and reacting in a world of mystery and the unknowable. In *Moby-Dick* this faith is highly individuated, emerging from the singular reflections of characters such as Ishmael and Ahab, reflections that are often akin to aesthetic responses. Again, they are not relativistic, as Hawthorne's theory of symbolism suggests, but nor are they scientifically objective. This kind of faith involves the subjective and emotional experience of the perceiver and is not necessarily manifest in religious systems and institutions in any consistent or systematic way. Melville in fact seems to distance himself from any one particular intellectual system, religious, philosophical, or scientific. Unlike Graham Greene, a devout Catholic, Melville remained heterodox in his religious and intellectual affiliations. Perhaps because of the various studies of mythology that emerged in the twentieth century, writers and poets of faith such as Greene, T. S. Eliot, Evelyn Waugh, and later Flannery O'Connor often adopted traditional religious positions with a new sense in which the mythologies that defined them were the embodiment of the divine understood in human terms. But Melville the Victorian precedes this pattern of thinking, and as such his reflection on the epistemic value of faith led him to explore with greater flexibility the potential nature of the divine. Ahab's contention that the metaphysical force behind the pasteboard mask is evil is one example of this broad and potentially heretical speculation. But elsewhere the book presents a figuration of God that is equally unconventional though significantly more palatable.

This comes into play in the figure of the weaver-god, which appears first in "The Castaway," in which a young boy, Pip, is lost from a whale boat and, sinking in the depths, has a vision: "He saw God's foot upon the treadle of a loom, and spoke it; and therefore his shipmates called him mad" (321–22). In a vision that occurs as he is near drowning, he sees God weaving the world from a loom, the world and all its creatures as well as the thread of history itself emerging as a single grand tapestry. Melville associates this vision with madness, with the absence of reasoning intellect and the propositions that constitute rational belief. In fact, it is an insanity that may in fact be the engine of faith itself: "So man's insanity is heaven's sense; and wandering from all mortal reason, man comes at last to that celestial thought, which, to reason, is absurd and frantic; and weal or woe, feels then uncompromised, indifferent as his God" (322).

Ahab takes the mad Pip on as his companion, recognizing the divinity of his madness, the profound insight that he has experienced. But the weaver-god is an ambiguous figure, not the beneficent deity of the Judeo-Christian tradition or the agent of evil Ahab conceives. In "A Bower in the Arsacides," Melville develops the weaver-god more completely:

> Oh, busy weaver! unseen weaver!—pause!—one word!—whither flows the fabric? what palace may it deck? wherefore all these ceaseless toilings? Speak, weaver!—stay thy hand!—but one single word with thee! Nay—the shuttle flies—the figures float from forth the loom; the freshet-rushing carpet forever slides away. The weaver-god, he weaves; and by that weaving is he deafened, that he hears no mortal voice; and by that humming, we, too, who look on the loom are deafened; and only when we escape it shall we hear the thousand voices that speak through it. (345)

The weaver-god is not Ahab's god of malevolence, nor is he preoccupied with the pleas and concerns of the human beings who comprise a part of his tapestry. In some sense, he appears similar to the designer god of the Enlightenment, that divine figure whom Melville suggested people dislike because they "rather distrust His heart." The weaver-god seems himself to be subject to the limitations of the grand mystery of his own creation. He is deafened to the concerns of his creation by the act of creation itself.

This perspective is not as unorthodox as it may sound, since it posits the self-limitation of God explored by many modern theologies, particularly process theology.[3] But it does point to the freedom with which Melville dealt with the issues of religion and metaphysics in *Moby-Dick*. Aside from the more indefinable qualities that make it a great work, part of *Moby-Dick*'s value emerges from the manner in which it anticipates the intellectual culture of the twentieth century, the primary concerns and interests of modern writers, who dealt with religious questions in the context of change, variety, and crisis. The symbol of the great white whale is not relative and void of content; it streams forth with meaning and implies metaphysical realms that transcend human understanding. But it is also evasive and open to various readings and misreadings. Ultimately, it is a sublime symbol of mystery.

Moby-Dick is in many ways a book like no other. Few novel-length works of literature look exactly like it. It contains a novel: the story of Ishmael, Ahab, and the many characters who pursue the white whale into the remote and vast Pacific. It contains a sermon, a short story, a brief play, and a series of chapters that are basically works of natural philosophy. Theological and philosophical questions are an integral part of the entire book. All of these genres integrate around a host of themes, and it would be a vast overstatement to privilege one over another. But metaphysics and religion were certainly at the core of Melville's concerns in the work, and in this sense *Moby-Dick* becomes perhaps one of the most distinctly human works of literature ever written.

Since the birth of consciousness, human beings have struggled with the question of their origin and their future. It is the blessing and the curse of the human experience to be aware of oneself as a mortal being and to intimate that we are perhaps something more. Melville's book is in this sense the gift of an age, the grand expression of those concerns as they confronted the changes and modern patterns of thinking that in many ways defined the nineteenth century. Melville was no philosophical relativist. The quest itself is essential because there are truths and realities to be sought, even if they are never fully to be grasped and held. But the great white whale, one of the grandest and most profound symbols in Western literature, suggests that to seek knowledge of the metaphysical involves the subjective and personal apprehension of truth that involves but transcends the probing empirical mind of the Enlightenment.

In considering Melville's late poem *Clarel*, Stan Goldman deals directly with Melville's unique religiosity, arguing that "rebellion can be a theological search, and, quite often, it is only the near-believer who thinks deeply about faith" (12). As an artist of profound if unorthodox religious sensibility, Melville understood the inherent relationship between religion and art, that the sublime figuration of images and symbols from the natural world involves understanding that the deepest forms of knowledge have a relationship to beauty. To seek the metaphysical, then, is to pursue not merely objective understanding but what the German romantic philosopher Immanuel Kant called "pure reason," which contrasts with the reason associated with rationality and logic. One of the most generative ways to seek the ultimate is through the act of artistic creation, which involves a deeper apprehension both religious and aesthetic.[4] The metaphysical quest takes us beyond even the vastness of the sea. Ishmael ends an "orphan," alone yet living, and in telling us his story he has had the courage to grapple with a thing more real than sense. Like him, in Melville's own words, the true seeker must cast off from the lee shore, journey beyond the limits of intellectual convention and rational scientific inquiry, and "wrestle with the angel—Art."[5]

Notes

1. The term "Victorian" is often used to describe the culture in England during the reign of Queen Victoria in the late nineteenth century. However, one aspect of the intellectual and literary culture of the time involved significant changes that occurred as a result of the birth of modern science. Thus, to refer to Melville as an American Victorian is to claim that he was preoccupied with many of the same concerns as his British and European contemporaries.

2. Epistemology is the branch of philosophy that deals with knowledge. The primary epistemological questions are: What is knowledge? How do we know what we know? How do we discover knowledge? In the scientific age, the primary epistemological approach is empiricism, what is often termed the "scientific method," which yields objective knowledge gathered through the senses. Religious knowledge, gathered through personal experience or "divine revelation," is what may be called subjective, in that it cannot be proven empirically.

3. A twentieth-century theological perspective posited by thinkers such as Alfred North Whitehead (1861–1947) and Charles Hartshorne (1897–2000), process theology deemphasizes the coercive nature of God and argues for his persuasive nature. According to this view, God self-limits his influence over the universe and the events that occur within it, allowing for development over time.

4. It is important to note that, like many of his contemporaries in European and American romanticism, Melville was much engaged in the metaphysical considerations of the German romantic philosophical tradition. In his October 22, 1849, journal entry, he recounts an enriching conversation he had on board ship with two German professors: "*Last night* about 9 ½ P.M. Adler & Taylor came into my room, & it was proposed to have whiskey punches, which we *did* have, accordingly. Adler drank about three table spoons full—Taylor four or five tumblers &c. We had an extraordinary time & did not break up till after two in the morning. We talked metaphysics continually, & Hegel, Schegel [*sic*], Kant &c were discussed under the influence of whiskey." See Jay Leyda, 322.

5. This is the last line from Melville's 1891 poem "Art."

Works Cited

Braswell, William. *Melville's Religious Thought: An Essay in Interpretation*. Durham: Duke UP, 1943.

Delbanco, Andrew. *Melville: His World and Work*. New York: Knopf, 2005.

Franchot, Jenny. "Melville's Traveling God." *The Cambridge Companion to Herman Melville*. Ed. Robert S. Levine. Cambridge: Cambridge UP, 1998.

Goldman, Stan. *Melville's Protest Theism: The Hidden and Silent God in* Clarel. DeKalb: Northern Illinois UP, 1993.

Greene, Graham, and Marie-Francoise Allain. *The Other Man: Conversations with Graham Greene*. New York: Simon, 1983.

Hawthorne, Nathaniel. *The Scarlet Letter*. New York: Norton, 1988.

Huxley, T. H. *Agnosticism and Christianity*. *The Norton Anthology of British Literature*. 7th ed. Vol. B. New York: Norton, 2000.

Melville, Herman. *Correspondence*. Ed. Lynn Horth. Evanston and Chicago: Northwestern-Newberry, 1993. Vol. 14 of *The Writings of Herman Melville*.

_____. *Journals*. Ed. Howard C. Horsford with Lynn Horth. Evanston and Chicago: Northwestern-Newberry, 1989. Vol. 15 of *The Writings of Herman Melville*.

_____. *Moby-Dick; or, the Whale*. New York: Norton, 2002.

Thompson, Lawrence. *Melville's Quarrel with God*. Princeton: Princeton UP, 1952.

Turner, James. *Without God, Without Creed: The Origins of Unbelief in America*. Baltimore: Johns Hopkins UP, 1985.

Pierre and the Ambiguities of Antebellum America

Peter West

On September 7, 1852, an item appeared in the New York *Day Book* under the headline, "Herman Melville Crazy." Melville had published his seventh novel, *Pierre; or, The Ambiguities*, in July of that year, and the *Day Book* was not impressed. After citing a friend's description of *Pierre* as "the ravings and reveries of a madman," the article continued: "We were somewhat startled at the remark, but still more at learning, a few days after, that Melville was really supposed to be deranged, and that his friends were taking measures to place him under treatment. We hope one of the earliest precautions will be to keep him stringently secluded from pen and ink" (qtd. in Howard and Parker 380–81). Other reviewers shared the opinion that the novel was laughably inscrutable. The *American Whig Review* decided that Melville's "fancy is diseased," and the New York *Lantern* mockingly reported on "an intelligent young man" seen entering a local bookstore to purchase a copy of Melville's latest: "He has, of course, not since been heard of" (qtd. in Delbanco 179, Howard and Parker 381). Only three months after the novel appeared in the marketplace, the influential *Graham's* magazine stated that the novel was "generally considered a failure" (qtd. in Howard and Parker 382).[1]

Today, *Pierre* is still thought of by many readers to be an odd, nearly unreadable work. A novel seemingly at war with itself, it invokes the familiar conventions of established literary tradition, even as it fights, in typical Melvillean fashion, against conventionality. The characters read almost as stock figures from various nineteenth-century genres: Delly is the morally "ruined" protagonist of the seduction novel; Lucy the sentimental heroine, loyal to her male lover even in the face of her family's outrage; and Isabel the dark, mysterious double who emerges out of the shadows in so many works of gothic fiction. Even Pierre himself can be read as a romantic protagonist in the tradition of Byron's Manfred, or

Melville's own Captain Ahab.[2] But as the narrative invokes the story-telling practices of familiar traditions, *Pierre* evokes truth too elusive, too ambiguous, for conventional modes of storytelling. The novel ultimately defies the categories and expectations invoked in its own pages, and thus appears the product of a "deranged" mind.

In the discussion that follows, I want to argue that the strangeness of Melville's novel reflects the unresolvable contradictions not only of its creator, but of the historical moment in which it was written. If *Pierre* is an ambiguous book, it was the product of an ambiguous age. The antebellum era in the United States was a period of rapid economic development and great social upheaval, and the literary imaginations of Melville and his contemporaries were profoundly shaped by these forces of history. In the North, the linked processes of industrialization and modernization were changing the working habits of Americans, and giving rise to new metropolitan centers such as New York. Furthermore, while Washington Irving and James Fenimore Cooper proved that American writers could make a living with the pen, the emerging profession of authorship brought with it the new challenge of feeding a popular marketplace while navigating a burgeoning publishing industry often unfriendly to innovation or experimentation.

Another force acting on antebellum authors was the legacy of America's Revolutionary past, which loomed as both an inspiration and a shadow. Like Pierre Glendinning, Melville was born into an illustrious family with connections to Revolution-era heroism. His paternal grandfather, Major Thomas Melvill, took part in the Boston Tea Party, and his maternal grandfather, General Peter Gansevoort, was a hero at the Battle of Saratoga. But the nineteenth century was tough on the Gansevoort and Melvill clans. The author's father, a merchant, struggled throughout his life to build a stable business, dying when Herman was only twelve and leaving his family penniless. If ancestry often meant economic and social stability in England, in the young American republic, both wealth and status were increasingly subject to the vicissitudes of the marketplace.

As Melville built his literary career in the late 1840s, he quickly grew frustrated by an audience of readers that wanted authentic (but also well-crafted) tales of his time living among cannibals. A young, boldly creative inheritor of his family's legacy, Melville learned that to be a visionary artist and a professional author were very different things. As both an imaginative, autonomous being and a laboring subject at the mercy of a fickle literary marketplace, Melville was a divided soul. He complained, in a now-famous letter written to Nathaniel Hawthorne while Melville was composing *Pierre*, "What I feel most moved to write, that is banned,—it will not pay. Yet, altogether, write the *other* way I cannot. So the product is a final hash, and all my books are botches" (Melville, *Correspondence* 191).

Of course, Melville was not the only American author of his time being pulled back to the heroic exploits of the nation's founding days while also confronting the new economic realities of a modernizing America. Ralph Waldo Emerson's "Nature," one of the most influential texts to appear in America in the first half of the nineteenth century, began with an insight about 1830s America that was also an admonition: "Our age is retrospective," Emerson wrote, seeking both to inspire a new generation with the example of the nation's founders, and to embarrass them by revealing how little they had accomplished in comparison. Similarly, the Young America movement of the 1840s (with which Melville associated briefly before moving away from New York at the end of the decade) sought to bring to the realm of letters a nationalistic energy and vitality that might spark a literary tradition worthy of the American nation.

But the author who shared Melville's sense of the clash of old and new America most intensely was Nathaniel Hawthorne, a neighbor and friend during the relatively brief stretch of time that produced both *Moby-Dick* and *Pierre*. Hawthorne, of course, is celebrated for his dark, moral explorations of America's Puritan history, a project fueled both by careful research and the author's own genealogical link to Puritan violence. Like Melville, he was born into a once-proud family struggling to find its footing in a modernizing nation. One of many parallels between them is that both the Melvilles and Hawthornes changed the spelling of the family name early in the nineteenth century, suggesting the fraught relationship each writer had with his familial identity. Melville's mother is supposed to have done so to distance her own family from the stigma of the ignoble death of her husband, Allan Melvill, and Nathaniel added a final "e" to his surname to distance himself from a Hawthorn lineage that went straight back to the violent persecutions of the Salem witch trials.

By 1851, just as Melville was turning his attention from *Moby-Dick* to *Pierre*, Hawthorne gave his Berkshire neighbor a copy of his latest novel, *The House of the Seven Gables*, in which old Hepzibah Pyncheon is forced to turn a corner of her family's aging home into a cent shop. In what is today seen as a provocative moment in American literary history, a proud but fading American family is forced to come out into the Main Street of nineteenth-century commerce. Hawthorne wrote *The House of the Seven Gables* on the heels of *The Scarlet Letter*, and many critics have read the novel as the author's conscious attempt at the popular genre of domestic fiction.[3] Like Hepzibah Pyncheon herself, Hawthorne turned his attention from the deeds and sins of his forefathers to the more pragmatic details of mid-nineteenth-century life. Or, more accurately, he merged these two very different kinds of subject matter into his tale of a cursed and corrupt family that is forced to reckon with the economic, social, and political realities of the present day.

Hawthorne's turn toward domestic fiction in *Seven Gables* offers a helpful context for thinking about the novel that his neighbor began writing following the publication of *Moby-Dick* near the end of 1851. Melville's first six books had all been set either at sea or in distant, exotic realms; in *Pierre*, however, his literary imagination made landfall in the Berkshires, before taking his reader into the belly of the American beast: the often violent, alien streets of New York City. What *Seven Gables* and *Pierre* have in common is that each is the product of its author's willful, if uncertain, turn toward the realities of his age. Both novels address the preoccupations of a literary marketplace that each author repeatedly claimed never really to understand. But beneath their similar surfaces, these two novels are as different as the men who wrote them. Hawthorne's blend of gothic and domestic storytelling neatly concludes (too neatly, for many critics) with the union of the Maule and Pyncheon families, and the apparent reconciliation of the dark national past and the sunlit world of daguerreotypes, telegraphy, and railroads. On the other hand, Melville's novel unravels into nihilistic rage, violence, and, ultimately, suicide. While the sins of the Pyncheon family are atoned for in *The House of the Seven Gables*, in *Pierre* the past and the present remain unreconciled.

Much like the story of the Pyncheon clan, Pierre Glendinning's journey from his rural ancestral home to the hostile streets of lower Manhattan dramatizes the era's disorienting clashes between the old and new. When the reader is first introduced to Pierre, he is emerging "from the embowered and high-gabled old home of his father" (3). In this crucial first chapter, Melville's narrator takes great pains to describe the "patriotic and family associations of the historic line of Glendinnings" (5). We learn, for example, that in the meadows behind the Glendinning mansion an "Indian battle" had been fought, in which Pierre's great-grandfather, "mortally wounded, had sat unhorsed on his saddle on the grass, with his dying voice, still cheering his men in the fray" (5–6). Only a few miles away "rose the storied heights, where in the Revolutionary War his grandfather had for several months defended a rude but all-important stockade fort, against the repeated combined assaults of Indians, Tories, and Regulars" (6). Carefully presenting the heroic legacy associated with the Glendinning name as a psychological rather than historical phenomenon, Melville's narrator reports, "All the associations of Saddle-Meadows were full of pride to Pierre" (7).

Just as his ancestor reportedly sat on a saddle with no horse beneath it, the young Pierre rides into adulthood atop a family legacy that is largely an illusion. Meaning here hinges on the duality of the word "saddle": the stable, comfortable seat that "Saddle Meadows" promises Glendinning men quickly turns into a burden with which the young Pierre is himself saddled. For in the sentence that follows the above description of Pierre's fond associations with his family name, we are told that only Pierre's youth keeps him from knowledge of "that maturer and larger interior development, which should forever deprive these things of their full power of pride in his soul" (7). The power of the Glendinning name is a psychological fiction saddling Pierre with an ideal of male heroism—even as he abandons the aristocratic Lucy for the lower-class Isabel, and leaves the rural grandeur of Saddle Meadows for the democratic streets of New York City.

To the careful reader, Pierre's familial identity is problematic long before the young protagonist learns of his father's secret past.[4] Pierre recalls, for example, that his grandfather, "during a fire in the old manorial mansion, with one dash of his foot . . . had smitten down an oaken door, to admit the buckets of his negro slaves" (29). In this one anecdote, we glimpse the complexity of a Glendinning legacy marred by the injustice of slavery and the grandiose performance of white male heroism: The elder Pierre Glendinning bravely kicks open a door so that his human property can save the family estate. When we learn that this "mildest hearted, and most blue-eyed gentleman in the world . . . a gentle white-haired worshiper of all the household gods" had also "annihilated two Indian savages by making reciprocal bludgeons of their heads," it becomes clear that the Glendinning family legacy reflects the nation's own historical mingling of nobility and injustice, piety and violence (29–30).

As the inheritor of the Glendinning mantle, Pierre can only imagine himself through the logic of noble white masculinity. But, as Melville's novel continually implies, masculinity itself is a rather precarious foundation for defining the self—not only because it is dependent on its linguistic counterpart, the feminine, but also because white masculinity was in crisis during the antebellum years. Even though nineteenth-century gender roles attributed to white males an unquestioned physical, legal, and political authority, the articulation of this dominance required the male subject's location within (and above) a community in which women represented a new kind of threat. Thus, the appearance of Isabel's mysterious face at the sewing circle instantly makes it a challenge for Pierre "to regain the conscious possession of himself" (47). Before he can plausibly solve the mystery of this unknown female other—a mystery that must be resolved for Pierre to answer the deeper puzzle of his own identity—he attempts to regain his footing by playing the familiar part of the dominant man:

> Disguising his wild reveries as best he might from the notice of his mother, and all other persons of her household, for two days Pierre wrestled with his own haunted spirit; and at last, so effectually purged it of all weirdnesses, and so effectually regained the general mastery of himself, that for a time, life went with him, as though he had never been stirred so strangely. Once more, the sweet unconditional thought of Lucy slid wholly into his soul, dislodging thence all such phantom occupants. Once more he rode, he walked, he swam, he vaulted; and with new zest threw himself into the glowing practice of all those manly exercises, he so dearly loved. It almost seemed in him, that ere promising forever to protect, as well as eternally to love, his Lucy, he must first completely invigorate and embrawn himself into the possession of such a noble muscular manliness, that he might champion Lucy against the whole physical world. (50)

Describing Pierre's struggle to regain his own self-mastery, Melville highlights the dependence of masculine dominance on female subjects who must both witness and prop up manhood. The sentimental language on display—Pierre's "sweet unconditional thought of Lucy," his romantic desire to "champion Lucy against the whole physical world"— is in subtle tension with the passage's account of male dominance as both process and performance. Pierre must "embrawn himself" by going through the "glowing practice of all those manly exercises" that purge all "weirdnesses" from a sustainable masculine identity.

Though this is merely one small moment in Pierre's development, it offers a helpful glimpse into the ambiguities of Melville's language throughout the novel. Here and elsewhere, our narrator combines generic convention with a more philosophical perspective that exposes the limitations of contemporary literary practices. In the above excerpt, Pierre functions as the traditional hero of a sentimental novel, even as sentimentalism is exposed as a superficial realm of mere mythmaking. Indeed, Pierre's crisis of masculinity stems from the character's own investment in a vocabulary of gender that is nothing more than a sentimental fiction. Just as the Glendinning legacy exists only as a series of "associations" that Pierre initially buys into, masculinity emerges here as an idea promising our character a coherent way of defining and maintaining a viable self. He will soon embrace the role of Isabel's brother and protector precisely because the certainty of this role offers him a stable-seeming identity in an otherwise ambiguous world.

If masculine self-mastery and dominance is a lie in *Pierre*, such a gender crisis (to use a twenty-first-century phrase) brings us down to the solid ground of antebellum America, with its complex social and economic landscapes. As many scholars of the era have revealed, the emergence of a market economy made possible two related but at times contradictory social phenomena. On the one hand, the processes of industrialization gave rise to the influential and profoundly gendered ideal of domesticity, in which the home was elevated to an exalted place in the popular imagination. Women were increasingly seen as the emotional and spiritual caretakers of the family unit, and men were defined by their economic and political power outside the home. On the other hand, the economic value of labor in the northern free marketplace also meant that men had to "earn" their manhood by proving their ability to compete in the marketplace and support a family. To be sure, gender roles developed throughout the nineteenth century in ways that largely reinforced the patriarchal dominance of earlier periods, but the male laborer was now subject to the power dynamics of the marketplace, where autonomy and self-determination were no longer birthrights of gender.

While the story of Pierre replaces the aristocratic values of the Revolutionary era with the nineteenth-century ideal of democratic individualism, it also betrays an anxiety about the meaning of manhood in this new social landscape. Melville's novel depicts a protagonist caught between a patriarchal past and a present in which high-born men like him are at a disadvantage in the marketplace. Pierre, after all, becomes the noble protector of three vulnerable women who each seem better suited for economic survival than their male champion. Read solely in the context of a sentimental novel, Isabel represents the kind of dependent, socially inferior being who allows Pierre an opportunity to invent himself as a chivalric male. "When thou lookest on me," he tells her in Book VI, "thou beholdest one, who in his soul hath taken vows immutable, to be to thee . . . thy protecting and all-acknowledging brother" (113). And yet this same crucial scene suggests that Pierre's need to play the part of the protecting brother emerges out of his awareness of Isabel's economic power. As he bends down to kiss her brow, Pierre clasps Isabel's hand:

> All his being is now condensed in that one sensation of the clasping hand. He feels it as very small and smooth, but strangely hard. Then he knew that by the lonely labor of her hands, his own father's daughter had earned her living in the same world, where he himself, her own brother, had so idly dwelled. Once more he reverently kissed her brow, and his warm breath against it murmured with a prayer to heaven. (113)

His newfound sister's "strangely hard" hand calls into consciousness the "lonely labor" allowing Isabel to survive in the very world in which Pierre himself "had so idly dwelled." In another example of the narrative's preoccupation with the dependence of masculine identity upon feminine, Pierre sees in Isabel's economic independence a reminder of his own economic powerlessness. Though he is born into a substantial family fortune, the shifting ideals of the time required that American men must "embrawn" themselves in the marketplace. Pierre spends the remainder of the novel attempting to rescue Isabel, Delly, and Lucy, all of whom bring to the marketplace an ability to work—Isabel's sewing, or Lucy's painting—that renders Pierre's exertions something of a farce.

Like the author who created him, Pierre attempts to earn both his livelihood and his manhood in the realm of letters. Melville's choice of profession for his hero is significant not only because it reflects his own, but because the literary marketplace was one realm where women succeeded in achieving and maintaining careers that rivaled, and at times overshadowed, those of their male counterparts. Many of the most popular and successful authors of the 1840s and 1850s were women, much to the chagrin of many male writers of the era. Writing to his editor in the early 1850s, Hawthorne complained that

> America is now wholly given over to a d_____d mob of scribbling women, and I should have no chance of success while the public taste is occupied with their trash—and should be ashamed of myself if I did succeed. What is the mystery of these innumerable editions of the *Lamplighter*, and other books neither better nor worse?—worse they could not be, and better they need not be, when they sell by 100,000. (*Letters* 304)

Melville himself was keenly aware of the fact that for a male author to succeed in the literary marketplace, he needed to cultivate an audience of the opposite sex. As difficult as it is to imagine in retrospect, he seems to have felt that *Pierre* would allow the author of the hypermasculine *Moby-Dick* to break through to a female readership thought to prefer domestic, sentimental fictions.

We can glimpse Melville's thinking about the gendered tastes of his readers in a letter he wrote to Hawthorne's wife, Sophia, just as he was completing *Pierre*. Sophia Hawthorne had written to Melville praising *Moby-Dick* for its allegorical richness (she especially admired the "Spirit-Spout" chapter), and Melville was now promising something very different for his next literary offering. "My Dear Lady," Melville writes in a chivalric tone that seems to mock itself, "I shall not again send you a bowl of salt water. The next chalice I shall commend will be a rural bowl of milk" (*Correspondence* 219). That Melville could imagine *Pierre* in such benign terms strains the imagination, but what is even more suggestive here is the tone the author takes in speaking to his friend's wife. The Hawthornes had just moved from the Berkshire region to West Newton, Massachusetts, and thus Melville immediately follows his comments about *Pierre* with inquiries about the state of the Hawthorne home: "And now, how are you in West Newton? Are all domestic affairs regulated?" Coming at the end of an intense burst of work on his new novel, Melville's letter addresses Mrs. Hawthorne as the clear caretaker of the domestic realm and implies that his soon-to-be-completed book will be more appropriate for a wife and mother than his previous novels.

Melville being Melville, he could in practice never wholly commit to the literary conventions that antebellum audiences would demand from domestic fiction. Indeed, the narrative of *Pierre* offers a suggestive glimpse into the career-long battle that Melville waged with the literary marketplace. His "disordered," truth-seeking protagonist barges into Lucy's chamber at the beginning of book 11, confronts "her terrified and virgin aspect" (183), and boldly tells her that he has married another. Here and elsewhere, the "snow-white" conventions of sentimental storytelling are too fragile, too unreal to contain the power of masculine truthtelling. In a scene that reads very much like a sexual violation, Lucy is described as "no more pale, but white as any leper; the bed-clothes trembled to the concealed shudderings of all her limbs" (183). Like the countless sentimental heroines of nineteenth-century novels who are physically unable to confront the reality of their conditions, Lucy falls "over toward him in a swoon" (183).

When we read such moments of symbolic violence alongside what I have already suggested is Pierre's crisis of masculinity, the novel's inscrutability itself comes into focus as its author's refusal to privilege the terms of the literary marketplace. Like Pierre aggressively confronting his lover with a piece of news he seems to hope she will not be able to handle, Melville flouts convention in so many ways that his contemporary readers assumed he had simply gone mad. It is only, however, when Pierre embarks on his career as an author that the dimensions of Melville's own rebellion in the novel come into focus. For once we see the nineteenth-century world of publishing through the eyes of Pierre Glendinning, the novel looks like an act of hostility by an author who believed there was no place for masculine truthtelling in the antebellum literary marketplace.[5]

Because we first learn of Pierre's ambitions as an author well over halfway through the novel, some critics have argued that the chapters on the antebellum literary scene were hastily added by Melville as a kind of afterthought.[6] And yet as jarring as it is to first learn of Pierre's "poetic nature" at the start of book 17, the entirety of *Pierre* reflects that chapter's view of traditional novels as superficial products of a profit-minded marketplace. In a passage that calls to mind the "rural milk" of his letter to Sophia Hawthorne, Pierre finds his "social placidity . . . ruffled by polite entreaties" from "young ladies" who seek out his autograph for their albums (250). And later the young author comes to recognize what Melville's narrator calls the "penalty of celebrity" in a popular marketplace that treats writing as a form of fashion (255). So perfect is the analogy in *Pierre* that our hero receives a letter, written on "the daintiest scalloped-edged paper, and in the neatest possible, and fine needle-work hand," from "two young men, recently abandoning the ignoble pursuit of tailoring for the more honorable trade of the publisher" (246). Describing Pierre's literary output, these tailors-turned-editors write, "The fine cut, the judicious fit of your productions fill us with amazement. The fabric is excellent—the finest broadcloth of genius" (247). In a literary environment that sees books as material objects to be exploited for profit, Pierre's genius can only be articulated by railing against the effeminate superficiality of editors and publishers.

Of course, the more pressing problem facing Pierre is the one that hounded his creator throughout his own literary career. As our narrator describes this dilemma, "It may have already been inferred, that the pecuniary plans of Pierre touching his independent means of support in the city were based upon his presumed literary capabilities. For what else could he do? He knew no profession, no trade. Glad now perhaps might he have been, if Fate had made him a blacksmith, and not a gentleman, a Glendinning, and a genius" (260). Trapped in a very different world from his grandfather's, Pierre comes to recognize that reputation and security are dependent on a democratic marketplace in which the categories of "genius" and "gentleman" have no currency.[7] With no profession or trade to turn to, Pierre has no means for rescuing his trio of imperiled damsels. One might even say that it is not the unmarried young women of the unpropertied classes who are most vulnerable to the fluctuations of antebellum economic life—as popular novels such as Fanny Fern's *Ruth Hall* and Maria Susanna Cummins's *The Lamplighter* argued throughout the 1850s—but the brilliant young male genius who is too noble and too passionate to compromise artistic and intellectual integrity in the name of fashion or in the interest of profit.

If this were simply the story of a high-born American youth trapped in a modernizing and commercializing America, *Pierre* would hardly be seen as a "deranged" or "mad" book. Countless works of fiction published in the nineteenth century appear to riff on this theme—from Washington Irving's "Rip Van Winkle," to Hawthorne's "My Kinsman, Major Molineux," to Edgar Allen Poe's "The Fall of the House of Usher." Melville's novel goes off the tracks of the familiar narrative by turning this theme into an ontological crisis in which the very outlines of the self dissolve into ambiguity. Melville's complex mode of narration, in which the reader has access both to Pierre's consciousness and to an Ishmael-like narrator who keeps the characters' beliefs at arm's length, allows him to simultaneously descend into the melodrama of Pierre's righteous violence and retain the aloof posture of the nonbeliever, looking disdainfully down at a young romantic who mistakes fictions for truths.

Consider, for example, the way our protagonist sees the rejection of the Glendinning past as a foundation for a genuine kind of self-knowledge. When he throws "repeated packages of family letters, and all sorts of miscellaneous memorials" upon the fire in a climactic moment from book 12, our narrator briefly celebrates Pierre's break from the past as a moment of Emersonian self-reliance: "Henceforth, cast-out Pierre hath no paternity, and no past" (199). He stands, like the "American Adam" figure so prominent in nineteenth-century literature, with the world before him: "The future is one blank to all; therefore twice-disinherited Pierre stands untrammeledly his ever-present self!—free to do his own self-will and present fancy to whatever end!" (199) In the chapters that follow, however, the narrator increasingly counters Pierre's revolutionary rhetoric with a more agnostic vision of the self as a fiction invented and protected by the mind to cover up the void at the center of existence.[8]

When read in the context of the narrator's skepticism, Pierre's dramatic self-invention as the noble and heroic genius ultimately reaffirms his entrapment within the feminized world of both domesticity and domestic fiction. In the opening paragraphs of book 21, with Pierre and his crew "permanently lodged in three lofty adjoining chambers of the Apostles," the narrator employs the perspective familiar to readers of the traditional domestic novel. Writing in an extended dependent clause, Melville writes perhaps the longest sentence of a notoriously overwritten novel ("overlooking the hundred and one domestic details, of how their internal arrangements were finally put into steady working order; how poor Delly, now giving over the sharper pangs of her grief, found in the lighter occupations of a handmaid and familiar companion to Isabel..." [282]). After drifting over the mundane details of this scene of improvised urban homemaking, the narrator turns to the seemingly more profound business of Pierre writing "a book, which the world should hail with surprise and delight" (283). Soon the narrator informs us that "because Pierre began to see through to the first superficiality of the world, he fondly weens he has come to the unlayered substance"

(285). Coming on the heels of the chapter's opening rejection of the petty concerns of domestic fiction, Pierre's own writing appears as the expression of what Melville earlier called the "untrammeledly . . . ever-present self." Freed from the entanglements of family, history, and literary convention, Pierre sees himself at what Melville elsewhere called "the very axis of reality."[9]

And yet at this crucial moment in the novel, Melville's narrator highlights the delusional nature of Pierre's romantic self-importance. While the fictional author sitting at his desk imagines that he "has come to the unlayered substance," our narrator tells us that "as far as any geologist has yet gone down into the world, it is found to consist of nothing but surface stratified on surface. To its axis, the world being nothing but superinduced superficies" (285). The novel's nihilistic refusal to accept the very premise of a buried truth emerges here as an equally nihilistic view of the self as an emptiness: "By vast pains we mine into the pyramid; by horrible gropings we come to the central room; with joy we espy the sarcophagus; but we lift the lid—and no body is there!—appallingly vacant as vast is the soul of a man!" (285).

Melville's novel must have been exasperating for the contemporary reader because it refuses to buy into the very terms it employs. On the one hand, the book claims to tell a story of noble action, in which Lucy can write to Pierre: "Oh, give to me of thine own dear strength! I am but a poor weak girl, dear Pierre; one that didst once love thee but too fondly, and with earthly frailty. But now I shall be wafted far upward from that; shall soar up to thee, where thou sittest in thine own calm, sublime heaven of heroism" (310). On the other hand, his narrator takes great pains to portray Pierre's faith in a pure, untrammelled self beyond the contingencies of past and present as naive. Thus, when he feels his "dark, triumphant joy" in the novel's final chapters, we see him in much the way that Ishmael witnesses the vengeance of Ahab—not as righteous and heroic, but as righteous and heroic in the mind of the believer. And thus, when Pierre confronts Glendinning Stanly in the novel's climactic scene, he does so at "a large, open, triangular space, built round with the stateliest public erections;—the very proscenium of the town" (359). To see this urban space as a proscenium is to see the social world as a theater.[10] Any assertion of human agency—including Melville's own attempt at writing a novel—can only be seen as a performance that validates the world's false beliefs. Just like the "public erections" that invent a past to give the present a coherent meaning, Pierre's dramatic killing of Glen is noble only according to a logic that the narrator himself looks in on from the outside. Like Ishmael, who sees not just the doubloon but what his shipmates see when looking at the doubloon, the narrator of *Pierre* occupies a realm from the perspective of which the novel's own storytelling conventions are seen as meaningless.

It is of course tempting to link the agnostic narrative persona of *Pierre* to the agnosticism of Melville himself. Years after the public failure of *Pierre* (and only months before the disaster of *The Confidence-Man*, the last novel he would publish in his lifetime), Melville took a trip to Europe and the Holy Land, stopping on the way to visit his old friend Nathaniel Hawthorne in Liverpool. Here is how Hawthorne described this visit in his notebook:

> Melville, as he always does, began to reason of Providence and futurity, and of everything that lies beyond human ken, and informed me that he had "pretty much made up his mind to be annihilated"; but still he does not seem to rest in that anticipation; and, I think, will never rest until he gets hold of a definite belief. It is strange how he persists—and has persisted ever since I knew him, and probably long before—in wandering to and fro over these deserts, as dismal and monotonous as the sand hills amid which we were sitting. He can neither believe, nor be comfortable in his unbelief; and he is too honest and courageous not to try to do one or the other. (*English Notebooks* 432–33)

In this brief but suggestive portrait, one recognizes those very forces that shape the conflict between the hero and narrator of *Pierre*: courage (Pierre) and disbelief (narrator), truthtelling (Pierre) and uncertainty (narrator). At its most basic level, Melville's narrative follows the attempt of a noble-minded young man attempting to rescue three fallen women from an unjust society. But it does so in such a contradictory manner that the author can neither tell the tale, nor be comfortable in rejecting the terms by which it is told.

Ultimately, however, it is too limiting to read the ambiguities of *Pierre* solely as evidence of Melville's own spiritual or philosophical restlessness. As I suggested at the outset, this notoriously inscrutable novel has the most to teach us when we ask what its indeterminacies suggest about the antebellum era. For even if we read *Pierre* as the idiosyncratic creation of an author who could neither believe nor be comfortable with his unbelief, such a spiritual dilemma brings us back down into the circumstances of mid-nineteenth-century America. This, after all, was an age when traditional Christianity scrambled to reconcile its doctrines with the moral questions of slavery, urban poverty, and countless other issues of public debate. The influence of Unitarianism and Quakerism in the North reflected a generation of believers seeking out a balance between the pragmatic concerns of human society and the established doctrines of Protestant Christianity.

And so we should not be surprised to find in *Pierre* a fictional clergyman named Falsgrave, who argues that "by one universal maxim, to embrace all moral contingencies,—this is not only impossible, but the attempt, to me, seems foolish" (102). For Falsgrave, faith in the nineteenth century requires a doctrinal flexibility. For Pierre Glendinning, who listens disdainfully as his mother's minister recalibrates the heavens to accommodate mere "contingencies," truth is universal or it is not truth at all. Looming somewhere above this debate is the author of *Pierre*, who left his reader with no clear path out of such uncertainty: To seek out truth in solitude, like Plotinus Plinlimmon, is to be forever burdened with "the heavy unmalleable element of mere book-knowledge" (283); to conform to the terms of the world, like Glen Stanly, is to become a "dishonorable" imposter of one's own self; and to take up arms against an unjust society, like Pierre himself, is merely to strike through the masks of a pasteboard world.

If such a vision of humanity anticipates the naturalist and modernist fictions of the late nineteenth and early twentieth centuries, it is too simplistic to merely suggest that the author of *Pierre* was a visionary. As I have attempted to reveal, Melville's "botch" of a novel makes for such a challenging read precisely because it was of its time. In scrutinizing many of the era's most pervasive and complex ideals—individualism, democracy, domesticity, romanticism—the novel reflected back to antebellum readers the ambiguities of the age.

Notes

1. While most reviews of *Pierre* were hostile, there were a few significant exceptions. An excellent overview of the critical reception of Melville's novel can be found in Howard and Parker; see also Delbanco.

2. Samuel Otter explored the use of these various conventions in great detail in *Melville's Anatomies*. A highly influential study that explores the relevance of domesticity and the sentimental novel to *Pierre* is Gillian Brown's *Domestic Individualism*.

3. See, as examples, the readings of *The House of the Seven Gables* in Michael Gilmore's *American Romanticism and the Marketplace* and Walter Benn Michaels's *The Gold Standard and the Logic of Naturalism*.

4. For the most trenchant and influential study of the question of genealogy in *Pierre* and Melville's other works, see Michael Paul Rogin, *Subversive Genealogy*.

5. One study that sees Melville's writing (including *Pierre*) as a site of authorial hostility, and even violence, is Elizabeth Renker's *Strike Through the Mask*. In another reading focused on questions of the literary marketplace, John Evelev explores *Pierre* as a critique of the antebellum publishing industry.

6. Hershel Parker advanced such an argument in "Why Pierre Went Wrong," and then expanded on it with Brian Higgins in "The Flawed Grandeur of Melville's *Pierre*." Parker and Higgins are also the authors of the much more recent book-length study, *Reading Melville's* Pierre; or, The Ambiguities.

7. One might read the character of Charlie Millthorpe, whom Jonathan Crimmins describes as "Melville's representative of urban commercialism" (456), as a figure in whom the forces of inheritance and self-making are reconciled, however uneasily. Describing Millthorpe ("the son of a very respectable farmer—now

dead"), our narrator states, "The delicate profile of his face bespoke the loftiest aristocracy; his knobbed and bony hands resembled a beggar's" (*Pierre* 275).

8. Many critics of *Pierre* have noted that its narrator grows more and more cynical towards the novel's protagonist, creating an increasingly nihilistic tone throughout the course of the novel. Howard and Parker, for example, argue that at the start of Book IX, the narrator begins "to scold his hero in the manner of Carlyle" (372).

9. The phrase comes from Melville's essay "Hawthorne and His Mosses," in which he writes that "in this world of lies, Truth is forced to fly like a scared white doe in the woodlands; and only by cunning glimpses will she reveal herself, as in Shakespeare and other masters of the great Art of Telling the Truth,—even though it be covertly, and by snatches" (244).

10. The novel's depiction of New York City as a realm of theatricality and performance no doubt reflected an emerging urban culture. To learn more about how antebellum New York fostered this connection between urban identity and performativity, see David Scobey's "Anatomy of the Promenade." For a discussion of the meaning of the new American metropolis in *Pierre*, see Wyn Kelley, *Melville's City*.

Works Cited

Baym, Nina. "Melville's Quarrel with Fiction." *Publications of the Modern Language Association* 94.5 (1979): 909–23.

Brown, Gillian. *Domestic Individualism: Imagining Self in Nineteenth-Century America*. Berkeley: U of California P, 1990.

Crimmins, Jonathan. "Nested Inversions: Genre and the Bipartite Form of Herman Melville's *Pierre*." *Nineteenth-Century Literature* 64.4 (2010): 437–64.

Delbanco, Andrew. *Melville: His World and Work*. New York: Knopf, 2005.

Evelev, John. *Tolerable Entertainment: Herman Melville and Professionalism in Antebellum New York*. Amherst: U of Massachusetts P, 2006.

Gilmore, Michael. *American Romanticism and the Marketplace*. Chicago: U of Chicago P, 1988.

Hawthorne, Nathaniel. *The English Notebooks*. Ed. Randall Stewart. New York: Russell, 1962.

_____. *The Letters, 1853–1856*. Ed. Thomas Woodson, James A. Rubino, L. Neal Smith, and Norman Holmes Pearson. Columbus: Ohio State UP, 1987. Vol. 17 of *The Centenary Edition of the Works of Nathaniel Hawthorne*.

Howard, Leon, and Hershel Parker. "Historical Note." Appendix. *Pierre, or The Ambiguities*. By Herman Melville. Ed. Harrison Hayford, Parker, and G. Thomas Tanselle. Evanston and Chicago: Northwestern-Newberry, 1995. 365–410.

Kelley, Wyn. *Melville's City: Literary and Urban Form in Nineteenth-Century New York*. Cambridge: Cambridge UP, 1996.

Melville, Herman. *Correspondence*. Ed. Lynn Horth. Evanston and Chicago: North-western-Newberry, 1993. Vol. 14 of *The Writings of Herman Melville*.

_____. "Hawthorne and His Mosses." *The Piazza Tales and Other Prose Pieces 1839–1860*. Ed. Harrison Hayford et al. Evanston and Chicago: Northwestern-Newberry, 1971. Vol. 9 of *The Writings of Herman Melville*.

_____. *Pierre, or The Ambiguities*. Ed. Harrison Hayford et al. Evanston and Chicago: Northwestern-Newberry, 1995. Vol. 7 of *The Writings of Herman Melville*.

Michaels, Walter Benn. *The Gold Standard and the Logic of Naturalism: American Literature at the Turn of the Century*. Berkeley: U of California P, 1988.

Otter, Samuel. *Melville's Anatomies*. Berkeley: U of California P, 1999.

Parker, Hershel. "Why *Pierre* Went Wrong." *Studies in the Novel* 8.1 (1976): 7–23.

Parker, Hershel, and Brian Higgins. "The Flawed Grandeur of Melville's *Pierre*." *New Perspectives on Melville*. Ed. Faith Pullin. Edinburgh: Edinburgh UP, 1978.

_____. *Reading Melville's* Pierre; or, The Ambiguities. Baton Rouge: Louisiana State UP, 2006.

Renker, Elizabeth. *Strike Through the Mask*. Baltimore: Johns Hopkins UP, 1997.

Rogin, Michael Paul. *Subversive Genealogy: The Politics and Art of Herman Melville*. New York: Knopf, 1983.

Scobey, David. "Anatomy of the Promenade: The Politics of Bourgeois Sociability in Nineteenth-Century New York." *Social History* 17.2 (1992): 203–27.

Melville's Anatomy of American Belief:
*The Confidence-Man: His Masquerade*_____

Peter J. Balaam

> If any man among you seemeth to be wise in this world, let him become a
> fool, that he may be wise. For the wisdom of this world is foolishness with
> God. For it is written, He taketh the wise in their own craftiness.
>
> (St. Paul, I Corinthians 3:18–19)

"Odd fish!"

　"Poor fellow!"

　"Who can he be?" . . .

　"Bless my soul!"

　"Uncommon countenance" . . .

　"Humbug!" . . .

　"Piteous" . . .

　"Beware of him."

Passengers aboard a Mississippi steamboat murmur such judgments
in response to a stranger in a cream-colored suit in the early pages of
Melville's *The Confidence-Man: His Masquerade* (1857). The book
was Melville's tenth in eleven years and famously the last work of fiction he published in his lifetime. Ominous in their variety and their
speakers' conviction, these beliefs scroll down the page, enabling Melville to dramatize a curious degree of public alarm produced by a mild-
seeming stranger, and to hint that his second chapter will show "that
many men have many minds" (*Confidence-Man* 7).

　A similar list could perhaps be developed out of what has been said
of *The Confidence-Man* itself. The pity and alarm of the earliest reviews has been succeeded by the appreciation of twentieth-century
readers, hailed by Elizabeth S. Foster in her scholarly edition of 1954
as the readership for which *The Confidence-Man* had long waited.
Though now highly regarded by Melvilleans and critics of modernism,
we still have significant critical disagreement about "its author's inten-

tions, its title character's identity and motives, its structure, the relation of the parts to the whole—and even whether it amounts to a whole" (Branch, Parker, and Hayford 255). What we can say is the following: the *Fidèle*, a Mississippi River steamboat heading to New Orleans from St. Louis on April Fool's Day in the middle of the nineteenth century becomes the scene of several shifting conversations; passengers are let on and off at various stops along the way; these passengers are in some sense meant to stand as representative of humanity. Beyond these facts, as one of the book's most astute contemporary interpreters has observed, a "reader cannot be very sure about much of anything that happens in the book" (Quirk, "*Confidence*" 272). That claim may overstate the case, but not by much. It is my aim in what follows to provide new readers of the novel with the capacity to see that this very lack of certainty not only makes Melville's book difficult but makes it an important book worth wrestling with. Those who can acquire a taste for it will find an acute study of American character and a profound ethical meditation on the inescapability of faith in fiction and religion.

By any measure, *The Confidence-Man* is hard, probably the most difficult of all Melville's books, including *Pierre*. The sources of the difficulty are not mysterious, so we may describe them briefly. One source of the difficulty lies in its lack of a focal character and tractable plot; despite the title's apparent promise of a central character, readers expecting a novel will be disappointed. Melville actually presents a series of characters, men who enter from the wings, command our attention for a chapter, or two, or ten, and then (nearly always) pass out of the book for good. Moreover, while on stage, these characters and their conversation partners discuss matters of some urgency and familiarity to Melville's nineteenth-century readers, but, even if we pore over an edition's last footnote, the sheer number of such references will challenge all but well-read experts in the culture of the period.

Difficult in subject matter, then, the demands of these conversations are increased by the dramatized dialogue in which Melville conveys them, foregoing the conventional means of attribution that would enable readers to track with ease who is saying what. In a joking acknowledgment of this difficulty late in the book, one of Melville's confidence men observes with delight to another: "Our sentiments agree so, that were they written in a book, whose was whose, few but the nicest critics might determine" (158). Several chapters begin with dramatized voices in conversation, leaving the reader to sort out from internal clues who is on stage, what they are saying, and to whom. Answers to such uncertainties in this novel can take many, many pages. Finally, most readers will find Melville's narrator to compound their uncertainty with his guarded, obsessively qualifying style, from which the last buoyancies of Ishmael's wit and invention have been drained away. Consider the following attempt on the narrator's part to explain the sudden feelings of levity in a character we have known to be other than lighthearted:

> Meditation over kindness received *seemed* to have softened him something, too, *it may be*, beyond what *might*, *perhaps*, have been looked for from one whose unwonted self-respect in the hour of need, and in the act of being aided, *might* have appeared to some *not wholly unlike* pride out of place; and pride, in any place, is *seldom* very feeling. But *the truth, perhaps*, is, that those who are least touched with that vice . . . (24; emphasis added)

The barrage of subjunctives, double negatives, and clipped qualifiers seems almost a parody of Henry James's "major phase" still forty years away, except that it's funnier. The empty gesture of "the truth, perhaps" is both funny and a serious indicator of the direction Melville will take his "masquerade." With this style that parodies the shallow rhetorical posturing of a certain kind of literary man, it seems clear that our narrator, too, will be something of a confidence man.

Many have taken such uncertainties to indicate the sad end of Melville's career as a novelist. Others, including Foster and Hershel Parker, have conducted research into Melville's sources and religious ideas to try to decode in the book a fairly consistent allegory in the vein of John

Bunyan's *Pilgrim's Progress* or Edmund Spenser's *Faerie Queene*. As allegory, *The Confidence-Man* tells the story of the Devil come to America, taking various disguises and exposing the credulity and folly of the country's haplessly well-intentioned citizens. Melville's purpose, in the allegorical theory, is to voice his Calvinist disdain for the optimism of his era's liberal religious reforms and faith in human progress. But though hints of a theological allegory allure us, for a variety of reasons the book seems at best only teasingly allegorical, finally not susceptible to a single integrated interpretation. Others have seen the book as working far less consistently. Though their emphases differ, such critics agree that Melville's book makes brilliant literary use of the confidence man to anatomize the folly of pre–Civil War society, to theorize fiction-making as a kind of confidence game, to develop humor as an ethical and aesthetic alternative to scurrilous satire, or to cultivate in readers a fear-based wariness and then reveal the limitations of such defensiveness (see Bryant; Cook; Kuhlmann; Quirk).

Neither an allegory nor a novel exactly, the book is probably best seen as an "anatomy," or Menippean satire—a book-length prose work ridiculing attitudes as opposed to individuals. Melville knew the genre well from Robert Burton's *The Anatomy of Melancholy* and François Rabelais's *Gargantua and Pantagruel*. In many respects, Ishmael's "cetology chapters" in *Moby-Dick* constitute an "anatomy" of the whale and the whaling industry. Thinking of the book as an anatomy offers readers a means to bring its most puzzling features into focus. Literary theorist Northrop Frye observed that unlike highly narrative genres such as the romance, the anatomy is unconcerned with "the exploits of heroes, but relies on the free play of intellectual fancy and the kind of humorous observation that produces caricature." The anatomy presents readers "with a vision of the world in terms of a single intellectual pattern"—here, the confidence man—the structure of which "makes for violent dislocations in the customary logic of narrative" (Frye 309–10; qtd. in Quirk, *Melville's* 136).

Following Frye, we may and indeed must dispense with the genre expectations of novel reading and work to discern instead the "single intellectual pattern" within the world of the anatomy. So attuned, readers may expect and even welcome the "violent dislocations" that will occur in the logic of the narrative. Melville drew the intellectual pattern for his book from the confidence man; so let us turn toward this interesting figure in American cultural history.

Cultural and Historical Backgrounds

The bewildering pace of social change in the United States between 1790 and 1850 rendered it less a place than a process. As historian Carroll Smith-Rosenberg describes it:

> For half a century three massive revolutions—the commercial, transportation, and industrial—swept through American society. As the basic modes of economic production and institutional organization changed, so did the experience of time and space, the functions, structure and internal dynamics of the family, gender, and generational relations. Earlier visions of God, the apt mirrors of earlier experience, shattered. By the 1840s the world that colonial Americans had carefully crafted lay in fragments. Yet the form the new order would take was not yet clear. Conflicting economic, social, and ideological systems battled for hegemony. The obsolete coexisted with the novel. So much was new that all appeared uncertain. (79)

Melville wrote *The Confidence-Man* in this world of uncertainty, capitalizing on the deceptiveness and hungry amorality of his central figure. As patriarchally organized rural economies and social structures in the East gave way during Melville's lifetime to the more volatile and anonymous energies of the market, myriad young people left eastern villages and family farms to strike out for burgeoning cities and western regions. In doing so, they feared the shifty, opportunistic, and predatory confidence man that lay in wait for them, the mirror image of their own industriousness and ingenuity. In a fluid social world without fixed markers of class or identity, problems reading the social landscape were acute. Making matters more difficult, as William Lenz observes, were the clash of contradictory ideologies of autonomy and openness: on one side, Americans typically "want to trust everyone, to believe in the democratic promise that all people are equally good and equally engaged in cooperative and progressive personal and communal development"; on the other, Americans also typically "suspect that often within the hearts of strangers (and . . . close associates) lurks the very devil himself, wanting to spring upon [them] and rob [them] of [their] goods and good faith" (Lenz, "Confidence Men" 278).

New York City newspapers coined the term "confidence man" in 1849, almost a decade before Melville's book, in connection with the case of one William Thompson, who was arrested for the theft of several strangers' gold watches. Thompson became known as "the Confidence Man" through the scam he perpetrated in broad daylight on the streets of the city. Dressed in a genteel suit, Thompson would appear on a crowded thoroughfare, choose his victim from among the other well-dressed gentlemen in the street, hail and draw him into conversation, presuming familiarity with him. After some time, he would suddenly ask whether the other had enough confidence in him to lend him his watch for the day. By this ruse, several New Yorkers were parted with valuable watches that they had themselves placed into Thompson's hands. The so-called Confidence Man was eventually recognized by one of his victims and arrested, but not before his case became a sensation in the press (Halttunen 6; Lenz, *Fast Talk* 280).

To betray another's confidence in the mid-nineteenth-century United States would have been a powerful form of violation, especially in an ostensibly Christian and democratic order where "all men are created equal." But perhaps for his sheer effrontery and opportunism, the confidence man had an allure as well. He was hailed by one of Melville's reviewers as "one of the indigenous characters" of American city life, his deeds "form[ing] one of the staples of villainy and an element in the romance of roguery" (qtd. in Halttunen 7). Though the term was new, it quickly stuck, offering a standard label for a figure already long associated with the moral threats of America's constantly changing cities. The pervasive social instability of the American society Melville knew offered fine opportunities for confidence men of all stripes, and there were those who regarded this society with an eye so jaundiced they might have echoed Ishmael's "Who ain't a slave?" with the question, "Who ain't a confidence man?" Within four days of Thomson's arrest in New York, a reporter at the *Herald* had developed what Johannes Bergmann has called some of the "literary possibilities" of the situation, likening the low-grade genius of Thomson's chicanery to what successful Wall Street financiers did every day when they "pocketed millions" but ironically remained "exemplars of honesty," "cherished" by the communities they plundered (Bergmann 308).

Melville set his satirical investigation of American belief in the western regions that fueled the wealth and the growth of cities along the Eastern Seaboard. Throughout Melville's life, these were areas synonymous with the ideal of individual opportunity and collective visions of national destiny, along with their attendant anxieties. Such zones were associated with both boundless opportunity and lawlessness, where, as Lenz observers, new capacities, new identities, and new rules organized social forces but loosely (*Fast Talk* 1–2). Despite the sensation around William Thompson's arrest in New York, it was the area southwest of the Alleghenies that had seen the birth and growth of the literary progenitors of Melville's confidence man: August B. Longstreet's Yellow Blossom, Joseph Baldwin's Ovid Bolus, George Washington Harris's Sut Lovingood, and Johnson Jones Hooper's Simon Suggs (Lenz, "Confidence Men" 279).

How *The Confidence-Man* Works

Despite its flaws and the many unfruitful-seeming challenges it throws in the path of even the most willing readers, *The Confidence-Man* is neither the failure many readers have considered it nor the impenetrable chore it will initially seem to some. That it works—coherently, artfully—can be demonstrated. It works, first, in the dazzling ambiguities it renders in its depiction of nineteenth-century society and in the play of multiple possibilities. It works as well in the moral vision of Melville's satire, a comedy both light-hearted and cutting. Finally, it works in the unexpected transformation of the figure of the confidence man it enacts, a process by which the book bends at its poles to connect thematically the guileless man in cream colors to the book's arch deceiver, the Cosmopolitan.

The first of these achievements, the ambiguity that arises from the book's multiplication of possibilities, begins with the book itself. The opening two chapters serve as a kind of overture for the rest, Melville presenting there a world of pomp and vacuity, energy and instability, and confidently laying out the foundational themes and motifs on which he will build. The *Fidèle* is a bee-hive of activity, the chaotic variety of its "promenades, domed saloons, long galleries, sunny balconies, confidential passages, bridal chambers, state-rooms, and out-of-the-way retreats" bursting with the murmuring restlessness of mixing human types (8). The keynotes of this murmur are juxtaposition and desire. Peace-loving Quakers rub shoulders with soldiers; "fine ladies" with "squaws"; Mormons with "Papists"; "jesters" with "mourners"— and desire renders everyone in the throng some kind of human hunter; moreover, the pursuers are themselves pursued, as the "farm-hunters and fame-hunters; heiress-hunters, gold-hunters, buffalo-hunters, bee-hunters, happiness-hunters, [and] truth-hunters" are themselves the objects of "keener hunters after all these" (9).

Aboard the *Fidèle* crowded with strangers, pickpocket "chevaliers," and peddlers hawking penny-press lives of notorious outlaws, Melville situates the man in cream colors. For obvious reasons, readers have long held to a settled interpretation of this alluring stranger, but in fact Melville wastes no time in establishing through him his book's investment in multiple possibilities. The stranger's "fair," "downy," "flaxen," "white," "fur[red]," and "fleecy" qualities obviously associate him with lamb-like innocence. And in the message of love he scrawls on his slate and the rough treatment he receives in return from the crowd, he seems symbolically a martyr of true Christian vulnerability among cunning "foxes" (4, 5). But he may be too good to be true. It was a common dodge of nineteenth-century confidence men— witness the ruse of Twain's "duke" playing Peter Wilks's brother in *Adventures of Huckleberry Finn*—to pass themselves off as deaf and dumb. Moreover, within the space of these few pages Melville places the stranger among no fewer than three placards, each announcing a competing interpretive possibility. Standing near a "Wanted!" sign that announces a reward for the arrest of a mysterious imposter from the East, the man in cream colors publishes phrases from Paul's first letter to the Corinthians for the crowd—"Charity thinketh no evil" (4).

As such clues proliferate but never align to support any definitive judgment, readers find themselves stepping into Melville's interpretive trap. Does this odd man bear his message of Christian charity sincerely, as explanation of himself, as guide and guardian of others' innocence? Or does his plea to love instead of thinking evil express an imposter's self-interested wish to escape suspicion? While readers naturally crave an answer to this unfolding interpretive problem, the man in cream colors exits the book as swiftly as he entered, falling into exhausted sleep in a quiet spot on the forecastle deck. The crowd's rejection of him as a "simpleton" underscores his thematic similarity to Jesus, while, even in his absence from the stage, his mute appeals for the way of charity gain new interest in contrast with another placard, the barber's communication: "No Trust" (5). Literally announcing that the barber refuses to work except for ready payment, in the context of the stranger's appeal to "charity"—that is, generosity or philanthropic assistance— this sign registers an essentially hostile rejection of every man aboard the *Fidèle*. *The Confidence-Man* works in the case of the ambiguities it enacts because, though we get very few answers to our questions about the identity and meaning of these characters, through these uncertainties Melville builds the clear point that the paradoxical ethic of love at the core of Paul's biblical thought unsettles and in part enrages the crowd, representatives of their ostensibly Christian civilization, while the barber's open condemnation of humanity for lack of honesty provokes in them no "derision or surprise, much less indignation" (5). To the crowd, the lamb-like prophet seems dangerous or laughable, and when he cannot explain himself, they quickly reject him; meanwhile, the barber seems to them reasonable, trustworthy, and possibly, in his self-possession, even virtuous. For such wary self-interest and worldly wisdom as the barber's, no explanation is required.

The book also works in the coherence of Melville's comedy and the moral vision behind it. For all his ambition to investigate the moral range between vulnerability and defensiveness and to connect that investigation to religious paradoxes and his own fiction-making art, Melville works his subject—the moral problem of wanting to trust but fearing to be fleeced—for its essential comedy. And *The Confidence-Man* is, spottily, a very funny book. The progression of rogues presented in the book's first half (chapters 3 through 22) fully illustrates the idea of confidence man as knave: a crafty fellow devoted to parting people, many of them fools, from their money. Aboard the *Fidèle* we meet Black Guinea, a pathetic cripple who performs his own humiliation for the coins passersby toss into his open mouth (chapter 3); the sanctimonious Mr. Ringman, with a weed in his hat indicating mourning and a manner oozing manipulative sincerity (chapters 4–5); the man in gray, philanthropist and agent for the Seminole Widow and Orphan Asylum (chapters 6–8); Mr. Truman, in traveling cap with tassels, President of the Black Rapids Coal Company and developer for the New Jerusalem, a newly built community awaiting settlers in northern Minnesota (chapters 9–15); a scurrilous herb doctor, skeptical of modern medical science and peddler of the all-natural, strictly herbal Omni-Balsamic Reinvigorator (chapters 16–21); and a nameless representative of an "intelligence office" (the equivalent of an employment agency) significantly distinguished as the Philosophical Intelligence Office (chapter 22).

Never sharing the fictional stage, these confidence men seem the different guises of a single, shape-shifting entity whose basic method is to ape the culture's optimism, tempting his listeners to "embrace a cherished hope" that will turn out to be "a spike aimed at his breast" (Kuhlmann 109). The topics of their discussions with potential victims range through an array of mid-nineteenth-century cultural questions— to what degree character can be inferred from physical appearance, whether "Indian-hating" constitutes or contradicts virtue, whether materially aiding a friend in need sullies friendship. While few of these topics are funny in themselves, Melville builds the comedy out of the lengths to which the confidence man will go to provide verisimilitude sufficient to persuade his conversation partner to show confidence, act upon on his convictions, and open his wallet. Melville's investigation of the individual's capacity, in a world of strangers, to engage openly in a relation of candor and trust with another forces a trial of American selfhood that juxtaposes social ideals calling for self-possession with others dictating openness and generosity. As William Lenz observes, "Americans want to be trusting, but do not want to be gulled" ("Confidence Men" 278).

Accordingly, Melville draws his comedy out of carefully represented character. The righteousness of a muscular Methodist minister with charity on his lips becomes laughable when he finds himself challenged by a one-legged curmudgeon. Goaded by a few rounds of their exchange, the minister soon pronounces his opponent a "reprobate," threatens to "teach [him] charity on the spot," and shakes the man by his collar above the deck. As pleased onlookers praise the righteous "church militant," the Methodist regains composure by raising his hands to the crowd: "Oh, friends," he hails them, "oh, beloved, how are we admonished by the melancholy spectacle of this raver" (16). The transition into homily is so smooth, it reveals that the minister is himself half confidence man. The sheer chutzpah of the confidence men in their humbuggery is often very funny, as when the man with the weed says insinuatingly to Mr. Roberts, "Just now, an unpleasant distrust, however vague, was yours." Sadly spelling out the moral lesson of Mr. Roberts's failing—"Ah, shallow as it is, how subtle a thing is suspicion"—he leaves the hapless merchant lighter of both wallet and self-respect (23). Searching out his whole "intellectual pattern," Melville allows us to see the confidence man as pathetic as well, using humor to engender both sympathy and admiration. The old herb doctor, looking like a medieval alchemist in his brown overcoat, cries his wares on deck before a tough crowd that sees right through him. Since he doesn't have a chance with them, his persistence is not only funny but admirable, and all the more so when he invents out of thin air the following pitch, an unforgettable concoction of equal parts Jonathan Edwards and Professor Harold Hill:

"Ladies and gentlemen, might I, by your kind leave, venture upon one other small supposition? It is this . . . that the Samaritan Pain Dissuader is the one only balm for that to which each living creature—who knows?—may be a draughted victim, present or prospective. In short:—Oh, Happinesss on my right hand, and oh, Security on my left, can ye wisely adore a Providence, and not think it wisdom to provide? Provide!" (Uplifting the bottle.) (85)

Melville's comedy frequently turns on differences of class and gentility between characters who inhabit different geographical and philosophical worlds. This is true of the rich encounter between Pitch the Missouri misanthropist and Frank Goodman—notable name!—the lover of mankind who, in the guise of a "Cosmopolitan" is the confidence man's final avatar. Pitch is a western tough guy who affects a virtuous sobriety by subjecting everything to his literalistic scrutiny and skepticism. He believes in the essential rascality of people and cannot be brought to trust in anything that grows or changes. If in holding by the Medes and Persians (115), he is really just indulging a style like any other, he is unaware of it. But he has met his match in the Cosmopolitan, one who from his outlandish dress to his enthusiastic appetite

for all things human, exudes the confident spirit of the European Enlightenment and the lives of Franklin, Voltaire, and Hume: catholic instead of local, inquisitive and empirical instead of traditional, fraternal
rather than austere. The Cosmopolitan's dress and speech and attitudes
reveal a delight in the protean flexibility that makes Pitch's blood boil:
"Life is a pic-nic *en costume*," he tells Pitch: "One must take a part, assume a character, stand ready in a sensible way to play the fool" (133).
Just before the two meet, Pitch spends chapter 23 berating himself for
having allowed the man from the Philosophical Intelligence Office to
persuade him, when he was set against it, to contract to hire another
boy to work on his farm. Astonished at his own gullibility, Pitch re-
visits his fall as a military skirmish in which the PIO man assaulted
his self-fortress "on the south-facing, genial side, where Suspicion, the
warder, parleyed." Nothing in *The Confidence-Man* is more indicative
of Melville's sense of human folly in action, or funnier, than the plume
of tobacco smoke and voice from behind that interrupt Pitch's analogy-
rife review of how the PIO man used analogical rhetoric in deceiving
him: "A penny for your thoughts, my fine fellow" (130).

Finally, *The Confidence-Man* works in its unexpected transformation of the confidence man figure through the character of the Cosmopolitan, a process by which the book moves from social satire to
profound literary, religious, and philosophical possibility. Melville's
best comic lines are also thematically resonant. A bit of pious self-congratulation from Mr. Turner, president of the Black Rapids Coal Company—"I have my soft side, thank God!" (47)—is funny for seeming
to announce a weakness, while it is undoubtedly intended to lead the
sophomore to indulge his own least-defended impulses. Though it occurs innocuously and early on, this line heralds a shift in the book's
second half. According to Tom Quirk, Melville's shifting sense of his
own subject as he composed *The Confidence-Man* led him to transform
the confidence man "from a simple knave to a sort of knight-errant of
confidence." From a book that had begun in "bitter and narrow satire
and antireligious feelings," Quirk observes, this change brought for-

ward the "high literary ambition and deeply felt human sympathy" that we associate with Melville at his most far-seeing and capacious (*Melville's* 4–5). Having warned readers in the book's first half to fear and judge the confidence man, Melville turns the tables in the book's second half, revealing the humanity of his "soft side," his idealistic and undefended perspective.

To understand this reading of the book, we must grasp the moral spaciousness that Melville drew from the topsy-turvy ideals expressed in Paul's letter to the Corinthians. Though one cannot say so without running the risk of being taken in, when Mr. Turner expresses gratitude for his "soft side," and the Cosmopolitan suggests that a callous defendedness may be more damaging than vulnerability, they express a spirit akin to St. Paul's sense of the paradoxical triumph of folly over worldly wisdom: "Let no man deceive himself. If any man among you seemeth to be wise in this world, let him become a fool that he may be wise. For the wisdom of this world is foolishness with God. For it is written, He taketh the wise in their own craftiness" (I Corinthians 3:18–9). Foregoing law and tradition as forms of worldly wisdom in order to embrace the unmasterable paradoxes of love, St. Paul gains the benefits of folly: detachment, play, and a path beyond ego and understanding. To the Cosmopolitan, a man like Pitch, in laboring to make himself unassailable, has opted for a premature and negative certainty that in worldly quarters counts as wisdom and strength. Deceived by his own wariness, which he takes as proof of his virtue, Pitch knows nothing of the ethical path of folly that Paul marks out for the Christian. "See how distrust has duped you!" the Cosmopolitan cries to the wary Missouri skeptic: "For God's sake, get you confidence!" (138). Taking the pilgrim's stance of "charity" instead of judgment may be just the Cosmopolitan's latest ruse, but it inescapably expresses Paul's commitment to the paradox of folly, a spirit that replaces the deceptive false certainty of worldly "wisdom" with a mental and affective spaciousness—a tolerant but attentive not-knowing.

The challenge of reading the second half of the book lies in noting how the Cosmopolitan's "skeptical but humane state of mind" (Quirk, *Melville's* 4), especially an unwillingness to judge, emerges from his increasingly pained and alarmed reactions to others' baseless certainty. The Cosmopolitan's "soft side" emerges in a transformation at the end of his conversation with Pitch from which he walks with "ruefully altered mien" and a step "less lightsome" than when he approached (138). In scenes with the confidence man Charlie Noble (chapters 25 through 35), the Cosmopolitan resists the former's insinuations about Pitch's character by urging a charitable agnosticism. Dissociating "charity" from "mercy," he redefines it more simply as a just allowance for "the insensible leeway of human fallibility" (156). Though it stems from the paradoxes of Pauline charity, the Cosmopolitan's ethic of tolerance is grounded not in religious doctrine but in humane acceptance and acknowledgment of the mysteries of human motivations. Confronting the cold certainties of Egbert's whitewashing self-interest behind lofty principle, the Cosmopolitan cries, "Enough," and seems actually transformed from confidence man to human benefactor, offering Egbert a shilling (223). The Cosmopolitan's transformation alters the book's conception of the confidence man from a knave who would rob fools of their money to a beneficent trickster who would rob wise fools of their supposed wisdom, calling them into new and strange realities unimagined from behind their fearful defenses.

"Something Further": Themes and Literary Implications

While Melville should not be taken to espouse Paul's hyperboles on love and folly in a conventional religious way, it is apparent that he saw enormous possibility in their inherent paradoxes. Melville's satire emerges nowhere more palpably than in the misplaced certainty that grounds judgment of, and lack of confidence in, other people. A gossiping man aboard the *Fidèle* seems to waive all uncertainty regarding the herb doctor's sincerity as a first step to what he calls knowledge, encouraging others to "suspect first and know next." As he explains it: "True knowledge comes but by suspicion or revelation. That's my maxim" (92). While today such views would get this man elected to the House of Representatives in a trice, Melville's rueful point is that such certainty, passing itself off as reason, has been the basis for the whole range of human cruelties and calamities of church history from the crusades to the Spanish Inquisition. Melville dedicated *The Confidence-Man* to the "victims of *Auto-da-fè*," the "acts of faith" in which heretics and apostates were executed for their beliefs.

The novelist, too, must be guided by a lack of certainty in the creation of his art. Interrupting the action of *The Confidence-Man* three times—in chapters 14, 33, and 44—Melville sheds light on the fiction-writer's craft in attitudes resonant with the humility of Pauline folly and the Cosmopolitan's withholding of judgment. In brief, these essays argue that the fiction writer who would speak the truth must forego the shortcuts of the worldly wisdom that is readerly desire and deploy the folly that will enable the truth to come out. In chapter 14, the narrator defends himself against anticipated objections to inconsistency in his representation of characters. Since an actual person in possession of a consistent character is a "rare bird," novels that provide an impression of consistent character are fraudulent and possibly blasphemous (69). With the generous uncertainty that the Cosmopolitan wields in his defense of Pitch, the narrator observes that, like the divine character, the mysteries of human character are "past finding out" (70).

If the readerly novel that presents consistent characters is a confidence game, by rights fiction has a truth-telling capacity that makes it expressively analogous to religion. Melville had praised the power of Hawthorne's work in such terms, likening it to Shakespeare's indirect and "occasional flashings forth of the intuitive Truth" (Melville, "Hawthorne" 522). Melville conceived of the power of literary art as something akin to madness by which, in the raptures of displacement, a writer occasionally speaks "or sometimes insinuates the things, which we feel to be so terrifically true, that it were all but madness for any good man, in his own proper character, to utter, or even hint of them" (522). Anticipating in chapter 33 the complaints of typical nineteenth-century readers who crave realism from fiction, Melville's narrator counsels the truth telling that comes from displacement. Remarkably, for a book often regarded as utterly antireligious, Melville's sense is that, like religion, proper fiction must walk an uncertain line between the known and the created: "It is with fiction as religion," his narrator observes, "It should present another world, and yet one to which we feel the tie" (*Confidence-Man* 183).

This palpable tie between real and fictional worlds is the basis for Melville's curiously astringent stance in chapter 44 against the cult of the "original" character. His objection to this critical and readerly cliché is evidently just that such a character necessarily cuts the tie between reality and fiction that gives the latter its uncertainty and its capacity to speak the truth. These brief essays suggest that for Melville, fiction, like religion, is a two-way street, a negotiable uncertainty. In trafficking in readerly belief as the novelist does, he too is but a confidence man, though at his best he is a trickster-benefactor—one who, with playful rather than criminal intent, aims to rob idle readers of their convictions.

The Confidence-Man ends in a much-studied final scene that, amid ominous associations to darkness and midnight, revelation, apocalypse, and the lamp extinguished, has seemed to many readers to "put out the light" of belief in North America. Perhaps; but such a reading must overlook the Cosmopolitan's conversion to a temporary role as the old man's caretaker and his volunteering of his "indifferent eyes" to guide them down the hall to bed (251). The "indifference" of his vision is not just reasonably sharp vision but also an uncommitted openness altogether typical of the Cosmopolitan's skepticism and humanity. Like his confidence man, Melville's book is not at all free of quackery—in fact, both are evidently tissues of lies, bits of theatrical trumpery. Though not without a strong dose of Omni-Balsamic nonsense, the book succeeds in being some kind of Reinvigorator that reminds us that being a self, reading a novel, and knowing anything at all are matters that must engage us in the work of belief. In the fruitful latitude of its embrace of folly and uncertainty, *The Confidence-Man* leads us into the possibilities of a night without guarantees, in which, whatever language we choose, we can no longer rely on the solidities and certainties of previous eras. Given Melville's sense of belief as ubiquitous, perennial, inescapable, how could it be otherwise than that "something further may follow of this Masquerade" (251)?

Works Cited

Bergmann, Johannes Dietrich. "The Original Confidence Man." 1969. *The Confidence-Man: His Masquerade*. By Herman Melville. Ed. Harrison Hayford and Mark Niemeyer. New York: Norton, 2002. 304–12.

Branch, Watson, Hershel Parker, and Harrison Hayford. "Historical Note." Appendix. *The Confidence-Man: His Masquerade*. By Herman Melville. Ed. Harrison Hayford, Parker, and G. Thomas Tanselle. Evanston and Chicago: Northwestern-Newberry, 1984. 255–358.

Bryant, John. *Melville and Repose: The Rhetoric of Humor in the American Renaissance*. New York: Oxford UP, 1993.

Cook, Jonathan A. *Satirical Apocalypse: An Anatomy of Melville's* The Confidence-Man. Westport: Greenwood, 1996.

Foster, Elizabeth S. Introduction. *The Confidence-Man: His Masquerade*. By Herman Melville. New York: Hendricks House, 1954. xiii–xcv.

Frye, Northrop. *Anatomy of Criticism: Four Essays*. Princeton: Princeton UP, 1957.

Halttunen, Karen. *Confidence Men and Painted Women: A Study of Middle-Class Culture in America, 1830–1870*. New Haven: Yale UP, 1982.

Kuhlmann, Susan. *Knave, Fool, Genius: The Confidence Man as He Appears in Nineteenth-Century American Fiction*. Chapel Hill: U of North Carolina P, 1973.

Lenz, William. "Confidence Men" *American History through Literature, 1820–1870*. Ed. Janet Gabler-Hover and Robert Sattelmeyer. 3 vols. Detroit: Thomson, 2006. 277–81.

_____. *Fast Talk and Flush Times: The Confidence Man as a Literary Convention*. Columbus: U of Missouri P, 1985.

Melville, Herman. *The Confidence-Man: His Masquerade*. Ed. Harrison Hayford, Hershel Parker, and G. Thomas Tanselle. Evanston and Chicago: Northwestern-Newberry, 1984. Vol. 10 of *The Writings of Herman Melville*.

_____. "Hawthorne and His Mosses." 1850. *Moby-Dick*. Ed. Hershel Parker and Harrison Hayford. 2nd ed. New York: Norton, 2002. 517–32.

Quirk, Tom. *"The Confidence-Man." American History through Literature, 1820–1870.* Ed. Janet Gabler-Hover and Robert Sattelmeyer. 3 vols. Detroit: Thomson, 2006. 272–77.

_____. *Melville's Confidence Man: From Knave to Knight.* Columbia: U of Missouri P, 1982.

Smith-Rosenberg, Carroll. *Disorderly Conduct: Visions of Gender in Victorian America.* New York: Oxford UP, 1985.

Metrical Melville: The Career of an Obscure Poet

Brian Yothers

The poet Herman Melville's most forbidding rival has always been Herman Melville—in his capacity as author of *Moby-Dick*, "Bartleby, the Scrivener," and *Billy Budd*. Melville as the writer of three of the most revered pieces of prose in world literature naturally tends to overshadow the poet whose work, while eminently quotable, was neither popular during his lifetime nor a full beneficiary of the twentieth-century revival of interest in Melville that made *Moby-Dick* the most visible novel in all of American literature and placed "Bartleby, the Scrivener" and *Billy Budd* at the heart of the American canon as well. Unlike Melville's early fiction, meanwhile, the poetry has never lent itself easily to providing a context for his most famous prose works. To add insult to injury, one of the more common arguments for neglecting Melville's poetry is that his prose is simply much more poetic and lyrical than this verse. On the other hand, it is impossible to deny that we would be unlikely at this point to know of Melville's poetry at all if not for the triumphant apotheosis of his prose over the course of the early twentieth century.

Despite the ambiguous status of Melville's poetry in relation to the rest of his career, Melville has by this time assumed a fairly prominent place in the study of nineteenth-century American poetry. William Spengemann has published a tripartite study of American poetry in the nineteenth-century that groups Melville with Walt Whitman and Emily Dickinson as one of the three most influential and innovative American poets before the twentieth century. Unlike many of his predecessors in considering Melville's poetry, Spengemann makes Melville's use of poetic forms in his prose not a demonstration of why Melville was a better poet as a writer of prose than as a writer of verse, but as a sign that Melville was a poet from the start. The shift of emphasis is important: Melville's poetry can in this way be seen as central rather than peripheral to the arc of his career. Spengemann's choice to include Melville as the third member of his American poetic trinity had a venerable precedent: Robert Penn Warren, one of America's most prominent modernist poet-critics had likewise placed Melville with Whitman and Dickinson in the 1940s. Warren, Hennig Cohen, Walter Bezanson, William Shurr, and William Bysshe Stein all wrote extensively on Melville's poetry during the 1960s, and in recent years Douglas Robillard, Dennis Berthold, Elizabeth Renker, Hsuan Hsu, Cody Marrs, Lawrence Buell, Helen Vendler, Rosanna Warren, and Samuel Otter have all illuminated Melville's poetry in substantial studies and essays. If Melville the poet remains obscure relative to his fiction-writing double, it is nonetheless clear that he constitutes a significant portion of the story of nineteenth-century American verse.

Melville's career as a poet writing in verse seems to have begun as soon as his career as a novelist ended. Melville's last full-length novel, *The Confidence-Man*, was published in 1857, and by 1860, as Hershel Parker has established, Melville was ready to publish his first collection of poems, a collection which we now know (again as the result of Parker's 2008 study *Melville: The Making of the Poet*) to have been enabled by extensive reading in poetry and poetic theory throughout the 1850s. This collection ultimately remained unpublished, but the fact that it existed shows how decisively and determinedly Melville moved from prose to verse. Much of this earlier work was ultimately published in *Timoleon, Etc.*, the last collection of poetry that Melville published during his lifetime.

Melville's immersion in poetry and poetics bore fruit in his first published book of poetry, *Battle-Pieces and Aspects of the War* (1866), which was rendered distinctive both by his change of genre to poetry and by the massive changes occasioned in American life by the Civil War. Like his greatest contemporaries, Whitman and Dickinson, Melville allowed the changes that took place in the United States during the Civil War to shape his art profoundly. *Battle-Pieces* is distinguished by Melville's ability to create a sufficiently capacious poetic vehicle to embrace widely divergent reactions to the war, while combining them all under a broadly Unionist understanding of America. As Stanton Garner has pointed out, Melville combined in both his person and his poetry pacifistic objections to the Civil War and genuine belief in the Union cause (Garner 454–55).

Formally, *Battle-Pieces* showed Melville experimenting with a wide array of poetic subgenres. In some of his most frequently quoted poems, his model is elegiac: for example, in "Shiloh" we read about the carnage after one of the Civil War's bloodiest battles, and in "The Portent," we read about the execution of the antislavery radical John Brown. Melville also experimented with new forms: In "Donelson," Melville pieced together newspaper accounts and speeches by both staunchly pro-Union characters and Copperheads, who sympathized with the South. Frequently and insistently, Melville tapped into mythic imagery in his discussion of the Civil War. In "Gettysburg," for example, he identified the Confederate forces invading Pennsylvania with the Philistine god Dagon, who was worshipped by the Israelites' most formidable rivals in the Hebrew scriptures. Indeed, the tension between mythic understandings of warfare and the technology of killing in the modern nineteenth century is crucial to the shape of *Battle-Pieces*. This tension is most famously embodied in the frequently anthologized poem "A Utilitarian View of the Monitor's Fight," which acknowledges and laments the mechanization of warfare with the concluding lines:

> War shall yet be, and to the end;
> But war-paint shows the streaks of weather;
> War yet shall be, but warriors
> Are now but operatives; War's made
> Less grand than Peace,
> And singe runs through lace and feather. (lines 25–30)

At this moment, the poem, like the whole collection, dwells upon the way in which the brute facts of the war defied all attempts to make it part of a mythology while simultaneously acknowledging the psychological power of myth.

Because *Battle-Pieces* is so frequently excerpted and too rarely read as a whole, it is easy to lose sight of the truly panoramic view of the Civil War that we get from this collection. Over the course of the poems in *Battle-Pieces*, Melville moves from large historical moments to very personalized portraits of figures who can stand in for major social changes, most strikingly John Brown in "The Portent" and an aging woman who has been freed from slavery in "Formerly a Slave." *Battle-Pieces*, then, is not merely a substantial collection of occasional verse, but a cohesive if diverse whole. The collection communicates both ambivalence about the morality of war itself and confidence in the justice of the union cause and the resulting emancipation of the former slaves. It achieves this sense of diversity in unity through the varieties of formal qualities and allusions in poems that are ultimately tied together by a thematic focus on the concept of Union. In this way, the form of *Battle-Pieces* corresponds to the necessary reconstruction of the nation itself.

Battle-Pieces is Melville's most accessible book of poetry in terms of its historical themes, but Melville's largest and most idiosyncratic poetic achievement is one of the longest and strangest poems in American literature. *Clarel: A Poem and Pilgrimage in the Holy Land* (1876) is an 18,000-line verse travelogue that captures the anguish of the faith-doubt crisis of the nineteenth-century and the crisis of American democracy in the Gilded Age in an account of a pilgrimage to Jerusalem and its environs. *Clarel* represented the culmination of nearly two decades of work and reflection. Melville had visited Palestine in 1856, and he had recorded a series of idiosyncratic observations in his travel journal from the voyage that he later used in writing *Clarel*.

The most striking formal characteristic of *Clarel*, noted by interpreters from Walter Bezanson to Stan Goldman, is its creation of a multiplicity of contending voices that put forward religious, philosophical, and political positions in debate with each other. The voices in the poem represent both a variety of religious perspectives from within Protestantism and a range of perspectives from Catholic and Orthodox Christianity, Judaism, and Islam, and Melville also includes substantial references to Buddhism and Hinduism in the text. These voices also articulate the struggle between faith and doubt characteristic of the period throughout the Anglo-American world. Not only does Melville create a richly panoramic view of the contemporary American and global religious scene, he also creates characters in this poem that contain a range of these positions within their own capacious personalities. Most notably, Rolfe, a philosophical sailor who has often been identified with Melville himself by critics, manages to absorb, reimagine, and argue with the claims of nearly every other figure in the poem. The title character, Clarel himself, plays a similar role, although with less adroitness and confidence than Rolfe. It is almost as if Melville chose to insert two selves into the poem—one young, nervous, and troubled by doubt, and one who can courageously navigate the contraries around which the poem is structured. A third stand-in for Melville appears in the voice that narrates the poem as a whole, which is not limited to Clarel or any other individual character. This voice can be associated with a mature sense of wisdom, and at times disillusionment, that even Rolfe has yet to achieve. The rest of the cast of characters is enormous, but among the most frequently discussed is Vine, whom many critics have identified with Melville's friend and literary model Nathaniel Hawthorne.

Traditionally, criticism of *Clarel* has approached the poem as a verse novel of ideas, with religious, philosophical, and political concerns being paramount, but more recent criticism of *Clarel* has called attention to its remarkable visual properties, attributes that both continued Melville's interest in the visual in *Battle-Pieces* and extended this development considerably. Melville frequently referred to works from the visual arts in *Clarel*: In "How *Clarel* Works" (2005), Samuel Otter has called special attention to the sketches of Giambattista Piranesi, which Melville mentions explicitly through the narrator's commentary on the events in the poem. In emphasizing the visual so consistently in *Clarel*, Melville drew upon those aspects of his earlier work in the abortive collection *Poems* and in *Battle-Pieces* that focused on the close description of objects drawn from the visual arts. Here, however, the effect attempted is more ambitious: Rather than simply creating a series of brief, concentrated images, Melville attempts in *Clarel* to create a kind of visual panorama that parallels the sweeping survey of ideas that he undertakes in the same poem. It is this quality that ultimately renders one of the more frequent critiques of *Clarel* invalid: The poem is said to be excessively abstract and philosophical, yet Melville consistently captures throughout the poem the relationship between images and ideas, finding analogues between architecture and theology, landscape and metaphysics, and portraiture and psychology. In this way, *Clarel* extends the arc of Melville's poetic career that began with *Battle-Pieces*: Like the earlier collection, *Clarel* can seem loose and disconnected, but in fact achieves a different sort of unity from what we often expect in poetry, in no small part through its series of visual effects and their relation to the abstract thought that shapes the argument of the poem. The unity that *Clarel* achieves points toward a complex understanding of the nature of faith, an understanding which ultimately is embodied in the form of the poem itself. For Melville, dogmatic faith in a personal deity who grants or denies salvation according to his will is mostly alienating, but the sense of meaning that the act of belief itself conveys is a psychological necessity.

John Marr and Other Sailors, with Some Sea-Pieces (1888) marked Melville's return to the sea. While the self-conscious intellectualism of the earlier poetry was submerged in this collection, Melville's capacity for image-making and dialogue continued to expand. Here, the focus is not so much on the visual art of ancient history and elite modernity as the powerful visual images that make up the experience of nineteenth-century sailors around the globe. In poems like "Bride-Groom Dick," and "Tom Deadlight" Melville captured the voices of sailors and the culture of the sea in the nineteenth century, while in other poems like "To Ned" and "Crossing the Tropics," he provided polished lyrical reflections on the lives of sailors. In the concluding portion of *John Marr and Other Sailors*, "Sea-Pieces," Melville uses an imagistic approach that anticipates the methods of early modernist poets. One of the most striking examples of this appears in the series of poems entitled "Pebbles," which comprised a group of brief, vivid poems that reflected on the metaphysical meaning of the sea by means of intense physical imagery. "The Tuft of Kelp," which takes the substance identified in the title, is still more precise in its imagery:

> All dripping in tangles green,
> Cast up by a lonely sea,
> If purer for that, O Weed,
> Bitterer, too, are ye?

In other poems, such as "The Maldive Shark," "The Man of War Hawk," and "The Berg," Melville showed an almost naturalistic side, emphasizing the parts of life at sea that resist human intentions.

Timoleon, Etc. (1891), the last collection of poetry that Melville published during his lifetime, is a less thematically focused collection than *John Marr and Other Sailors*, but it organizes itself around several central principles, most notably Melville's interest in competing approaches to religious and philosophic truth, in the visual aspects of poetry, and in the relationship of the past to present as refracted through poetic forms. The long opening poem from *Timoleon* takes a classical family drama as its occasion, and many of the poems draw upon classical or Renaissance contexts and the artwork that emerged from those eras. In the substantial section "Fruits of Travel from Long Ago," Melville's attention is focused on the visual arts and the artistic theories connected with their production. As has been established by several scholars and affirmed most recently by Hershel Parker, much of this collection likely antedates the composition of the rest of the poems in *Timoleon*. Melville likely wrote some of these poems after his trip to Europe and the Holy Land, and may have initially planned to publish them as part of the 1860 volume that never ultimately appeared.

Timoleon thus provides us with a kaleidoscopic view of Melville's poetic career across three decades of writing. It illustrates his long-term fascinations with travel, with the Greek and Roman classical world, and with the implications of religious difference for the imagi-nation. Poems like "Buddha," "The Enthusiast," and "Fragments of a Lost Gnostic Poem of the Twelfth Century" illustrate the continuing range of Melville's religious interest, and poems like "The Bench of Boors," "Art," and "The Marchioness of Brinvilliers" point toward his intensifying obsession with the visual arts. There is perhaps no more representative or more haunting poem in *Timoleon* than the ambitious dramatic monologue "After the Pleasure Party." This poem is unusual in Melville's body of work in that the speaker is a woman. Like so many of the poems in the collection, it takes as its occasion an image drawn from the visual arts, in this case an image of "amor threaten-ing"—love being represented not only as attractive, but as vengeful and even violent. The primary speaker is a woman named Urania who laments her lost opportunities for sexual love as the result of her de-votion to abstract knowledge, and her reflections prompt a commen-tary by a presumably male speaker who takes Urania's lament as an occasion to reflect on what was lost when Christianity triumphed in the formerly pagan Roman empire. The poem thus becomes a com-plex reflection on the nature of poetic voice, the relationship between religious belief and art, and the meaning of sexuality. This haunting engagement with loss appears again in one of *Timoleon*'s briefest po-ems, "Monody," which has been frequently associated by readers with Melville's relationship with Nathaniel Hawthorne, although this as-sociation has often been challenged and is by no means regarded as definitive—as Douglas Robillard has noted, "It would be as valid to assume that Melville was writing of Malcolm, his eldest son, who, it is assumed, committed suicide" (*Poems*, 341). In this poem, we see Melville's ability to express powerful emotion through concrete visual images, as he writes in the second stanza,

> By wintry hills his hermit-mound
> The sheeted snow drifts drape,
> And houseless there the snow-bird flits
> Beneath the fir-trees' crape:
> Glazed now with ice the cloistral vine
> That hid the shyest grape. (7–12)

Whatever the poem's biographical implications, Melville's use of the visual imagery of snow and fir trees as a funeral shroud and of the contrast between the living grape and the killing ice on the vine demonstrate the way in which his poetry invites us to see powerful and unexpected metaphors in the landscape.

Melville's posthumously published poetry is the least explored portion of his body of work, but it offers tantalizingly personal suggestions about Melville's views and relationships toward the end of his life. *Weeds and Wildings, with a Rose or Two*, a collection Melville wrote for his wife, Elizabeth Shaw Melville, captures the way Melville's weighty philosophical themes could be addressed with a winsome touch at the end of his life, while at the same time retaining Melville's characteristic focus on intellectual and spiritual struggle and uncertainty. Melville is clearly deeply concerned with mortality in these poems, yet the tone is more witty and clever than morbid. Although this body of work continues to be insufficiently discussed, Robert Milder's essay "Old Man Melville: The Rose and the Cross" provides one of the finest introductions to the material. Much of Melville's late poetry remains quite difficult for most readers to access. Most recent collections of his poetry have focused on his published collections to the exclusion of unpublished and especially uncollected work, and for some of this material, readers must still turn to Howard Vincent's 1947 volume *Collected Poems of Herman Melville,* although John Bryant's 2001 collection *Herman Melville: Tales, Poems, and Other Writings* has made much of this material considerably more widely available. This reflects the work that still needs to be done in establishing definitive texts of both *Weeds and Wildings* and other uncollected poems, which were left in manuscript form, but the fact that these efforts are still in process should not drive students away from considering these poems.

What emerges in Melville's best uncollected poetry, as in the late published collections and *Weeds and Wildings* (left unpublished at the time of his death), is a restless and active mind in full possession of both its intellectual and poetic powers and its own sense of balance and self-assurance. One of Melville's more whimsical and touching poems, "Montaigne and His Kitten" takes the great sixteenth-century French essayist Montaigne as its speaker and his cat as its audience, with Montaigne playfully addressing the meaning of mortality in a monologue directed to the cat. Montaigne questions human arrogance in excluding animals from heaven, and concludes by suggesting that playfulness and humor may be the best response to mortality, with the line, "Wise ones fool it while they may" (32). Several other poems that were in manuscript form at the end of Melville's life are important for the light they shed on the degree to which Melville continued to develop as a poet up until his death: The two poems paired together as "The Marquis of Grandvin" ("At the Hostelry," which deals in an ambitious manner with the theory of the visual arts, and "Naples in the Time of Bomba," which is concerned with authority, democracy, and revolution) and "Pontoosuce," which, with its meditation on the "warmth and chill of wedded life and death" (96), have been read as one of Melville's very last statements on the problem of mortality.

Melville's last great accomplishment in prose grew out of his poetic endeavors. As Melville scholars have long known, *Billy Budd* grew out of the poem that concludes it, not the other way around. In "Billy in the Darbies," Melville adopts the voice of a sailor who is sleeping fitfully on the night of his execution. (In the context of *Billy Budd* itself, the personae become still more complex. The author of the poem is a sailor who makes the illiterate Billy the speaker in the poem, suggesting something about the artistic sophistication Melville attributed to the poetry of working men.) The sailor finds himself moving imaginatively between his past life and his looming death, and he adopts a tone that is both touching and stoic: He appreciates the fact that the ship's chaplain has come to see him, but is less interested in questions of faith than in a dreamlike rehearsal for his death and burial at sea itself. The poem includes images both haunting and oddly comical:

> A jewel-block they'll make of me tomorrow,
> Pendant pearl from the yard-arm end
> Like the ear-drop I gave to Bristol Molly—
> O, tis me, not the sentence they'll suspend. (7–10)

Characteristically, Melville plays with the image of Billy suspended in space as he is hanged as a kind of visual pun in which Billy resembles jewelry, at the same time that he generates admiration for the courage of a speaker who can address his rapidly approaching end with such grace. "Billy in the Darbies" thus fits quite naturally with a late poem like "Montaigne and His Kitten" in its embrace of a kind of whimsical humor in the face of death. This willingness to confront mortality without illusions and without despair functions as the unifying theme of much of Melville's later poetry.

Given the range and the idiosyncratic qualities of Melville's poetry, a central question for Melville scholars is how to categorize Melville's poetic achievement. The narrative that underlies most dismissive critiques of Melville's poetry regards his poetry as being hopelessly behind the times; in this view, Melville's capacity for inventiveness and originality failed him when he turned to poetry. The standard version of this view alleges that the fact that Melville's verse is metrical and rhyming, unlike much of Whitman's poetry, and less exuberantly experimental in its use of language than that of Emily Dickinson, means that Melville is essentially a less skilled, less popular, and less success-ful version of the Schoolroom Poets—Longfellow, Whittier, Lowell, and Holmes—rather than a major figure in the history of American poetry. Recent work by William Spengemann has called into question the idea that seeing Melville as a characteristic poet of his time has to mean dismissing his capacity as a poet, as Spengemann has carefully examined Melville's metrical innovations and emphasized his role within nineteenth-century American poetry as a poet who both worked within the American romantic tradition and transformed it by develop-ing new forms related to those already in circulation. Likewise, work by Helen Vendler on *Battle-Pieces* and *Clarel* and Rosanna Warren on *Battle-Pieces* has emphasized that even within his nineteenth-century context, Melville's use of prosody is impressive and adroit.

The more traditional riposte to the dismissal of Melville's poetry as conventional romanticism is to see him as being radically ahead of his time: In this telling, Melville is a great poet because of the ways in which he anticipated the rise of modernism with his extensive use of irony and ambiguity in his verse and with his pervasive attention to themes like alienation and anxiety. This reading extends from Rob-ert Penn Warren and Howard P. Vincent in the 1940s through William Shurr and William Bysshe Stein in the late 1960s and early 1970s. The view that Melville anticipated modernism in his form certainly has its strengths: Many of Melville's later poems show premonitions of Im-agism, and indeed could be mistaken for something out of William Butler Yeats or Ezra Pound from the 1910s. Moreover, the affective dimension to much of this poetry fits in nicely with modernism's em-phasis on alienation and fragmentation, and Melville's obvious rever-ence for art is highly characteristic of modernism. The very fact that the Italian artistic tradition is, as Dennis Berthold recently established so definitively, central to Melville's poetry places him firmly in a line of continuity with modernists like Pound and T. S. Eliot. Like Eliot, Melville found the literature of seventeenth-century England to be a particularly significant antecedent for his work, and Melville shares a love of irony, paradox, and punning with both the British metaphysical poets of the seventeenth-century, like John Donne and George Herbert, and twentieth-century Anglo-American modernists. Perhaps no poem captures the modernist Melville more succinctly and powerfully than his late poem "Art." In this poem, which requires quotation in full to illustrate the power of its meditation upon the nature of art, Melville explores the contraries that are essential to artistic creation:

> In placid hours well-pleased we dream,
> Of many a brave unbodied scheme.
> But form to lend, pulsed life create,
> What unlike things must meet and mate:
> A flame to melt—a wind to freeze;
> Sad patience—joyous energies;
> Humility—yet pride and scorn;
> Instinct and study; love and hate;
> Audacity—reverence. These must mate,
> And fuse with Jacob's mystic heart,
> To wrestle with the angel—Art.

In this poem, Melville highlights the contradictions that are the fundamental sources of art, whether visual or literary, and he employs the characteristic modernist gesture of using mythic symbolism with religious overtones when he invokes the biblical account of Jacob wrestling with the Angel of the Lord. The reverence for art and the emphasis on paradox and irony are characteristic of the literary modernism that the poem presages, but it also connects Melville to the romantic tradition that shaped his entire career, and the spare, precise language connects him with the literary realism in vogue when Melville was writing most of his poetry.

Connected to Melville's use of the sort of language we associate with realism is a more recent and still more persuasive reading of Melville's poetry than either his condemnation as an outdated romantic or his exaltation as a preemptive modernist that situates Melville within his own time period. In her essay "Melville the Realist Poet" (2005), Elizabeth Renker has argued that Melville, like Dickinson and Whitman, is preeminently a realist poet, and that we tend to ignore his poetry because we think of the realist era in American literature as an era of prose fiction. Renker further argues that this characteristic of Melville's poetry makes Melville a central American poet of the later nineteenth century. Renker's argument represents a breakthrough in the critical response to Melville's poetry, and it offers a compelling rationale for situating Melville at the center rather than the periphery of late nineteenth-century American poetry, and for viewing Melville's poetry as a major body of work in its own right, rather than as a curious adjunct to his superlative accomplishments in prose. Perhaps no poem better captures the realist (and even naturalist) Melville than his short poem "The Maldive Shark," a favorite of anthologists. This poem discusses the way in which pilot fish, seemingly harmless and endearing creatures, exist in a symbiotic relationship with the predatory Maldive shark, which is referred to in the poem as a "pale ravener of horrible meat" (16).

In addition to accounting for poetry like "The Maldive Shark," Renker provides a clearer narrative than is often ventured for how Melville's final prose masterpiece, *Billy Budd*, developed out of the years of writing poetry that preceded its composition, and indeed coincided with its composition. I would like to suggest, however, that a reading of Melville's poetry that attends still more closely to both the continuities in Melville's own career and the continuities in nineteenth-century American poetry can be the most illuminating path of all into Melville's poetry. The boundaries between movements like romanticism, realism, and naturalism are never quite so firmly and cleanly drawn as our anthologies suggest, as G. R. Thompson and Eric Carl Link demonstrated in their 1999 study *Neutral Ground: New Traditionalism and the American Romance Controversy*. Moreover, as early as the 1950s, Milton R. Stern was advocating a naturalist reading of Melville's body of work as a whole in his superb study *The Fine Hammered Steel of*

Herman Melville (1957). Ultimately, we best understand Melville's position as a poet in literary history when we take him seriously as a romantic *and* a realist *and* a naturalist *and* a protomodernist (and even proto-postmodernist) than when we try to limit his verse to one of these categories.

One way into Melville's poetry that demonstrates the continuity of his work is Melville's treatment of the visual arts. The importance of this topic in relation to Melville's poetry has been the subject of some brilliant scholarly work by Hsuan L. Hsu, Samuel Otter, Dennis Berthold, and Douglas Robillard. The concept of *ekphrasis* (a seemingly forbidding term, but one which simply refers to writing about an art object) has become especially important for recent criticism of Melville's poetry through the efforts of Robillard, who wrote a full-length monograph on the topic entitled *Melville and the Visual Arts: Ionian Form, Venetian Tint* (1997). Robillard argued that Melville's use of writing about the visual arts helped to define his specific approach to literary art, one characterized by a high level of concern for imagery and the act of seeing. Hsu extended this reading in relation to *Battle-Pieces*, and Otter and Berthold have done the same in relation to *Clarel*.

A second, and too often ignored, path to seeing the continuities in Melville's poetry and prose is through his reading. Work on Melville's reading has been an important part of Melville criticism from the start, from the pioneering work of Jay Leyda in *The Melville Log* (1951) to the decades-long efforts of Merton M. Sealts to establish a definitive list of works that we can be certain that Melville read in *Melville's Reading*. Nathalia Wright's work on Melville's use of the Bible, Walker Cowen's cataloguing of much of Melville's marginalia, and Walter Bezanson's work on the source material for *Clarel*, all contribute substantially to our knowledge of Melville's reading and serve to illuminate his achievement in poetry. Most recently, there has been a renaissance in the study of Melville's reading and marginalia under the auspices of Steven Olsen-Smith, Peter Norberg, and Dennis Marnon at *Melville's Marginalia Online*, producing substantial work on Melville's influences.

Indeed, Melville seemed to draw more heavily and directly on his reading in his poetry than he did even in his major fiction. In particular, as can be seen in the online edition of Melville's marginalia to the New Testament and the book of Psalms, for which I have provided the introduction and notes at *Melville's Marginalia Online*, Melville reproduced many of the passages that he annotated in the book of Psalms in identical or nearly identical form in *Clarel*. Nor was Melville's thoroughgoing use of sources restricted to sacred texts. In *Battle-Pieces*, he drew freely upon newspaper accounts of major battles in the Civil War, incorporating them in his poetry in ways that presaged the modernist use of pastiche as a characteristic poetic form. "Donelson," for example, takes the newspaper accounts of the battle from which it takes its name as the frame for the poem as a whole, and hints at the possibilities of such a method as it would be developed by Eliot, Pound, and H.D. in the twentieth century. Herman Melville the poet is thus intimately enmeshed with Herman Melville the careful reader and annotator of the work of others.

As William B. Dillingham showed in his study *Melville and His Circle: The Last Years* (1996), Melville's late poetry in particular is a revelation of how vigorous his reading and engagement with a variety of literary and intellectual traditions remained until the end. Melville spans the globe in the range of references that he employs in such collections as *John Marr and Other Sailors*, *Timoleon*, and *Weeds and Wildings*, as well as in his uncollected verse. In these works, Melville shows his close familiarity with French (Montaigne), Portuguese (Camoens), Spanish (Cervantes), Italian (Dante), and German (Goethe, Schiller, and Schopenhauer) authors, resulting in a body of poetry that is truly global in its scope. Melville's poetry thus represents a continuation and expansion of the cosmopolitan tendencies so often noted in his fiction.

Melville the poet, then, is not just a great prose poet who could never quite replicate this success in verse. Nor is he solely behind his time, ahead of his time, or in step with his time. Rather, Melville's poetry represents a continuation and amplification of his most characteristic themes and devices, and like *Moby-Dick* and "Bartleby, the Scrivener," the poetry is immersed in both nineteenth-century American experience and broader literary and artistic traditions that include but are not limited to those of Europe. A full and accurate portrait of Melville, and indeed of the growth of American literary culture in the nineteenth century, cannot do without the verse that Melville wrote from 1860 up until the final days of his life in 1891. If Melville remains to some degree an obscure poet for most readers of nineteenth-century American literature, he is also a poet whose body of work both represents and transcends his own time.

Works Cited

Berthold, Dennis. *American Risorgimento: Herman Melville and the Cultural Politics of Italy.* Columbus: Ohio State UP, 2009.

Bezanzon, Walter. "Introduction." *Clarel: A Poem and Pilgrimage in the Holy Land.* By Herman Melville. New York: Hendricks House, 1960.

Bryant, John, ed. *Herman Melville: Tales, Poems, and Other Writings.* New York: Modern Library, 2002.

Buell, Lawrence. "Melville the Poet." *The Cambridge Companion to Herman Melville.* Ed. Andrew Delbanco. Cambridge: Cambridge UP, 1998. 135–56.

Cohen, Hennig. *Selected Poems of Herman Melville.* New York: Doubleday, 1964.

Dillingham, William B. *Melville and His Circle: The Last Years.* Athens: U of Georgia P, 1996.

Garner, Stanton. *The Civil War World of Herman Melville.* Lawrence: UP of Kansas, 1993.

Goldman, Stan. *Melville's Protest Theism: The Hidden and Silent God in Clarel.* DeKalb: Northern Illinois UP, 1993.

Hsu, Hsuan. "War, Ekphrasis, and Elliptical Form in Melville's *Battle-Pieces.*" *Nineteenth Century Studies* 16 (2002): 51–72.

Leyda, Jay. *The Melville Log: A Documentary Life of Herman Melville, 1819–1891.* New York: Harcourt, 1951.

Melville, Herman. *Clarel: A Poem and Pilgrimage in the Holy Land.* Ed. Hershel Parker, Harrison Hayford, and Walter Bezanson. Evanston and Chicago: Northwestern-Newberry, 1991. Vol. 12 of *The Writings of Herman Melville.*

_____. *Published Poems.* Ed. Robert C. Ryan, Harrison Hayford, Alma MacDougall Reising, and G. Thomas Tanselle. Evanston and Chicago: Northwestern-Newberry, 2009. Vol. 11 of *The Writings of Herman Melville.*

Milder, Robert. "Old Man Melville: The Rose and the Cross." *New Essays on Billy Budd.* Ed. Donald Yannella. New York: Cambridge UP, 2002.

Olsen-Smith, Steven, Peter Norberg, and Dennis C. Marnon, eds. *Melville's Marginalia Online.* Melville's Marginalia Online, 2011. Web. 13 Jan. 2012.

Otter, Samuel. "How *Clarel* Works." *A Companion to Herman Melville.* Ed. Wyn Kelley. New York: Blackwell, 2005. 467–81.

Parker, Hershel. *Melville: The Making of the Poet.* Evanston: Northwestern UP, 2008.

Renker, Elizabeth. "Melville the Realist Poet." *A Companion to Herman Melville.* Ed. Wyn Kelley. New York: Blackwell, 2005. 482–96.

Robillard, Douglas. *Melville and the Visual Arts: Ionian Form, Venetian Tint.* Kent: Kent State UP, 1997.

_____. *The Poems of Herman Melville.* Kent: Kent State UP, 2000.

Sealts, Merton M. *Melville's Reading.* Rev. ed. Columbia: U of South Carolina P, 1988.

Shurr, William. *The Mystery of Iniquity: Melville as Poet, 1857–1891.* Lexington: UP of Kentucky, 1972.

Spengemann, William. *Three American Poets: Walt Whitman, Emily Dickinson, and Herman Melville.* South Bend: U of Notre Dame P, 2010.

Stein, William Bysshe. *The Poetry of Melville's Late Years: Time, History, Myth, and Religion.* Albany: State U of New York P, 1970.

Stern, Milton R. *The Fine Hammered Steel of Herman Melville.* Urbana: U of Illinois P, 1957.

Thompson, G. R., and Eric Carl Link. *Neutral Ground: New Traditionalism and the American Romance Controversy.* Baton Rouge: Louisiana State UP, 1999.

Vendler, Helen. "Desert Storm." Rev. of *Clarel*, by Herman Melville, and *Journals*, by Herman Melville. *The New Republic* 7 Dec. 1992: 39–42.

_____. "Melville and the Lyric of History." *Southern Review* 35.3 (1999): 579–94.

Vincent, Howard P. *Collected Poems of Herman Melville.* Chicago: Hendricks, 1947.

Warren, Robert Penn, Ed. "Introduction." *Selected Poems of Herman Melville.* New York: Random, 1967.

Warren, Rosanna. "Dark Knowledge: Melville's Poems of the Civil War." *Raritan: A Quarterly Review* 19.1 (1999): 100–21.

Wright, Nathalia. *Melville's Use of the Bible.* New York: Octagon, 1947.

Billy Budd, Sailor: Or, How to Read a Book _____

Wyn Kelley

Herman Melville's *Moby-Dick* stands at the center of his output as a writer, but *Billy Budd* is one of his most popular works, to judge by only one indicator, the online bookseller Amazon.com. While a recent search for *Moby-Dick* on Amazon predictably generated an astronomical 1,752 items (editions in different media as well as critical and secondary works), his other books range from the sparse (*Battle-Pieces* at 40, *Clarel* 60) to the highly respectable (*White-Jacket*, 108; *Mardi*, 138; *The Confidence-Man*, 157; *Redburn*, 163; *Omoo*, 174; "Bartleby," 310; and *Pierre*, 343) to the downright trendy: *Typee* 461 and *Billy Budd* 462. It would seem that *Billy Budd* is one of Melville's most widely published books after *Moby-Dick*.

But is it read? And do readers consume it with pleasure? Or is it one of those profound meditations on the human condition that seems necessary for educating the young and enlightening the foolish? With its long sentences, archaic diction, and incomprehensible characters, it may seem remote from the concerns of contemporary readers. Yet in one critical aspect—its confrontation with issues of reading and literacy—it speaks directly to readers in a digital age. For *Billy Budd* focuses on the questions that preoccupy many readers now: Why do books matter? What are the best ways to read? Can we adapt our reading practices to new media while maintaining the skills and sensitivities of the past? Thinking about *Billy Budd* in terms of reading implies that we are not alone in our concerns about the meaning and value of literary texts. The future of reading, Melville might say, lies in understanding the reading practices of the past.

I. What Is the Matter with the Character Billy Budd?

Although Melville's Billy Budd appears an ideal Handsome Sailor, icon of "strength and beauty," someone "such perhaps as Adam presumably might have been ere the urbane Serpent wriggled himself into his company," the narrator specifies that "there was just one thing amiss in him," namely, his stutter: "No visible blemish indeed, . . . but an occasional liability to a vocal defect" (*Billy Budd* 44, 52, 53). This defect, the narrator warns, suggests the interference of "the envious marplot of Eden" (i.e., Satan) and indicates that "the story in which he is the main figure is no romance" (53). Indeed, the story may be more like a tragedy, since Billy's inability to speak at the moment of crisis, when Claggart, the master-at-arms, accuses Billy of mutiny and Billy kills him with a single blow to the forehead, results in Billy's execution for a crime he seems too good to commit. Billy's testimony at the drumhead court convened by Captain Vere focuses on his stutter as the culprit: "Could I have used my tongue I would not have struck him. But he foully lied to my face and in presence of my captain, and I had to say something, and I could only say it with a blow, God help me!" (106).

It would appear from the way Melville structures the story that Billy's "vocal defect" is his only flaw. An observer might otherwise blame the passion in Billy that expresses itself in violence. Early in the book, when a sailor named Red Whiskers insults him with a "dig under the ribs," Billy explodes: "Quick as lightning Billy let fly his arm" (*Billy Budd* 47). This episode results in a "terrible drubbing," but instead of bloodshed it ends with peace and harmony: "They all love him" (47). At another moment of crisis, when the afterguardsman tries to bribe Billy into joining a mutiny, Billy's threats to "t-t-toss you over the r-rail" reveal his deep emotion, the "bonfire in his heart [that] made luminous the rose-tan in his cheek" (82, 77). These events may prepare readers for Billy's behavior in the face of Claggart's insinuations, but when Billy's final blow proves lethal, the narrator makes no mention of any character flaw. The killing results from his "violent efforts at utterance," not malice against Claggart (99).

Billy does have what might seem another defect: The narrator early reports that "he was illiterate" (*Billy Budd* 52). Billy's inability to read, in a world governed by military law and in a narrative saturated with references to texts of poetry, mythology, history, and legal doctrine, might seem a liability, if not a character flaw. But the narrator immediately converts it into a form of romantic pleasure: "He could not read, but he could sing, and like the illiterate nightingale was sometimes the composer of his own song" (52). Although such musical or even poetic talent may seem like a gift, some critics have noted a problem with Billy's illiteracy. Most influentially, Barbara Johnson has analyzed the different forms of reading in *Billy Budd*, seeing Billy as able in a sense to read—each character reads the others and his social environment—but as unable or unwilling to interpret what he observes. She contrasts Billy's naïve acceptance of Claggart—someone who always has a "pleasant word" for him (*Billy Budd* 71)—with Claggart's ironic and conspiratorial reading of Billy. Johnson argues that the story opposes two different kinds of unsuccessful reading: "It seems evident that Billy's reading method consists in taking everything at face value, while Claggart's consists in seeing a mantrap under every daisy" (Johnson 587). Readers beware! No one would want to stumble into either of these snares.

The character Vere would appear to be the more successful reader, or at least the one most explicitly a reader of texts: "His bias was toward those books to which every serious mind of superior order occupying any active post of authority in the world naturally inclines: books treating of actual men and events no matter of what era—history, biography, and unconventional authors like Montaigne, who . . . philosophize upon realities" (*Billy Budd* 62). As Johnson points out, Vere's deep literacy as well as his authority as captain allow him to judge and mediate between Billy's and Claggart's partial readings, although Melville's narrator also suggests that Vere's judgment is flawed.

If Vere's capacity to judge rests on or derives from his superior literacy, what does the text seem to be saying about reading? Does Billy's illiteracy contribute to his demise? Does Vere's literacy, on the other hand, make him a better captain (even if he dies unfulfilled, "the most secret of all passions, ambition, never [having] attained to the fulness of fame" [*Billy Budd* 129])? And what does it mean, after all, to be literate in Billy's world or in ours? What does it take to read *Billy Budd*?

Ironically the "illiterate nightingale" inhabits a text that for many readers can seem unreadable. The difficulties of *Billy Budd* raise questions not only about the author, narrator, and characters but also about readers. What kind of literacy is required of the readers of *Billy Budd*?

In the first seventy or so years after it was published, readers understood *Billy Budd* mostly in terms of a print-text world, where literacy is measured by the quantity and sophistication of texts readers have consumed. To read *Billy Budd* successfully in this context, one must have read many books. Twenty-first-century readers, operating in a world of digital texts and social reading practices, must judge texts in new terms. The literacy required for reading *Billy Budd* may not necessarily mean having read all the books mentioned in Melville's text. Rather, Melville's narrator suggests that individual reading and preparation are not enough; reading must be social to succeed, depending on all members of a society, not just a few.

II. What Is the Matter with the Book *Billy Budd*?

The difficulties of reading *Billy Budd* arise from a number of features of Melville's text, among them the state of the manuscript, the narrator's identity and writing style, the questions of genre the story raises, and the proliferation of references to other texts. These difficulties speak to *Billy Budd*'s requirements for different kinds of literacy as well.

First, it helps to know that Melville's text was not finished when he died, that it was still in manuscript form (in often illegible handwriting), and that he had not made up his mind about the final order of chapters, the names of his ships, or certain details about characters.[1] Until almost thirty years after Melville's death, when Raymond Weaver first read the manuscript presented to him by Melville's granddaughter Eleanor Melville Metcalf, it had not been finally edited for publication. When Weaver did edit and publish it, scholars subsequently found errors in his transcriptions and editorial decisions. Not until 1962, in a text edited and annotated by Harrison Hayford and Merton M. Sealts,

Jr., did *Billy Budd* appear in a form scholars might accept as reasonably close to what Melville intended.

Hayford and Sealts furthermore used manuscript evidence to show that the text had developed in stages over the years of its composition. As they revealed, the story had begun as a poem, "Billy in the Darbies [Irons]," like the sailor-portraits that appeared in Melville's poetry collection *John Marr and Other Sailors* (1888). By the time Melville developed a full-length story, Billy's character, envisioned in the poem as a seasoned mutineer, had evolved into the Billy condemned for raising his hand against an officer rather than leading an organized mutiny. Likewise, Claggart entered the story at a later stage, creating conflict, and after him Vere, complicating the plot even more. Because of Hayford and Sealts's work, any reader of *Billy Budd* must recognize that the book's difficulties may derive as much from the accidents of bad handwriting, pages poorly shuffled, and late-stage changes of heart as from the writer's consistent habits or intentions.

A second difficulty arises from Melville's choice of narrator. Who is this person and how are we to read him—i.e., to judge or trust his statements? We do know that the narrator is a living person, referring to himself and his experiences. For example, he has observed the world of the sailors, as he reveals in the second paragraph: "A somewhat remarkable instance recurs to me. In Liverpool, now half a century ago, I saw under the shadow of the great dingy sea-wall of Prince's Dock (an obstruction long since removed) a common sailor so intensely black" (*Billy Budd* 43). At another moment, he speaks directly to the reader and invites him or her into the narrative: "In this matter of writing, resolve as one may to keep to the main road, some bypaths have an enticement not readily to be withstood. I am going to err into such a bypath. If the reader will keep me company I shall be glad" (56). He also points to his own limits as a narrator: "His [Claggart's] portrait I essay, but shall never hit it" (64). He has memory problems as well, trying to recall a conversation forty years before with a "Trafalgar man" (66). In attempting to explain Claggart's obsession with Billy, he draws on the words of a certain "honest scholar, my senior" who taught him a thing or two about "obscure spiritual places" in the human heart (74, 75). Yet the narrator is not sure of what he learned: "At the time, my inexperience was such that I did not quite see the drift of all this. It may be that I see it now" (75). Or maybe he does not.

Melville's narrator is not just mysterious; he may be mistaken or even deliberately misleading. Hence, he seems capable of judging that Claggart is mad and even of describing from what kind of madness he suffers: "Now something such an one [a madman] was Claggart, in whom was the mania of an evil nature, not engendered by vicious training or corrupting books or licentious living, but born with him and innate, in short 'a depravity according to nature'" (*Billy Budd* 76). Yet when the surgeon later wonders "professionally and privately" whether Vere might have been seized with a sudden lunacy that causes him to condemn Billy, the narrator is less confident about his knowledge of madness: "Who in the rainbow can draw the line where the violet tint ends and the orange tint begins? . . . So with sanity and insanity" (102). Reading this narrator, then, would seem to require a degree of skepticism.

At the same time that the narrator arouses skepticism, his style seems to make such skepticism difficult. For he is the master of long, complex sentences, antiquated diction, double negatives, and dense layers of abstraction that confuse or lead the willing reader astray. How can one keep one's wits in sentences like this one?

> And here be it submitted that apparently going to corroborate the doctrine of man's Fall, a doctrine now popularly ignored, it is observable that where certain virtues pristine and unadulterated peculiarly characterize anybody in the external uniform of civilization, they will upon scrutiny seem not to be derived from custom or convention, but rather to be out of keeping with these, as if indeed exceptionally transmitted from a period prior to Cain's city and citified man. (*Billy Budd* 52–53)

Is the reader alert enough to wonder if "the doctrine of man's Fall" is truly "now popularly ignored" (Why? Because of Darwin? Because people are wicked?); or to ask how a "pristine" virtue could possibly exist "in the external uniform of civilization," a seeming paradox; or to imagine a period prior to "Cain's city and citified man" (in Eden? Or post-Eden pre-civilization)? Although the sentence delivers itself with rhetorical formality and seeming authority, the logic does not lead to a definite conclusion. Even with the ending flourish of quoting a Roman poet, the narrator seems to make nothing clear except that a creature as unsullied as Billy could never exist or be recognized by the tainted humans around him. Yet Billy exists.

The narrator's language is not always this complicated. Readers tend to forget the wealth of plain, homely, even beautiful sentences in the text: "What was the matter with the master-at-arms?" (*Billy Budd* 73); "Why, even spare buttons were not so plentiful at sea" (83); "As it was, innocence was his blinder" (88); "It was like handling a dead snake" (99); "It was like a gift placed in the palm of an outreached hand upon which the fingers do not close" (121); "Truth uncompromisingly told will always have its ragged edges" (128). But these islands of clarity in what many perceive as a swamp of assertions cautiously advanced, statements retracted and undermined, and observations rendered dubious or ambiguous, may be hard to notice. So along with skepticism, readers of this narrator's words must be armed with a dictionary and a large supply of patience.

A third problem the text presents has to do with genre. Books tend to require maps, and we use genre as a way of mapping a story. If we know that we are reading a detective novel, science fiction adventure, romantic comedy, or three-handkerchief melodrama, then we expect certain plot patterns, character types, and emotional responses. What kind of story is *Billy Budd*?[2] Many readers have viewed the work as tragedy but have disagreed over the question of whose tragedy it is. Is Billy Budd, the good man who dies unnecessarily, a tragic hero? But as Aristotle defines tragic hero, he must be ethically superior, capable of a choice that would doom him to certain death. Billy's fate, in contrast, is accidental, unsought for by a man who, though strong and good, seems almost a child. Vere better fits the role of tragic hero, but rather than dying as a result of his hubris, or tragic pride, he falls from a sniper's bullet in a meaningless, again accidental demise. Even modern tragedy of the kind attempted by Arthur Miller or Phillip Roth, while often complicating the tragic conflict or outcome, usually leaves no doubt about who the hero is.

Similar questions arise when we consider *Billy Budd* as biblical allegory. The narrator's language and symbolism make it clear that Billy is aligned with Adam, Claggart with the serpent, and Vere with God the Father. Or is Billy Christ? Like Christ, he suffers a martyr's death, the spar from which he is hanged appearing as a sacred emblem: to the sailors "a chip of it was as a piece of the Cross" (*Billy Budd* 131). Yet other references associate Billy with Abel, Joseph, Isaac, and Elijah. Even if we ignore the basic differences among all these figures—the innocence of Adam, Abel, Joseph, and Isaac contrasted with the wisdom of Elijah and the leadership of David or Jesus—the other figures in Melville's panoply complicate these Judeo-Christian associations. Billy also resembles Alexander the Great, Achilles, Hercules, Apollo, a British captive of the Roman empire, and a Tahitian islander in the era of Captain Cook. Where is the map for an allegory of such contending types? Can Billy be as violent as Achilles, as charismatic as Alexander, as strong as Hercules, and still as meek as Christ? Are we then in an epic, a tragedy, a war story, a legal fiction, or a story of religious sacrifice?

A reader of *Billy Budd* must retain a sense of balance, a certain openness to possibility, a willingness to entertain multiple readings at once. But then he or she faces another challenge: the wealth of historical, literary, legal, religious, and philosophical references in the text. It is not enough to be a smart, open-minded, and flexible reader; Melville's text also seems to assume a vast knowledge of the past, knowledge one can attain only by reading books. If the traits of literacy we have examined so far speak to the *quality* of a reader's abilities, this last point tests the *quantity* of books read, the depth of knowledge gained. How else to find one's way in a story that draws on the history of revolutions in France, England, and America? On an understanding of England's Mutiny Act, the mutinies at the Nore and Spithead, or the *Somers* mutiny in America? On knowledge of the conspiracies of Guy Fawkes and Titus Oates? Or the writings of Thomas Paine, Voltaire, Diderot, Nathaniel Hawthorne, William James (the naval historian), Tennyson, Andrew Marvell, Montaigne, Camoëns, Malory, Homer, Ann Radcliffe, Coke and Blackstone, Plato, Milton—not to mention the host of authors that scholars have detected as Melville's less explicit sources? *Billy Budd*, it would seem, requires the reader to be editor, critic, lexicographer, scholar, cartographer, historian—all at once. As Huck Finn says to his companion as they dig their way into the hut-prison from which they hope to rescue Jim: "This ain't no thirty-seven year job; this is a thirty-eight year job, Tom Sawyer" (Twain 273).

III. How to Read Like Billy

Reading *Billy Budd* indeed looks daunting if we apply one model of literacy, the one that has held sway for much of the twentieth century. According to this model, a literate person should be able not only to decode a text but to understand and master its meaning, using the methods of close reading developed by twentieth-century practitioners of New Criticism such as Cleanth Brooks, Robert Penn Warren, and William K. Wimsatt (see Davis). Such an approach assumes certain standard features of a text and the reading experience (see Jenkins, Kelley, et al.). First, a book is linear: You start at the beginning and go to the end. A book has a design that you can best appreciate by reading in a given order. Second, it is continuous: A book has a unity and cumulative effect you would lose by skipping around. Third, it is complete: You must read it all to get the meaning. And finally, it is deep: Your first reading gives you only surface understanding. You must read and reread, looking for significant patterns of language and theme, before you can say you understand the text.

Billy Budd would seem to demand and reward this kind of reading. But as we have seen, the challenges are deep and neverending. Start with the expectation of linearity. The book begins on Prince's Dock in Liverpool and ends with the poem that purports to represent Billy's thoughts on the night before his death. Yet we know that the story was written in a very different order, starting with the poem and layering in successive drafts, in which the characters and events changed with each new stage of composition. Where, then, is the beginning, where the end? Melville mischievously complicates this issue by providing us with three endings: chapter 28, narrating Vere's death and hence bringing to a close the lives of the three main characters; chapter 29, reporting how the story survived in the outside world as a misleading piece of journalism; and chapter 30, with "Billy in the Darbies," a step back in time, as it reconsiders Billy's thoughts before death, but a step forward in history as it records the sailor's memories of his life. Melville would seem not to have tremendous concern for readers' expectations of a linear narration.

Likewise, it would be hard to find continuity in *Billy Budd*. In perhaps the most obvious example, chapters 3 through 5 stop the story to speculate on the events at the Nore Mutiny, Nelson's behavior in battle, and his influence on the crew of the *Theseus*. Hayford and Sealts discuss the fact that Melville removed the manuscript leaves of what is now chapter 4 to a separate folder (*Billy Budd* 8); later editors restored them. Other digressions intervene in descriptions of Claggart's character (chapters 8 and 11). The discussion of insanity at the beginning of chapter 21 ("Who in the rainbow can draw the line . . . " (102) breaks into the story, and chapter 26, in which the surgeon and purser debate the question of how Billy really died, seems not only digressive but puzzling. Peter Stallybrass has described the history of discontinuous texts like the Bible, books that may be read in parts or against the linear flow of narrative or thought—an almanac or encyclopedia, *The Decameron* or *The Arabian Nights*, where the reader experiences the pleasure of wandering at will throughout the text (Stallybrass; Kelley

76). Melville's narrator invites such possibilities when he beckons the reader into the "by-path" of digression.

An errant reader would risk missing important parts of the story, however, and would experience the anxiety that comes with the expectation of completeness in a literary text. Good readers, that is, must cover the whole book to get its meaning. Yet who is not tempted to skim sections of *Billy Budd* and get to the murder and trial scene? Who might not consider certain parts of Melville's long exposition dispensable? As in his earlier *Moby-Dick*, Melville includes many observations and musings that a reader pressed for time might find unnecessary to the plot. Furthermore, what we know about Melville's habits of reading suggests that he was not always himself a careful reader, nor as writer did he tie up all his loose ends: As he wryly remarks in *Moby-Dick*, "There are some enterprises in which a careful disorderliness is the true method" (324). Reading *Billy Budd* completely, then, might not satisfy all one's questions—about the characters' backstories, about intriguing minor figures like the Dansker or Squeak or hidden events below decks. And Melville does not seem to have weighed this expectation very seriously.

One other expectation of a worthy literary text is that it be deep, and in this sense Melville seems to meet standard criteria. He even includes a fictional scholar telling the narrator that characters like Claggart's require extraordinary care and attention: "Yes, X— is a nut not to be cracked by the tap of a lady's fan. . . . I think that to try and get into X—, enter his labyrinth and get out again, without a clue derived from some source other than what is known as 'knowledge of the world'— that were hardly possible, at least for me" (*Billy Budd* 74). When the narrator argues that knowledge of the world may be useful for studying human nature, the scholar replies, "Yes, but a superficial knowledge of it, serving ordinary purposes. But for anything deeper, I am not certain whether to know the world and to know human nature be not two distinct branches of knowledge, which while they may coexist in the same heart, yet either may exist with little or nothing of the other" (75). His reply (if it is not one of Melville's characteristically sly jokes) suggests the extraordinary depth of knowledge and perception necessary for understanding character, and especially a complex character like that of Claggart. Melville's narrator, then, seems to signal the importance of depth for successful reading of *Billy Budd*.

Yet his text does not satisfy this demand. His characters are not knowable. No matter how deeply one reads the text, one will probably never fully understand Billy's innocence, Claggart's depravity, or even Vere's upright adherence to the law. Each character is specifically identified as "exceptional" but not comprehensible (*Billy Budd* 53, 62, 74). Entering the "labyrinth" of their characters, then, does not lead to knowledge (74). Readers never fully understand why Claggart accuses Billy, why Vere condemns him to death, why Billy cries out, "God bless Captain Vere!" (123).

A traditional model of reading, then, will probably not work for a fuller and, it needs to be said, more pleasurable experience of reading *Billy Budd*. But fortunately, with the advent of new technologies of reading, new media for texts to live in, notions of literacy have changed, and these new reading practices prove immensely fruitful for reading *Billy Budd* (see Jenkins, Kelley). These practices include shared, social reading spaces; easy access to remote texts; and deliberate errancy (admittedly a paradox). That is, readers can meet online at fan sites or discussion groups to share their interpretations of a literary text; they can track down arcane allusions and sources with a click; and they can wander through texts at will, reading them nonlinearly, discontinuously, incompletely, and superficially.

One paradox of the new reading practices enabled by digital media is that they are in fact quite old. Take the social world of reading. We think of reading as an individual enterprise, a contract between one author and one reader that takes place in the private space of an individual mind and heart. Although this kind of reading has always been available to the wealthy few, it has only recently become accessible to anyone with a primary school education. In Melville's period, families still spent time reading books together, partly for the pleasure of communal entertainment, partly to save money on expensive products, partly to educate the young, partly to instill values considered important to authority figures (Davidson; Hedrick; Zboray). Since middle-class reading often took place in a social setting and with copies nearby of Webster's dictionary, the Bible, and most likely a popular encyclopedia or almanac or McGuffey's *Reader* with examples of respected authors' writings, one could consult a family member or a handy book for guidance to puzzling references. And since one might well be multitasking while listening to another member of the group read—sewing, repairing tools, writing letters, doing accounts—the experience of reading might include the errancy of contemporary web surfing, as one's attention wandered freely.

Even in *Billy Budd*, Melville's narrator gives glimpses of the social world of reading. The sailors are "men whose reading was mainly confined to the journals" (*Billy Budd* 63). How did they get and read these journals? A ship's library contained a small but choice collection of books like those in the family library described above, along with copies of whatever newspapers and magazines were available.[3] These might be read and passed from hand to hand or read aloud by one sailor to friends who, like Billy, are "illiterate." Yet all have access to printed matter. Furthermore, as the last chapter indicates, they sometimes pick up a pen themselves, and the "rude utterance" of one of the sailors gets "rudely printed at Portsmouth as a ballad" (131). The sailors participate in an active literary culture, then, that includes fiction, journalism, and poetry, not perhaps as genteel as Captain Vere's reading, but no less meaningful.

What would it mean to read *Billy Budd* more as the sailors might read and less as Vere and Claggart do? Let's go back to Barbara Johnson's argument and its implications for thinking about literacy in *Billy Budd*. Johnson suggests that there is not one kind of literacy in the story but three. Vere's form of literacy might be understood as a version of the twentieth-century close-reading model that prizes linearity, continuity, completeness, and depth. He looks for a rational structure in the complex web of motives and emotions that produces Billy's fatal blow. Although he cannot understand Claggart's intentions and has only a partial comprehension of Billy's behavior, he closely observes what has taken place, he sees the implications, and he proceeds, "under the law of Mutiny Act" to address the crisis logically, thoroughly, and lawfully, as Melville's long and patient narration of the drumhead court scene displays (*Billy Budd* 111). His adherence to this logical structure ends in Billy's death, the loss of a beautiful boy, but we see that he has read and interpreted the events of Claggart's death as disruptive to order on the ship and has acted according to his training to contain the crisis. If we read the book the way Vere reads, we will come away with the sense of a logical text that rewards patience, effort, and faith in a set of firm principles—what Johnson calls the "testament of acceptance," quoting critics who see the book as coming to a tragic but resigned recognition of turbulent reality (Johnson 574).

What if we read as Claggart does? He is Johnson's "ironic" reader who sees double meanings everywhere. His form of literacy is conspiratorial, subversive, looking for the riotous energies that threaten social order. Quoting critics who speak of Melville's "testament of resistance," Johnson suggests that a Claggart reading would see the irreconcilable differences in the text (586). Such a reading would view Vere's solution as self-interested, protecting established power and punishing insurgent potential in the crew. But like Vere's form of literacy, Claggart's depends on the expectation that a text be linear, continuous, complete, and deep. His reading style would undermine that textual structure but would depend on it for meaning. Claggart, after all, resembles Guy Fawkes, who plotted to blow up the Houses of Parliament. His plot would be meaningless without those authoritative structures in place. In that sense, then, both Vere and Claggart assume a world of order, a readable world, which they variously uphold or subvert according to their natures.

To read *Billy Budd* as a Vere or a Claggart is to assume that it is a whole text, an orderly story with a logical structure, a central narrative authority, a clear, discernible intention. What would it be like to read it as an "illiterate nightingale" would? Billy, remember, is plucked from his ship, the *Rights of Man*, and deposited on the *Bellipotent*, with no more chance to protest than would be offered to a "goldfinch popped into a cage" (*Billy Budd* 45). This state of affairs might not seem inconsistent to one who started life in a "pretty silk-lined basket" hanging on a "good man's door in Bristol" (51). Billy looks around him, notices that sailors on a warship get regularly flogged, and betakes himself to the rigging. "Life in the foretop well agreed with Billy Budd," for he can lounge at his ease, look down on the sailors below, and enjoy the company of friends, as he did on the *Rights of Man* (68). Billy's life, then, and his likely reading style, resemble the errancy of the narrator who beckons the reader into a "bypath." Billy has no plan, no path, no certain logic or structure to guide him. As a result he is "illiterate" in the ways of the *Bellipotent*, and he suffers, but he is also the only person on the ship, for the time, who seems to be enjoying himself.

A reader might try approaching *Billy Budd*, then, as Billy might. What would such an approach entail? First of all, one must have friends. Instead of reading alone, as Vere might, or in the dark like Claggart, one would read in a social space like the sailors' forecastle quarters, the nineteenth-century parlor or lyceum, or the twenty-first-century classroom, reading group, or online discussion. In such a reading environment, one can share expertise and learn from others. Secondly, one would jettison or at least weigh the expectation of a text that it be linear, continuous, complete, and deep, and look for a *Billy Budd* that more resembles "Billy in the Darbies"—"rude," spontaneous, affectionate, and direct. "Billy in the Darbies" is out of place, in the sense that it does not fit with the Billy who appears in *Billy Budd* and does not arrive with the correct forms of narrative point of view, diction, genre, and, perhaps, literary taste. But "Billy in the Darbies" also speaks movingly of the bonds that hold the sailors together. The Billy of the poem reflects that his mates will give him a parting handshake, and he asks the sentry to "ease these darbies at the wrist" (*Billy Budd* 132), a final act of kindness. Unlike the Billy of *Billy Budd*, or other characters in the story, the Billy of "Billy in the Darbies" also speaks poetically of death: "I am sleepy, and the oozy weeds about me twist" (132). Nothing else in the story communicates so immediately the terror and beauty of death as that line. In the poem's "rude utterance," its "illiterate" expression of emotion, it tells a more profound story of human experience than the "deep" narrative can. Yet this line appears in a throwaway piece, an ephemeral ballad written by an unschooled poet and distributed on flimsy paper among sailors whom no one in the literate world of the text cares about.

To read as Billy would is to honor these sailors and to understand that Melville, who began his text with the poem, honors them too. We may not fully understand why he has made it difficult to hear their voices in the text, why *Billy Budd* is difficult to read. But we can start by refusing to read in the styles of the most destructive characters—Claggart, who plots Billy's death, and Vere, who executes him. To read as Billy does is to surrender the expectation of mastering the text, as a master-at-arms or a captain would.

To read as Billy is furthermore to be a nightingale, to sing and occasionally to compose one's own song. The reading practices on display in *Billy Budd* would seem to leave little room for sailor creativity, the kind that would sing or compose a ballad. Vere speaks unwittingly of this kind of creativity when he notes ironically of the drums that beat the men to quarters (in a phrase that recalls both punitive beating and musical beats) that "forms, measured forms" organize human beings (*Billy Budd* 128). He is talking about the forms of military, legal, and civilized order that keep social animals in place. But his speech reminds readers that these forms are also like the music of Orpheus that enchanted the forest animals and kept them still. To read as a Billy is likewise to be entranced by the text, to hear the music in language that is at times harsh and discordant but nevertheless rings with a certain "chime" (45). Such a form of reading leaves behind the expectation of mastering a text. Instead it yields to it, as Billy submits to his experience of being "impressed" (see Westover).

In the military world of Melville's story, being "impressed" means being seized against one's will to labor in a harsh and forbidding world of hierarchy and power. In the world of social reading, where errancy and "rude utterance" are encouraged, being "impressed" implies not necessarily understanding what one has stumbled into but nevertheless agreeing to abide there for a while. Billy's tragedy was that he was "illiterate" in the reading practices that governed the world of Vere and Claggart. But he offers another kind of literacy, one generous, flexible, creative, and loving, that should impress us all.

Notes

1. The full discussion of the growth of *Billy Budd* appears in Hayford and Sealts's "Editors' Introduction" to the novel (1–39).
2. For a fuller treatment of *Billy Budd* and the problems of genre, see Kelley 181–87.
3. In chapter 41 ("A Man-of-War Library") of *White-Jacket*, Melville supplies details of sailor reading and habits of literacy.

Works Cited

Davidson, Cathy N. *Revolution and the Word: The Rise of the Novel in America*. New York: Oxford UP, 2004.

Davis, Garrick, ed. *Praising It New: The Best of the New Criticism*. Athens: Ohio UP, 2008.

Hedrick, Joan D. *Harriet Beecher Stowe: A Life*. New York: Oxford UP, 1995.

Jenkins, Henry, Wyn Kelley, et al. *Reading in a Participatory Culture*. Language and Literacy Series. New York: Teachers College Press. Forthcoming in print.

Johnson, Barbara. "Melville's Fist: The Execution of *Billy Budd*." *Studies in Romanticism* 18.4 (1979): 567–99.

Kelley, Wyn. *Herman Melville: An Introduction*. Oxford: Blackwell, 2008.

Melville, Herman. *Billy Budd, Sailor (An Inside Narrative)*. Ed. Harrison Hayford and Merton M. Sealts, Jr. Chicago: U of Chicago P, 1962.

_____. *Moby-Dick: A Longman Critical Edition*. Ed. John Bryant and Haskell Springer. New York: Longman, 2009.

_____. *White-Jacket: Or the World in a Man-of-War.* Ed. Harrison Hayford, Hershel Parker, G. Thomas Tanselle. Evanston and Chicago: Northwestern-Newberry, 1970. Vol. 5 of *The Writings of Herman Melville.*

Stallybrass, Peter. "Books and Scrolls: Navigating the Bible." *Books and Readers in Early Modern England.* Ed. Jennifer Andersen and Elizabeth Sauer. Philadelphia: U of Pennsylvania P, 2002. 42–79.

Twain, Mark. *The Adventures of Huckleberry Finn.* 1885. San Francisco: Ignatius, 2009.

Westover, Jeff. "The Impressments of Billy Budd." *Massachusetts Review* 39.3 (1998): 361–84.

Zboray, Ronald J. *A Fictive People: Antebellum Economic Development and the American Reading Public.* New York: Oxford UP, 1993.

RESOURCES

Chronology of Herman Melville's Life_____

1819	Herman Melville is born on August 1 in New York City, the third child of Allan Melvill and Maria Gansevoort. (The family would add the concluding *e* to their name in the 1830s.)
1830	A once-prosperous merchant, Allan Melvill's business fails and he is forced to declare bankruptcy. The Melvill family moves to Albany, New York.
1832	Having grown ill during pursuit of another failed business venture, Allan Melvill dies.
1839	In June, Herman Melville sails to Liverpool, England, and back as a deck hand on the ship *St. Lawrence*.
1841	On January 3, Melville sails from New Bedford, Massachusetts, on the whaling vessel *Acushnet*, bound for the South Seas.
1842	In July, Melville and Richard Tobias Greene desert the *Acushnet* at the island of Nukuheva in the Marquesas. Lives for a month with the natives in the Taipi Valley.
1842	In August, Melville is able to leave the Marquesas by boarding the Australian whaler *Lucy-Ann*. Conditions about the *Lucy-Ann* are poor.
1842	In October, Melville, having participated in a nonviolent work stoppage aboard the *Lucy-Ann*, is shackled and put ashore in Tahiti to stand trial for mutiny. Allowed the freedom to wander during the day provided he return to his cell at night, Melville escapes by canoe to the neighboring island of Eimeo, where he works for a short time on a potato farm.
1842	In November, Melville joins the crew of the Nantucket whaler *Charles & Henry*.
1843	In May, Melville leaves the crew of the *Charles & Henry* with no complications in Hawaii. Works temporarily as a bookkeeper in a shop in Honolulu.

1843	In August, Melville enlists in the U.S. Navy and boards the frigate *United States*.
1844	In October, Melville is discharged from the navy and disembarks in Boston, Massachusetts.
1845	Melville lives at his mother's home in upstate New York; begins writing *Typee*.
1846	*Typee* is published.
1847	*Omoo* is published. Melville marries Elizabeth Shaw and moves to New York City.
1849	*Mardi* is published. Melville's first child, Malcolm, is born.
1849	*Redburn* is published. Melville travels to England and France.
1850	*White-Jacket* is published. Melville returns from Europe; begins to research and write *Moby-Dick*. In August, meets Nathaniel Hawthorne during a trip to Pittsfield, Massachusetts; in October, the Melville family purchases and moves into a 160-acre farm, which Melville calls Arrowhead, near Pittsfield.
1851	*Moby-Dick* is published. Melville's second child, Stanwix, is born.
1852	*Pierre* is published. Disappointing sales of *Moby-Dick* and *Pierre* contribute to growing financial difficulties for Melville.
1853	Melville's third child, Elizabeth, is born. He works on the stories later to appear in *The Piazza Tales*; several of these stories are published in magazines from 1853 to 1855.
1854	*Israel Potter* begins to appear in serialized form in *Putnam's Monthly Magazine*.

1855	Book publication of *Israel Potter*. Melville's fourth child, Frances, is born.
1856	*The Piazza Tales* is published. Melville, in increasingly poor health, travels to Europe and the Holy Land, stopping along the way to visit Hawthorne in England.
1857	*The Confidence-Man* is published. Melville returns to the United States, attempts to increase his income through lecturing from 1857 to 1860, with little success.
1860	Sails aboard the clipper *Meteor* (captained by his brother, Thomas) to San Francisco.
1863	Struggling with his health and finances and unable to keep up Arrowhead any longer, Melville trades Arrowhead (losing money in the bargain) to his younger brother Allan for Allan's home in New York City.
1864	Visits an army camp on the front lines during the Civil War.
1866	Publishes the poetry collection *Battle-Pieces and Aspects of the War*. Appointed inspector of customs at New York, for which he is paid about four dollars a day.
1867	Melville and his wife have marital difficulties and contemplate separation. In September, Malcolm Melville dies of a self-inflicted gunshot wound, widely believed to be suicide.
1876	*Clarel* is published.
1885	Melville resigns his position at the custom house.
1886	Stanwix Melville dies.
1888	Melville privately publishes *John Marr and Other Sailors, with Some Sea-Pieces*, and begins working on *Billy Budd, Sailor*.

1891	Melville privately publishes *Timoleon*.
1891	Melville dies on September 28.
1924	*Billy Budd* is published.

Works by Herman Melville_____

Novels

Typee: A Peep at Polynesian Life (1846)
Omoo: A Narrative of Adventures in the South Seas (1847)
Mardi: And a Voyage Thither (1849)
Redburn: His First Voyage (1849)
White-Jacket; or, The World in a Man-of-War (1850)
Moby-Dick; or, The Whale (1851)
Pierre; or, The Ambiguities (1852)
Israel Potter: His Fifty Years of Exile (1855)
The Confidence-Man: His Masquerade (1857)
Billy Budd, Sailor (1924)

Short Stories

The Piazza Tales (1856)

Poetry

Battle-Pieces and Aspects of the War (1866)
Clarel: A Poem and Pilgrimage in the Holy Land (1876)
John Marr and Other Sailors (1888)
Timoleon, Etc. (1891)

Bibliography

Allen, Gay Wilson. *Melville and His World*. New York: Viking, 1971.

Balaam, Peter. *Misery's Mathematics: Mourning, Compensation, and Reality in Antebellum American Literature*. New York: Routledge, 2009.

Bellis, Peter J. *No Mysteries Out of Ourselves: Identity and Textual Form in the Novels of Herman Melville*. Philadelphia: U of Pennsylvania P, 1990.

Bercaw, Mary K. *Melville's Sources*. Evanston: Northwestern UP, 1987.

Bernstein, John. *Pacifism and Rebellion in the Writings of Herman Melville*. Hague: Mouton, 1964.

Berthold, Dennis. *American Risorgimento: Herman Melville and the Cultural Politics of Italy*. Columbus: Ohio State UP, 2009.

Bickley, R. Bruce, Jr. *The Method of Melville's Short Fiction*. Durham: Duke UP, 1975.

Bowen, Merlin. *The Long Encounter: Self and Experience in the Writings of Herman Melville*. Chicago: U of Chicago P, 1960.

Branch, Watson G., ed. *Melville: The Critical Heritage*. London: Routledge, 1974.

Brodhead, Richard H. *Hawthorne, Melville, and the Novel*. Chicago: U of Chicago P, 1976.

Bryant, John. *Melville and Repose: The Rhetoric of Humor in the American Renaissance*. New York: Oxford UP, 1993.

Budd, Louis J., and Edwin H. Cady, eds. *On Melville: The Best from American Literature*. Durham: Duke UP, 1988.

Canaday, Nicholas, Jr. *Melville and Authority*. Gainesville: U of Florida P, 1968.

Chase, Richard. *Herman Melville: A Critical Study*. New York: Macmillan, 1949.

_____, ed. *Melville: A Collection of Critical Essays*. Englewood Cliffs, NJ: Prentice-Hall, 1962.

Colatrella, Carol. *Literature and Moral Reform: Melville and the Discipline of Reading*. Gainesville: UP of Florida, 2002.

Cook, Jonathan A. *Satirical Apocalypse: An Anatomy of Melville's* The Confidence-Man. Westport, CT: Greenwood, 1996.

Davis, Clark. *After the Whale: Melville in the Wake of* Moby-Dick. Tuscaloosa: U of Alabama P, 1995.

Delbanco, Andrew. *Melville: His World and Work*. New York: Knopf, 2005.

Dillingham, William B. *An Artist in the Rigging: The Early Work of Herman Melville*. Athens: U of Georgia P, 1972.

_____. *Melville's Later Novels*. Athens: U of Georgia P, 1986.

_____. *Melville's Short Fiction, 1853–1856*. Athens: U of Georgia P, 1977.

Dimock, Wai-chee. *Empire for Liberty: Melville and the Poetics of Individualism*. Princeton: Princeton UP, 1989.

Dowling, David. *Chasing the White Whale: The* Moby-Dick *Marathon; or, What Melville Means Today.* Iowa City: U of Iowa P, 2010.

Dryden, Edgar A. *Melville's Thematics of Form: The Great Art of Telling the Truth.* Baltimore: Johns Hopkins, 1968.

_____. *Monumental Melville: The Formation of a Literary Career.* Stanford: Stanford UP, 2004.

Duban, James. *Melville's Major Fiction: Politics, Theology, and Imagination.* DeKalb: Northern Illinois UP, 1983.

Evelev, John. *Tolerable Entertainment: Herman Melville and Professionalism in Antebellum New York.* Amherst: U of Massachusetts P, 2006.

Fisher, Marvin. *Going Under: Melville's Short Fiction and the American 1850s.* Baton Rouge: Louisiana State UP, 1977.

Fogle, Richard. *Melville's Shorter Tales.* Norman: U of Oklahoma P, 1966.

Franklin, H. Bruce. *The Wake of the Gods: Melville's Mythology.* Stanford: Stanford UP, 1963.

Gale, Robert L. *A Herman Melville Encyclopedia.* Westport, CT: Greenwood, 1995.

Garner, Stanton. *The Civil War World of Herman Melville.* Lawrence: U of Kansas P, 1993.

Garner, Stanton, and John Wenke. *The Two Intertwined Narratives in Herman Melville's Billy Budd: A Study of an Author's Literary Method.* Lewiston, NY: Mellen, 2010.

Goldman, Stan. *Melville's Protest Theism: The Hidden and Silent God in* Clarel. DeKalb: Northern Illinois UP, 1993.

Hayes, Kevin J. *The Cambridge Introduction to Herman Melville.* Cambridge, UK: Cambridge UP, 2007.

Heflin, Wilson, Mary K. Bercaw Edwards, and Thomas Farel Heffernan. *Herman Melville's Whaling Years.* Nashville: Vanderbilt UP, 2004.

Hetherington, Hugh W. *Melville's Reviewers, British and American, 1846–1891.* Chapel Hill: U of North Carolina P, 1961.

Higgins, Brian. *Herman Melville: An Annotated Bibliography, 1846–1930.* Boston: Hall, 1979.

_____. *Herman Melville: A Reference Guide, 1931–1960.* Boston: Hall, 1987.

Higgins, Brian, and Hershel Parker, eds. *Herman Melville: The Contemporary Reviews.* Cambridge, UK: Cambridge UP, 1995.

_____. *Reading Melville's* Pierre; or, The Ambiguities. Baton Rouge: Louisiana State UP, 2006.

Hillway, Tyrus. *Herman Melville.* New York: Twayne, 1963.

Kelley, Wyn, ed. *A Companion to Herman Melville.* Malden, MA: Blackwell, 2006.

_____. *Herman Melville: An Introduction.* Malden, MA: Blackwell, 2008.

_____. *Melville's City: Literary and Urban Form in Nineteenth-Century New York.* Cambridge, UK: Cambridge UP, 1996.

Kier, Kathleen. *A Melville Encyclopedia: The Novels*. Troy, NY: Whitston, 1994.

Kirby, David. *Herman Melville*. New York: Continuum, 1993.

Krauthammer, Anna. *The Representation of the Savage in James Fenimore Cooper and Herman Melville*. New York: Lang, 2008.

Lebowitz, Alan. *Progress into Silence: A Study of Melville's Heroes*. Bloomington: Indiana UP, 1970.

Levin, Harry. *The Power of Blackness: Hawthorne, Poe, Melville*. New York: Knopf, 1958.

Levine, Robert S., ed. *The Cambridge Companion to Herman Melville*. Cambridge, UK: Cambridge UP, 1998.

Lewis, R. W. B. *Herman Melville*. New York: Dell, 1962.

Leyda, Jay. *The Melville Log: A Documentary Life of Herman Melville*. 2 vols. New York: Harcourt, 1951.

Maxwell, D. E. S. *Herman Melville*. London: Routledge, 1968.

McCarthy, Paul. *"The Twisted Mind": Madness in Herman Melville's Fiction*. Iowa City: U of Iowa P, 1990.

McWilliams, John P., Jr. *Hawthorne, Melville, and the American Character: A Looking-Glass Business*. Cambridge, UK: Cambridge UP, 1984.

Milder, Robert, ed. *Critical Essays on Melville's* Billy Budd, Sailor. Boston: Hall, 1989.

_____. *Exiled Royalties: Melville and the Life We Imagine*. Oxford: Oxford UP, 2006.

Miller, Edwin H. *Melville*. New York: Braziller, 1975.

Miller, James E., Jr. *A Reader's Guide to Herman Melville*. New York: Farrar, 1962.

Mumford, Lewis. *Herman Melville: A Study of His Life and Vision*. New York: Harcourt, 1962.

Otter, Samuel. *Melville's Anatomies*. Berkeley: U of California P, 1999.

Pardes, Ilana. *Melville's Bibles*. Berkeley: U of California P, 2008.

Parker, Hershel. *Herman Melville: A Biography*. 2 vols. Baltimore: Johns Hopkins UP, 1996–2002.

_____. *Melville: The Making of the Poet*. Evanston: Northwestern UP, 2008.

Potter, William. *Melville's* Clarel *and the Intersympathy of Creeds*. Kent: Kent State UP, 2004.

Renker, Elizabeth. *Strike through the Mask: Herman Melville and the Scene of Writing*. Baltimore: Johns Hopkins UP, 1996.

Samson, John. *White Lies: Melville's Narratives of Facts*. Ithaca: Cornell UP, 1989.

Sanborn, Geoffrey. *The Sign of the Cannibal: Melville and the Making of a Postcolonial Reader*. Durham: Duke UP, 1998.

Sanborn, Geoffrey, and Samuel Otter, eds. *Melville and Aesthetics*. New York: Macmillan, 2011.

Sealts, Merton M., Jr. *Melville's Reading*. Columbia: U of South Carolina P, 1988.

_____. *Pursuing Melville: 1940–1980*. Madison: U of Wisconsin P, 1982.

Selby, Nick. *Herman Melville:* Moby-Dick. New York: Columbia UP, 1998.

Sherrill, Rowland A. *The Prophetic Melville: Experience, Transcendence, and Tragedy*. Athens: U of Georgia P, 1979.

Short, Bryan C. *Cast by Means of Figures: Herman Melville's Rhetorical Development*. Amherst: U of Massachusetts P, 1992.

Shurr, William H. *The Mystery of Iniquity: Melville as Poet, 1857–1891*. Lexington: UP of Kentucky, 1972.

Spanos, William V. *The Exceptionalist State and the State of Exception: Herman Melville's* Billy Budd, Sailor. Baltimore: Johns Hopkins UP, 2011.

_____. *Herman Melville and the American Calling: The Fiction After* Moby-Dick, *1851–1857*. Albany: State U of New York P, 2008.

Spengemann, William C. *Three American Poets: Walt Whitman, Emily Dickinson, and Herman Melville*. Notre Dame: U of Notre Dame P, 2010.

Stafford, William T. *Melville's* Billy Budd *and the Critics*. San Francisco: Wadsworth, 1961.

Sten, Christopher. *The Weaver-God, He Weaves: Melville and the Poetics of the Novel*. Kent: Kent State UP, 1996.

Stern, Milton R. *The Fine Hammered Steel of Herman Melville*. Urbana: U of Illinois P, 1957.

Stuckey, Sterling. *African Culture and Melville's Art: The Creative Process in* Benito Cereno *and* Moby-Dick. Oxford: Oxford UP, 2009.

Thompson, Lawrance. *Melville's Quarrel with God*. Princeton: Princeton UP, 1952.

Tolchin, Neal L. *Mourning, Gender, and Creativity in the Art of Herman Melville*. New Haven: Yale UP, 1988.

Wenke, John Paul. *Melville's Muse: Literary Creation and the Forms of Philosophical Fiction*. Kent: Kent State UP, 1995.

West, Peter. *The Arbiters of Reality: Hawthorne, Melville, and the Rise of Mass Information Culture*. Columbus: Ohio State UP, 2008.

Yothers, Brian. *Melville's Mirrors: Literary Criticism and America's Most Elusive Author*. Rochester: Camden House, 2011.

CRITICAL
INSIGHTS

About the Editor _____

Eric Carl Link is professor of American literature and chair of the Department of English at the University of Memphis. He is the author of several books, including *The Vast and Terrible Drama: American Literary Naturalism in the Late Nineteenth Century* (2004), *Understanding Philip K. Dick* (2010), and *Neutral Ground: New Traditionalism and the American Romance Controversy* (1999; coauthored with G. R. Thompson). He is also the founder and editor of the journal *ALN: The American Literary Naturalism Newsletter* and is the coeditor (along with Donald Pizer) of the *Norton Critical Edition of* The Red Badge of Courage, fourth edition. He is the editor of several collections, including *Taming the Bicycle: Essays, Stories, and Sketches* by Mark Twain and *Critical Insights: The Red Badge of Courage*. Aside from these studies, he has published numerous essays on figures such as Charles Brockden Brown, Stephen Crane, Frank Norris, Mark Twain, and others, as well as articles on a variety of topics related to nineteenth-century aesthetic theory. He is a two-time Fulbright Senior Scholar: in 2008 he lectured at Lesya Ukrainka Volyn National University in Lutsk, Ukraine; and in 2011 he lectured at the University of Fribourg in Fribourg, Switzerland.

Contributors_____

Eric Carl Link is professor of American literature and chair of the Department of English at the University of Memphis. He is the author of several books, including *The Vast and Terrible Drama: American Literary Naturalism in the Late Nineteenth Century* (2004), *Understanding Philip K. Dick* (2010), and *Neutral Ground: New Traditionalism and the American Romance Controversy* (1999; coauthored with G. R. Thompson), as well as numerous articles and book chapters. He is also the founder and editor of the scholarly journal *ALN: The American Literary Naturalism Newsletter*, and has served as a Fulbright Senior Scholar in Ukraine (2008), and Switzerland (2011).

Greg Conley is a doctoral candidate in English literature studying and teaching at the University of Memphis. He has a forthcoming essay in *Extrapolation* about Stanislaw Lem and his conception of godlike aliens and alien gods. His research focuses on transatlantic Gothic literature in the nineteenth century, Darwinian evolution, and their combined contributions to Victorian fantasy and science fiction. Occasionally he fences.

John David Miles is an assistant professor of English at the University of Memphis specializing in colonial and nineteenth-century American literature. He received his PhD from Duke University in 2009 for a dissertation entitled "The Afterlives of King Philip's War: Negotiating War and Identity in Early America." His cowritten essay "Those We Don't Speak Of: Indians in *The Village*" was published in *PMLA* in 2008, and he has also published book reviews in *American Literature*. He is currently at work on essays that investigate the production of the West as a literary space, as well as a book project tracing the role of historical writing in the construction of early American communities. Miles currently resides in Memphis, but continues to call rural central Kentucky his home.

John Samson is associate professor and director of sophomore literature in the Department of English at Texas Tech University. He received his PhD from Cornell University in 1980 and is the author of *White Lies: Melville's Narratives of Facts* (1989) and articles and book chapters on nineteenth- and twentieth-century American fiction and nonfiction, as well as literary criticism and theory. From 1995 to 2003 he contributed the "Melville" chapter to *American Literary Scholarship*. He is currently engaged in a project tracing the cultural roots of the movement from realism to modernism in the American novel from 1870 to 1920; this project focuses on the novels of Mark Twain, Jack London, and Willa Cather in their relation to their political and philosophical contexts.

Clark Davis is professor of English and chair of the Department of English at the University of Denver. He is the author of *After the Whale: Melville in the Wake of* Moby-Dick (1995) and *Hawthorne's Shyness: Ethics, Politics, and the Question of Engagement* (2005).

Nicole de Fee received her PhD from the University of Nebraska–Lincoln in 2008. Her dissertation, "From Colony to Empire: The Decolonization of National Literary Identity in Antebellum American Literature," focused on the development of a post-colonial literary identity in the works of Washington Irving, James Fenimore Cooper, Edgar Allen Poe, and Herman Melville. She is currently an assistant professor of English at Louisiana Tech University in Ruston, Louisiana, where she teaches American literature.

David Dowling, lecturer in English at the University of Iowa, has published numerous books and articles on nineteenth-century American literary history and culture, with a special interest in the economics of authorship and the politics of the publishing world. His books include *Capital Letters: Authorship in the Antebellum Literary Market* (2009), *Chasing the White Whale: The* Moby-Dick *Marathon; or, What Melville Means Today* (2010), *The Business of Literary Circles in Nineteenth-Century America* (2011), and *Literary Partnerships and the Marketplace: Writers and Mentors in Nineteenth-Century America* (2012). His latest book, *Emerson's Protégés: Mentoring and Marketing Transcendentalism's Future*, is under review at a major academic press.

Gale Temple received his PhD in 2001 from Loyola University of Chicago. He is currently associate professor and director of graduate studies in the Department of English at the University of Alabama at Birmingham, specializing in early American literature and culture. He has published on writers such as Charles Brockden Brown, Nathaniel Hawthorne, Fanny Fern, Herman Melville, and Henry James. He is currently working on a book about early American literary and cultural portrayals of what today we might call addiction. His wife, Cheryl Temple, also teaches English at UAB, and together they have three children: Samuel, Sophie, and Simon; a cat named Hattie; and an Australian cattle dog named Comet.

John Wenke is professor of English at Salisbury University in Maryland, where he teaches American literature and literary writing. His books include *J. D. Salinger: A Study of the Short Fiction* (1991) and *Melville's Muse: Literary Creation and the Forms of Philosophical Fiction* (1995). He has published numerous scholarly essays and chapters, short stories, creative nonfiction essays, and reviews. He is currently completing a book-length manuscript, "American Proteus: Providence, Self-Fashioning and the Creation of Charles Brockden Brown." He has twice won Salisbury University's Distinguished Faculty Award.

Shelby L. Crosby is an assistant professor of English at the University of Memphis. She received her doctorate from the State University of New York at Buffalo with a focus on nineteenth-century African American and women's literature. Her research and teaching interests include nineteenth-century African American literature, twentieth-century black women's science fiction, and critical race theory. Currently she is working on an essay examining Paul Laurence Dunbar's construction of black femininity in *The Sport of the Gods* and a book manuscript that examines black female representation and the construction of black womanhood in nineteenth-century African American literature, particularly in African American men's writing.

Jonathan A. Cook has a PhD from Columbia University and is the author of *Satirical Apocalypse: An Anatomy of Melville's* The Confidence-Man (1996). He has published numerous articles and reviews on Melville, Hawthorne, Irving, Poe, and other nineteenth-century American writers and has prepared the introductions and notes for Melville's annotations of Hawthorne's books for the website *Melville's Marginalia Online*. He has also written the introduction and notes for the Barnes and Noble Classics edition of Thomas Hardy's *Far From the Madding Crowd*. Forthcoming are a book-length study of *Moby-Dick* and the Bible, and an essay on Melville's final poetry collection, *Timoleon*, in an essay collection devoted to American authors' last works. He is chair of the English Department at Middleburg Academy in Middleburg, Virginia, and an adjunct professor at Lord Fairfax Community College.

Anna Krauthammer received her PhD from the Graduate Center, City University of New York. She teaches literature and composition at Touro College in New York City. Her published dissertation, *The Representation of the Savage in James Fenimore Cooper and Herman Melville* (2008), is a comparative study of the representation of non-Euro-American others in these writers' major works. In addition to her own writing, she reviews books and articles for several journals.

Steven Frye is professor of English at California State University, Bakersfield. He is the author of *Understanding Cormac McCarthy* (2009), *Historiography and Narrative Design in The American Romance* (2001), and editor of *Critical Insights: The Tales of Edgar Allan Poe* (2010) and *Critical Insights: The Poetry of Edgar Allan Poe* (2011). He is president of the Cormac McCarthy Society and associate editor of *ALN: The American Literary Naturalism Newsletter*, as well as the author of a variety of articles on Herman Melville, Cormac McCarthy, and other authors of the American romance tradition.

Peter West, assistant professor of English at Adelphi University, is the author of *The Arbiters of Reality: Hawthorne, Melville, and the Rise of Mass Information Culture* (2008). He has published essays and reviews on nineteenth-century literary topics at *ATQ*, *South Atlantic Review*, *American Literature*, and *Resources for American*

Literary Study. In addition, he has published an article exploring the meaning of Kentucky's Mammoth Cave in the nineteenth-century racial imagination (at the online journal *Southern Spaces*), and another on Otis Bullard's moving panorama of New York City (at *Common-place*, the online journal of the American Antiquarian Society). He is currently working with a team of coeditors on a multivolume collection of texts related to the panorama in England and the United States, to be published by Pickering and Chatto.

Peter Balaam is assistant professor of English at Carleton College in Minnesota, where he teaches courses in U.S. literature and culture from the colonial era to 1900. A scholar of U.S. religious culture, he is the author of *Misery's Mathematics: Mourning, Compensation, and Reality in Antebellum American Literature* (2009). He is currently at work on projects treating Emerson and Kierkegaard, Emerson and old age, and the cultural life of animals in the antebellum United States.

Brian Yothers is associate professor of English and director of the literature program at the University of Texas at El Paso. He is the author of *Melville's Mirrors: Literary Criticism and America's Most Elusive Author* (2011) and *The Romance of the Holy Land in American Travel Writing, 1790–1876* (2007) and a coeditor of *Journeys: The International Journal of Travel and Travel Writing*. He is a contributing scholar to *Melville's Marginalia Online*, where he has written the introduction and notes to Melville's marginalia to the New Testament and the book of Psalms. He is currently working on a book on religious difference in Melville's fiction and poetry.

Wyn Kelley, of the literature faculty at the Massachusetts Institute of Technology, is author of *Melville's City: Literary and Urban Form in Nineteenth-Century New York* (1996) and of *Herman Melville: An Introduction* (2008). Former associate editor of the Melville Society journal *Leviathan*, and editor of the Blackwell *Companion to Herman Melville* (2006), she has published in a number of journals and collections, including *Melville and Hawthorne: Writing a Relationship* (2008), *Ungraspable Phantom: Essays on* Moby-Dick (2006), *Melville and Women* (2006), *"Whole Oceans Away": Melville in the Pacific* (2007), and *The Cambridge Companion to Herman Melville* (1998). A founding member of the Melville Society Cultural Project, she has worked closely with the New Bedford Whaling Museum on a number of initiatives: lecture series, conferences, exhibits, and a scholarly archive. She is also associate director of *MEL* (Melville Electronic Library), an NEH-supported interactive digital archive for reading, editing, and visualizing Melville's texts.

Index

slavery, 38, 39, 215, 219
   Dred Scott v. Sanford (Supreme
      Court case), 40
   Fugitive Slave Act, 163
Stowe, Harriet Beecher, 40
Swift, Jonathan, 195

Timoleon (Melville), 289–90
transcendentalism, 32–34, 68, 73
"Tuft of Kelp, The" (Melville), 4, 289
Typee (Melville), 17, 70, 82, 180
   cannibalism in, 130, 132, 202–3
   Christianity in, 145, 186, 198–99
   critical reception, 44
   cultural identity in, 92–96
   as gothic fiction, 125–33
   imperialism in, 86, 92, 197–99

   indigenous religion in, 194
   landscape in, 85, 187
   "noble savage," concept in, 195–96
   race in, 89
   sexuality in, 129, 184, 191–92

Uncle Tom's Cabin (Stowe), 40
"Utilitarian View of the Monitor's Fight,
   A" (Melville), 285

whaling, 28–29, 102
White-Jacket (Melville), 18
   critical reception, 45
Whitman, Walt, 3, 283–84, 293, 296

Young America movement, 37–38